D1796381

Recasting Culture and Space in Iberian Contexts

SUNY series in National Identities

Thomas M. Wilson, editor

Recasting Culture and Space in Iberian Contexts

edited by Sharon R. Roseman and Shawn S. Parkhurst

State University of New York Press

Published by
State University of New York Press, Albany

© 2008 State University of New York

All rights reserved

Printed in the United States of America

No part of this book may be used or reproduced in any manner whatsoever without
written permission. No part of this book may be stored in a retrieval system or
transmitted in any form or by any means including electronic, electrostatic, magnetic
tape, mechanical, photocopying, recording, or otherwise without the prior permission in
writing of the publisher.

For information, contact State University of New York Press, Albany, NY
www.sunypress.edu

Production by Kelli W. LeRoux
Marketing by Anne M. Valentine

Library of Congress Cataloging-in-Publication Data

Recasting culture and space in Iberian contexts / edited by Sharon R.
   Roseman, Shawn S. Parkhurst.
       p. cm. — (SUNY series in national identities)
   Includes bibliographical references and index.
   ISBN 978-0-7914-7311-5 (hardcover : alk. paper)
   ISBN 978-0-7914-7312-2 (pbk. : alk. paper)
   1. Spain—Civilization.   2. National characteristics, Spanish.
3. Portugal—Civilization.   4. National characteristics, Portuguese.
I. Roseman, Sharon R., 1963–   II. Parkhurst, Shawn S.

DP48.R425 2008
946—dc22   2007011277

10 9 8 7 6 5 4 3 2 1

Contents

Acknowledgments   ix

Chapter 1
Culture and Space in Iberian Anthropology   1
      Sharon R. Roseman and Shawn S. Parkhurst

PART 1: Colonial Spaces and National Identities   33

Chapter 2
The Hidden Empire: Peasants, Nation Building, and the Empire
in Portuguese Anthropology   35
      João Leal

Chapter 3
Displaced Identities among the Malacca Portuguese   55
      Brian Juan O'Neill

Chapter 4
Imperialist Ideology and Representations of the Portuguese
Provinces during the Early Estado Novo   81
      António Medeiros

PART 2: Fascism, Cultural Spaces, and Memory Politics   101

Chapter 5
Re-presenting the Fascist Classroom: Education as a Space
of Memory in Contemporary Spain   103
      Susan M. DiGiacomo

Chapter 6
Cursillos and *Concursos* in Rural Galicia: The Sección Femenina
and the Modernizing Project of the Franco Dictatorship   129
    Sharon R. Roseman

Chapter 7
Crossing Borders, Reconfiguring Lives: A Catalan Exile
Family in Wartime London   151
    Oriol Pi-Sunyer

PART 3: Regionality and Space   177

Chapter 8
The City and the Countryside: The Virgin of Sonsoles   181
    María Cátedra

Chapter 9
Race and Space in Interpretations of Portugal: The
North-South Division and Representations of Portuguese
National Identity in the Nineteenth and Twentieth Centuries   205
    José Manuel Sobral

Chapter 10
Local Correspondence: A Village Writer's Contribution to the
Cultural Production of Regionality in the Alto Douro of
Northern Portugal   225
    Shawn S. Parkhurst

PART 4: Cultural Politics and the Global   251

Chapter 11
Kafe Antzokia: The Global meets the Local in Basque
Cultural Politics   253
    Jacqueline Urla

Afterword
Displacements: The Experience of Vectored Spaces in
Peninsular Places   271
    James W. Fernandez

Contributors   291

Index   295

Acknowledgments

To the contributors: thank you for your enthusiasm for this project, your patience, and your writing. We are all indebted to three anonymous reviewers for their careful comments and suggestions on earlier drafts of these essays. To Susan DiGiacomo, your generous assistance at the last hour with our final argument in chapter 1 is most appreciated. Thank you as well to Oriol Pi-Sunyer and Jackie Urla for your assistance with nuances in chapter 1. Although we regret that their work could not be included here, we want to thank Joseba Zulaika and Mary Orgel for the stimulating and important papers that they presented at the conference session of the American Anthropological Association at which earlier versions of these essays were presented. We are grateful to Jim Fernandez and Michael Herzfeld for the lucid and provocative comments that they delivered during the session as our discussants; their suggestions and questions were most helpful in modifying our original drafts.

Our warm thanks to Tom Wilson for supporting our idea that we propose a book based on our panel to SUNY Press for Tom's series on National Identities. We offer our sincere gratitude to Michael Rinella, Senior Acquisitions Editor at SUNY Press for his superb assistance at every stage involved in the manuscript review process. Thank you as well to Kelli W. LeRoux, Senior Production Manager at SUNY Press for her helpful advice and the care she took with the manuscript.

Shawn would like to thank Sharon for being the brains, brawn, and moving spirit behind this book, and for being such a generous teacher and collaborator on matters Iberian and anthropological. The University of Louisville has provided various kinds of support. Particular members of that institution to be thanked: Tom Byers, of the Commonwealth Center for the Humanities and Society, and Elaine Wise of the Division of Humanities. Julie Peteet, Chair of the Department of Anthropology, contributed sage advice, intellectual comradeship, and a

congenial departmental environment for work on this volume. Thanks
to the University of Louisville's Committee on Academic Publication
for financial support in the preparation of the manuscript and to Lindsay Taylor for her assistance with its production. Jean Lave opened a
door for me that led to Portugal. By carefully reading and critiquing
my work on the Alto Douro, Paul Duguid has helped shape the way
I understand the place. Caroline Brettell has graciously helped me to
understand Portugal in social scientific terms. I want to thank the many
institutions and people in Portugal who have made my work there so
gratifying and illuminating. Many of these (especially the good people
of Socalcos) must remain unnamed in this context, but it is crucial to
record my debt to José Manuel Sobral, João de Pina Cabral, Luísa
Pedroso de Lima, Gaspar Martins Pereira, Brian Juan O'Neill, Paula
Mota Santos, Dulce Freire, Deolinda Adão, António Medeiros, Xerardo
Pereiro Pérez, Chris Gerry, and the late Stephen Stoer. Brett Williams
and José Manuel Sobral were always there for intellectual and moral
support. Thanks to Lisa Borgen for just about everything.

Sharon would like to thank Wayne Fife for his intellectual com-
panionship, insightfulness, and unwavering support in all ways. To Shawn:
thank you for all the ideas, shared commitment to the study of Portugal,
Galicia, and Spain, and steadfastness. I am grateful to the Social Sciences
and Humanities Research Council of Canada and Memorial University
of Newfoundland for their financial and logistical support. In particular,
our sincere thanks to Jill Allison for her meticulous assistance with copy
editing and the preparation of the book's index. The efficiency, knowledge, and helpfulness of the staff at the Arquivo Histórico Provincial de
Lugo and the Arquivo do Reino de Galicia are unmatched and much
appreciated. I would also like to thank the many individuals in Galicia
and elsewhere in Spain who have been so encouraging of my research
on the Franco period, despite the discomfort that discussion of the
dictatorship often brings to a conversation. In particular, thank you to
my colleagues Xaquín Rodríguez, Nieves Herrero, María Cátedra, Susan
DiGiacomo, Carmen Blanco, Claudio Rodríguez Fer, and Susana de la
Gala. To my research participants: although I have promised you anonymity, I shall do my best to continue to write about what you have
recounted to me in good faith. Your commitment to engage the past
is what makes it possible to seek an understanding of it.

Finally, we must sincerely thank the *Revista de Antropología Social*
for permission to reprint a much altered English-language version of

chapter 8, "The City and the Countryside: The Virgin of Sonsoles," by María Cátedra. An earlier version of this paper was published in 2001 as "La ciudad y su tierra: la Virgen de Sonsoles," *Revista de Antropología Social* 10:71–121.

Thank you as well to Gabriel Gatti and *Papeles del C.E.I.C./I.K.I.* for permission to reprint a slightly altered version of chapter 11, "Kafe Antzokia: The Global meets the Local in Basque Cultural Politics," by Jacqueline Urla. An earlier version of this paper was originally published in *Papeles del C.E.I.C./I.K.I.*, No. 10 (October 2003), an electronic publication of the Centro de Estudios sobre la Identidad Colectiva/ Identitate Kolektiboen Ikertegia, University of the Basque Country (http://www.ehu.es/CEIC/papeles/marcospapeles.htm).

CHAPTER 1

Culture and Space in Iberian Anthropology

SHARON R. ROSEMAN AND SHAWN S. PARKHURST

How are people's politics forged through attending museums or plays about the past? What are the processes through which folk material and expressive culture become essentialized as typical markers of particular nations, regions, and time periods—including in colonized spaces? How did the distinction between the geographical North and South emerge as such a key symbolic division in different parts of Europe? How did the idea of Empire impact the development of explanatory frameworks in fields such as anthropology in former colonial powers such as Portugal? How do dictatorships and other forms of authoritarian government organize ordinary citizens to transmit new cultural idioms to their counterparts? What part do irony and ambivalent nostalgia play in memory and cultural politics? How can regions and nations gradually be delineated in part through the circulation of accounts of localities? What can struggles over the control of religious sites tell us about social differentiation and politics in particular locales and regions? How do the homes of people living in political exile become part of counter-spaces created as part of the reconstitution of everyday life? How do seemingly well-defined spaces for everyday socializing such as public cafés become sites for acts of "ex-centric" political resistance?

These are the kinds of questions that drive this dynamic collection of essays. The contributors are all concerned with the role played by struggles to define the cultural meanings attached to physical spaces in the formation of people's subjectivities. The settings for their examinations of the interplay of space, culture, and power are particular periods and geographical locations in nineteenth-, twentieth- and twenty-first-

1

century Iberia. We denominate our spatial field of interest as *Iberia* to provide a useful intellectual disruption, to challenge our readers from the outset to question easy assumptions about combined spatial and cultural meanings, especially those inculcated by nation-state institutions.

This book takes up a number of debates that are currently at the forefront of theoretical discussions in anthropology and a number of its sister fields: how to depict and explain the workings of power in different contexts, particularly in modern states during periods of authoritarian rule and as part of global fields of influence (e.g., Verdery 1991; Wolf 2001); how to bring together examinations of meaning and of materiality (e.g., Donham 1999; Lem 1999; Maddox 1993; Trouillot 1995); and how to illustrate the impacts of people's lived experiences of space and time in the face of critical challenges to stable mappings (e.g., Appadurai 1992; Clifford 1997; Donnan and Wilson 1999; Fernandez and Huber 2001; Gupta and Ferguson 1997; Low and Lawrence-Zúñiga 2003; Ong 1999). As with the postsocialist societies of central and eastern Europe, Iberian spaces provide an important focus for considering these sorts of questions between the late nineteenth and early twenty-first centuries (e.g., Berdahl 1999). In this ongoing historical period, the legacies of colonialism retain a grim profile; struggles for national self-determination within and beyond the borders of the Iberian Peninsula continue apace; struggles for hegemony—at times leading to war—among those with widely ranging political ideologies (e.g., monarchism, republicanism, liberalism, socialism, anarchism, communism, fascism, and neoliberalism) fluctuate in combined and uneven forms. The dictatorships of Primo de Rivera, Salazar, and Franco, as well as the periods prior to and following them, are the subject of a rich body of recent studies in various disciplinary specialties. The present collection of essays fits into this recent reengagement by providing anthropological considerations on the making of culture and space by those who lived through the last century and a half in Iberian contexts.

RESPATIALIZING ANTHROPOLOGY

Over the past few decades, geographical theory has come to have a renewed influence on anthropology and other fields (e.g., Appadurai 1988; Birdwell-Pheasant and Lawrence-Zúñiga 1999; Buchli 2002; Caldeira 2000; Christian 1972; Darby 2000; Herzfeld 1991; Redfield

2000; Stewart 1996; Tsing 1993). Drawing on a series of rich cases that all relate to the Iberian Peninsula, the authors of this volume demonstrate that questions about space,[1] mappings, and texts are also about social identities and power. They focus largely on the late nineteenth and twentieth centuries, a period marked by a drive toward grandiose ideological conceptualizations that affected the production of ideas about modern geographical space (Lefebvre 1991 [1974]). The authors are interested in the links between this historical context and the emergence both of specific intellectual traditions, and of everyday discourses and practices. This collection thereby explores the making-of-conflicted-spaces in Portugal and Spain, and in foreign sites impacted by Iberian-origin exile or colonial settlement. The essays in this book compel readers to consider exactly how people's political identifications have been forged through cultural struggles over the uses and meanings of physical spaces, whether these are in Barcelona, Bilbao, villages in the Alto Douro of Portugal or in Galician Spain, Malacca, the countryside lying on the edge of Ávila (the "City of the Saints"), in Spain, or Catalans' wartime London.

All of the contributors to this book work from the premise that spatial specificity contributes enormously to our understanding of the relations between power and culture. At roughly the same time that different modalities of power were being added to the agenda of cultural analysis, the question of spatial relations was raised as one that both political-economic and more culturalist styles of anthropology had neglected while intensifying their emphasis on historical process. Geographers had begun looking at human space as highly plastic and power-laden in the 1970s, and came to have an influence on anthropologists in the 1990s. David Harvey had played a role in geography closely analogous to Eric Wolf's in anthropology, by bringing Marxist political economy into geographical analysis and by "spatializing" Marx (Harvey 1973, 1982). Other geographers criticized Harvey's emphasis on Marx's model of capitalism for treating modern space as fully colonized by capital (echoing the many anthropologists who viewed various "modernized" cultures as having their own logics despite their long contact with capitalism). Geographer Edward Soja broke important conceptual ground by drawing on Michel Foucault and the Marxist Henri Lefebvre as resources for "reasserting space" in a social theory that challenged the "historical" emphasis he viewed as dominating social thought since the late nineteenth century. Foucault had characterized the late twentieth century as "the epoch of space": "the epoch of juxtaposition, the epoch of the side-by-side, of the dispersed" (Foucault 1986:22). Soja claimed that the postmodern capitalism of the late twentieth century revealed space to be not simply an inert context for, or reflection of, society, but rather both a "social product . . . and a shaping force (or medium) in social life" (Soja 1989:7). Other contemporary geographers, more interested in human spatial practices than in sweeping forces such as capitalism, have emphasized how cultural histories depend on spatial practices, and vice versa, with power relations always also in the mix: As Allan Pred puts it, "Through their participation in a multitude of practices and associated power relations, through their participation in a multitude of structuring processes, people make a plurality of histories and construct a plurality of human geographies" (Pred 1990:14). Feminist anthropology reevaluated how the division between "public" and "private" often encouraged stereotyped treatments of cross-cultural similarities and differences instead of probing understandings of gender, power, and subjectivity (e.g., see Lamphere 1997; Rosaldo 1980). The relative neglect of concrete space and place in much of the anthropology of the 1970s and 1980s was a likely influence on the acceptance of the public/private split within much feminist anthropology of the period. Whatever the historical reasons for the reassertion of space in social theory, this shift has taken place, as evidenced by the role geographical questions have played—sometimes implicitly—in anthropology since the early 1990s (e.g., see Rodman 1992; Rotenberg and McDonogh 1993; Tsing 1993). In this spatially sensitive anthropology, power is a conceptual lynchpin; and while it can intersect with capital, it has more than a merely economic modality.

In 1997, Akhil Gupta and James Ferguson published their co-edited *Culture, power, place*, a collection of essays (expanded from a special issue of the journal *Cultural Anthropology* published in 1992) that consolidated themes and forms of analysis focused on spatial categories and presuppositions in anthropology (also see Alonso 1994; Appadurai 1988; Marcus 1995). In the book's first and second chapters, the editors lay out their agenda as one of evaluating how "the renewed interest in theorizing space in postmodernist and feminist theory . . . forces us to reevaluate such central analytic concepts in anthropology as that of 'culture' and, by extension, the idea of 'cultural difference' " (Gupta and

Ferguson 1997:33). Culture areas and nations had served as concepts through which space, place, and culture took on an "assumed isomorphism" that has sometimes worked to silence questions about the culture of people living on frontiers, about cultural difference within nations and localities, and about the cultural constitution of postcolonial spaces (Gupta and Ferguson 1997:34–35). Most importantly, for Gupta and Ferguson, "spaces have *always* been hierarchically interconnected, instead of naturally disconnected" (Gupta and Ferguson 1997:35; italics in original), meaning that established notions of cultural change as stimulated mainly through exogenous contact had to be rethought. The upshot was that while capitalism and colonialism could still be viewed as dislocating particular societies, those societies were best viewed as always already "integrated" through power: one "spatial distribution of hierarchical power relations" (ibid.:36) often became another such distribution through preestablished, but shifting, articulations. Gupta and Ferguson argued, then, that power relations must always be included in attempts to reconceptualize space (also see Lomnitz-Adler 1992; Stewart 1996; Tsing 1993).

While a new sensitivity to questions of space has worked to disarticulate culture and space as concepts, sociocultural anthropologists generally understand that power must play a role in rearticulating them. It is important to emphasize, of course, that we need to relativize power, and examine how it might actually be more significant in some contexts than others. As Marshall Sahlins has recently stressed, an old anthropological lesson worth remembering is that culture is empowering to the species as a whole, and we would be ill-advised to reduce it to hegemony (Sahlins 2004:146). That said, an important recognition of the specific force of power informs key analyses of change through time in historical anthropology (e.g., Mintz 1985; O'Brien and Roseberry 1991; Sider 1986, 2003; Wolf 1982, 2001). Often influenced by theoretical debates taking place within and between political economy, poststructuralism, postmodernism, and feminism, most of the ethnographic treatments of culture in space published in the 1990s examine power relations carefully. In his historical ethnography of Mexican regions, for example, Lomnitz-Adler argues that "the various 'cultural spaces' within a regional culture can be analyzed in relation to the hierarchical organization of power in space" termed a "power region" (Lomnitz-Adler 1992:22). In her evocative and groundbreaking treatment of marginality,

Anna Lowenhaupt Tsing recounts how in the Meratus mountains of Indonesia "marginality is shaped" by "state rule, the formation of regional and ethnic identities, and gender differentiation" (Tsing 1993:5). Kathleen Stewart presents the "space on the side of the road" in West Virginia coal country as " 'occupied,' exploited, and minoritized," even as it offers room to maneuver free of the smooth hegemonic surface of an American cultural highway built for the hurtling vehicle of bourgeois social life (Stewart 1996:3, 205). Daphne Berdahl explicates the attachment of East German villagers to the memory of the Wall that had so effectively contained and oppressed them as in part a reaction to their post-wall domination by West Germany (Berdahl 1999:229).

SPACE, CULTURE, AND POWER: EXAMPLES FROM IBERIAN ANTHROPOLOGY

The anthropology of Spain and Portugal includes in-depth treatments of the dynamics of space, culture, and power ranging from some of the classic works of the mid-twentieth century to more recent publications. James Fernandez reminded us in 1988 that, as elsewhere in the world, figurative representations of Iberian areas such as Andalusia had through "metonymic misrepresentation" (Fernandez 1988:22) come to stand as stereotyped markers for broader spaces (i.e., "Spain") and as symbols playing off against the heterogeneity of lived practice. On a related topic and at about the same time, João de Pina-Cabral called anthropologists of "the Mediterranean" to account, asking questions such as, "Are the Algarve mountaineers more like Moroccans than like *minhotos*?" (Pina-Cabral 1989a:399), while inviting readers to consider that "the notion of the Mediterranean Basin as a 'culture area' is more useful as a means of distancing Anglo-American scholars from the populations they study than as a way of making sense of the cultural homogeneities and differences that characterize the region" (ibid:399; also see Fernandez 1983b).

As already indicated, we strategically chose the term *Iberia* to define this collection in order to provide a broad, challenging starting point for an exploration of space and culture in various historical moments. Most often used today as a geographic term denoting the peninsula that incorporates the mainland areas of the countries of Spain and Portugal, the concept of Iberia is linked to the Latin *Hiberus* or *Iberus* that was used to refer to the river later known as the Ebro

(Machado 1967:1247; Marchant and Charles 1948:250). The term *Iberian*, deriving from the same root, was used to refer to ancient populations that lived in a portion of what is now part of the country of Spain and the language that they spoke (Real Academia Española 1992:802; see Ruiz and Molinos 1998). In his comprehensive ethnological works on Spain, in addressing the etymological and historical basis for the idea of Iberia, Julio Caro Baroja refers to use of the designation in the writings of authors from the classical period such as Herodotus and Polybius (e.g., Caro Baroja 1991). In *Los pueblos de la península ibérica*, Caro Baroja emphasizes that he is drawing closely on Adolf Schulten's references to classical sources in his *Fontes Hispaniae Antiquae*, although he does not agree with all of Schulten's arguments, specifically that the river Ebro was named after the people known as the Iberos and not vice versa (Caro Baroja 1991:130–31). Reminding us that there were other rivers in that region of Europe named Hiberus and that rivers were often personified in the Classical Period, Caro Baroja also notes that, as with other cultures affected by Hellenization, Íber was a son of Hercules in Greek mythology, along with his brother Keltis: "The Hellenization of [core] concepts is something that serves to help us understand the [idea of] Iberian culture . . ." (ibid.:131).[2] Caro Baroja is interested in suggestions that the Iberians, who from the sixth century BC until the first century lived in the northeastern part of the Iberian Peninsula, were not only littoral but also seafaring peoples who had traveled to Sicily and the African continent, sometimes apparently even working as mercenaries for the Greeks (ibid.:131–32; Ruiz and Molinos 1998). Of course numerous peoples occupied different areas of the peninsula through the centuries; our intention here is to briefly trace aspects of the legacy of the Iberian concept rather than provide an overview of the movements of the Carthaginians, Lusitanians, Visigoths, Muslim populations, and so on. Two very different recent treatments of the historical legacy of "the peoples of Spain" discourse include work by Carrie Douglass and Susana Narotzky. Douglass's book is an in-depth symbolic analysis of the bullfighting cycle in Spain, in which she argues that differing, often vigorously expressed, reactions to bullfighting can signify people's views on both "the place of 'Spain' in Europe" (Douglass 1997:7) and the relationship among the "many Spains" (ibid.). Narotzky (2001), in contrast, argues for a more materialist approach in which the political economy of spatial specificities are always at the forefront of inquiry. Her critical reading of Caro Baroja's "peoples of Spain" includes the point that his approach relies on "a tautological vision of history" (ibid:12) which allows for various essentialisms and omissions, including a minimizing of the impact of Islam in Spain (ibid.).

The later emergence of mixed populations that came to be designated as Celtiberians, and the continuing struggles over territorial control and cultural domination throughout the Iberian Peninsula, associated islands, and colonized lands led to the emergence of new terminologies deriving from the root *Hiberus*, including that of Iberoamericans (Real Academia Española 1992:802). In both Portuguese and Spanish, a link is also made between the terms *Iberia* and *Hispania* (e.g., Machado 1967:1247). Although their focus is clearly on providing what constitutes an important, rigorous synthesis of the archaeological findings relating to the Iberian populations living from the sixth century BC until Romanization, Arturo Ruiz and Manuel Molinos are careful to contextualize what they are doing by providing an initial framing discussion of the politically charged and sometimes shifting uses of both archaeological data as well as core denominations. They comment, for example, that "[p]ortrayed by some, because of their strong autochthonous tradition, as a model of 'the Hispanic,' or by others as the fountainhead of the various peoples of Spain, the Iberians have ranged through the history of Spain in the past century as contemporary parties to the historical debate that led to the civil war in 1936" (Ruiz and Molinos 1998:1).

The idea of shifting "Iberian" spaces relating to ancient population movements, political struggles, and texts does not of course provide us with unambiguous connotations in the early twenty-first century; however, we contend that with the term's use, the cultural meanings of various spaces are opened up to consideration. Using Iberia, rather than solely the denominations of political states such as Spain and Portugal, or a "Hispania" always too readily conflated with "Spain," can create a useful intellectual counterpoint to assumed meanings. By referring to Iberia, we point to the peninsula and places in the world relevant to it such as former colonies, island spaces such as the Azores and Mallorca, the locations of political exiles, and even border countries situated on the peninsula such as the Principality of Andorra (e.g., Comas d'Argemir and Pujadas 1997). The term *Iberia* can also serve to point to the ongoing dynamics of struggles for national as well as regional rights and identities within contemporary Spain and Portugal. Indeed, a recent edition of one dictionary of the Spanish language refers to the term "*iberismo*," defining it as not only relating to the "study of the history and culture of the Iberos" (Moliner 1999:1) but as sometimes used to refer to "a doctrine favouring the union of Spain and Portugal or an increased integration between these two countries" (ibid.). While we are by no means using Iberia in this explicit sense, we do hope that employing the multifaceted concept to frame this volume will highlight the constant struggles over the contours and meanings of both geographical and political mappings. One very recent example of this is of course Catalonia's reform of its statute of autonomy in 2005 and the highly negative tone of the reactions to this proposal not only in the Spanish parliament but in the Spanish mass media, the military, the Church, and the business community, just as other stateless nations such as Galicia and Euskal Herria also work toward revised arrangements with the Spanish state. Moreover, debate in Catalonia over modifications to crucial aspects of the statute text forced by the Spanish parliament points to the continuing saliency of historical referents and the "Iberianness of the issues at stake," "at least on the Catalan left" (DiGiacomo 2006). As Susan DiGiacomo explains, the leftist Esquerra Republicana de Catalunya party chose to recommend a "no" in the referendum (for very different reasons than those driving the right-wing Partido Popular party), having come to the conclusion that "since there was apparently no negotiating with the state, even under a government of the left, *'l'autonomia que ens cal és la de Portugal'*—the autonomy we need is the one Portugal has, a reference to 1640, when Catalans won an important battle but lost the war that resulted in Portugal regaining its status as an independent state" (ibid.). Additional good examples of similar struggles over mappings are the current debates over the future shape and direction of the European Union in the context of rejections of the new European Constitution through processes such as the referendum in France in 2005, and very public discussions about applications of countries such as Turkey to be part of the EU's ongoing enlargement.

Anthropologists' interventions into public and academic debates about nationalities within Spanish borders and struggles for territorial, linguistic, and other political rights have been among the most relevant contributions to the study of space and culture. Indeed, this area of inquiry has been a research focus for a number of the contributors to this volume (for example, DiGiacomo 1986, 1999, 2001; Pi-Sunyer 1985a, 1985b, 1995; Roseman 1995, 1997; Urla 1988, 1993, 1995). The tensions between the central government of the Spanish state and the various parts of the country it has governed in recent centuries did not of course begin with the repressions of the Franco years. Some have argued that the liberal regimes of Spain's nineteenth and early twentieth centuries did not succeed in their efforts to "forge a nation-state" (Smith and Mar-Molinero 1996:3), in contrast to developments in other Western European states such as France. In response to claims for the right to self-determination after the end of the Franco dictatorship, the 1978 Spanish Constitution allowed for the creation of Autonomous Community levels of government. In this process, the Basque Country, Catalonia, and Galicia were recognized to be "historic nations"; accordingly, these three areas, or parts of them, were the first to be granted Autonomous Community status within the new democracy. Subsequently, other regions established their own Autonomous Community jurisdictions, ranging greatly in size of territory and population as well as in the ideological and historical referents for autonomy. Today, there are seventeen Comunidades Autónomas within the Spanish polity.[3] Despite Portugal's smaller size, greater ethnic homogeneity, and increased political centralization relative to Spain, the country is considered by many historians, geographers, and anthropologists to harbor important regional differences and felt regional identities. One common way of discussing broad divisions within Portugal has been to focus on north/south or (related) Atlantic/Mediterranean dichotomies (e.g., Brettell 1979, 1990; Brøgger and Gilmore 1997; Dias 1963, 1964; Mattoso 1991; O'Neill 1995; Ribeiro 1991 [1945]) based in climatological, ecological, topographical, economic, social, political, and religious patterns.[4] Another way has been to focus on named subareas with "historically legitimated categories of social identity and actual sociocultural unity" (Pina-Cabral 1989b:12), such as the Minho and Trás-os-Montes in the northern part of the country, or the Algarve in the south (Bastos 1988, 1993). This work is similar to the by now classic twentieth-century ethnological works by Julio Caro Baroja; Caro Baroja is known for his close attention to the Basque Country and also for his numerous volumes charting the "peoples" who occupied various geographical regions within both Spain and Portugal through prehistoric and historic periods (e.g., Caro Baroja 1946, 1973, 1991). Since the publication of his first overviews of Iberian space during the Franco regime in the 1940s, Caro Baroja's method of ethnological comparison has solidified the idea of arranging discussions of cultural, social, and linguistic variation within a framework of geographical blocs. Over the many years of his writing career, he employed a range of such frameworks, including that of the "south," "east," "center," "west," and "north" of the peninsula in "ancient times" as well as what he termed in the 1940s "the contemporary regions" such as: "the provinces of Vascongada and Navarra" to "the central *meseta*: Old Castille and the ancient Castilianized provinces of the Reign of León" (Caro Baroja 1946). It was authors such as Caro Baroja who laid the groundwork for the continued discussions over the last several decades not only of the *"lusitano"* connection between Galicia and Portugal but distinctions such as the *"área atlántica"* (the Atlantic area), the *"área pirenaica"* (the area of the Pyrenees), the *"zona central"* (the central zone) and *"los pueblos del sur"* (the people of the south) (Caro Baroja 1991). As Rodríguez Campos (2002a) has emphasized, the Mediterranean/Atlantic distinction became important ideologically at the end of the nineteenth and in the first few decades of the twentieth century in the writings of prominent intellectuals such as José Ortega y Gasset (1964 [1914]), Vicente Risco (1920, 1980 [1930]), and Victoriano García Martí (1933). In many ways, the Portuguese historian Joaquim Pedro Oliveira Martins can be considered a forerunner of studies that attempted to link an overall "Iberian civilization," conceived of as a "superorganism" (Oliveira Martins 1930 [1880]), to important regional differentiation in terms of cultural practice (Oliveira Martins 1879, 1880).

As with Spain, while much of the more recent anthropological field studies in Portugal have dealt with specific settlements (Brito 1996; O'Neill 1987; Almeida 1996), there are also older studies that deal with larger spaces such as parishes, "lands," districts, or even entire provinces and "regions" (see Leal 2000:27–61; Medeiros 1998), as well as recent studies that focus on the same, with an emphasis on the parish level (Brettell 1986; Cutileiro 1971; Leal 1994; Pina-Cabral 1986; Silva 1998; Sobral 1999; Wall 1998).[5] In this, the Portuguese literature has much in common with many of the classic works in the anthropology of Spain (e.g., Lisón Tolosana 1983 [1979], 1987 [1979]).

It is important to remember that much of the ethnographic work of the last several decades of the twentieth century attended closely to the level of the "local," whether it involved studies of rural or urban spaces. Julian Pitt-Rivers's emphasis on the "boundaries of the community"—on the ways in which patron saints, ballads, collective nicknames, and other means of ascribing insider/outsider identities to people—in Andalusian agro-towns is echoed in many ethnographies of towns, villages, and urban neighborhoods in Portugal and Spain (e.g., Brandes 1975; Brito 1996; Cordeiro 1997; Freeman 1970; Gilmore 1987; Kavanagh 1994a, 1994b; Lisón Tolosana 1973; Maddox 1993; Pina-Cabral 1986; Press 1979; Riegelhaupt 1973; Tenorio 1982). The local importance of boundaries and borders is also highlighted in ethnographic work focusing on Iberian crossroads and intersections. Christian, for example, remarks on the "gravitation of apparitions and shrines towards boundaries" (Christian 1972:73; also see Lisón Tolosana 1987 [1979]:127).

Boundedness and spatial as well as social exclusion are important concepts in studies of divided populations and the consequences of social isolation and xenophobia in urban Iberia, as Teresa San Román (1976) and her colleagues demonstrated thirty years ago in their ambitious study of social life in nucleated settlements occupied largely by Romani families [in Castilian, *gitano*; in English translation, Gypsy] in the greater Madrid area. Some of these settlements, such as Barrio de la Celsa situated on the highway between the towns of Villaverde and Vallecas, were characterized by the poor and makeshift quality of the dwellings known as *chabolas* or shacks (ibid.:38–41). Several decades later, San Román provides an important challenge to our ideas about space and sociality in her detailed analyses of the reality of the "transterritorial community" (San Román 1996:12) of Romani people with "diffused identities" (ibid.) living in Spain. In her recent theoretical volume on racism, antiracism, anti-antiracism, and "*alterofobia*," she argues incisively that in the context of Spain "it took the arrival of immigrants from Africa and people's celebration, with varying degrees of shame, of the quincentenaries for there to be a renewed preoccupation with the 'other.' For some anthropologists, 'the reencountered subject,' in my view" (San Román 1996:59). She then turns to an even more direct comment on assumptions about spatiality and (social) distance reflecting on how she has long

> protested against the temerity and impertinence that was implied in calling the 500,000 Gypsies [Roma] of the Spanish state 'an exotic

theme.' I have repeated many times and will continue to do so:
culturally, Gypsies are not much further from me and those around
me than the community of "*gente guapa*" (pretty people) of the
Mediterranean. Politically I am, clearly, much closer . . . (ibid.)

In a recent book charting the emergence of "landscapes of inequality" (Suárez-Navaz 2004:79) in the case of Senegalese and other
immigrants from Africa settling in the Andalusian province of Granada,
Liliana Suárez-Navaz provides an important ethnographic account rooted
in "a consideration of the global political economy underlining the
rebordering of the Mediterranean" (ibid.:221). She demonstrates the
dialectical construction of shifting social identities in a context in which
the "racialization of class relations" (ibid.:222) is occurring alongside
forms of individual and collective resistance on the part of immigrants.
In this penetrating examination, Suárez-Navaz analyzes how processes
of "sociospatial segmentation" (ibid.:78) carried over from prior forms
of socioeconomic hierarchy in rural Andalusia were recast in the 1990s,
as "security and control of local spaces became the dominant idiom for
reorganizing the place of immigrants in the [Alfaya] valley" (ibid.:89).

In her analysis of the Basque *korrika* ritual, Teresa del Valle (1994)
addresses how physical borderlands can become the focus for resistance.
The *korrika* is a relay footrace of 2,080 kilometers in length that was
initiated in 1980 as a way to support the Basque language movement
as well as to mark the territory of Euskal Herria on both sides of the
French/Spanish border in the western Pyrenees. Del Valle demonstrates
that this movement through physical space is underpinned by not just
a celebration of Basque unity but also by an "atemporality" and an
explicit "symbolic attempt . . . to abolish the border" (del Valle 1994:xxvii,
71; also see Douglass 1978; Fernandez 1983b; Gómez-Ibáñez 1975;
González Reboredo and Fernández de Rota 1990).[6] In their study of
Andorra as a "border" country, Dolors Comas d'Argemir and Joan Josep
Pujadas remind their readers that although "frontier spaces" are often
considered from the outside to be spaces characterized by "transition
and liminality," "[f]or those who live on borders, these are not [like] a
wall of separation but a bridge over which a community of interests is
established and system for living is organized" (Comas d'Argemir and
Pujadas 1997:39).

Some of the most penetrating work in the ethnographic corpus
on Iberia attending to the making of culture and power through space

deals with ongoing processes of charged boundary making and contestations over ritual and "tradition." William Christian, for example, has produced a series of important studies demonstrating that a full understanding of Catholicism in Spain requires research into the appearance of the divine in the natural landscape and the human politics connected with such sightings (e.g., Christian 1972, 1996). Accounts of the emergence and continuity of rural shrines "often involve tension between town and landscape" (Christian 1996:302). In addition, "[t]he divine will repeatedly foils attempts by clergy and civil authorities to capture images. . . . Images return mysteriously to their place of origin; shrine building materials move at night; a half-constructed shrine collapses if it is not in the right place" (ibid.). For the contours of social relations—whether they are between laypeople and the hierarchy of the Catholic church, people from particular locales or neighborhoods, kin and neighbors of the same socioeconomic class, workers and employers, or activists in social movements and state officials—are often reinforced, parodied, or contested outright via struggles over space and culture (e.g., Brettell 1990; Cátedra 1992; Kaplan 1993; Kasmir 1996; Roseman 1996, 2003; Sanchis 1983). Manuel Delgado Ruiz makes a related argument in his book on iconoclasticism and anticlericalism in Spain, where he suggests that, in addition to the existing analyses of the political framework bearing on the anticlerical actions during the Spanish Civil War (1936–39), it is crucial to provide a detailed historical understanding of the broad social and symbolic context for violence against symbols of the sacred within Spanish Catholicism. He argues that there are important links between a pattern of violence (both verbal and physical) against non-Catholic religious communities—both within Spain and in colonized areas—and the abundance of blasphemic, iconoclastic, and anticlerical practices directed at God, the saints, and sacred locations linked to Catholicism. According to Delgado Ruiz, iconoclasticism has an ongoing relationship with iconophilism, but in moments such as the Civil War, the "very same violence that has been feeding the system" can take on "the task of annihilating it" (Delgado Ruiz 2001:173). He suggests that one of the aspects that must be considered in such an analysis relates to "a topographic logic" (ibid.:46) whereby a "willingness to erase the sacred can be observed in the painstaking action taken with regard to toponymy. Place names are, in effect, another of the strategies related to territorialization" (ibid.:48; also see Delgado Ruiz 2002, 2003).

Another key area of research on space and culture in Iberia deals with kinship, property, inheritance patterns, and house form. A portion of this literature highlights commonalities between Portugal and Spain, with multigenerational households and impartible inheritance being associated with parts of the "north" and neolocal postmarital residence, nuclear family households, and partible inheritance being associated with the "south" of the peninsula, as well as with urban areas (on this issue, see the papers in Douglass 1988). The prevalence of uxorilocality and female preferential inheritance among peasant and fishing households has been associated with male labor migration in northern coastal Portugal and coastal Galicia (e.g., Brettell 1986; Cole 1991; Lisón Tolosana 1983 [1979]), with natolocality, single mothers, and unmarried cohabitation significant among those with lower-class status (e.g., Cutileiro 1971; Dias 1963; Kelley 1991; O'Neill 1984, 1987; Parkhurst 2003; Pina-Cabral 2003). Recent research has taken up a theme prevalent in the early ethnology and folklore of the peninsula (e.g., Dias 1984 [1953]; Risco 1933) by returning to the topic of household architecture. In this new work, the commitment to incorporating historical depth into anthropology has been combined with a renewed attention to spatiality, even at the most microscopic level. Caroline Brettell, for example, has traced how the *casa* (house) of one family in Viana do Castelo (northwestern Portugal) has durably served to symbolize the integration "of a well-to-do and respected peasant family" through various generations due to its architectural design, which conditioned the "processes of consolidation and exclusion" leading to its social meaning (Brettell 1999:66). This theme is found in accounts from other parts of the peninsula, including Ruth Behar's (1986) "archaeology of the house" in central León, Spain, wherein a system of partible inheritance may result in dwellings being "sliced down the middle" (Behar 1986:62; also see Fernandez 1990; Fernández de Rota y Monter 1984). Fernandez and Fernandez (1988:136) consider how a long-standing commitment "to accommodate all one's descendants under one roof" in Asturias has led to two generations of the same family frequently living in high-rise buildings on separate floors, a pattern also found in other parts of the peninsula, including Catalonia and Galicia. Denise Lawrence-Zúñiga (1999) explores how formal changes in the new housing being erected in places such as Vila Branca (southern Portugal) both coincide with and serve to transform family members' access to privacy and patterns of sociability.

In an influential ethnography of a European elite, Gary McDonogh (1986) demonstrates that one can observe the relations among the powerful families of Barcelona and between elite individuals and other city residents by attending to the design and use of the Cementiri Vell (Old Cemetery) and the Gran Teatre del Liceu (the opera house). Whereas in both the cemetery and the opera house, "class membership and boundaries are clearly demarcated" (McDonogh 1986:166), "the interaction of living Barcelonins at the opera has also made it an arena in which boundaries are crossed by acts of violence that spring from social and economic inequality" (ibid.). In one of the most important European studies of the "politics of tradition," Richard Maddox (1993) examines how one cannot study the hegemonic uses of the past in the Andalusian town of Aracena without taking into account the intersections between everyday spaces in the town and the "complex cultural space" (Maddox 1993:8) of "El Castillo," the latter including the archaeological remains of a fortress standing on a hilltop (*monte*) as well as "the monte itself, the church, and the most popular of the town's lay religious brotherhoods" (Maddox 1993:8; for an important related study of "tradition" in Andalusia see Collier 1997). In Portugal, Kimberly Holton demonstrates how during Lisbon's stint as Cultural Capital of Europe during 1994 the city's half-reconstructed avenues, plazas, and performance venues exposed "the costs of modernity, the tenuousness of liberty, and the scars of underdevelopment" for the country (Holton 1998:191). Analyzing Portugal's Expo '98, Timothy Sieber reveals a spatial concretization of different perspectives on Portuguese history and culture. The dominant perspective—on Portuguese history as the work of home-grown "Discoverers" such as Vasco da Gama, or on "Portuguese music" as superior to an emigrant, (national) working-class, or (international) Lusophone sound—can be successfully read, argues Sieber, from "the exclusion of local immigrant communities and associations in the Expo" (Sieber 2001:574), and from the fact that "Expo's ten performance venues for music were segregated by type of music" (Sieber 2002:170). While officialized, prestigious arts occupied raised stages, emigrant and working-class musics were relegated to lower, informal spaces (ibid.:172).[7]

Iberia has served as an anthropological proving ground for the spatial analysis of gender relations. Stanley Brandes's (1980) analysis of "metaphors of masculinity" in 1970s Andalusia provided us with key insights into space and gender within Iberia by exploring the intense social life of men in bars (also see Driessen 1983; Gilmore 1991; McDonogh 2003), as well as how gender relations are symbolically both affirmed and reversed in the physical space of olive groves at harvest time (Brandes 1980:137–56; also see Brandes 1987). In his recent engagement with the production of "hegemonic masculinities" in Pardais, a village in Portugal's Alentejo region, Miguel Vale de Almeida complements the Andalusian examples by reminding us that among male workers one needs to consider the "time-space of work and that of domestic life" (Almeida 1997:149), as well as the "compulsory" (ibid.) café where "drinking, smoking, talking, competing, playing and argu-ing—are coercive activities" (ibid.:150) that mark off a specific social time (Almeida 1996:89).

In counterpoint to Vale de Almeida's findings, however, Joyce Riegelhaupt had earlier demonstrated that, despite formal legal restrictions focused on women and the "appearance" of women's social subordination in the Portugal of the 1960s, women in São João das Lampas parish, near Lisbon, in fact played key political and economic roles. Their relative power resulted from these women's prominent positioning in public space and their consequent ability to cultivate strategic cross-household and cross-community networks (Riegelhaupt 1967). A highly significant book by del Valle interprets the contested politics of space and gender in the Basque cities of Bilbao and Donostia (or San Sebastián) by recounting how the association Independent Women (Mujeres Independientes) advocates reclamation of Donostia's urban space, partly through the substitution of place names chosen to honor aristocrats, saints, military leaders, and politicians with those commemorating the contributions of workers, non-Basque heroines such as Mother Teresa of Calcutta, and different kinds of plant life (del Valle 1997).

The anthropology of Iberian contexts has also attended extensively to movement through space and the interconnections between locales that accompany processes such as permanent and temporary migration, transhumance, pilgrimage, tourism, and the delineation of parklands (e.g., Brandes 1975; Brettell 1982, 1986, 2003a, 2003b; H. C. Buechler 1987; J-M. Buechler 1975; Buechler and Buechler 1984; Crain 1996, 1997; Douglass 1975; Freeman 1979; Frey 1998; Greenwood 1977; Klimt 1989, 2000a, 200b; Leeds 1987; Fernandez 1984; Mintz 1978; Nogués Pedregal 1996; Pi-Sunyer 1973, 1977; Rodríguez

Campos 2002b). As Caroline Brettell has pointed out, although it was clear to herself and George Gmelch (1986) in the late 1970s that "return migration" was as important to study as emigration, the significance of "an ideology of return" was not widely recognized in anthropology at that time (Brettell 1998:81). Determining the impacts of such ideological underpinnings on demographic patterns across space and time became an integral aspect of much of the ethnographic work on Portugal and Spain (e.g., Brettell 1986; Douglass 1971; Gilmore 1980; Greenwood 1976; Hansen 1977; Harding 1984; Klimt 2000a; O'Neill 1984, 1987). Through his close comparison of life in the village of Ramosierra in the province of Soria and parish of San Martín in the capital city of Madrid, Michael Kenny's (1966 [1961]) treatment of "rural" and "urban" spaces in Castile had demonstrated that ongoing contacts between rural and urban people as well as a regular migration of people from villages to Madrid and other cities resulted in a number of commonalities. As relevant was the existence of "two parallel channels linking town and country . . . the one set up by the official State and Church structures, the other established by patronage" (ibid.:236). However, he also identified some important points for drawing both contrasts and comparisons such as the following: "The sense of coexistence—strong in the village parish, weak in the city parish—has a permanent static quality. It is based on a constant, territorial relationship. The sense of loyalty, on the other hand, is based on a variable, social relationship and is an abstract sentiment" (ibid.: 235). Kenny's astute observations on the complexity of urban and rural spatiality are also paralleled in studies such as Ignasi Terradas Saborit's (1979, 1987) historical anthropology of class and culture in the industrial colonies that operated in Catalonia in the nineteenth and twentieth centuries in support of the growing textile trade. When these colonies emerge in the nineteenth century, in L'Ametlla de Merola, the subject of Terradas Saborit's detailed illustrative case study, as in other colonies, the wider context is the link between the "de-urbanization of industry" (Terradas Saborit 1979:56) and the "privatization of public functions" (ibid.) that were not being provided by the state. In one article Terradas Saborit argues that one of the most significant aspects of the mid–nineteenth century establishment of such colonies was the fact that, although some of the workers lived full-time in these organized social spaces, many others, "and especially women and youth . . . came and went from the outside" (Terradas Saborit 1987:78); as rural peasants from settlements in the vicinity, these workers not only practiced a multioccupational livelihood but, in Kenny's terms, participated in more than one arrangement of both coexistence and loyalty. It was only in the 1990s that generalized anthropological paradigms had caught up to such innovations that had emerged out of empirical "area studies"; at this time the need for cautious analysis of both the cultural and socioeconomic impacts of population movements finally received due attention in the field as a whole (e.g., Clifford 1997; Ong 1999; Schiller, Basch, and Blanc-Szanton 1992). In a recent book, Holton makes an intricate argument that there has been a substantial recasting of significant spaces in Portugal, and that understanding popular aesthetic practices requires a comprehension of this shift. While during the Salazar regime the national level overshadowed all other spatial registers, in the years following the dictatorship a dialectical "glocality" has arisen as the spatial preoccupation of the epoch. There is increasing cultural concentration on promoting the identities of village, town, and city neighborhood, not as synecdoches of the nation, but as entities that bypass much national bureaucratic regulation in reaching into diasporic Portuguese communities across the globe. The spatial dialectic informs the most intimate of social practices, such as folkloric dance, a highly sensual means of cultural transmission (Holton 2006:51). Anticipating the paradigmatic shift in anthropology that led to books such as Holton's, in his pioneering treatments of change and continuity in rural Asturias James Fernandez (e.g., 1986) had long been developing a theoretically innovative way to write about space, culture, and movement. Fernandez introduced "the notion of semantic space" (Fernandez 1986:137). This "organizes our experiences, which may be quite other, by a spatial metaphor" (ibid.). For Fernandez, experiences of movement in physical space have cultural entailments in that they can be accessed through the very "territoriality of words" (ibid.): "[I]f one wishes to become real friends with an Asturian one has to walk the paths and byways of Asturias"; at the same time, "[t]o know Asturias, one is told, is to learn the Asturian names associated with the peaks where the chamois hide or the river pools where the trout lie" (Fernandez 1986:137–38; also see Delgado Ruiz 1999 on movement and urban space).

In this collection of essays, we take up a number of these themes that have been introduced in earlier writings on Iberia. In order to highlight them, the volume is divided into four sections: Colonial Spaces and National Identities; Fascism, Cultural Spaces, and Memory Politics; Regionality and Space; and Cultural Politics and the Global. For each of these sections, we provide a brief introduction to the theme and outline some key interconnections among the various contributions that are grouped together under it. The volume concludes with a final word (for now) from James Fernandez, where he takes up this volume's engagement with the highly charged politics being played out in diverse Iberian cultural sites at the present time as well as in the past. In all the sections of this book, we aim to emphasize how space and culture continue to be recast in an era characterized by both global "flows" and a renewed concern with political borders. Overall, these essays on culture and space in Iberian contexts bring to the forefront the importance of anthropologists keeping in mind histories of empire, colonialism, and other forms of hegemony as well as people's resistances to oppression, struggles for political self-determination, and formulations of new cultural strategies over time.

NOTES

1. We agree with Patricia Yaeger (1996:5) that it is not sufficient to circumscribe "places" as meaningful, human-made locations that are easily distinguished from other physical spaces: "In a global economy where multiple places converge in a single space, where the space/place binary becomes porous and provisional, we need to destabilize the organicism and integrity that place-centered analysis sometimes assumes, to recognize within a transnational economy the strange effects that happen in the margins between 'space' and 'place.' "

2. Throughout this volume, all translations into English from other languages is that of the contributors, unless otherwise indicated.

3. These include: Andalucía, Aragón, Asturias, Canarias, Cantabria, Castilla y León, Castilla-La Mancha, Cataluña, Comunidad de Madrid, Comunidad Valenciana, Extremadura, Galicia, Islas Baleares, Navarra, País Vasco, La Rioja, Región de Murcia. There are also two contested "autonomous cities" in African territories that continue to have a colonized status as Spanish enclaves: Ciudad Autónoma de Ceuta and Ciudad Autónoma de Melilla.

4. For an instructive critique of Dias (an anthropologist) and Ribeiro (a geographer), early proponents of this kind of geocultural division within Portugal, see Leal (1999).

5. Brettell, Pina-Cabral, and Wall focus on the level of the parish, largely because of the spatial organization of social life in northwestern Portugal,

commonly known as "the world of the parishes," as opposed to the "world of the villages" found in the northeast, where Brito and O'Neill worked. Sobral also focuses on the parish, but his field site lies outside of "the world of the parishes." Leal's spatial focus moves between that of parish, set of parishes, and island in the Açores. While Silva and Wall are both sociologists, their work is heavily influenced by anthropological theory and method.

6. Compare with the impact that state policies can have on the creation of border "wars" between neighboring communities, over both land and sea resources (Meltzoff 1995:31). Also see Sahlins (1989) on the Catalan communities living in the borderland of the eastern Pyrenees.

7. On the Seville '92 Expo, see Harvey (1996) and Maddox (2004).

References

Almeida, Miguel Vale de. 1996. *The hegemonic male: Masculinity in a Portuguese town*. Providence and Oxford: Berghahn Books.

———. 1997. Gender, masculinity, and power in southern Portugal. *Social Anthropology* 5, no. 2:141–58.

Alonso, Ana María. 1994. The politics of space, time and substance: State formation, nationalism, and ethnicity. *Annual Review of Anthropology* 23:379–405.

Appadurai, Arjun. 1992. Global ethnoscapes: Notes and queries for a transnational anthropology. In *Recapturing anthropology: Working in the present,* ed. Richard Fox, 191–210. Santa Fe: School of American Research.

Appadurai, Arjun, ed. 1988. Place and voice in anthropological theory. Special theme issue. *Cultural Anthropology* 3, no. 1:16–96.

Bastos, Cristiana. 1988. The northeastern Algarve and the southern Iberia family pattern. *Journal of Family History* 13, no. 1:111–22.

———. 1993. *Os montes do nordeste algarvio*. Lisbon: Edições Cosmos.

Behar, Ruth. 1986. *Santa María del Monte: The presence of the past in a Spanish village*. Princeton: Princeton University Press.

Berdahl, Daphne. 1999. *Where the world ended: Re-unification and identity in the German borderland*. Berkeley: University of California Press.

Birdwell-Pheasant, Donna, and Denise Lawrence-Zúñiga, eds. 1999. *House Life: Space, place, and family in Europe*. Oxford and New York: Berg.

Brandes, Stanley H. 1975. *Migration, kinship, and community: Tradition and transition in a Spanish village*. New York: Academic Press.

———. 1980. *Metaphors of masculinity: Sex and status in Andalusian folklore*. Philadelphia: University of Pennsylvania Press.

———. 1987. Sex roles and anthropological research in rural Andalusia. *Women's Studies* 13:357–72.

Brettell, Caroline B. 1979. Emigration and its implications for the revolution in northern Portugal. In *Contemporary Portugal: The revolution and its antecedents,* ed. Lawrence S. Graham and Harry M. Makler, 281–98. Austin: University of Texas Press.

———. 1982. *We have already cried many tears: The stories of three Portuguese migrant women.* Cambridge, MA: Schenkman Publishing Company.

———. 1986. *Men who migrate, women who wait: Population and history in a Portuguese parish.* Princeton: Princeton University Press.

———. 1990. The priest and his people: The contractual basis for religious practice in rural Portugal. In *Religious orthodoxy and popular faith in European society,* ed. Ellen Badone, 55–75. Princeton: Princeton University Press.

———. 1991. Kinship and contract: Property transmission and family relations in northwestern Portugal. *Comparative Studies in Society and History* 33:443–57.

———. 1998. Returning with the emigrants: A journey in Portuguese ethnography. In *Europe in the anthropological imagination,* ed. Susan Parman, 80–93. Upper Saddle River: Prentice-Hall.

———. 1999. The *casa* of José dos Santos Caldas: Family and household in a northwestern Portuguese village, 1850–1993. In *House Life: Space, place, and family in Europe,* ed. Donna Birdwell-Pheasant and Denise Lawrence-Zúñiga, 39–72. Oxford: Berg.

———. 2003a [1993]. The emigrant, the nation, and the state in nineteenth- and twentieth-century Portugal: An anthropological approach. In *Anthropology and migration: Essays on transnationalism, ethnicity, and identity,* 9–21. Walnut Creek: Altamira Press.

———. 2003b [1983]. Emigration, the church, and the religious *festa* in northern Portugal. In *Anthropology and migration: Essays on transnationalism, ethnicity, and identity,* 75–99. Walnut Creek: Altamira Press.

Brito, Joaquim Pais de. 1996. *Retrato de aldeia com espelho: Ensaio sobre Rio de Onor.* Lisbon: Publicações Dom Quixote.

Brøgger, Jan, and David D. Gilmore. 1997. The matrifocal family in Iberia: Spain and Portugal compared. *Ethnology* 36:12–30.

Buchli, Victor, ed. 2002. *The material culture reader.* Oxford and New York: Berg.

Buechler, Hans Christian, and Judith-Maria Buechler. 1984. Four generations in Spanish Galicia: A developmental analysis of socioeconomic options. In *Culture and community in Europe: Essays in honor of Conrad Arensberg,* ed. Owen M. Lynch, 150–74. New Delhi: Hindustani Press.

Buechler, Hans Christian. 1987. Spanish Galician migration to Switzerland: Demographic processes and family dynamics. In *Migrants in Europe: The role of family, labor, and politics,* ed. Hans Christian Buechler and Judith-Maria Buechler, 221–64. New York: Greenwood Press.

Buechler, Judith-Maria. 1975. The Eurogallegas: Female Spanish migration. In *Being female,* ed. Dana Raphael, 207–14. The Hague: Mouton.

Caldeira, Teresa P. R. 2000. *City of walls: Crime, segregation, and citizenship in São Paulo.* Berkeley: University of California Press.

Caro Baroja, Julio. 1946. *Los pueblos de España: ensayo de etnología.* Barcelona: Editorial Barna.

———. 1963. The city and the country: Reflexions on some ancient commonplaces. In *Mediterranean countrymen: Essays in the social anthropology of the Mediterranean,* ed. Julian Pitt-Rivers, 27–40. Paris and La Haye: Mouton.

———. 1966. *La ciudad y el campo.* Madrid and Barcelona: Ediciones Alfaguara.

———. 1973. *Los pueblos del norte de la península ibérica (análisis histórico-cultural).* 2nd edition. San Sebastián: Editorial Txertoa.

———. 1991. *Los pueblos de la península ibérica.* San Sebastián and Barcelona: Editorial Txertoa and Editorial Crítica.

Cátedra, María. 1992. *This world, other worlds: Sickness, suicide, death, and the afterlife among the Vaqueiros de Alzada of Spain.* Trans. William A. Christian Jr. Chicago: The University of Chicago Press.

Christian, William A. Jr. 1972. *Person and God in a Spanish valley.* New York: Seminar Press.

———. 1996. *Visionaries: The Spanish Republic and the reign of Christ.* Berkeley: University of California Press.

Clifford, James. 1997. *Routes: Travel and translation in the late twentieth century.* Cambridge: Harvard University Press.

Cole, Sally. 1991. *Women of the praia: Work and lives in a Portuguese coastal community.* Princeton: Princeton University Press.

Collier, Jane Fishburne. 1997. *From duty to desire: Remaking families in a Spanish village.* Princeton: Princeton University Press.

Comas d'Argemir, Dolors, and Joan Josep Pujadas. 1997. *Andorra, un país de frontera: Estudi etnogràfic dels canvis econòmics, socials i culturals.* Barcelona: Editorial Alta Fulla.

Cordeiro, Graça Índias. 1997. *Um lugar na cidade: Quotidiano, memória e representação no Bairro da Bica.* Lisbon: Publicações Dom Quixote.

Crain, Mary M. 1996. Contested territories: The politics of touristic development at the shrine of El Rocio in southwestern Andalusia. In *Coping with tourists: European reactions to mass tourism,* ed. Jeremy Boissevain, 27–55. Providence: Berghahn Books.

———. 1997. The remaking of an Andalusian pilgrimage tradition: Debates regarding visual (re)presentation and the meanings of "locality" in a global era. In *Culture, power, place: Explorations in critical anthropology,* ed. Akhil Gupta and James Ferguson, 291–311. Durham and London: Duke University Press.

Cutileiro, José. 1971. *A Portuguese rural society*. Oxford: Clarendon Press.

Darby, Wendy Joy. 2000. *Landscape and identity: Geographies of nation and class in England*. Oxford and New York: Berg.

del Valle, Teresa. 1994. *Korrika: Basque ritual for ethnic identity*. Trans. Linda White. Reno: University of Nevada Press.

————. 1997. *Andiamos para una nueva ciudad: Lecturas desde la antropología feminista*. Madrid: Instituto de la Mujer.

Delgado Ruiz, Manuel. 1999. *El animal público: Hacia una antropología de los espacios urbanos*. Barcelona: Editorial Anagrama.

————. 2001. *Luces iconoclastas: Anticlericalismo, espacio y ritual en la España contemporánea*. Barcelona: Editorial Ariel.

————. 2002. *Disoluciones urbanas: Procesos identitarios y espacio público*. Medellín: Editorial Universidad de Antioquia.

————, coord. 2003. *Carrer, festa i revolta: Els usos simbòlics de l'espai públic a Barcelona (1951–2000)*. Barcelona: Departament de Cultura, Generalitat de Catalunya.

Dias, Jorge. 1963. Algumas considerações acerca da estrutura social do povo português. In *Actas do 1.º Congresso de Etnografia e Folclore. Vol. 1*. Lisbon: Biblioteca Social e Corporativa.

————. 1964 Portugal: Land and people. In *Portuguese contribution to cultural anthropology*, 62–78. Johannesburg: Witwatersrand University Press.

————. 1984[1953]. *Rio de Onor: Comunitarismo agro-pastoril*. Lisbon: Editorial Presença.

DiGiacomo, Susan M. 1986. Images of class and ethnicity in Catalan politics, 1977–1980. In *Conflict in Catalonia: Images of an urban society*, ed. Gary W. McDonogh, 72–92. Gainesville: University of Florida Press.

————. 1999. Language ideological debates in an Olympic city: Barcelona, 1992–1996. In *Language ideological debates*, ed. J. Blommaert, 105–42. Berlin: Mouton de Gruyter.

————. 2001. 'Catalan is everyone's thing': Normalizing a nation. In *Language, ethnicity and the state. Volume 1: Minority languages in the European Union*, ed. Camille C. O'Reilly, 56–77. Basingstoke and New York: Palgrave.

————. 2006. Personal communication.

Donham, Donald L. 1999. *History, power, ideology: Central issues in Marxism and anthropology*. Berkeley: University of California Press.

Donnan, Hastings, and Thomas M. Wilson. 1999. *Borders: Frontiers of identity, nation and state*. Oxford and New York: Berg.

Douglass, Carrie B. 1997. *Bulls, bullfighting, and Spanish identities*. Tucson: University of Arizona Press.

Douglass, William A. 1971. Rural exodus in two Spanish Basque villages: A cultural explanation. *American Anthropologist* 73, no. 5:1100–14.

————. 1975. *Echalar and Murelaga: Opportunity and rural exodus in two Spanish Basque villages*. New York: St. Martin's Press.

————. 1978. Influencias fronterizas en un pueblo Navarro. *Ethnica* 14:39–52.

Douglass, William A., ed. 1988. Iberian family history. Special theme issue of *Journal of Family History* 13, no. 1.

Douglass, William A., and Joseba Zulaika. 1990. On the interpretation of terrorist violence: ETA and the Basque political process. *Comparative Studies in Society and History* 32, no. 2:238–57.

Driessen, Henk. 1983. Male sociability and rituals of masculinity in rural Andalusia. *Anthropological Quarterly* 56, no. 3:125–33.

Fernandez, James W. 1983a. Consciousness and class in southern Spain. *American Ethnologist* 10, no. 1:165–73.

————. 1983b. Convivial attitudes: The ironic play of tropes in an international kayak festival in northern Spain. In *Text, play, and story: The construction and reconstruction of self and society*, ed. Edward M. Bruner, 199–229. Proceedings of the American Ethnological Society.

————.1986. *Persuasions and performances: The play of tropes in culture*. Bloomington: Indiana University Press.

————. 1988. Andalusia on our minds: Two contrasting places in Spain as seen in a vernacular poetic duel of the late 19th century. *Cultural Anthropology* 3, no. 1:21–35.

————. 1990. Enclosures: Boundary maintenance and its representation over time in Asturian mountain villages (Spain). In *Culture through time: Anthropological approaches*, ed. Emiko Ohnuki-Tierney, 94–127. Stanford: Stanford University Press.

Fernandez, James W., and Renate Lellep Fernandez. 1988. Under one roof: Household formation and cultural ideals in an Asturian mountain village. *Journal of Family History* 13, no. 1:123–42.

Fernandez, Renate Lellep. 1984. Cheesemaking as a living culture resource in Covadonga National Park, Spain. In *International perspectives on cultural parks. Proceedings of the First World Conference*, 335–341. Denver: U.S. National Park Service and Colorado Historical Society.

Fernandez, James W., and Mary Taylor Huber, eds. 2001. *Irony in action: Anthropology, practice, and the moral imagination*. Chicago: The University of Chicago Press.

Fernández de Rota y Monter, José Antonio. 1984. *Antropología de un viejo paisaje gallego*. Madrid: Centro de Investigaciones Sociológicas y Siglo XXI de España Editores.

Foucault, Michel. 1986. *Of other spaces*. Trans. Jay Miskowiec. *Diacritics* 16, no. 1:22–27.

Freeman, Susan Tax. 1970. *Neighbors: The social contract in a Castilian village*. Chicago: The University of Chicago Press.

————. 1979. *The Pasiegos: Spaniards in no man's land.* Chicago and London: The University of Chicago Press.

Frey, Nancy Louise. 1998. *Pilgrim stories: On and off the road to Santiago.* Berkeley: University of California Press.

García Martí, Victoriano. 1933. *De la zona atlántica.* Madrid: Sociedad Española de Librería.

Gilmore, David D. 1980. *The people of the plain: Class and community in lower Andalusia.* New York: Columbia University Press.

————. 1987. *Aggression and community: Paradoxes of Andalusian culture.* New Haven: Yale University Press.

————. 1991. Commodity, comity, community: Male exchange in rural Andalusia. *Ethnology* 30, no. 1:17–30.

Gmelch, George. 1986. Return migration. *Annual Review of Anthropology* 9:135–59.

Gómez-Ibáñez, Daniel Alexander. 1975. *The western Pyrenees: Differential evolution of the French and Spanish borderland.* Oxford: Clarendon Press.

González Reboredo, X. M., and X. A. Fernández de Rota, eds. 1990. *Lindeiros da galeguidade—I. Simposio de Antropología.* A Coruña: Consello da Cultura Galega.

Greenwood, Davydd J. 1976. *Unrewarding wealth: The commercialization and collapse of agriculture in a Spanish Basque town.* Cambridge: Cambridge University Press.

————. 1977. Culture by the pound: An anthropological perspective on tourism as cultural commoditization. In *Hosts and guests: The anthropology of tourism,* ed. Valene L. Smith, 129–38. Philadelphia: University of Pennsylvania Press.

Gupta, Akhil, and James Ferguson, eds. 1997. *Culture, power, place: Explorations in critical anthropology.* Durham and London: Duke University Press.

Hansen, Edward C. 1977. *Rural Catalonia under the Franco regime: The fate of regional culture since the Spanish Civil War.* Cambridge: Cambridge University Press.

Harding, Susan Friend. 1984. *Remaking Ibieca: Rural life in Aragon under Franco.* Chapel Hill: University of North Carolina Press.

Harvey, David. 1973. *Social justice and the city.* Baltimore: Johns Hopkins University.

————. 1982. *The limits to capital.* Chicago: The University of Chicago Press.

————. 2001. *Spaces of capital: Towards a critical geography.* New York: Routledge.

Harvey, Penelope. 1996. *Hybrids of modernity: Anthropology, the nation state, and the Universal Exhibition.* London and New York: Routledge.

Herzfeld, Michael. 1991. *A place in history: Social and monumental time in a Cretan town.* Princeton: Princeton University Press.

Holton, Kimberly DaCosta. 1998. Dressing for success: Lisbon's year as Cultural Capital of Europe. *Journal of American Folklore* 111, no. 440:173–96.

————. 2006. *Performing folklore: Ranchos folclóricos from Lisbon to Newark.* Bloomington: Indiana University Press.

Kaplan, Temma. 1993. *Red city, blue period: Social movements in Picasso's Barcelona.* Berkeley: University of California Press.

Kasmir, Sharryn. 1996. *The myth of Mondragon: Cooperatives, politics, and working class life in a Basque town.* Albany: State University of New York Press.

Kavanagh, William. 1994a. Symbolic boundaries and "real" borders on the Portuguese-Spanish frontier. In *Border approaches: Anthropological perspectives on frontiers,* ed. Hastings Donnan and Thomas M. Wilson, 75–87. Lanham, MD: University Press of America.

————. 1994b. *Villagers of the Sierra de Gredos: Transhumant cattle-raisers in central Spain.* Providence: Berg.

Kelley, Heidi. 1991. Unwed mothers and household reputation in a Spanish Galician community. *American Ethnologist* 18, no. 3:147–62.

Kenny, Michael. 1966 [1961]. *A Spanish tapestry: Town and country in Castile.* New York: Harper & Row.

Klimt, Andrea. 1989. Returning "home": Portuguese migrant notions of temporariness, permanence, and commitment. *New German Critique* 46:47–70.

————. 2000a. European spaces: Portuguese migrants' notions of home and belonging. *Diaspora* 9:259–85.

————. 2000b. Enacting national selves: Authenticity, adventure, and disaffection in the Portuguese diaspora. *Identities: Global Studies in Culture and Power* 6, no. 40:513–50.

Lamphere, Louise. 1997. The domestic sphere of women and the public world of men: The strengths and limitations of an anthropological dichotomy. In *Gender in cross-cultural perspective,* ed. Caroline B. Brettell and Carolyn F. Sargent, 82–92. Upper Saddle River, NJ: Prentice-Hall.

Lawrence-Zúñiga, Denise. 1999. Suburbanizing rural lifestyles through house form in southern Portugal. In *House Life: Space, place, and family in Europe,* ed. Donna Birdwell-Pheasant and Denise Lawrence-Zúñiga, 157–75. Oxford: Berg.

Leal, João. 1994. *As festas do Espírito Santo nos Açores: Um estudo de antropologia social.* Lisbon: Publicações Dom Quixote.

————.2000. *Etnografias portuguesas (1870–1970): Cultura popular e identidade nacional.* Lisbon: Publicações Dom Quixote.

————. 1999. Mapping Mediterranean Portugal: Pastoral and counter-pastoral. *Nar. Umjet.* 36, no. 1:9–31.

Leeds, Anthony. 1987. Work, labor, and their recompenses: Portuguese life strategies involving "migration." In *Migrants in Europe: The role of family, labor, and politics,* ed. Hans C. Buechler and Judith-Maria Buechler, 9–59. New York: Greenwood Press.

Lefebvre, Henri. 1991. *The production of space*. Trans. Donald Nicholson-Smith. Malden, MA, and Oxford: Blackwell Publishers. Original version published by Éditions Anthropos in 1974.

Lem, Winnie. 1999. *Cultivating dissent: Work, identity, and praxis in rural Languedoc*. Albany: State University of New York Press.

Lisón Tolosana, Carmelo. 1973. Some aspects of moral structure in Galician hamlets. *American Anthropologist* 75, no. 3:823–34.

———. 1983[1979]. *Antropología cultural de Galicia*. Madrid: Akal Editor.

———. 1987[1979]. *Brujería, estructura social y simbolismo en Galicia*. Madrid: Akal Editor.

Lomnitz-Adler, Claudio. 1992. *Exits from the labyrinth: Culture and ideology in the Mexican national space*. Berkeley: University of California Press.

Low, Setha M., and Denise Lawrence-Zúñiga, eds. 2003. *The anthropology of space and place: Locating culture*. Malden and Oxford: Blackwell Publishing.

Machado, José Pedro. 1967. *Dicionário etimológico da língua portuguesa*. 2ª Edição. Vol. II. Lisbon and São Paulo: Editorial Confluência and Livros Horizonte.

Maddox, Richard. 1993. *El Castillo: The politics of tradition in an Andalusian town*. Urbana and Chicago: University of Illinois Press.

———. 2004. *The best of all possible islands: Seville's Universal Exposition, the New Spain, and the New Europe*. Albany: State University of New York Press.

Marchant, J. R. V., and Joseph F. Charles. 1948. *Cassell's Latin dictionary*. London and Toronto: Cassell and Company.

Marcus, George E. 1995. Ethnography in/of the world system: The emergence of multi-sited ethnography. *Annual Review of Anthropology* 24:95–117.

Mattoso, J. 1991. *Identificação de um país: Ensaio sobre as origens de Portugal. Volume 1—Oposição*. Lisbon: Editorial Estampa.

McDonogh, Gary Wray. 1986. *Good families of Barcelona: A social history of power in the industrial era*. Princeton: Princeton University Press.

———. 2003. Myth, space, and virtue: Bars, gender, and change in Barcelona's *Barrio Chino*. In *The anthropology of space and place: Locating culture*, ed. Setha M. Low and Denise Lawrence-Zúñiga, 264–83. Malden and Oxford: Blackwell.

Medeiros, António. 1998. Pintura dos costumes da Nação: Alguns argumentos. *Trabalhos de Antropologia e Etnologia* XXXVIII, no. 1–2:131–69.

Meltzoff, Sarah Keene. 1995. Marisquadoras of the shellfish revolution: The rise of women in co-management on Illa de Arousa, Galicia. *Journal of Political Ecology* 2:20–38.

Mintz, Jerome. 1978. *Pepe's family*. Documentary film. Indiana University Audio-Visual Center.

Mintz, Sidney W. 1985. *Sweetness and power: The place of sugar in modern history*. New York: Viking.

Moliner, María. 1999. *Diccionario de uso del español*. Madrid: Editorial Gredos.

Narotzky, Susana. 2001. *La antropología de los pueblos de España. Historia, cultura, y lugar.* Barcelona: Icaria editorial.

Nogués Pedregal, Antonio Miguel. 1996. Tourism and self-consciousness in a South Spanish coastal community. In *Coping with tourists: European reactions to mass tourism,* ed. Jeremy Boissevain, 56–83. Providence: Berghahn Books.

O'Brien, Jay, and William Roseberry, eds. 1991. *Golden ages, dark ages.* Berkeley: University of California Press.

Oliveira Martins, Joaquim Pedro. 1879. *História de Portugal.* Lisbon: Livraria Bertrand.

———. 1880. *História da civilização ibérica.* Lisbon: Livraria Bertrand.

———. 1930 [1880]. *A history of Iberian civilization.* Trans. Aubrey Bell. London: Oxford University Press.

O'Neill, Brian Juan. 1984. *Proprietários, lavradores e jornaleiros: desigualdade social numa aldeia transmontana, 1870–1978.* Lisbon: Publicações Dom Quixote.

——— 1987. *Social inequality in a Portuguese hamlet: Land, late marriage, and bastardy, 1870–1978.* Cambridge: Cambridge University Press.

———. 1995. Diverging biographies: Two Portuguese peasant women. *Ethnologia Europaea* 52:97–118.

Ong, Aihwa. 1999. *Flexible citizenship: The cultural logics of transnationality.* Durham: Duke University Press.

Ortega y Gasset, José. 1964[1914]. *Meditaciones del Quijote.* Madrid: España Calpe.

Parkhurst, Shawn S. 1999. In the middle of the myth: The problem of power in gender relations and the Alto Douro region of northern Portugal. *Anthropologica* XLI, no. 2:103–15.

———. 2003. Portugal. In *International Encyclopedia of Marriage and Family.* Second Edition. Volume 3, ed. James J. Ponzetti Jr., 1241–45. New York: Macmillan Reference USA.

Pina-Cabral, João de. 1986. *Sons of Adam, daughters of Eve.* Oxford: Clarendon Press.

———. 1989a. The Mediterranean as a category of regional comparison: A critical view. *Current Anthropology* 30, no. 3:399–406.

———. 1989b. Sociocultural differentiation and regional identity in Portugal. In *Iberian identity,* ed. Richard Herr and J. R. Polt, 3–18. Berkeley: Institute of International Studies, University of California.

———. 2003. Lei e paternidade: As leis de filiação portuguesas. In *O homem na família: Cinco ensaios de antropologia.* Lisbon: Imprensa de Ciências Sociais.

Pi-Sunyer, Oriol. 1973. Tourism and its discontents: The impact of a new industry on a Catalan community. *Studies in European Society* 1:1–20.

———. 1977. Through native eyes: Tourists and tourism in a Catalan maritime community. In *Hosts and guests: The anthropology of tourism,* ed. Valene L. Smith, 149–56. Philadelphia: University of Pennsylvania Press.

————. 1985a. The 1977 parliamentary elections in Barcelona: Primordial symbols in a time of change. *Anthropological Quarterly* 58, no. 2:108–19.

————. 1985b. Catalan nationalism: Some theoretical and historical considerations. In *New nationalisms of the developed West,* ed. Edward Tiryakian and Ronald Rogowski, 253–76. Boston: Allen and Unwin.

————. 1995. Under four flags: The politics of national identity in the Barcelona Olympics. *Political and Legal Anthropology Review* 18, no. 1:35–55.

Pred, Allan. 1990. *Making histories and constructing human geographies: The local transformation of practice, power relations, and consciousness.* Boulder: Westview Press.

Press, Irwin. 1979. *The city as context: Urbanism and behavioral constraints in Seville.* Urbana and Chicago: University of Illinois Press.

Real Academia Española. 1992. *Diccionario de la lengua española.* Madrid: Real Academia Española.

Redfield, Peter. 2000. *Space in the tropics: From convicts to rockets in French Guiana.* Berkeley: University of California Press.

Ribeiro, Orlando. 1991[1945]. *Portugal, o Mediterrâneo e o Atlântico.* Lisbon: Livraria Sá da Costa.

Riegelhaupt, Joyce F. 1967. Saloio women: An analysis of informal and formal political and economic roles of Portuguese peasant women. *Anthropological Quarterly* 40, no. 3:109–26.

————. 1973. Festas and padres: The organization of religious action in a Portuguese parish. *American Anthropologist* 75, no. 3:835–52.

Risco, Vicente. 1920. O sentimento da terra na raza galega. *Nós* 27:4–9.

————. 1980[1930]. *El problema político de Galicia. Obra completa I,* 11–231. Madrid: Akal.

————. 1933. *Terra de Melide.* Santiago de Compostela: Seminario de Estudos Galegos.

Rodman, Margaret Critchlow. 1992. Empowering place: Multilocality and multivocality. *American Anthropologist* 94, no. 3:640–56.

Rodríguez Campos, Joaquín S. 2002a. Ideas on Atlantic culture in the northwest Iberian Peninsula. *Journal of the Society for the Anthropology of Europe* 2, no. 2:35–44.

————. 2002b. Los parques naturales como paradigma para la modernización cultural: El caso gallego. In *Identities, power, and place on the Atlantic borders of two continents,* ed. Sharon R. Roseman, 37–50. St. John's: Faculty of Arts, Memorial University of Newfoundland.

Rosaldo, Michelle Z. 1980. The uses and abuses of anthropology. *Signs* 5, no. 3:389–417.

Roseman, Sharon R. 1995. "Falamos como falamos": Linguistic revitalization and the maintenance of local vernaculars in Galicia. *Journal of Linguistic Anthropology* 5, no. 1:3–32.

————. 1996. "How we built the road": The politics of memory in rural Galicia. *American Ethnologist* 23, no. 4:836–60.

————. 1997. Celebrating silenced words: The "reimaginings" of a feminist nation in late twentieth century Galicia. *Feminist Studies* 23, no. 1:43–71.

————. 2003. Spaces of production, memories of contention: An account of local struggle in late-20th century rural Galicia (Spain). *Dialectical Anthropology* 27:19–45.

Roseman, Sharon R., and Heidi Kelley. 1999. Introduction. Special theme issue on "Ethnographic Explorations of Gender and Power in Rural Northwestern Iberia." *Anthropologica* XLI, no. 2:89–101.

Rotenberg, Robert, and Gary McDonogh, eds. 1993. *The cultural meaning of urban space*. Westport: Bergin and Garvey.

Ruiz, Arturo, and Manuel Molinos. 1998. *The archaeology of the Iberians*. Trans. Mary Turton. Cambridge: Cambridge University Press.

Sahlins, Marshall. 2004. *Apologies to Thucydides: Understanding history as culture and vice versa*. Chicago: University of Chicago Press.

Sahlins, Peter. 1989. *Boundaries: The making of France and Spain in the Pyrenees*. Berkeley: University of California Press.

San Román, Teresa, et al. 1976. *Los gitanos al encuentro de la ciudad: del chalaneo al peonaje*. Madrid: Editorial Cuadernos para el Diálogo.

San Román, Teresa. 1996. *Los muros de la separación: Ensayo sobre alterofobia y filantropía*. Barcelona: Editorial Tecnos.

Sanchis, Pierre. 1983. *Arraial: Festa de um povo*. Lisbon: Publicações Dom Quixote.

Schiller, Nina Glick, Linda Basch, and Cristina Blanc-Szanton, eds. 1992. *Towards a transnational perspective on migration: Race, class, ethnicity, and nationalism reconsidered*. New York: Academy of Sciences.

Sider, Gerald M. 1986. *Culture and class in anthropology and history: A Newfoundland illustration*. Cambridge: Cambridge University Press.

————. 2003. *Between history and tomorrow: Making and breaking everyday life in rural Newfoundland*. Peterborough: Broadview Press.

Sieber, Timothy R. 2001. Remembering Vasco da Gama: Contested histories and the cultural politics of contemporary nation-building in Lisbon, Portugal. *Identities* 8, no. 4:549–81.

————. 2002. Composing Lusofonia: Multiculturalism and national identity in Lisbon's 1998 musical scene. *Diaspora* 11, no. 2:163–88.

Silva, Manuel Carlos. 1998. *Resistir e adaptar-se: Constrangimentos e estratégias camponesas no noroeste de Portugal*. Porto: Afrontamento.

Smith, Angel, and Clare Mar-Molinero. 1996. The myths and realities of nation-building in the Iberian Peninsula. In *Nationalism and the nation in the Iberian Peninsula*, ed. Clare Mar-Molinero and Angel Smith, 1–30. Oxford and Washington: Berg.

Sobral, José Manuel. 1999. *Trajectos: O presente e o passado na vida de uma freguesia da Beira.* Lisbon: Imprensa de Ciências Sociais.

Soja, Edward W. 1989. *Postmodern geographies: The reassertion of space in critical social theory.* London and New York: Verso.

Stewart, Kathleen. 1996. *A space on the side of the road: Cultural poetics in an "other" America.* Princeton: Princeton University Press.

Suárez-Navaz, Liliana. 2004. *Rebordering the Mediterranean: Boundaries and citizenship in southern Europe.* New York and Oxford: Berghahn Books.

Tenorio, Nicolás. 1982. *La aldea gallega.* Vigo: Edicións Xerais de Galicia.

Terradas Saborit, Ignacio. 1979. *La colònia industrial com a particularisme històric: L'Ametlla de Merola.* Barcelona: Editorial Laia.

———. 1987. Les característiques històriques de les colònies industrials catalanes. *Revista de Catalunya* 5 (Febrer):72–83.

Trouillot, Michel-Rolph. 1995. *Silencing the past: Power and the production of history.* Boston: Beacon Press.

Tsing, Anna Lowenhaupt. 1993. *In the realm of the diamond queen: Marginality in an out-of-the-way place.* Princeton: Princeton University Press.

Urla, Jacqueline. 1988. Ethnic protest and social planning: A look at Basque language revival. *Cultural Anthropology* 3, no. 4:379–94.

———. 1993. Cultural politics in an age of statistics: Numbers, nations, and the making of Basque identity. *American Ethnologist* 20, no. 4:818–43.

———. 1995. Outlaw language: Creating alternative public spheres in Basque free radio. *Pragmatics* 5, no. 2:245–61.

Verdery, Katherine. 1991. *National ideology under socialism: Identity and cultural politics in Ceausescu's Romania.* Berkeley: University of California Press.

Wall, Karin. 1998. *Famílias no campo: Passado e presente em duas freguesias do Baixo Minho.* Lisbon: Publicações Dom Quixote.

Wolf, Eric R. 1982. *Europe and the people without history.* Berkeley: University of California Press.

———. 2001. *Pathways of power: Building an anthropology of the modern world.* Berkeley: University of California Press.

Yaeger, Patricia. 1996. Introduction: Narrating space. In *The geography of identity*, ed. Patricia Yaeger, 1–38. Ann Arbor: University of Michigan Press.

PART 1

Colonial Spaces and National Identities

The chapters in this part of the book provide unique treatments of the way images of a divided, but conquering, Portuguese nation infused the work of prominent anthropologists and other intellectuals writing accounts or orchestrating enactments of culture and place throughout the twentieth century. Leal's chapter examines how Portuguese anthropology has been influenced by "hidden empire" discourses over the last hundred years, beginning with the negative depictions of Portuguese folk culture around the turn of the twentieth century—depictions that became part of what Leal terms a "nation-questioning" rather than a "nation-building" anthropology. Leal also demonstrates how the dominant theme of *saudade* or "nostalgic longing" so closely associated with Portuguese folk culture can also be seen as a political nostalgia for the lost period of Portuguese imperial might. His survey of the intersections between notions of Empire, the Portuguese nation, and key studies of Portuguese "folk culture" provides not only a superb overview of twentieth-century Portuguese history but also an ideological analysis of key thinkers in Portuguese anthropology. Brian O'Neill's chapter takes readers far away from the Iberian Peninsula to the Kristang community of Catholic Eurasians in the Portuguese Settlement of Malacca. In his account of the intersections of ethnonational habitus, place, and power O'Neill leads us away from simplistic notions of disremembering or assimilation. He describes how the small linguistic and cultural minority of Malacca Portuguese has reproduced itself as ethnically Other. This has been achieved through various cultural practices including, since the 1940s, the imitation of Portuguese folk styles, which he contends reflects a habitus of effusive "hyper-Portuguese" identity. O'Neill's chapter outlines the processes underlying national identification on the part of extraterritorial partial descendants of migrants whose mobility had been enabled by Portuguese imperialism. This contribution also provides a model for future research on the reinscription of national culture by those who are displaced and who do not necessarily have local signposts demarcating the "mother country." António Medeiros's chapter details the importance of the visual representation of "ethnographic" differences for the organization of political power during António Salazar's New State, inaugurated in the 1930s, and lasting until 1974. Medeiros analyzes the First Portuguese Colonial Exhibition, put on in Porto in 1934, as a proving ground for a new type of cultural intervention within Portuguese politics. With the inauguration of the Salazar regime came increased emphasis on control in the African colonies, which had been weak. Accompanying this emphasis was a new stress on well-produced images that pass rapidly in parades but stick in the minds of spectators. From the beginning of the twentieth century nationalized Portuguese middle-class culture focused heavily on parodying the everyday life of provincials and colonial "others," with little effort at ethnographic accuracy. For Medeiros, the 1934 Exhibition represents a key transition in the "ethnographic" component of this culture. In July 1934, a procession in the Exhibition relied on conventional cultural parody to draw participants. Yet the September procession closing the Exhibition was personally directed by Henrique Galvão, the main architect of New State cultural policy. Galvão successfully conveyed the new notion that the empire comprised twenty-one provinces, stretching from Africa to the Minho, in northwestern Portugal. Stressing the imperial whole seems to have required highlighting strict ethnographic (imagistic) accuracy in depicting each component province. Medeiros claims that the last procession in the 1934 Exhibition can be understood retrospectively as a dress rehearsal for later forms of cultural representation, many of which are found today in parish or municipal Portuguese folklore festivals.

CHAPTER 2

The Hidden Empire

Peasants, Nation Building,
and the Empire in Portuguese Anthropology

João Leal

The difference between *völkerkunde* and *volkskunde*, between the anthropological study of foreign "primitive cultures" and the anthropological study of local "folk traditions and customs," is central to the history of European anthropology. George Stocking (1982) has related the development of these distinct anthropological traditions to political and ideological circumstances prevailing in nineteenth- and early twentieth-century Europe. *Völkerkunde* studies, or "anthropologies of empire building," developed in countries that ruled over a colonial empire, such as France and Great Britain, while *volkskunde* studies, or "anthropologies of nation building," developed in countries that had a classical national problem, that is, countries involved in a process of national autonomy and/or independence.

This distinction is doubly paradoxical when applied to the history of Portuguese anthropology. The first paradox is that, despite the existence of an empire that lasted until 1974, no systematic tradition of colonial social anthropology emerged in Portugal until the late 1950s, when Salazar's totalitarian regime (which ruled Portugal from 1926 to 1974), in the face of the increasing threat of independence movements and decolonization, favored the development of social anthropological studies in the former Portuguese colonies. The second and correlated paradox is that, despite the fact that Portugal has been defined as one of the "old continuous nations" of the West (Seton-Watson 1977), with no national problem, Portuguese anthropology emerged and developed,

35

from 1870 until 1970, as an intellectual project committed to the study of folk traditions, and to a search for Portuguese national identity.

The first paradox was addressed by Rui Pereira (1998) in a paper on Jorge Dias, one of the most important twentieth-century Portuguese anthropologists, who, after a period devoted to the study of Portuguese folk culture, eventually conducted extensive research among the Makonde of Northern Mozambique (Dias 1964; Dias and Dias 1964, 1970). Besides stressing the links between Dias's Africanist interests and the new attitude toward social anthropological research in the former Portuguese colonies adopted by Salazar's regime in the late 1950s, Pereira points out that before that period there was no systematic interest among Portuguese anthropologists in the social and cultural study of the different populations living in the territories of the colonies. This lack of interest is contrasted by Pereira with the commitment to the study of the "colonial other" shown by Portuguese physical and biological anthropologists and is explained both as a result of the "underdeveloped nature" (Pereira 1998:XI) of Portuguese colonialism and as a consequence of the policies of the Portuguese state. Pereira stresses, in particular, the connections between the development of biological and physical anthropology and the need to quantify "indigenous labor" (ibid.: XVII), which was one of the main tenets of the policy of intensive exploitation of indigenous labor developed by Portuguese colonial authorities until the 1950s.

The second paradox has been addressed by several researchers, including myself, who stress the nation-building nature of Portuguese anthropology. For Pina-Cabral, for instance, Portuguese anthropology was of great "importance in the development of the notion of nationality in the context of bourgeois hegemony. . . . As in other European countries during the 19th and the early 20th centuries, [Portuguese] anthropology was associated . . . with a quest for national identity" (1991:33). I argued that "Portuguese anthropology [between 1870 and 1970] developed as a discipline oriented towards the study of Portuguese folk culture, and centered on the discussion of Portuguese national identity" (Leal 2000a:28).[1] Both myself and Pina-Cabral, albeit in different ways, address the different periods of development of Portuguese anthropology, indicate the authors who were central in that process, discuss the several definitions of folk culture given by Portuguese anthropologists and ethnographers, and focus on the distinct methodological and theoretical issues they faced.

Several other studies have completed this picture of Portuguese anthropology.[2] What emerges from it is, again, the dual commitment of Portuguese anthropology between 1870 and 1970 to the study of Portuguese folk culture and to the discussion of Portuguese national identity. As in other European traditions of nation-building anthropology, peasant customs and traditions were seen as the remote and solid soil upon which Portuguese national identity rested.

Despite confining itself to the restricted space of rural Portugal and its apparent indifference to the colonial dimension of the country, Portuguese anthropology was nevertheless haunted by the empire. In the interstices of this folk-centered discourse, the imperial dimension of Portugal was often to be found. It was not an overt presence, but a hidden one, something that could not be seen immediately. It is this hidden presence of the empire in Portuguese anthropology that this chapter seeks to disclose.

In the first part of the chapter, I address the negative judgments of Portuguese folk culture produced by turn-of-the-century Portuguese anthropologists. I then move to the analysis of anthropological discourses on Portuguese national character. In both cases, I argue, behind an explicit interest in Portuguese folk culture one can find hidden assumptions and judgments on the Portuguese Empire. In the final part of the chapter, I stress the way in which the empire has haunted other episodes of twentieth-century Portuguese intellectual life and can also be viewed as an important part of everyday discourses on national identity.

The Hidden Empire I: Folk Culture and National Decline

One of the best examples of this imperial subtext can be found in turn-of-the-century Portuguese anthropology. The main Portuguese anthropologists at the time were Adolfo Coelho[3] and Rocha Peixoto. After concentration on folk literature and folk traditions, which had been the main topics of research throughout the 1870s and 1880s, Portuguese anthropology became a more open field of research and issues such as traditional material culture, folk art, and the social and economic organization of rural communities were integrated into the research agenda. At the same time, it also became a more sophisticated intellectual endeavor, both in methodological and in theoretical terms. The first attempts to establish fieldwork as the key methodology in the study of

Portuguese folk culture were made then. In theoretical terms, as in other European countries, evolutionism became the dominant influence in Portuguese anthropology. However, the main feature of this period in the development of Portuguese anthropology was the emergence of a negative image of Portuguese folk culture. This image stood in sharp contrast to the image of Portuguese folk culture that had prevailed in the 1870s and 1880s and that would again dominate Portuguese anthropology after 1910. In fact, instead of a romantic approach to peasant customs and traditions, viewed as the faithful trustees of the nation's soul, Coelho and Peixoto represented the Portuguese folk as a negative entity, depicting its customs and traditions in strongly critical terms.[4] Adjectives such as "rude," "unrefined," "gross," and "barbaric" were commonly used by both authors to characterize peasant customs, and the evaluations of the various items of folk culture researched were generally pervaded by a negative tone.

Writing about traditional pottery in northern Portugal, for instance, Rocha Peixoto characterized it, both in technological and aesthetic terms, as "close to some of the grossest types in primitive pottery and . . . incomparably inferior to some barbaric ones" (Peixoto 1967a [1900]:112). Portuguese folk tile was also qualified as "barbaric . . . devoid of creativity, . . . gross and rude, using very bad material" (Peixoto 1967b:135). Similar adjectives and assessments can also be found in Peixoto's papers on traditional jewelry, ex-votos or folk architecture (Peixoto 1967c [1904], 1967d [1906], 1967e [1908]). Peixoto's depiction of the interior of the Portuguese rural house, in particular, was extremely critical. According to Peixoto, it reflected

> the traditional poverty, the rude and violently utilitarian temperament and the mental indigence of [the Portuguese] folk, absolutely lacking in artistic aptitudes, simultaneously sentimental and egoistic, irreducibly heathen although fanatically pious, slave by origin and historical habitude, but eternally grateful and conformist. (Peixoto 1967c [1904]:160)

It was in his paper on Portuguese *fado* (Peixoto 1997 [1897]), a musical genre originating in the lower-class quarters of Lisbon that would eventually become the Portuguese "national song," that Peixoto characterized Portuguese folk culture in the most negative terms. His concluding remarks constitute one of the most disenchanted and pessimistic depictions of the Portuguese folk ever produced in Portugal:

Yesterday on the streets there were men playing guitar, plaintive, emaciated, with drunken eyes and dishevelled hair. . . . One of them was singing a well-known theme of a typical *fado*, the lyrics and music of which vividly reflect the temperament of the [Portuguese] people: dirty, vagabond, hypocritical, idle. . . . Contemplating these groups, one can come only to one sad conclusion: there goes the Nation. (ibid.:335–36)

Coelho used a more cautious tone. Nevertheless, his papers on folk pedagogy were characterized by a similar approach to Portuguese folk culture (Coelho 1993c [1898], 1993d [1910]), and the ethnological and anthropological programs he wrote in 1890 and 1896 (Coelho 1993a [1890] and 1993b [1896]) were also very skeptical about the qualities of the Portuguese folk, viewed as afflicted by a kind of "ethnic *maladie*" (Coelho 1993a [1890]:692) and depicted as "raw material of a people and not a people [in the full sense of the word]" (Coelho 1993b [1896]:705).

The main reason for this negative image of folk culture had to do with the general atmosphere then prevalent in the Portuguese intellectual scene, characterized by a gloomy ideology that foretold the national decline of Portugal. Coelho and Peixoto were strongly influenced by this ideology, and their negative depictions of Portuguese folk culture can be seen as a direct result of it. According to them, Portuguese folk culture was strongly affected by the general decline of the country and was itself in a state of decadence, which the two anthropologists tried to portray. For them, thus, Portuguese anthropology, rather than being a "nation-building" anthropology, was a "nation-questioning" anthropology, concerned with the symptoms of decay among the Portuguese folk. From a romantic token of national identity, folk culture was turned into an expression of the country's decline.

The dominance of this ideology of national decline was linked to a more comprehensive pattern of *fin de siècle* Western thought: as Herman (1997) has recently argued, Western decadence and national decline were then leading topics in Western humanities and social sciences. However, in the Portuguese case, this ideology of national decadence was also decisively fueled by a series of events, perceived as "traumatic" for Portuguese national pride. Among them was the British *Ultimatum* (1890). As is well known, the *Ultimatum*, which drastically limited Portuguese colonial claims on Africa, allowed for the British takeover of areas, roughly corresponding to the territories of contemporary Zimbabwe and Malawi, which were also claimed by the Portuguese crown. This directly affected the country's imperial status. Besides generalized and strong anti-British protests (Ramos 1994), the *Ultimatum* also gave rise to a series of skeptical reflections on the nation's viability built around the idea of national decline.

Coelho's and Peixoto's writings can be seen as an anthropological translation of the pessimistic ideas directly stemming from the *Ultimatum*. This means that their negative portrayals of Portuguese folk culture, rather than having a direct connection to the peasant customs and traditions that were the object of their research, were ultimately linked to issues related to the imperial condition of Portugal. Although hidden, the empire was thus the determinant factor in the questioning of national identity that developed in Portuguese folk-centered anthropology at the turn of the century.

Besides being the main explanation for the pessimistic tone of Portuguese anthropology in the 1890s and early 1900s, the empire was also used as a major rhetorical tool in some of the anthropological writings of that period. In his essay on folk pedagogy in Portugal, for instance, Coelho (1993c [1898]) stressed the importance of addressing the ideal notion of personhood transmitted through everyday teaching. For Coelho, the traditional Portuguese notion of personhood at one time emphasized the importance of values such as "frankness," "loyalty," "tenacity," and "coherence between thought and action" (Coelho 1993c [1898]:222). Traditionally expressed by the Portuguese phrase *o português velho* (literally "the old Portuguese"), this notion of personhood, according to Coelho, stressed the moral qualities of "the Nunos, Albuquerques and Pachecos alike" (ibid.:223). However, due to the general decline of the country, this notion of personhood was on the brink of extinction.

The imperial connotations of Coelho's language must be stressed. "The old Portuguese" was an expression coined during the Portuguese Discoveries of the sixteenth century to describe the qualities of the Portuguese navigators and conquerors. "The Nunos, Albuquerques, Pachecos" were such illustrious men as Nuno Álvares Pereira, Afonso de Albuquerque, or Duarte Pacheco Pereira,[5] directly or indirectly linked to the development of the Portuguese overseas empire. So, although explicitly addressing issues related to contemporary folk pedagogy, Coelho was in fact commenting on the decline of Portugal since the glorious days of Portuguese overseas expansion up to the contemporary gloomy situation of the country. Writing about peasants, he was actually thinking about the empire.

Another essay based in similar reasoning is Peixoto's paper on *fado*. As I have indicated, this paper was one of the most cynical essays ever written by a Portuguese about the Portuguese. Centered on a folk musical genre, the essay included several other references to folk culture, from beliefs about werewolves to traditional poetry. But what strikes the contemporary reader are its multiple references to Portuguese expansion and to the imperial condition of the country.

Some of the main episodes in Portuguese overseas expansion— the military occupation of northern Africa in the fifteenth century, the maritime voyages to India, the eighteenth-century exploitation of Brazilian gold and precious stones—are used as illustrations of the inconstant nature of the Portuguese soul, of which the *fado* is supposed to be the contemporary expression. Portuguese expansion is proposed as a metaphor for the sorry fate of the Portuguese nation, driven by a "delirium of greatness" and a "collective hallucination" which led to neglect of hard work and saving: "Everybody wanted to be a sailor, a merchant, a pirate; the land stood almost abandoned; there was no bread left for those who had stayed at home; there was even nobody to weave the clothing" (1997:333). For Peixoto, the decadence of the Portuguese nation, which folk culture so vividly expressed in contemporary times, had started long ago, and the Portuguese expansion was its first and most powerful evidence.

To sum up: the threat to the Portuguese empire was not only the ultimate explanation for the pessimistic tone of folk-centered Portuguese anthropology at the turn of the century; it was also with direct reference to the empire that the decline of Portuguese folk culture was explained. Although explicitly addressing issues related to Portuguese folk culture, Portuguese anthropologists were implicitly commenting on the imperial condition of Portugal.

THE HIDDEN EMPIRE II: PORTUGUESE ETHNIC PSYCHOLOGY

This hidden presence of the empire can also be found in the writings of Portuguese anthropologists on ethnic psychology. In fact, in their attempts to root Portuguese national identity in the solid ground of peasant custom and tradition, Portuguese anthropologists, like their counterparts in the rest of Europe, devoted a lot of energy to the task of characterizing Portuguese national character. For them, the existence of the nation rested decisively on a common "national soul or mentality," derived mainly from folk culture.[6]

The first Portuguese ethnologist to address issues related to this spiritual makeup of the nation was Teófilo Braga, who was active in the 1870s and 1880s and is considered one of the founding fathers of Portuguese anthropology. His early approaches to Portuguese ethnic psychology developed around a nationalist interpretation of folk literature, one of his favorite topics of research (Braga 1985 [1885] and 1894). After Braga, the issue was also addressed at the turn of the century. As we have seen, Coelho's and Peixoto's thoughts on national decadence were strongly associated with a negative assessment of Portuguese national character. However, the main anthropologist to address the topic was Jorge Dias, the leading Portuguese anthropologist between 1930 and 1970.[7] One of Dias's main concerns was which factors explained both the diversity and the unity of Portuguese folk culture. In order to explain the diversity of Portuguese folk culture, Dias turned to the model proposed by the human geographer Orlando Ribeiro (1963 [1945]), who had pointed out the existence of three main geographical areas in Portugal: the Mediterranean, the Northwest, and the Northeast. For Dias those geographical areas were also to be seen as culture areas linked to a number of particularities related to material culture, settlement patterns, family form and social organization, religious beliefs, etc. Despite this diversity, according to Dias, Portuguese folk culture exhibited a strong cultural unity. This cultural unity rested upon Portuguese national character, which Dias analyzed in "Os elementos fundamentais da cultura portuguesa" ("The fundamental elements of Portuguese culture") (1990 [1953]), a short essay that stands as one of the most influential essays ever produced by a Portuguese anthropologist. As I have shown elsewhere (Leal 2000b), his essay was influenced by the national character studies done by American anthropologists such as Ruth Benedict and Margaret Mead. But it was also strongly influenced by the theories regarding the role of *saudade* (which can be loosely translated as "homesickness," "nostalgia," "missing someone or something beloved," "remembering and longing for a past state of well being") in Portuguese national identity.[8]

All the different approaches to Portuguese ethnic psychology I have mentioned were based on folk culture. The various authors discussed Portuguese national character from the point of view of peasant customs and traditions. Braga's evidence was mainly based on genres of folk literature such as traditional poetry or folk tales. For Coelho and Peixoto, as we have seen, the empirical support was provided by folk pedagogy, *fado*, and similar folk-centered materials. Finally, Dias based his analysis on such items as folk religion, details of family and social organization, customary law, and so on.

Despite this firmly folk-centered approach, however, the different analyses were also pervaded by the shadow of the empire. We have already seen that Peixoto's and Coelho's pessimistic views on the nation's decline took the form of criticisms of the Portuguese national soul punctuated by several references to the imperial condition of Portugal. In the case of Braga, it is possible to find the same feeling for the Empire. In *O povo português nos seus costumes, crenças e tradições* (*Portuguese folk customs, beliefs, and traditions*) (Braga 1985 [1885]), an ambitious study of Portuguese folk culture that is usually considered his magnum opus, Braga offered a detailed view of Portuguese national character. That view stressed the emotional character of the Portuguese temperament, and, among other qualities, "the adventurous character" of the Portuguese and their "special inclination towards overseas exploration" (Braga 1985 [1885]:73). In *A pátria portuguesa. O território e a raça* (*Portuguese fatherland. Race and territory*) (1894), the topic was again addressed by Braga. Among the qualities of the Portuguese soul that Braga listed one finds such features as the "easy adaptation to new environments," "cosmopolitanism," "ethnic eclecticism," and a "tendency towards the rapid assimilation of new ideas" (Braga 1894:26). The "inclination towards overseas exploration" and "the adventurous character" of the Portuguese, allegedly of Celtic origin, were addressed in some detail by Braga (ibid.).

What must be stressed with respect to Braga's approaches to Portuguese ethnic psychology is again the hidden presence of the empire. In the case of *O povo português*, this presence is a discreet one. The "adventurous character" of the Portuguese and their "special inclination toward overseas exploration" are only two among a number of features taken to characterize the Portuguese soul (Braga 1985 [1885]:73). However, in the case of *A pátria portuguesa* this presence is more overt. The portrayal of Portuguese ethnic psychology that Braga offered there, in fact, rested almost exclusively on a list of features strongly connected to the imperial condition of the country.

However, it is in Dias's essay that this presence of the empire in the depictions of Portuguese national character stands out most clearly. In fact, one of the first ideas of "Os elementos fundamentais da cultura portuguesa" has to do with the "expansive nature of Portuguese culture" (Dias 1990 [1953]:141): "[T]he attraction towards the Atlantic Ocean was the soul of the nation and the driving force behind Portugal's history" (ibid.). According to Dias,

> The main achievements of the Portuguese creative genius—Camões's *Lusíadas*, the Jerónimos monastery, Nuno Gonçalves's *Políptico* and Manuel Coelho's *Tentos*[9]—are the four truly superior and original expressions of the Portuguese people, which for more than a century ventured into every sea on earth and delighted in the most diverse and exotic forms of nature. (ibid.:142)

After this eulogistic opening, the presence of the figure of the empire seems to disappear from Dias's essay. In fact, one of Dias's main arguments had to do with the complexity of Portuguese personality, which he linked to the diverse ethnic backgrounds of the Portuguese people: "The Portuguese personality is complex and is based on a series of deep antinomies which can be explained by the different psychological tendencies of the populations that have formed the country" (ibid.). It is around this idea that the bulk of Dias's essay is structured. Portuguese national character combined, for instance, "a strong capacity for dreaming" with "a powerful will to action," "an intrinsic goodness" with "violence and cruelty," "a strong feeling for individual freedom" with "powerful values of solidarity," "a lack of a sense of humor" with "an intense irony" (ibid.:145–46), etc. Dias's evidence for these different antinomies centered on Portuguese folk culture: the presence of the empire seems to be a vanishing one.

A closer look brings the empire back into view. Indeed, for Dias, one of the main contradictions of Portuguese national character was that between "a remarkable capacity for adapting to different surroundings" (ibid.:146)—allegedly expressed in a colonization process distinct from that of other European countries in that it promoted assimilation and miscegenation—and "a strong capacity for keeping its own character" (ibid.:146). The antinomy between a "strong capacity for dreaming" and "a powerful will to action" was also offered as the explanation for the Portuguese overseas expansion, with its mixture of dream and action (ibid.:145).

The overall contradictory nature of Portuguese temperament was also addressed in revealing terms. Dias saw it as responsible for the alternation in Portuguese history "of apogees of great achievement and periods of pronounced decay" (ibid.:146). The qualities of Portuguese national character, according to Dias, revealed themselves in particular historical circumstances: "[I]f the Portuguese are called to play a mediocre role, which does not satisfy their imagination, they lose courage and only do what is indispensable in order to stay alive" (ibid.:146–47). The apogee referred to by Dias is, of course, the period of Portuguese expansion overseas and the decay he mentions is the decline of Portuguese imperial glory.

To sum up: the approaches to Portuguese ethnic psychology show a similar pattern to the one we have found in turn-of-the-century anthropological discussions of the declining nature of Portuguese folk culture. In both cases, despite its folk-centered orientation, Portuguese anthropology actually had the empire as one of its main concerns.

Other minor examples of this trend can be found in some isolated episodes in the history of Portuguese anthropology. Let me give two examples. One of the seminal texts on Portuguese folk art, which was the main field of interest of Portuguese anthropologists and ethnographers during the 1910s and 1920s, was Baldaque da Silva's paper, "Nacionalização da arte portuguesa" ("The nationalization of Portuguese art") (Silva 1999 [1895]). Following "Arts and Crafts" teaching on the importance of folk art to the national renewal of arts, Silva gave several examples of specific folk items that could be used as inspiring motifs for erudite artists. Being a specialist on Portuguese fishing communities, Silva's proposals were based on such items as contemporary fishing boat decorations, fishing nets, etc. However, in order to stress the artistic and national value of those items, Silva presented them as part of a major Portuguese artistic tradition, going back to the sixteenth-century *manuelino* style,[10] and to its connections with Portuguese overseas expansion. Actual Portuguese fishermen, mostly illiterate, were thus transformed into the modern heirs of the sixteenth-century Portuguese navigators.

Another example of the empire as a subtext in Portuguese folk-centered anthropology can be found in the writings of the Azorean ethnographer Luís Ribeiro, who was the major figure in the development, during the twentieth century, of a strong regionalist tradition of anthropology in the Azores.[11] Addressing the particularities of Azorean ethnic psychology from the standpoint of peasant traditions and customs, Ribeiro basically viewed the Azorean folk as the twentieth-century heirs to the Portuguese navigators of the Age of Discoveries, but heirs "not yet bewildered by the conquests, nor corrupted by the gold of the East, faithful to the virtues of our race and to the great qualities that have made our history a glorious one" (Ribeiro, L. 1983 [1919]:4). Ribeiro's implicit reference to Coelho's statements on the decline of the "old Portuguese" notion of person (Coelho 1993c [1898]) in continental Portugal indicate the extent to which studies of peasants intermingled with an imperial subtext in the history of Portuguese anthropology.

Concluding Remarks

This weird mixture of folk-centered anthropology and hidden imperial concerns invites us to stress, at least in the Portuguese case, the limits of the sharp distinction established in the history of European anthropology between "nation-building" anthropology and "empire-building" anthropology (Stocking 1982), between folk-centered "local ethnology" and a "cosmopolitan anthropology" focused on the "primitive" (Gerholm 1995). Indeed, the Portuguese case shows that the boundaries between the two disciplines are less definitive and more porous than is usually thought.

However, in these concluding remarks, instead of addressing issues related to general problems in the history of anthropology, I would like to discuss some aspects of Portuguese national identity that can help explain this finally not-so-hidden presence of the empire in folk-centered Portuguese anthropology.

My first point concerns the general importance of the empire in the discourses of Portuguese national identity. This importance is so great that even when the empire is not the issue its presence cannot be avoided. Portuguese anthropology is not an isolated case. If we look at other important episodes in the discussion of Portuguese national identity in the twentieth century, we find the same pattern.

I have mentioned the importance of *saudade* in twentieth-century discussions of Portuguese national identity. *Saudade* was proposed by Teixeira de Pascoaes in a number of essays published between 1912 and 1926 as the structuring theme of the nation's soul (Pascoaes 1978

[1915], 1986 [(1912]). At first, his ideas met strong resistance from other Portuguese intellectuals committed to nation building. However, in the long run, *saudade* became a widespread stereotype in the national-identity discourses and practices of the Portuguese.[12]

As I have pointed out elsewhere (Leal 2000b), Pascoaes's approach to *saudade* had strong ethnographic and anthropological underpinnings. Though mainly a poet, Pascoaes used extensive evidence from Portuguese folk culture, especially folk poetry and folk religious rituals such as *Encomendação das almas*,[13] in his attempts to demonstrate the dominant place of *saudade* in Portuguese culture. In his view, the common people were the most accomplished poets of *saudade* and the urban poets should follow their example.

At the same time, however, his thoughts on the subject were also characterized by a vision of Portuguese history in which the empire figured as the major event. For instance, in his view, *saudade* had been the driving force behind the major episodes in Portuguese history, particularly those connected to Portuguese overseas expansion. The main objective of *Saudosismo*, the cultural and intellectual movement he founded, was to restore the lost splendor to Portuguese social and cultural life by replacing foreign influences, held to be responsible for the decline of the country since the Age of Discoveries, with a cult of "Portuguese things" reflective of the true "Portuguese soul." To sum up, his *saudade* was the nostalgic longing for a time when Portugal was great because of the empire.

The same dialectic between folk-based considerations of Portuguese national identity and the omnipresent shadow of the empire can be found in most of the writings of the so-called school of Portuguese Philosophy, closely influenced by Pascoaes's ideas, the main goal of which was to develop a purely Portuguese philosophy. The cases of Cunha Leão and Agostinho da Silva are particularly interesting. Following in the footsteps of Dias's "Os elementos fundamentais da cultura portuguesa," Cunha Leão (Leão 1971, 1973 [1960]) devoted his writings to a thorough discussion of Portuguese ethnic psychology. Agostinho da Silva (Silva 1994a, 1994b) had a passion for the Holy Ghost Festival, a complex folk ritual that takes place in the rural parishes of the Azores archipelago. Leão transformed Dias's main ideas on Portuguese national character in his psychological portrait of the Portuguese of the Discoveries and overseas expansion. Agostinho da Silva analyzed the Holy

Ghost Festivals as rituals connected to the Portuguese dream of the Fifth Empire, in which the lost grandeur of the nation would be recovered.[14] In both cases, as in Pascoaes's case, what seems to be at stake is the little Portugal of folk culture and rural customs. However, what is actually addressed is the great Portugal—colonial, expansionist, imperial—that the country once was.

The cases of Pascoaes and Portuguese Philosophy are not isolated phenomena with interest only for intellectual historians. In fact, it can be argued that some of the more important contemporary reflections on Portuguese national identity are still haunted by the empire. Although the 1974 Revolution and the emergence of new independent states in the former Portuguese colonies have put an end to Portuguese dreams of imperial grandeur, discourses and practices of national identity are still pervaded by the hidden empire.

Miguel Vale de Almeida has shown, for instance, that nostalgia for the colonial empire lies just beneath the surface of the contemporary ideology of *Lusofonia* (literally "Lusophony")—the central tenet of the policies of the Portuguese state regarding its former colonies (Almeida 2000). For Almeida, Portuguese popular support for the East Timorese struggle for independence from Indonesia can also be viewed as part of the same nostalgic postcolonial trend (ibid.). I myself have argued that the attempts by Santos, one of the most important contemporary Portuguese sociologists, to address the issue of Portuguese national identity in fresh sociological terms have remained attached to some of the main tropes regarding the Portuguese empire used by Dias and other Portuguese writers. In an essay entitled "Modernidade, identidade e cultura de fronteira" ("Modernity, identity, and boundary culture") (Santos 1994a [1993]), for instance, Santos characterizes Portuguese culture as a "boundary culture" in terms that strongly echo Dias's remarks on the "remarkable capacity of [the Portuguese to] adapt to different surroundings" (Dias 1990 [1953]:146).[15] Although inspired by contemporary world system theories, Santos's analysis is thus more directly indebted to Dias's ideas on the way in which the empire has shaped Portuguese "ethnic psychology" than Santos is actually ready to concede. Recent widespread criticisms in the media of the allegedly subaltern position of Camões's *Lusíadas* in the Portuguese high school curriculum have also as their main subtext the place of the Age of Discoveries in Portuguese national identity.

My second point is a more general one. If the empire has such a powerful presence in Portuguese culture, it pervades everyday discourse on national identity. In fact, it could be argued that a structuring idea of Portuguese national identity is summarized in the expression: "We are small, but once we were great." In other words, nostalgia for the empire is one of the main features of the shared discourse on national identity. It is not so clearly articulated as the rather stereotyped public discourses on *saudade* or hospitality as distinguishing features of Portuguese culture, but it is a much more powerful one. Renan once wrote that every nation rested on an agreement based not only in remembrance but also in amnesia. In the Portuguese case, one of the major agreements upon which Portuguese national identity seems to rest is founded in a kind of hyperamnesia, or excessive remembering (Roth 1989), regarding the Age of Discoveries.

The empire's lost grandeur can in fact be viewed not only as an important element of Portuguese "cultural literacy"—"the kind of cultural competence needed for participation in public discourse" (Löfgren 1989:13)—but also, more elusively, as one of the main bases for the implicit "associations, references and memories" (ibid.:15) that permeate the daily discourses and practices of Portuguese national identity.

Notes

A preliminary version of this paper was given as a lecture at ISCTE's Masters Program in Anthropology: Colonialism and Post-Colonialism. I thank Miguel Vale de Almeida and Marcia Wolff for their comments on an early version.

1. An English synthesis of my main ideas can be found in Leal (1999) and Leal (2001).

2. A synthesis of recent trends of development in the history of Portuguese anthropology can be found in Leal (1999).

3. On Adolfo Coelho, see Leal (1993a, 1993b).

4. I had the opportunity to analyze these negative images of Portuguese folk culture in greater detail in Leal (1995).

5. Nuno Álvares Pereira was the constable of King John the First. Although King John initiated Portuguese overseas expansion, Nuno Álvares Pereira had only an indirect relation to the event. Afonso de Albuquerque, Vice-Governor of Portuguese India in the sixteenth century, was one of the major protagonists in the development of Portuguese military power in the East. Duarte Pacheco Pereira (1954 [1508]) was a humanist who devoted his

book *Esmeralda de Situ Orbis*, first published in 1508, to the new scientific developments associated with Portuguese overseas expansion.

6. On the topic of Portuguese ethnic psychology, see Leal (2000a:83–104) and Leal (2000b).

7. For a selection of Dias's texts in English translation, see Dias (1973/74).

8. On the invention of *saudade* see Leal (2000b).

9. The *Lusíadas* is the Portuguese national epic written by Luís de Camões in the sixteenth century. The Jerónimos monastery, built in the so-called *manuelino* style, partially inspired by the Portuguese maritime expansion, is one of the most important Portuguese national monuments. Nuno Gonçalves painted one of the masterpieces of Portuguese art, the so-called *Políptico do Infante*.

10. On *manuelino* style see note 9.

11. On Ribeiro and the Azoreanist ethnographic and anthropological tradition, see Leal (2000a:227–44).

12. For instance, *saudade* is a widespread symbol of Portugueseness among Portuguese immigrants. See Feldman-Bianco (1992).

13. *Encomendação das almas* (literally "praying for the souls") is a specifically Portuguese ritual that takes place during Lent and is centered on remembrance of the dead.

14. The myth of the Fifth Empire originated in medieval utopian thought and predicted the coming of an age, ruled by the Holy Ghost, where material and spiritual plentifulness, universal peace and fraternity, etc., were supposed to reign. According to several Portuguese interpreters of the myth, Portugal was to have a crucial role on the advent of the Fifth Empire.

15. In another of his essays, Santos refers explicitly to the "*ponta de verdade* [kernel of truth]" in the idealist characterizations of the Portuguese as an "octopus" (Unamuno), with "a remarkable capacity to adapt to different surroundings" (Jorge Dias), and as "strongly cosmopolitan" (Fernando Pessoa) (Santos 1994b:60).

References

Almeida, Miguel Vale de. 2000. *Um mar da cor da terra: Raça, cultura e política de identidade*. Oeiras: Celta.

Braga, Teófilo. 1894. *A pátria portuguesa: O território e a raça*. Porto: Livraria Internacional de Ernesto Chardron.

———. 1985 [1885]. *O povo português nos seus costumes, crenças e tradições*. Lisbon: Publicações Dom Quixote.

Coelho, Adolfo. 1993a [1890]. Esboço de um programa para o estudo antropológico, patológico e demográfico do povo português. In *Obra etnográfica, vol. 1*, 681–701. Lisbon: Publicações Dom Quixote.

————. 1993b [1896]. Exposição etnográfica portuguesa. Portugal e ilhas adjacentes. In *Obra Etnográfica, vol. 1*, 703–36. Lisbon: Publicações Dom Quixote,.

————. 1993c [1898]. A pedagogia do povo português. In *Obra Etnográfica, vol. 2*, 173–250. Lisbon: Publicações Dom Quixote.

————. 1993d [1910]. A cultura mental no analfabetismo. In *Obra etnográfica, vol. 2*, 253–71. Lisbon: Publicações Dom Quixote.

Dias, A. Jorge. 1964. *Os Macondes de Moçambique. Aspectos históricos e económicos, vol. 1*. Lisbon: Junta de Investigações do Ultramar.

————. 1973/74. Aspects of ethnology. *Ethnologia Europaea* VII, no. 2:133–82.

————. 1990 [1953]. Os elementos fundamentais da cultura portuguesa. In *Estudos de antropologia, vol. 1*, 135–57. Lisbon: Imprensa Nacional-Casa da Moeda.

Dias, A. Jorge, and Margot Dias. 1964. *Os macondes de Moçambique. Cultura material, vol. 2*. Lisbon: Junta de Investigações do Ultramar.

———— and ————. 1970. *Os macondes de Moçambique. Vida social e ritual, vol. 3*. Lisbon: Junta de Investigações do Ultramar.

Feldman-Bianco, Bella. 1992. Multiple layers of time and space: The construction of class, ethnicity, and nationalism among Portuguese immigrants. In *Towards a transnational perspective on migration: Race, class, ethnicity and nationalism reconsidered*, ed. Nina Glick Schiller, Linda Basch and Cristina Blanc-Szanton. New York: Annals of the New York Academy of Sciences, Volume 645.

Gerholm, Tomas. 1995. Sweden: Central ethnology, peripheral anthropology. In *Fieldwork and footnotes: Studies in the history of European anthropology*, ed. H. A. Vermeulen and A. Alvarez Roldan, 159–70. London: Routledge,

Herman, Arthur. 1997. *The idea of decline in western history*. New York: Simon and Schuster.

Leal, João. 1993a. Prefácio. In Adolfo Coelho, *Obra etnográfica, vol. 1.*, 13–36. Lisbon: Publicações Dom Quixote.

————. 1993b. Prefácio. In Adolfo Coelho, *Obra etnográfica, vol. 2*, 13–23. Lisbon: Publicações Dom Quixote.

————. 1995. Imagens contrastadas do povo. Cultura popular e identidade nacional na antropologia portuguesa oitocentista. *Revista Lusitana (n.s.)* 13/14: 125–44.

————. 1999. The history of Portuguese anthropology. *History of Anthropology Newsletter* XXVI, no. 2:10–18.

————. 2000a. *Etnografias portuguesas (1870–1970): Cultura popular e identidade nacional*. Lisbon: Publicações Dom Quixote.

————. 2000b. The making of "saudade": National identity and ethnic psychology in Portugal. In *Roots & rituals. The construction of ethnic identities*, ed. Ton Dekker, John Helsloot, and Carla Wijers, 267–87. Amsterdam: Het Spinhuis.

————. 2001. "Tylorian professors and Japanese corporals": Anthropological theory and national identity in Portuguese anthropology. In *L'anthropologie et la Méditerranée. Anthropology of the Mediterranean*, ed. Dionigi Albera, Christian Bromberger, and Anton Blok, 645–62. Paris: Maisonneuve et Larose—Maison Méditerraniénne des Sciences de l'Homme.

Leão, Francisco Cunha. 1971. *Ensaio de psicologia portuguesa*. Lisbon: Guimarães.

————. 1973 [1960]. *O enigma português*. Lisbon: Guimarães.

Löfgren, Orvar. 1989. The nationalization of culture. *Ethnologia Europaea* XIX: 5–24.

Pascoaes, Teixeira de. 1978 [1915]. *Arte de ser português*. Lisbon: Roger Delvaux.

————. 1986 [1912]. O espírito lusitano ou o saudosismo. In *Filosofia da saudade*, ed. Afonso Botelho and António Braz Teixeira, 21–35. Lisbon: Imprensa Nacional-Casa da Moeda,.

Peixoto, Rocha. 1967a [1900]. Etnografia portuguesa. Indústrias populares: As olarias de Prado. In *Obras, vol. 1*, 89–132. Póvoa do Varzim: Câmara Municipal.

————. 1967b [1901]. Uma iconografia popular em azulejos. In *Obras, vol. 1*, 133–140. Póvoa do Varzim: Câmara Municipal.

————. 1967c [1904]. A casa portuguesa. In *Obras, vol. 1*, 153–65. Póvoa do Varzim: Câmara Municipal.

————. 1967d [1906]. Etnografia portuguesa. Tabulae votivae. Excerto. In *Obras, vol. 1*, 187–216. Póvoa do Varzim: Câmara Municipal.

————. 1967e [1908]. Etnografia portuguesa. As filigranas. In *Obras, vol. 1*, 262–312. Póvoa do Varzim: Câmara Municipal.

————. 1997 [1897]. O cruel e triste fado. *Etnográfica* I, no. 2:332–36.

Pereira, Duarte Pacheco. 1954 [1508]. *Esmeralda de Situ Orbi, 1505–1508*. Third edition. Lisbon: Academia Portuguesa de História.

Pereira, Rui. 1998. Introdução. In Jorge A. Dias, *Os Macondes de Moçambique, vol. 1*, V–LII. Lisbon: Comissão Nacional para a Comemoração dos Descobrimentos Portugueses—Instituto de Investigação Científica Tropical.

Pina-Cabral, João de. 1991. A antropologia em Portugal hoje. In *Os contextos da antropologia*, 11–41. Lisbon: Difel.

Ramos, Rui. 1994. A Segunda Fundação (1890–1926). In *História de Portugal, vol. 6*, ed. José Mattoso. Lisbon: Círculo de Leitores.

Ribeiro, Luís da Silva. 1983 [1919]. Os Açores de Portugal. In *Obras, vol. 2*, 1–17. Angra do Heroísmo: Instituto Histórico da Ilha Terceira—Secretaria Regional da Educação e Cultura.

Ribeiro, Orlando. 1963 [1945]. *Portugal, o Mediterrâneo e o Atlântico*. Lisbon: Sá da Costa.

Roth, Michael. 1989. Remembering forgetting: "Maladies de la mémoire" in nineteenth-century France. *Representations* 26:49–68.

Santos, Boaventura de Sousa. 1994a [1993]. Modernidade, identidade e cultura de fronteira. In *Pela mão de Alice: O social e o político na pós-modernidade*, 119–37. Porto: Afrontamento.

———. 1994b [1991]. Onze teses por ocasião de mais uma descoberta de Portugal. In *Pela mão de Alice: O social e o político na pós-modernidade*, 49–76. Porto: Afrontamento.

Seton-Watson, Hugh. 1977. *Nations and states. An inquiry into the origins of nations and the politics of nationalism*. London: UCL Press.

Silva, Agostinho. 1994a. *Ir à Índia sem abandonar Portugal, considerações, outros textos*. Lisbon: Assírio & Alvim.

———. 1994b. *Vida conversável*. Lisbon: Assírio & Alvim.

Silva, Baldaque da. 1999 [1895]. A nacionalização da arte portuguesa. *Etnográfica* III, no. 2:404–406.

Stocking, George W. Jr. 1982. Afterword: A view from the center. *Ethnos* 57:172–86.

CHAPTER 3

Displaced Identities among the Malacca Portuguese

BRIAN JUAN O'NEILL

The Malacca Portuguese[1] are a unique and fascinating group of Eurasians whose nucleus of residence is located within a seafront neighborhood on the outskirts of the city of Malacca in Western Malaysia designated as the "Portuguese Settlement." Particularly during the last three decades of the twentieth century, the amalgam of external images of this urban community created by journalistic, touristic, and academic onlookers has conferred on it an aura evocative of the notion of a kind of exotic human zoo, from which residents are displayed to thousands of visitors as yet one more proof of Malaysia's pluriethnic and multicultural past. For instance, the *Information Malaysia Yearbook* (Berita 1994) states that "[t]he outstanding characteristic of Malaysia's population today is its highly variegated ethnic mix that makes it one of the prime examples of a multi-racial society in the whole world" (Berita 1994:50–51). Eurasians figure as one of the country's sixty-four population groups (ibid.),[2] the Portuguese Eurasians focused on in this chapter comprising one among a number of subcategories of the larger number of Eurasians (see Note 6 below).

Born between 1926 and 1934 as a quite literally fabricated entity resulting from the philanthropic efforts of two priests, the twenty-eight-acre neighborhood's reputation was founded upon two somewhat diverging images: one pointing to a series of features suggestive of the poverty associated with urban ghettos (despite the rather minuscule scale of the Settlement), and another stressing its picturesque character as a languid fishing-oriented village whose "happy-go-lucky" residents stubbornly defy modernization and development. Father Manuel Joaquim

55

Pintado, a priest resident in Malacca for almost fifty years, painted the following image some decades back: "A visitor may find this out for himself by strolling through the streets with Portuguese names, or by taking a quiet meal in one of the three restaurants in the settlement. He may experience a strange, nostalgic but pleasant feeling—the Latin atmosphere of a Mediterranean seaside village, evoked by the music played or sung by its inhabitants, or, if he pays a visit to the San Pedro restaurant, he may feel the nostalgia of a Lisbon *Casa de Fados*" (Pintado 1980:60–61).

Within its confines were supposedly gathered the surviving descendants of the first Portuguese colonizers who arrived in the city in 1509 and then seized it under the leadership of Afonso de Albuquerque, in 1511. The community[3] accounts for some thousand out of a total of approximately 2,800 Portuguese Eurasians resident in the city (Batalha 1986 [1981]).

Some decades ago (mid-century), the community was viewed as divided into two "halves" (Santa Maria 1982: 98–101), termed *kasta altu* (upper group) and *kasta bassu* (lower group), the first composed primarily of civil servants and the second of full-time fishermen. Today, a scarce two dozen residents fish full-time, although a few hundred do so on a part-time basis, within a diversified occupational structure that includes factory workers, teachers, musicians, hotel supervisors, and a large group of retired civil servants. The community is led by a *regedor* or *rejidó* and his community panel. The majority of inhabitants speak—albeit with variations in fluency—a creole language termed *Kristang* or *papiá kristang* deriving 95 percent of its vocabulary from Portuguese and some grammatical influences from Malay (Baxter 1988; Hancock 1969, 1975). It is intelligible to speakers of the Creoles of the Cape Verde Islands and Guiné-Bissau and has a number of similarities with Galician. Indeed, the term for their language (Kristang) is also a generic term for their ethnic group. The roots of the word lie in the historical use of the term *cristão*, which originally referred to the (Catholic, Christian) Portuguese colonists: the word referred both to the persons as well as to the language used by them—literally, "speaking Portuguese" meant speaking the language of Christians (Baxter 1998a:44–46; Pintado 1974:39–42).

Today, the term *Kristang* has three meanings: (1) the Creole spoken by the Malacca Portuguese, (2) a person of the Catholic faith, or

(3) a member of the ethnic group of Portuguese Eurasians. Clearly, some oscillation may occur between the second and third usages indicated here, depending on the social situation, or social group, in question.[4] The New State attempted to incorporate within its colonial empire all remote Asian communities with presumed Portuguese heritage (República Portuguesa/Ministério do Ultramar 1954). However, these European performative imprints from the twentieth century are actually quite recent importations and should not cloud our vision. The exaggerated nostalgic umbilical cord to Portugal may be explained as a recent phenomenon, subtly superimposed upon an older Malay element. Since Independence (*Merdeka*) in 1957, one strand among many of the Kristangs' multiple identities has been suppressed, while simultaneously another strand (injected from outside) was inflated. A formerly creole identity with a more explicit Malay element was displaced by a newly adopted Portuguese identity with subliminal discriminatory undertones. I maintain that the marginalization of the neighborhood and the Kristang minority following 1957, in occupational and ethnic terms, followed immediately upon the period of transplantation of Portuguese folklore in Malacca, after 1952. This succession provided Kristangs with a positive identity evaluation from the outside. But a political and ideological strand also operated: while everything Portuguese was hailed, everything Malay was devalued. As Portuguese, instead of simply Portuguese Eurasians, therefore, Kristangs faced the possibility of cultivating a more efficient marketing label as tourism flourished in the 1960s and 1970s.

I view this process as one of the displacement and superimpostition of identities. As the Kristangs' history involved various gradations of contributions from Malay, Portuguese, and other sources (Baxter 1998b), the 1950s saw the emphasis of one strand at the expense of another. A creole identity was displaced by a European Portuguese identity fomented by the efforts of representatives of the New State in Portugal: priests, political figures who visited Malacca in 1952, neighborhood leaders, and middle-class Portuguese Eurasians dedicated to the development of folklore (Sarkissian 2000). Identities may be superimposed: this process neither annihilates a former identity, nor does it totally substitute one identity with another. Some areas are carried over in similar shape, while others are magnified, and yet others simply muffled. Let us look more closely at how this process took place.

Neither objectivist, nor subjectivist or purely situationist, our hyper-modernist stance evokes as carefully as possible the kaleidoscopic nature of the Kristangs' divergent allegiances, even if these be at once contradictory, incongruous, or illusory. But social agents do not simply possess free rein in abstract arenas; they are not ethnic chameleons shifting at will. The exaggerated nostalgic umbilical cord to Portugal may thus be explained as a recent phenomenon, subtly superimposed upon an older Malay element.

PORTUGUESE, PORTUGUESE EURASIANS?

Are we confronted, then, with Portuguese or with Portuguese Eurasians? Our nouns and adjectives are loaded. Quintessential to its nature as a sort of Lusophone bastion in the Orient is the self-image held by the vast majority of members of the Kristang ethnic group. Liberal relations with most other local ethnic groups are the rule: these include minorities with whom they interrelate and intermarry freely—Chinese, Tamils, Gujaratis, Sikhs, Europeans/Australians, and two other creole groups specific to Malacca: the Baba-Nyonyas (Malay-speaking Buddhists) and the Chitties (Malay-speaking Hindus). They affirm perennially, however, in a fashion reminiscent of Maryon McDonald's (1989) volume *"We are not French!" Language, culture and identity in Brittany*, that they are not ethnic Malays, but rather culturally and historically pertaining to their real, original *nassang* (people)—Portugal. Deterritorialized, if you will, for four and one-half centuries, delocalized, and disidentified with the Malay majority, the Kristangs have been on innumerable occasions termed a "people without a country," a survival from the sixteenth century.[5] One simplistic form of query might pose the problem: At what point in time, and for what reasons, did Kristangs adopt so enthusiastically an identity associated with the label *Portuguese*, closely linked to European dance, music, and costume motifs?

The essence of my analysis of displaced identities has to do with the extent to which the group under study perceive themselves today, ethnically, as the Malacca Portuguese rather than simply another sort of Malay or a subcategory of a wider Malay ethnic group. Questioned concerning their ethnic background, Kristangs will usually admit that they are partly Malay: one frequent phrase indicating this in Creole is *"sangi malayu, ng póku!"* ("We have a little Malay blood!"). However, this kind of admission is followed perennially by phrases such as "*nussa nassang, Portugal*" ("Portugal is our homeland/We are a Portuguese people") or "*Iou portugés, ng'ka malayu*" ("I am Portuguese, not Malay"), thereby reinforcing the notion that Kristangs should not be considered as Malays. They have succeeded in obscuring or repressing their partially Malay ancestry. Everything coming from Portugal is swallowed up as inherently benevolent. At extreme moments, parents will threaten to disinherit a daughter or son should they court and end up marrying a Malay. The phrase most common in these cases is: "*Iou sa filu kazá malayu, ng podi rentá más nussa kaza!*" (literally: "If my daughter/son marries a Malay, s/he will never set foot in my house again!"). Very few of the neighborhood's residents ever stress their elements of Malay ancestry or links to Malay culture in general. When such relationships are mentioned, they are established in a timid fashion. Nevertheless, the vast majority of Kristangs seem to maintain a firm distance between themselves and the Malays, who are conceived as an "ethnic Other." Differences are also stressed in reference to the broad categories of Chinese, Indian, Sikh, or European, but none of these groups provoke the firm reservations with respect to religious or family values associated with the Malays. When I mentioned in conversation with residents the term *Luso-Malay* (cited by Fernandis 1998:92), many of these simply laughed. I verified a generalized idea that the Portuguese Eurasians perceive themselves as a non-Malay ethnic group with a remote link to Europe, crystallized in the word Eurasian. In other words, no problem is raised by the recognized fact that Kristangs constitute a subminority within the country's minority of "Other" ethnic populations; in general, Kristangs do not aspire to "assimilate" into Malay culture or the Malay ethnic group: this would indeed imply major shifts in their own conceptualizations of their identity. Between these two extremes (rejection of Malay-ness and almost blind emulation and adoption of Portuguese-ness) lies a third, yet more complex level of identity, at once genuinely hybrid, creole, and highly elusive and obscure, both to our eyes as well as theirs.[6]

I suggest that these three distinct identities have, at different moments in the recent history of the group and its neighborhood, suffered multiple displacements in the sense of being replaced and superimposed, one upon another, in an oblique and spiraling fashion. Note that from the early decades of the inception of the neighborhood up to the late twentieth century, the term *Eurasian* disappeared from the epithet (or was it amputated?): the former Portuguese Eurasian Settlement became simply the Portuguese Settlement. This may not have been an innocent alteration; we recall that the New State aspired to turn the Malacca residents into members of the imperial community of all the formerly Portuguese-influenced areas of Asia. Did this subtle process constitute an attempt to "nationalize" the Eurasians of Malacca, as somehow more "Portuguese" than Portuguese Eurasian?[7] That the Malacca Portuguese possess one and only one identity thus seems preposterous; at least three levels of intertwined identities are at play. The argument has implications for an analysis of both power relations (from the point of view of the dominated) as well as physical place and social space.

The crux of the matter lies in the gulf between 1641, when formal Portuguese administration of Malacca ceased, and the mid-twentieth century, when the Portuguese New State, as it were, successfully infused their long-lost Malaccan cousins with "genuine" Portuguese folklore. This aesthetic transplanting campaign in the 1950s resulted in a two-pronged process: it approximated the Malacca Portuguese to their European forefathers, while it distanced them severely from the Malays. But it also contributed via tourism to the recuperation of certain dimensions of a creole identity, formerly invisible or virtually mute. It was at this moment that a nondescript cultural enclave rapidly turned into a kitsch showpiece. A positive element accompanied a negative one. The "pull" from the Portuguese world implied a "push" away from the Malay world; this process made the group more superficially visible but simultaneously discouraged identification with the Malay element in the Kristangs' creole background. How can we account for this shift? In other words, are we dealing with a genuinely (or symbolically) Portuguese people, or, alternatively, with a more subtly obscured Portuguese Eurasian creole ethnic group which has been cajoled, redefined, and relabeled "Portuguese" by external agents over the past six decades? Would our acceptance of a Portuguese epithet merely contribute to a reproduction of nationalist, colonialist categories applied by the fascist New State to its subjects within the former Portuguese empire?[8] A rephrased query might ask: Should the Kristangs be considered Portuguese merely on the basis of their own affirmations that they are indeed "the Malacca Portuguese"? How might we define what it means to be Portuguese in this Asian niche characterized by such multiplex colonial domination throughout the early modern period?

Most Kristangs will, as we have seen, figuratively, agree that some Malay elements characterize their identity, despite their predominantly Portuguese ancestry. How to be more Portuguese than the Portuguese might well characterize a large part of their aesthetic activity. One is struck by the effusive, exaggerated nature of their asseverations of Portuguese character. We are tempted to call this hyper-identity. A surprising number of Kristangs are highly talented musicians and chefs, and perform as such professionally. Three areas where they have, at least since the early 1980s, carved out preferential space within the context of urban Malacca are precisely the hotel industry (a number of Malacca's luxury hotels are directed by Kristang individuals), the culinary world, and the world of music. In the latter two cases, specifically Portuguese music and specifically Portuguese cuisine[9] have provided greater visibility for the group. In fact, it is Kristang cuisine (termed "Portuguese") that has gained prizes within and outside Malacca for a number of talented local chefs, while the folklore troupes have also provided a wider image for the group via trips to and performances in Macau, Thailand, and Singapore. In other words, the term *Portuguese* has been as it were grafted onto a series of cultural activities in which Kristang individuals and groups have dedicated special energy over the past decades. Why? Can we search for an answer in a concept such as Bentley's term *ethnic habitus* (Bentley 1987; also see Bentley 1991; Yelvington 1991)? Do the Kristangs succeed in obtaining abundant aesthetic and symbolic space amidst their reduced geographic and ethnic space as a marginalized group within the city of Malacca?

Numerous authors have noted the sometimes idiosyncratic, ambiguous, elusive nature of the self-image held by Kristangs (Guimarães and Ferreira 1996; Santa Maria 1982; Sarkissian 2000; Shelley 1991; even Padre António da Silva Rêgo in 1942). One parish priest (from Normandy), unpopular among some Kristangs, claimed to me once, angry with his "pampered" Portuguese Catholics and their superiority complex vis-à-vis other Catholics of non-Portuguese ethnic origin, that "these 'Portuguese'—they have no identity at all!" Following the logic of this volume in the sense of pinpointing historical processes, are there key dates that signpost these processes of shifting group identification?

THE NOTION OF "DISPLACED IDENTITIES"

Let me now explain the notion of displaced identities I am developing. The Malacca Portuguese (objectively) do not have one and only one identity, nor do they (subjectively) view themselves, their culture, and their heritage uniformly via one and only one concept of self-identification. The three major levels of identity are expressed through different kinds of cultural grammars or codes; the latter do not always coincide. These three frequently contradictory codes of selfhood cannot be explained sufficiently by traditional theories of unitary identity. I balk at defining identity in a systematic fashion (Gomes da Silva 1989; Handler 1994; Lévi-Strauss 1983 [1977]): but I use it obviously in neither a static fashion nor as totally plastic and conjunctural.[10]

The only way to try to locate what this weird creole sense of belonging nowhere really is seems to be through a term such as non-self-identification. Now, we might simply say that this group maintains (1) a bland or weak national identity as Malaysian citizens, (2) a highly exaggerated cultural identity directed toward Portugal and Portuguese culture, and (3) a supremely vague ethnic identity deriving from the group's complex creole history as a Eurasian population as it were with "one foot in Europe" and another in Asia. Each of the three vectors of identity has accompanying linguistic attitudes. National identity is echoed by a very weak form of identification with the Malay language; cultural identity linked to Portugal is buttressed by a positive identification with two European languages (Portuguese and English); ethnic or creole identity is associated with the group's ambiguous but constant use of their own uncodified, oral creole language, never linked in the past to schools, dictionaries, or glossaries.

Nevertheless, surviving since the conquest date of 1511, we cannot affirm that the same format of triple identity need have been present necessarily in earlier historical periods. Thus, the "erasing" of "colonized histories" mentioned by Nicholas Dirks (1993:280) can be confronted with James Clifford's affirmations (1997 [1994]): "The language of diaspora is increasingly invoked by displaced peoples who feel (maintain, revive, invent) a connection with a prior home. This sense of connection must be strong enough to resist erasure through the normalizing processes of forgetting, assimilating, and distancing. . . . Diaspora consciousness is thus constituted both negatively and positively. It is

constituted negatively by experiences of discrimination and exclusion . . ."
(ibid.:255–56) and produced positively "through identification with
world-historical cultural/political forces, such as 'Africa' or 'China' "
(ibid.:256). (Could we state something similar in relation to the Portuguese empire?) These communities "thus mediate, in a lived tension,
the experiences of separation and entanglement, of living here and
remembering/desiring another place" (ibid.:255). See also, along these
lines, Robin Cohen's delineation of seven key "fibres" of the diasporic
rope (1997:180–87).

Kristangs gravitate toward anything originating in Portugal: language, people, clothing, customs, music, dance, religion, and traditions.
Of a total of 164 households, only one had an open copy of the Koran
and a tapestry of Mecca hanging on the wall. Indeed, I was flatly
refused entrance into one *kaza* while elaborating a census with genealogies. I only later found out that the reason was linked to a brother-
in-law of the household head, who had married a Malay, and who
resided off and on inside the neighborhood. I was told that the family
was ashamed (*teng bergonya*). Everything originating in Portugal is inherently "good." Nowadays even audio cassettes, video cassettes, and
personal letters arriving from the formerly colonizing country are prized
items. One Portuguese linguist has noted this devouring attitude: "[T]he
sentimental leaning of the Malacca Christians toward their Portuguese
fatherland is quite moving. There are children whose wildest dream is
to visit Portugal some day, and who hoard everything Portuguese that
is given to them: postcards, stamps, coins" (Batalha 1986 [1981]:58).
Portugal serves as a sort of ideological cradle, name giver, and provider
of religion, language, and cultural traditions.

We may now annex the concept of displaced identities to a series
of four sequential processes.

A

The period from 1948 through 1953 was a crucial one. Father Manuel
Joaquim Pintado, a missionary ordained in Macau and arriving in Malacca in 1947, began to promote the recreation of Portuguese folklore.
The birth of the first of these folklore troupes, which for the first time
consciously sang and danced European Portuguese repertoires, played a
decisive role. This is the first moment of displacement: an identity as

"Portuguese" was adopted, thereby replacing to a certain degree their former Kristang identity. Admittedly nothing actually precludes a double identity at this point—Kristang on the one hand and Portuguese on the other. The key point is that the role of music and dance had a dramatic effect, once the Kristangs began to use public performances (Fernandez 1986; Turner 1992 [1987])[11] as a means toward developing and cultivating their image as a tourist attraction. A newly adopted Portuguese identity displaced an earlier Kristang identity.

Note, however, that while this appears to be an infusion of European aesthetics into regularly organized public events, those on the extreme receiving end of the infusion were not simply "indigenous," but inherently semi-European to begin with, due to their ambiguous status as Eurasians. So, we must look at precisely who is infusing whom with what. Another event is also significant. In 1953, two Malacca teenagers went to Portugal by invitation to an international colonial Jamboree meeting, organized following the visit in 1952 to the Oriental Provinces by the then Overseas Minister of Portugal, Sarmento Rodrigues (República Portuguesa/Ministério do Ultramar 1954). One of the two girls—today a music teacher in Singapore—recalls with nostalgia, in reference to this trip, her audience with the Pope in Rome and the tea she was offered by Salazar. She brought back to Malacca, among other texts, a copy of Rodney Gallop's *Portugal: A book of folkways* (1936). For anyone not from Portugal, the performances by these troupes are perceived to be truly and authentically Portuguese. But they are clearly not the result of a process of the "invention of tradition" (Hobsbawm and Ranger 1983), because they were copied, adapted and reproduced. Note that this regime is exactly the same as the one António Medeiros (chapter 4 in this volume) has referred to for 1926–74, simply viewed from the other extreme, on the margins of the empire, where Michael Herzfeld's (1997) "iconicity," and the totalitarian-tinged rural motifs Medeiros has pointed to, were identical in folkloric form. As Edward Bruner affirms in his provocative essay on tourism in Bali, "The Other becomes domesticated, reworked for the tourists, frozen in time, or out of time, in past time or no time, performing a Western version of their culture, essentially as entertainers" (1996:161).

Sarkissian (2000) has argued that the Kristangs have invented a tradition of Portuguese folklore that telescoped their European identifications four centuries back in time. But did this process consist of an invention, or rather a transplanting of folklore and an accompanying identity? Did an ethnic group invent, reinvent, or simply copy Portuguese traditions recreated in Malaysia? Was this a voluntary group strategy, or the result of a conscious effort on the part of agents of the New State in Portugal to implant European Portuguese aesthetic forms, thereby transforming Portuguese Eurasian practices into "purely" Portuguese ones?

But it is crucial to bear in mind that within Portugal itself, profound transformations had been set under way during the first decades of fascism between 1926 and the 1940s, and that these changes had direct echoes in Malacca via the activating of intertwined artistic and political links. Precisely how did this occur? One detailed study of the manipulation of "popular culture" by the Portuguese totalitarian regime (Melo 2001) has demonstrated exactly how the New State concretized a large-scale plan of reviving folklore traditions for nationalistic purposes. Particularly after 1933, a wide array of elements were expanded within this national strategy: municipal festivals, literary competitions, tourism, museums, the 1st Colonial Exhibition of 1934 in Porto, the Exhibition of the Portuguese World in 1940, and various Ethnography and Folklore Conferences (Melo 2001; Branco and Castelo-Branco 2003; cf. also Paulo 1994—note 8 above). One particularly colorful element was regional folklore troupes (*ranchos folclóricos*), which gained great visibility following their appearance in 1924–25 (Melo 2001:188–89). Music, song, dance, and costume were highlighted as keystones in these troupes: "Under the pretext of defending the authenticity of popular culture, Salazarism was responsible for an operation involving a shift in cultural references linked to song and dance (and dress as well), as the effort to infuse the style of the folklore troupe with national expressions had as a consequence the disfigurement of regional ethno-folkloric characteristics" (ibid.:188–89). By the 1940s, what the government defined as *ethnography* "served as an intermediary for this ideological encounter between the regime and the people, a scientifically legitimated factor of symbolic approximation and ideological classification of contents" (ibid.:66). Blocking the formal development of "ethnography and folklore" as a recognized academic discipline in Portugal, the regime thus managed to hold the reins of a marvelously effective visual and musical propaganda weapon, both within as well as outside the country.

During the 1950s—at the height of the fascist period—these folklore troupes experienced such success throughout Portugal that the process merited the term "explosion" (ibid.:193). In 1952 when the Portuguese Overseas Minister Sarmento Rodrigues paid his historic visit to Malacca, this entire process was well under way. On the day of his visit (19 May), it is important to note that beside the local creole songs sung by Kristangs a Portuguese song *Olá, Marinheiro* was included, and that the Malaccan choral group *Três Amigos* performed the Portuguese dance number *O Tiroliroliro*, which was "executed by a group of [local] boys and girls in regional Portuguese costume. This number aroused great interest and merited much applause due to the elegance of its movements and the charm of its costume" (República Portuguesa/Ministério do Ultramar 1954:14; 22–23). In other words, specifically Portuguese folkloric elements had already been incorporated within the Kristangs' own performative repertoire for this rare public occasion, at which they obtained direct personal contact with representatives of their homeland.

This process must be seen, however, within a transnational context: one of the Portuguese regime's key propaganda organs—the SNI, or *Secretariado Nacional da Informação, Cultura Popular e Turismo*—viewed the situation in these terms: Portugal was composed of "a series of provinces to all effects identical, by the rights and duties that the Homeland—into which they are habitually integrated—confers upon them. No element differentiates the Continental Portuguese from those of India, the Portuguese of Africa from those of Timor . . ." (Melo 2001:83, citing a 1955 publication of the SNI). Salazar's successor himself, Marcelo Caetano, affirmed in an early publication that "[a]lthough respecting the *modus vivendi* of the natives, the Portuguese have always endeavored to impart their faith, their culture and their civilization to them, thus calling them into the Lusitanian community" (Caetano 1951:34). This community of supposed Portuguese nationals was antithetical to what we would today term multicultural: Melo stresses that the New State achieved its objectives by fostering a monolithic, totalistic dimension (*uma dimensão omnímoda*) that went hand in hand with a strategy of combating "competing external universes" (Melo 2001:376). If not de jure citizens, many African and Asian populations with some form of Portuguese heritage were encompassed as de facto cultural members of this enormous Portuguese imperial community. The visit by the Overseas Minister and his accompanying coterie to Malacca in 1952 cannot be divorced from this wider process under way at the time, both inside Portugal as well as in the rest of the colonial empire.

Or to put it another way, we can see clear examples of the nationalizing strategy of the Portuguese regime in the details of the articulation between local Malaccan musical groups and the European Portuguese folklore troupes, which the former adopted, copied, and reproduced. The political strand cannot be separated from the artistic one. The attempt to incorporate remote populations in Asia within the circle of an empire-wide Lusitanian community reached Malacca at this time; cultural and artistic expressions thus played a crucial role in cementing the notion that the Kristangs were—instead of hybrid Creoles—truly and genuinely *Portuguese.*[12]

B

A second displacement concerns the Kristangs' relations with the Malays. 1957 constitutes a watershed date. With Malaysia's independence from Great Britain, Kristangs encountered a distancing from the Malay ethnic group and Malay culture in general. Significantly, a certain number of genealogies (dated well prior to 1957) of Kristang informants indicate Malay ascendants (some in fact being converts to Christianity). This would be virtually unheard of after that date. We find a second displacement distinctly away from the "close by" Malays following 1957, after a first displacement toward the "remote" European Portuguese following 1948. We must nevertheless be careful not to imply that all Kristangs share the same notion of identity—there may be two or more grand conceptions operative in parallel fashion or even in opposition.

C

These two displacements had the effect of muffling an apparently bilateral or double creole identity of the Kristangs as part-Portuguese and part-Malays. We hesitate to label this phenomenon something like an "original Kristang identity" (how can we prove it existed? when? what do we mean by original?). In other words, the two displacements set in motion following 1948 and 1957 make it quite a bit more difficult to determine clearly just what Kristang identity in fact ever was in the first place. This third process, rather than another displacement proper, might be viewed more exactly as a consequence of the two prior processes.

D

The first two displacements have also obscured a third and more subtle element in Kristang identity—the contributions from non-Portuguese and non-Malay ethnic groups. This is an important point, because it counters the traditional image of creole societies as simple hybrid products of only two cultures in contact—the colonizers and the indigenous colonized. The Malacca case indicates that a multiple set of mixtures prevails. Non-Malay and non-Portuguese traits remain occult or mute. This is yet another consequence.

Jean-Loup Amselle, in his *Mestizo logics: Anthropology of identity in Africa and elsewhere*, would suggest "a continuist approach that would emphasize an originary sycretism or lack of distinctness" (1998 [1990]:1). The latter will have altered its nature systematically since the first two moments of contact in 1509 and 1511. Identities, therefore, are not only mutable, manipulable, and dissolvable, but more significantly they can be displaced, substituted, and virtually suffocated. We repeat that we are not implying that the Kristangs have no identity, or no clear conception of their various identities (two very different affirmations). Rather, we suggest that their identities have been transformed by a dialectical process involving factors both external and internal to the group. Displaced identities are the fruit of simultaneously objective and subjective processes. This is certainly clear if we pay careful attention to some of the stimulating studies that have recently focused specifically on various angles of meaning afforded by the notion of displacement (Bammer 1994; Kaplan 1996; Wood 1999). Oriol Pi-Sunyer (chapter 7 in this volume) has captured yet another strand of processes of displacement by pointing to the complexities of the reconfiguration, restructuring, and rearticulation of the lives of exiles in alien environments. The experiences he describes reveal parallels with the multiple cultural worlds lived in by the Malacca Kristangs, who are themselves, indeed, a kind of "exiled" population cornered within a very singular cultural enclave within Malaysia. A number of identities may be sustained at the same time, and one or more of these may be displaced in one or another direction. This process leads me to the term *disjunctive* when I refer to varying dimensions of the lived experiences of Kristangs. While their relations with other local minorities are generally cordial, the link with the Malays is highly problematic and fraught with tension. Kristangs do, nevertheless, have a Malay heritage. We are reminded of the phrase: *"sangi malayu, ng póku!"* ("We have a little Malay blood!").

This fourth process, therefore, does not connote exile, forced migration, or refugee status: it is a social and psychological mechanism for the replacement of one identification by another. The idea needs a consistent definition, but gains some initial inspiration from work by Clifford (1988; 1997 [1994]), Gérard and Jolivet (1994), and Robertson et al. (1994). The identities of the Malacca Portuguese could also be termed elusive, equivocal, uncertain, divergent, discontinuous, or superimposed.

A second signification of the word has to do with place in two senses: firstly, it refers to physical or geographical space (Tilley 1994) and the removal or transferral of groups between territories. Secondly, it suggests social or mental space, and the shifting of identities from one "place" or niche to another. The notion of displacement carries both of these connotations simultaneously: a group of persons can maintain a permanent relationship of distance or removal from a remote place granted particular symbolic and emotive value. There need not thus be any specific local spatial referent for a displaced identity to develop or indeed to flourish.

Indeed, even outside the neighborhood, Kristangs have a wide range of monuments harking back to the Portuguese colonists' presence in Malacca, with which we do not hesitate in affirming that they identify. Examples are St. Paul's Church on St. Paul's Hill (erected as a chapel in 1521 [Pintado 1980:39]), the *Porta de Santiago* ("*A Famosa*") (Santiago Gate or St. James's Gate) first mentioned in 1586 but probably built somewhat earlier, according to Pintado (1980:38), St. Peter's Church (1710), *Jalan Portugis* (Portuguese Street), the marine museum inaugurated in 1994 (*Muzium Samudera*), constructed following the form of the Portuguese caravel *Flor de la Mar*. Four of the seven lanes inside the Portuguese Settlement are named after key historical figures: d'Albuquerque, Eredia, Teixeira, and Sequeira. In other words, not only culturally, but monumentally, the Malacca Portuguese can point to concrete spatial symbols of the presence of their ancestors, indelibly marking Malacca's urban landscape.

Let us recapitulate the processes under scrutiny:

A. First displacement: adoption of a "Portuguese" identity (1948–1953);

B. Second displacement: rejection of the Malay element in this newly replaced Portuguese identity (post-1957);

C. Third process: A and B obscure the definition of a prior Kristang identity;

D. Fourth process: A and B—at the same time—muffle a third element in Malacca Portuguese identity: the contributions of other ethnic groups (Chinese, Indian, Javanese, Baba-Nyonya, Chitty, etc.). We are impelled thus toward adoption of extreme caution in searching for any "original" Kristang identity, which has probably undergone numerous transformations (and earlier displacements?) since 1511.

AN INDIRECT ORIENTALISM?

Let us invoke here the notion of a hypothetical indirect orientalism. It may begin to clarify some of the power mechanisms at work in parallel with these displacements. Via propaganda and the conscious efforts of civil and ecclesiastical agents, the Portuguese New State as it were orientalized the Malays, through a kind of "Portuguesification" of the Kristangs. But this took place in an indirect fashion, indeed through the circuits of a vast network, taking advantage of the partially European component of their identity. Admittedly, we are only looking, as it were, backward through a telescope or magnifying glass. A key question would be: To what extent did Kristangs—prior to the strategies of the New State in the 1940s and 1950s—view their Malay neighbors as Others? Did the swallowing up of a Portuguese identity in the 1950s, in and of itself, stimulate a form of orientalizing of the Malays on the part of Kristangs? The New State thus fabricated a Portuguese diaspora. Kristangs were simultaneously recipients of an ideologically charged orientalism of sorts, as well as agents of a kind of filtered orientalism denigrating Malays. They thus played an oblique orientalist role.[13]

A second process derives from the shift in regional and national power domains occurring in 1957, and the effects of such on the local status of the Portuguese Eurasians. Informants systematically hail the British administration as a Golden Age in comparison to what they view as a generalized Malay fundamentalism following independence. Phrases such as "*Ingrés sa tempo, bong*" ("Things were good under the British") or "*Nus falá English muytu bong*" ("We spoke English very well"), implying that the Kristangs spoke English more fluently than

Malays, indicate a positive evaluation of the British epoch, with respect to the new period inaugurated under Independence following 1957. The Malaysian geographer Chan Kok Eng also refers to this shift:

> Prior to the country being granted political independence in 1957, the Eurasians in Melaka occupied an intermediate position in the colonial hierarchy, lower than the politically and economically powerful Europeans but somewhat higher than the Asians who formed the bulk of Melaka's population. The Asians, other than a few influential Chinese, were generally less well-placed in terms of access to the colonial administration, being composed primarily of Malays, who were less conversant with the language of the colonial power as well as being dispersed mainly through the rural areas remote from the seat of administration in Melaka Town—where, of course, the majority of the Eurasians were to be found. The Eurasians, by virtue of their command of English and their greater familiarity with Western manners and customs—which were in fact consciously adopted by middle-class Eurasians—were able to secure more important appointments in government service than were open to most Asians. They were also able to obtain employment in clerical, technical, subtechnical, and sub-managerial capacities in both government and private Western enterprises. (Chan 1983:275)

Chan thus insists on "the unduly high concentration of Eurasians in services that prevailed under colonial rule" (ibid.).

What I suggest here is that following independence, the Kristangs became rapidly marginalized in a different fashion than heretofore. We cannot simply blindly apply Said's (1978) (or others') binary notions of the dominant and the dominated; Kristangs were sequentially dominated in different epochs, while they appear to have achieved some degree of intermediate dominance under the British. After the Portuguese defeat by the Dutch in 1641, a spiraling of subaltern statuses can be said to have impinged on the Kristangs. An entire series of sequential layers of colonialist domination must be highlighted; the last of these was the taking over of national and State government institutions by a Malay majority. Inverse orientalism pops up again, because the Malay element in the Kristangs' ethnic profile was hastily downgraded. This process de-orientalized (or de-Asianized) them. Or, they deorientalized themselves. Yes, these inverted labels seem a bit fanciful. It sounds veritably like an ethnic Dr. Jekyll and Mr. Hyde complex. When Kristangs employ the derogatory term *natibu* (native/indigenous person) to refer to Malays, they are retaliating. This could be seen as a crystalline example of James C. Scott's (1985, 1990) notion of resistance to domination. The term is a weapon, or hidden transcript, providing indirect ammunition for the oppressed.

Another element worth highlighting is publications by Kristang authors concerning the Kristangs in general, among which we might refer to four recent books by two brothers from the Santa Maria family and two sisters from the Marbeck family. See Bernard Santa Maria (1982), Joseph Santa Maria (1994), Joan Marbeck (1995), and Celine Marbeck (1998). However partial and idiosyncratic they may be, these texts indicate a fine-tuned consciousness and concerted efforts toward publicizing Kristang culture well beyond the limits of the neighborhood. One patron (the Orient Foundation in Lisbon) has an ongoing program of scholarships for Kristang students completing their secondary schooling and entering university. Finally, tourism has—again, very indirectly—stimulated not only the copying of Portuguese dance, costume, and verses but also the resurgence of properly Kristang creole music and dance. The latter were, formerly, virtually dormant. You can now buy audio cassettes exclusively sung in Creole. This is an important development: up to this point, a number of audio cassettes had mixed Creole and Portuguese songs somewhat indiscriminately. The fact that there now exist entirely Creole cassettes indicates a novel conceptualization concerning the differences between Kristang music and the formerly dominant Portuguese songs.

In conclusion, this entire process should not be viewed as totally abstract or "objective"—just as the agents of the New State employed specific strategies of incorporation and identity definition, the Kristangs themselves have exerted strategies of accommodation and adaptation. The Estado Novo undertook to integrate the Kristangs within a transnational community of "Portuguese" that included the inhabitants of such outlying Asian colonial places as Goa, Damão, and Diu in India, Macau, and East Timor. Other areas, although not formally under Portuguese administration in the mid-twentieth century, such as Malacca as well as some small communities in Indonesia (Larantuka, Tugu) and Sri Lanka, bore the imprint of a former "Portuguese presence" (*presença portuguesa*) either in the form of monuments or immaterial culture (vestiges of the Portuguese language, folklore, religious practices, culinary traditions). This "Europeanization" brought about in Malacca a kind of indirect orientalism, turning the Kristangs into orientalists of sorts: they deformed the image of their Malay neighbors and, in so doing, also that of their own creole culture, obscuring virtually all of its non-Portuguese components.

The Kristangs have nevertheless persisted tenaciously within a kind of cultural enclave (Castile 1981), managing to maintain their creole identity—albeit somewhat mutely—beneath the surface of their adopted Portuguese masks. One of the costs, however, has been the denigration of their own partially Malay ethnic element: in simple terms, the effects of fascism "orientalized" their own view of the Malays and their own Malay heritage. A negative view of Malays cleared the ground for a positive view of the European Portuguese.

Our ethnographic recordings of social facts should not merely follow in the style of Stendhal's (1953 [1831]) observant traveler holding up a mirror to a passing landscape—this is simple ethnographic realism.[14] Rather, we should, according to Said's directives, pay closer attention to the creative and positive elements in minorities' actions and aspirations. This would be another angle of indirect orientalism, pointing to forms of constantly renewed processes of redefining and "re-scripting" the remote Portuguese culture that is viewed to be the group's cradle. So, following Smadar Lavie and Ted Swedenburg (1996), these creative and expressive forms of resistance seem to warn us of the dangers of reproducing colonialist stances via disguised forms of Othering. Displaced identities can thus be viewed as constructive, albeit sometimes purely reactive, praxis.

NOTES

1. Earlier versions of this chapter were presented respectively at the II° Colóquio de Antropologia: "Portugal (Pré/Pós) Moderno e Globalização"—Session 'Relações Interétnicas e Globalização' moderated by Jean-Yves Durand (Braga, Portugal: 18–19 May 1999) and in the seminar "From Orientalism to Postcolonialism: Towards a Debate on Portuguese Oriental Perspectives" organized by Rosa Perez and António Hespanha (Arrábida, Portugal: 14–16 July 1999), the latter version under the title "We Are Not Malay! Inverse Orientalism among the Malacca Portuguese."

2. Later in the same volume, Portuguese Square is mentioned as one of the nine major "tourist attractions developed in Melaka"; it comprises "a

number of restaurants serving local seafood and Portuguese cuisine as well as a stage for traditional and cultural shows. Some evenings on weekends and public holidays, the square takes on a carnival atmosphere. Colourful cultural shows are staged featuring traditional Portuguese songs and dances including the famous *beranyo* in which the audiences are invited to participate" (Berita 1994:572).

3. The term *community* is maintained here, although Anderson's (1991 [1983]) and Cohen's (1985, 2002) critical warnings and revisions are well heeded. Three basic levels of community are operative: (1) the residential neighborhood, (2) the social and "ethnic" category of Portuguese Eurasian as an identity marker, and (3) the wider and more diffuse former Portuguese empire (within which the authoritarian Estado Novo [New State] sought to encompass the "Portuguese" inhabitants of Malacca). These three levels of community operate—need it be overly stressed?—on levels that are neither temporally nor spatially always coincident. See Halperin's novel notion of *Practicing community* (1998), which builds upon Bourdieu's practice theory, for a fascinating revival of the word *community*, incorporating but also going well beyond Anderson's and Cohen's notions.

4. For example, the Creole terms *muru kristang* (an Indian Catholic) or *tchina kristang* (a Chinese Catholic) only invoke the second meaning (an ethnically based subcategory of Catholic). In general I have used the word *Creole* with upper case spelling when referring to the language or to an individual (speaking Creole, Malacca Creole Portuguese, a Creole [person], Europeans and Creoles), and lower case where the term serves as an adjective (creole identity, creole cuisine, creole culture, creole traditions).

5. This is certainly the thrust of two texts from the mid-1970s, the first entitled "People Without a Country: Portuguese in Malacca Seek Self-Identity" (Abrams 1974) and the second "Eurasians—An Identity in a Nonidentity" (Ganesan 1976). Both articles stress not only the difficulty—experienced by Kristangs themselves—of pinpointing a precise series of identity markers for this creole group, but also the urge toward expressions of a complex, multiple identity through aesthetic and folkloric styles.

6. There are a number of subcategories of the term *Eurasian*: Portuguese Eurasians, Dutch Eurasians, British Eurasians, "mixed" Eurasians, etc. A simplistic original meaning, referring to the children of European and Asian spouses, is obviously as dangerous as it is archaic (see Crabb's curious 1960 book), while the modern sense of the terms usually refers to a person who chooses to identify some form of genealogical background in which Portuguese, Dutch, or British surnames (or two of the latter) predominate.

7. Terminology in Creole reflects this interplay of multiple identities: I attended local committee meetings of the Regedor's Panel, which are held periodically or convoked for specific conjunctural reasons, during which a

half-dozen terms were discussed as proper designations for the group: Kristang, Portuguese Eurasian, Malacca Portuguese, Malaysian Portuguese, Portuguese Malaysians, Luso-Malays, etc. These discussions tend to be endless.

8. Paulo's study of the propaganda campaigns of the New State in Portugal and Brazil is elucidative: analyzing the SPN/SNI (*Secretariado de Propaganda Nacional/Secretariado Nacional de Informação, Cultura Popular e Turismo*), the author refers to "[a]n individuality mainly 'fabricated' by the ideology of the regime, based upon the appropriation of certain regional stereotypes and singularized images from Portuguese ethnography, presented via national and international exhibitions, festivals, competitions [*concursos*], conferences, 'cultural missions,' theatrical stagings, musical and dance spectacles, and other manifestations, symbols of 'officialized' popular traditions. During the decade of the 1950s, greater care was taken with Portugal's image in foreign contexts, while this was accompanied by an increasing interest in external propaganda and Tourism" (Paulo 1994:80; my translation).

9. Concerning hybrid cuisine, note the final sentence in the following quote from Father M. J. Pintado in 1980: "The ethnic origin of the settlers—a mixture of Malay and Portuguese, their patois and their religious festivals give them an identity of their own. The blend is most striking, as it comes from two races living far apart, in the Malay and Iberian Peninsulas. This blend of East and West is even apparent in the cuisine of the settlers" (1980:60). See also Celine Marbeck's Kristang cookbook (1998).

10. Three levels can be identified, as I have suggested. Portuguese Eurasians exhibit: (1) a largely negative disidentification with Malays, bordering at times on a fierce social poise of cultural separation; (2) a virtually blind, positive, and totalistic overidentification with the Portuguese, a people, "culture" if you like, or nation so distant in time and space as to foster almost automatically fabrication and invention; and (3) a very shifty, chameleon-like sense of pertaining to a kind of vague ethnic blob that has managed to survive and persist over time, but whose actual objective characteristics remain largely undelineable. Also see O'Neill (1995, 1997, 1999, 2002).

11. Note that on the stage within Portuguese Square, in the heart of the Settlement, two folklore troupes perform regularly every Saturday night from 8:30 to 9:30 p.m. Portuguese dances and music are interspersed with Malay performances executed by a Malay troupe. Tourists from Portugal invariably form part of the audience. These performances merit special attention, and have been analyzed in detail by Sarkissian (2000).

12. This notion is quite evident even in the language of the Overseas Minister's speech delivered in Malacca in 1952: "Portugal had two objectives in view when its ships set sail in search of the unknown World: to spread the Faith and the Empire. Today, four hundred years later, when Portugal has lost her dominions in this part of the world, but when the light of faith still reigns

alive within your souls, brought by our missionaries . . . you continue firm in your devotion to the old Homeland, and we feel satisfied and proud" (República Portuguesa/Ministério do Ultramar 1954:11).

13. Speaking of the VHP (Vishva Hindu Parishad) in Britain, the United States, the Caribbean, Fiji, and Holland, Van der Veer notes: "In an ironic twist of history, orientalism is now brought by Indians to Indians living in the West" (1993:42–43). The reverse seems to be true among the Malacca Portuguese: "[The Portuguese language] . . . has since been spoken by the Portuguese Eurasians of Malacca, though in a somewhat ungrammatical form with a mixture of Malay and other Asiatic words. . . . It is interesting to note that even after the conquest of Malacca by the Dutch, the Dutch language has never been learnt by our people. Up to the present day in Malacca the Portuguese language is spoken in certain homes inter familia . . . . With the advance of English education here it is feared that, in say another 15 or 20 years, the Portuguese language may die out here unless steps are taken to teach this language properly" (República Portuguesa/Ministério do Ultramar 1954:23–24).

14. Space allowing, we could extend this point farther by comparing differing styles of ethnographic naturalism and ethnographic surrealism. The famous quotation from chapter 19 of Part Two of Scarlet and black begins: "Why, my good sir, a novel is a mirror journeying down the high road. Sometimes it reflects to your view the azure blue of heaven, sometimes the mire in the puddles on the road below . . ." (Stendhal 1953 [1831]:365).

References

Abrams, Arnold. 1974. People without a country: Portuguese in Malacca seek self-identity. *The Asia Magazine* 14, no. 37–38:10–13.

Amselle, Jean-Loup. 1998 [1990]. *Mestizo logics: Anthropology of identity in Africa and elsewhere.* Stanford: Stanford University Press.

Anderson, Benedict. 1991 [1983]. *Imagined communities: Reflections on the origin and spread of nationalism.* London: Verso.

Bammer, Angelika, ed. 1994. *Displacements: Cultural identities in question.* Bloomington: Indiana University Press.

Batalha, Graciete Nogueira. 1986 [1981]. Malaca: O chão de padre e seus moradores 'portugueses.' Macau: Imprensa Oficial, 2ª edição (Offprint from *Biblos* LVII), 63 pp.

Baxter, Alan. 1988. *A grammar of Kristang (Malacca Creole Portuguese).* Canberra: Australian National University/Research School of Pacific Studies— Pacific Linguistics, Series B, 95.

————. 1998a. The linguistic reflexes of the historical connections between the Malay and Portuguese language in the Malay world. In *Save Our*

Portuguese Heritage Conference 95—Malacca, Malaysia, ed. Gerard A. Fernandis, 40–64. Malacca: author's edition.

———. 1998b. Introdução. In António da Silva Rêgo, *Dialecto português de Malaca e outros escritos [1942]*, 11–44. Lisbon: Comissão Nacional para as Comemorações dos Descobrimentos Portugueses.

Bentley, G. Carter. 1987. Ethnicity and practice. *Comparative Studies in Society and History* 29, no. 1:24–55.

———. 1991. Response to Yelvington. *Comparative Studies in Society and History* 33, no. 1:169–75.

Berita. 1994. *Information Malaysia 1994 Yearbook*. Kuala Lumpur: Berita Publishing Sdn. Bhd.

Branco, Jorge Freitas, and Salwa El-Shawan Castelo-Branco, eds. 2003. *Vozes do povo: A folclorização em Portugal*. Oeiras: Celta.

Bruner, Edward. 1996. Tourism in the Balinese borderzone. In *Displacement, diaspora, and geographies of identity*, ed. Smadar Lavie and Ted Swedenburg, 157–79. Durham: Duke University Press.

Caetano, Marcelo. 1951. *Colonising traditions, principles and methods of the Portuguese*. Lisbon: Agência Geral do Ultramar.

Castile, George Pierre. 1981. Issues in the analysis of enduring cultural systems. In *Persistent peoples: Cultural enclaves in perspective*, ed. George Castile and Gilbert Kushner, xv–xxii. Tucson: University of Arizona Press.

Chan, Kok Eng. 1983. The Eurasians of Melaka. In *Melaka: The transformation of a Malay capital c.1400–1980. Vol. 2*, ed. Kernial Singh Sandhu and Paul Wheatley, 264–81. Kuala Lumpur: Oxford University Press/Institute of Southeast Asian Studies.

Clifford, James. 1988. On orientalism. In *The predicament of culture: Twentieth-century ethnography, literature, and art*, 255–76. Cambridge: Harvard University Press.

———. 1997 [1994]. Diasporas. In *Routes: Travel and translation in the late twentieth century*, 244–77. Cambridge: Harvard University Press.

Cohen, Anthony. 1985. *The symbolic construction of community*. London: Tavistock.

———. 2002. Epilogue. In *Realizing community: Concepts, social relationships, and sentiments*, ed. Vered Amit, 165–70. London: Routledge.

Cohen, Robin. 1997. *Global diasporas: An introduction*. London: UCL Press.

Crabb, C. Henry. 1960. *Malaya's Eurasians—An opinion*. Singapore: Eastern Universities Press.

Dirks, Nicholas. 1993. Colonial histories and native informants: Biography of an archive. In *Orientalism and the postcolonial predicament: Perspectives on South Asia*, ed. Peter Van der Veer and Carol Breckenridge, 279–313. Philadelphia: University of Pennsylvania Press.

Fernandez, James W. 1986. *Persuasions and performances: The play of tropes in culture*. Bloomington: Indiana University Press.

Fernandis, Gerard A., ed. 1998. *Save Our Portuguese Heritage Conference 95—Malacca, Malaysia.* Malacca: author's edition.

Gallop, Rodney. 1936. *Portugal: A book of folkways.* Cambridge: The University Press.

Ganesan, Mages. 1976. Eurasians—An identity in a nonidentity. *Asean Review* 12 (June):24–25.

Gérard, Bertrand-F., and Marie-José Jolivet, eds. 1994. *Cahiers des Sciences Humaines* 30, no. 3 (Incertitudes identitaires). Paris: Orstom.

Gomes da Silva, José Carlos. 1989. *L'identité volée: Essais d'anthropologie sociale.* Brussels: Éditions de l'Université de Bruxelles.

Guimarães, João Pedro de Campos, and José Maria Cabral Ferreira. 1996. *O bairro português de Malaca.* Porto: Afrontamento.

Halperin, Rhoda. 1998. *Practicing community: Class culture and power in an urban neighborhood.* Austin: University of Texas Press.

Hancock, Ian. 1969. The Malacca Creoles and their language. *Afrasian* III:38–45.

———. 1975. Malacca Creole Portuguese: Asian, African, or European? *Anthropological Linguistics* 17, no. 5:211–36.

Handler, Richard. 1994. Is "identity" a useful cross-cultural concept? In *Commemorations: The politics of national identity,* ed. John R. Gillis, 27–40. Princeton: Princeton University Press.

Herzfeld, Michael. 1997. Structural nostalgia: Time and the oath in the mountain villages of Crete. In *Cultural intimacy: Social poetics in the nation-state,* 109–38. London: Routledge.

Hobsbawm, Eric, and Terence Ranger, eds. 1983. *The invention of tradition.* Cambridge: Cambridge University Press.

Kaplan, Caren. 1996. *Questions of travel: Postmodern discourses of displacement.* Durham: Duke University Press.

Lavie, Smadar, and Ted Swedenburg, eds. 1996. *Displacement, diaspora, and geographies of identity.* Durham: Duke University Press.

Lévi-Strauss, Claude, ed. 1983 [1977]. *L'identité.* Paris: PUF.

Marbeck, Celine. 1998. *Cuzinhia Cristang: A Malacca-Portuguese cookbook.* Kuala Lumpur: Tropical Press.

Marbeck, Joan. 1995. *Ungua adanza—An inheritance.* Malacca: Author's edition/Loh Printing Press.

McDonald, Maryon. 1989. *"We are not French!" Language, culture and identity in Brittany.* London: Routledge.

Melo, Daniel. 2001. *Salazarismo e cultura popular (1933–1958).* Lisbon: Imprensa de Ciências Sociais.

O'Neill, Brian Juan. 1995. Emular de longe: O povo português de Malaca. *Revista Lusitana* N.S. 13/14:19–67 (Actas do Colóquio Interdisciplinar "Retratos do País," Jorge Freitas Branco, and João Leal, eds.).

————. 1997. Forgotten Malacca (Review of Joseph Santa Maria, *Undi nos by di aki? Portuguese land title dilemma*). *Revista do Gabinete de Comunicação Social de Macau/Journal of the Government Media Bureau*) Special 97:114–21.

————. 1999. La triple identité des créoles portugais de Malaca. *Ethnologie Française* XXIX, 2 (Avril–Juin) [Portugal du Tage à la Mer de Chine]; 237–53.

————. 2002. Multiple Identities among the Malacca Portuguese. In *Review of Culture/Revista de Cultura* 4 (International edition). Macau: Instituto Cultural de Macau: 83–107.

Paulo, Heloísa. 1994. *Estado Novo e propaganda em Portugal e no Brasil: O SPN/SNI e o DIP*. Coimbra: Livraria Minerva.

Pintado, Father Manuel Joaquim. 1974. *Survival through human values: Religion, culture, language*. Malacca: St. Peter's Church.

————. 1980. *A stroll through ancient Malacca*. Malacca: Loh Printing Press/author's edition.

Rêgo, Father António da Silva. 1942. *Dialecto português de Malaca: Apontamentos para o seu estudo*. Lisbon: Agência Geral das Colónias.

República Portuguesa/Ministério do Ultramar. 1954. *Relação da primeira viagem do Ministro do Ultramar às províncias do Oriente 1952*. Volume II. Ed. Barradas de Oliveira. Lisbon: Agência Geral do Ultramar ["A Caminho de Malaca" and "Em Singapura"; 7–49].

Robertson, George, et al., eds. 1994. *Travellers' tales: Narratives of home and displacement*. London: Routledge.

Said, Edward W. 1978. *Orientalism*. Harmondsworth: Penguin.

Santa Maria, Bernard. 1982. *My people, my country: The story of the Malacca Portuguese community*. Malacca: Malacca Portuguese Development Centre.

Santa Maria, Joseph. 1994. *Undi nos by di aki? (Where do we go from here?): Portuguese land title dilemma*. Malacca: Author's edition/Sakti Bersatu.

Sarkissian, Margaret. 2000. *D'Albuquerque's children: Performing tradition in Malaysia's Portuguese settlement*. Chicago: University of Chicago Press.

Scott, James C. 1985. *Weapons of the weak: Everyday forms of peasant resistance*. New Haven: Yale University Press.

————. 1990. *Domination and the arts of resistance: Hidden transcripts*. New Haven: Yale University Press.

Shelley, Rex. 1991. *The shrimp people*. Singapore/Kuala Lumpur: Times Books International.

Stendhal, Henri Marie Beyle. 1953 [1831]. *Scarlet and black: A chronicle of the nineteenth century*. Trans. Margaret R. B. Shaw. Harmondsworth: Penguin. (Original: *Le rouge et le noir: Chronique de 1830*. Paris: Levavasseur, 1831).

Tilley, Christopher. 1994. *A phenomenology of landscape: Places, paths, and monuments*. Oxford: Berg.

Turner, Victor. 1992 [1987]. *The anthropology of performance*. New York: PAG
     Publications.
Van der Veer, Peter. 1993. The foreign hand: Orientalist discourse in sociology
     and communalism. In *Orientalism and the postcolonial predicament: Perspec-
     tives on South Asia*, ed. Peter Van der Veer and Carol Breckenridge, 23–
     44. Philadelphia: University of Pennsylvania Press.
Wood, Houston. 1999. *Displacing natives: The rhetorical production of Hawai'i*.
     Lanham, MD: Rowman and Littlefield.
Yelvington, Kevin. 1991. Ethnicity as practice? A comment on Bentley. *Com-
     parative Studies in Society and History* 33, no. 1:158–68.

CHAPTER 4

Imperialist Ideology and Representations of the Portuguese Provinces during the Early Estado Novo

ANTÓNIO MEDEIROS

The First Portuguese Colonial Exhibition was held in the northern Portuguese city of Porto from June 15 to the end of September, 1934. The event attracted much attention at the time. Today it is rarely remembered.[1] About 1.5 million people visited the exhibition grounds that were designed around "The Palace of the Colonies," the name given the Crystal Palace (*Palácio de Cristal*) for the summer of 1934, when it was covered with a temporary façade reflecting the modernist influences of the time.[2] The numbers in attendance register the importance and suggest the social impact in northern Portugal of this first mass propaganda initiative by the Estado Novo (the New State), which had only recently been legally consolidated. The Colonial Act of 1930 and the new Constitution of 1933 were the mainstays of the new authoritarian regime's legal order (Rosas and Brito 1996).

During the 1930s "ethnographic" processions became a regular means of transmitting ideology under strict control of the state. The main interest of the 1934 Exhibition lies here: it was one of a set of experiments in representing Portugal and its overseas colonies to the public.[3] In the light of the ideology being developed at the time, a very broad, inclusive space of community was envisaged: the empire. Prior to the Exhibition, attention had certainly been paid to representing the various colonies. But in the 1930s, displaying this empire seemed to require representing the "*Metrópole*" (Portugal proper) and its internal diversity. Much of the literature published for the Colonial Exhibition suggests the reason for this: the colonies were coming to be seen as "overseas provinces."[4] The new emphasis on representing both internal and overseas "provinces" was particularly evident in two great processions: the Entre-Douro-e-Minho Regional Parade and the Colonial Procession, both high points in the Exhibition calendar.

The state-sponsored events in Porto offered the broad public newly accessible (because condensed and formulaic) images of a regionally varied Portuguese national culture, and thus represent an important juncture in the "invention of tradition" (Hobsbawm and Ranger 1983). Indeed, representations of the Portuguese provinces as having distinctive "folk cultures," introduced in 1934, are still widely considered valid today, though in the intervening seventy years many political changes have taken place in Portugal (cf. the suggestions in Branco 1999).

I first became interested in the First Colonial Exposition while doing fieldwork in two rural parishes in the Minho during the 1990s. I encouraged an elderly informant to recount the earliest local uses of the stereotyped folkloric representations so common today in the northwest of Portugal. His earliest memory was of a Sunday in 1934, when virtually his entire village followed the local priest to Porto. All had been asked to wear old-style clothes for participation in the Parade of Entre-Douro-e-Minho Region. My informant stayed at home that day due to his youth and the possibility of disorder in the city.

MEMORY TRACES OF A ONCE NEW CULTURE

Most of the informants with whom I spoke in Porto during research in 1999 knew almost nothing about the Colonial Exhibition. However, their childhood recollections of weekend trips to the Crystal Palace gardens revealed certain traces of that distant initiative: for example, a soaring white limestone monument symbolizing "the Portuguese colonial effort," an island "monkey village" in the small lake hosting the "Bijagó Lake Village" in 1934, a lion that for decades lived a miserable life in execrable conditions, and a foul-smelling aviary with exotic birds. In June 1934 a journalist noted the following, with no hint of conscience: "The exoticism of the Colonial Exhibition is mainly supplied by the indigenous peoples and the zoological specimens. They have roused exceptional curiosity among the visitors" (O Comércio do Porto Colonial, June 16, 1934:3).

Today, almost every trace of the authoritarian state's initiative of 1934 has disappeared from the Crystal Palace gardens. Perhaps the 1934 Exhibition has been obscured largely because of changes in Portuguese policy on colonies and former colonies occurring in the intervening years, particularly following the fall of the dictatorship on April 25, 1974. Two years after this date, the former colonies achieved official independence. Additionally, in the 1990s membership in the European Union brought new ways of objectifying Portuguese culture (see Handler 1988 on objectifying national culture). These new efforts at objectification differ significantly from the efforts made in 1934 to impart an "imperial mentality" to the masses, as I saw during fieldwork in Porto in the fall of 1999 with the preparation of cultural events for the European Capital of Culture celebrations scheduled for 2001. Yet we need to ask why folkloric processions stressing rural Portuguese cultural specificities continue to take place even in the twenty-first century. What might such representations of "Portuguese" space and culture tell us about the staying power of iconic knowledge (Herzfeld 1997:73), even in the face of minimally retrievable narratives of specific earlier events?

Though obscured, significant records of the Exhibition can be uncovered, and former visitors' memories of the event, though often hazy, can be recovered. My field visit in Porto had nothing of Geertz's "Balinese cockfight"—when a chance incident in daily life allows a foreign anthropologist to get involved in the "webs of significance" of a culture not his or her own—about it (Geertz 1973). I did research in libraries and photographic archives and talked with people who remembered the changes in the Crystal Palace gardens in the decades following the Colonial Exhibition. Meetings in various parts of northern Portugal with people who visited the event in 1934 provided anecdotal records of the disparity between the promoters' intentions of imparting an "imperial mentality" and the learning that actually took place. The documentary and oral evidence represented variations on a cultural core that I, as a native anthropologist, also shared.

With a certain irony, Burton Benedict says of the great exhibitions: "They were presenting an ordered world. Many of these ideas could be seen in concrete (or at least plaster) form at the expositions" (1983:2). Given that one of the most important historians of the period calls the 1930 Colonial Act a "centralizing and *nationalizing* turning point" (Rosas 1994:202; my emphasis), it seems especially appropriate to follow Benedict Anderson's famous (1991 [1983]) formulation and consider the 1934 Porto Exhibition part of an effort to create an "imagined community"—in this case of an immense, variegated empire.[5] The Colonial Exhibition certainly "represented" economic interests, but it was above all an exercise in imperial and nationalist pedagogy carried out under the aegis of the state to legitimize the recently installed authoritarian regime. The target of this display was the Portuguese people as a whole. However, the relative modesty of the resources available limited the Exhibition's impact. Lisbon press coverage of the Exhibition was minimal. The number of visitors from the capital and the southern provinces must have been fairly low. There were no foreign exhibitors and very few foreign visitors. Though actual attention from abroad was limited, it was a fairly atypical "great exhibition." Projecting the image of a nation outward is one of the most consistent features of this type of event (Benedict 1983; Greenhalg 1988), and the organizers boasted of successfully promulgating the event internationally (cf. Galvão 1935).

New Representations of the Overseas Empire and the Rural

All European colonial exhibitions[6] spotlighted living human beings uprooted and placed in large-scale plaster of Paris settings representing their distant homelands. These living dioramas reflected the political domination and economic exploitation orchestrated from the imperial metropoles; they showcased the central powers' capacity for both organized colonial rule and technical and commercial innovation. In the Porto exhibition, the government's "ethnographic section" constructed a tale of progress culminating in the achievements of a colonial economy committed to modernization. But in 1934 the political and economic control actually exercised by Portugal in the colonies was weak (as it had been throughout the history of the Portuguese empire) (Chabal et al. 2002:30; also Anderson 1962:98–99). In part the Exhibition was meant to strengthen this control. Yet there were few technical and material resources in Portugal for the representational advance imagined. Also lacking was a critical mass of willing, middle-class exhibition-goers, the most common type of visitors to the great international exhibitions in many other Western countries (Benedict 1983).

Henrique Galvão, the main organizer, recognized that most visitors to Porto's Crystal Palace gardens in 1934 would not consume the images of the "exotic" on offer with sophistication, although he counted on the preliminary effectiveness of the "lesson in colonialism" that he wished to transmit:

> They came in the same spirit of joy and amusement with which they attend public festivities or the theatre, a bullfight or a football match. Some said: Let's go and see the blacks . . . .
>
> Those who had come only to see the blacks and have fun in the fairgrounds actually saw a little more besides. (Galvão 1934:1)

At this time many Europeans associated the ideas of "tribal" and "primitive" with positive aesthetic values (Clifford 1988; França 1974; Golan 1995). In the Portuguese context, however, the rationale for ethnographic representations of the colonies was generally connected more explicitly to imperialist ideology than to avant-garde aesthetic values:

> It is beyond my comprehension that the aim of mounting an exhibition in a European city of the savage way of life followed by the indigenous people in our colonies is to present our civilized people with examples that deserve imitation. . . . Instead, the aim should be displaying the greatness of the nation and its dominions beyond the tiny metropole. (Costa Júnior 1934; underlining in original)

These views appear in an article by J. R. Costa Júnior entitled "The revival of rural life." The title of the article is characteristic of an age marked by great change and a sense of general crisis in values. In the 1910s and 1920s, various proposals for Portuguese national redemption emerged from the most diverse political quarters. These represented not only the salience of the idea of empire (see Leal's chapter in this volume) in early-twentieth-century Portugal, but also refractions of antimodernist ideologies circulating internationally. For the generation coming of age with the Great War, what Peter Gay identified as "the hunger for wholeness" was very clear, and perhaps best articulated among right-wing intellectual groups.[7] It can be seen as a direct consequence of the anguish accompanying the most destructive aspects of modernity (Gay 1968). The author of "The revival of rural life" conveys a lack of cosmopolitan "old bourgeois" readiness to consume the exotic. Also missing from the passage cited, it should be noted, is a readiness to understand that representing empire was consistent with new ways of conceiving the rural zones of the metropole: the empire and the rural zones of the home territory were parts of a whole. During the period analyzed here, the ideologists of the authoritarian regime produced a coherent representation of this whole.

During the course of the 1934 Exhibition, new ethnographic motifs were developed that would coexist with and in a way mimic the more established forms used to represent the colonies. Various news reports document this process. The following account is an especially good example of the documentation available to researchers. It is a commentary on the Colonial Procession, the great parade that brought the Exhibition to a close on September 30:

> All those who attended the procession recall the interesting, well-organized depiction of farming life. The regional and folkloric groups unabashedly added a colorful, picturesque note of national popular culture. They would have made an interesting parade by themselves.
>
> The procession included motifs and representatives from the provinces of Minho, Trás-os-Montes, the demarcated wine region of the Douro, Beira Alta and Beira Baixa, Ribatejo, Alentejo, Estremadura and the Algarve. These counterbalanced the overseas ethnographic segments. (Author anonymous, "Ecos do cortejo colonial: A representação da lavoura," *Ultramar* 18:2)

ICONICITY AND MIMESIS IN THE EARLY ESTADO NOVO

Based on the news reporting, it seems that few of the journalists and members of the intended general audience grasped the principles of the modernist grammar available for exhibiting provincial cultures. More noteworthy, perhaps, is how few of the Exhibition organizers seem to have achieved such a grasp. Judging from available documents, only the technical director, Henrique Galvão, managed to apply the modernist discourse systematically in the Colonial Exhibition. Galvão was closely attuned to what modern propaganda techniques offered for the transmission of a new popular culture.

At the beginning of the 1930s some members of the state elite introduced very rapid changes in the ways the country was represented. They proposed new forms of historical and ethnographic synthesis as components of a mass culture to be based in an authoritarian ideology and the extensive use of images. In 1931 António Ferro, along with Galvão a key figure in the new regime's propaganda apparatus, used a

Baudelairean metaphor that suggests a radical awareness of the changes the propaganda work could bring about. "It is true," he said, "that Salazar has saved the country... he has almost completely remodeled the nation's façade" (Ferro 1933:1).[8]

With the exception of the work of a very few specialized ethnographers (Leite de Vasconcelos, Rocha Peixoto, Vergílio Correia, for example), representations of Portuguese cultural specificity were generally crafted somewhat carelessly, their aim being to entertain. At the turn of the twentieth century, the leisure and literary habits of the middle classes encouraged the burlesque mimesis of rural customs and the systematization of the fantasized images of rural life created via this mimesis. Such images appeared in particular connection with one province, the Minho, which was especially highlighted in turn-of-the-century Portuguese nationalist representations (Medeiros 2002, 2003).

It is worth giving an example of how these ethnographically inattentive representations persisted beyond 1930. Ethnographic motifs redolent of the Minho underlay the proposed mimesis of rural customs for consumption by summer vacationers in search of "national" amusement.[9] I quote below from a report in the newspaper *O Comércio do Porto* on the festivities at the spa town of Caldas de Vizela in August 1934, while the Colonial Exhibition was being held in Porto.

> As could be expected, the magnificence of the purely national festivities put on yesterday by the owners of the Cruzeiro do Sul Hotel for their guests has never been seen before. . . . A large group of ladies and gentlemen appeared unexpectedly, dressed in the costumes of the Minho and the Marias of Portugal, and put the spectators in a cheerful mood . . . .
> At two in the morning the Portuguese-style supper began with the traditional *caldo verde* soup of potato and kale. . . . Set with large dishes, three-armed candleholders, small saucers with *tremoços* [edible lupine seeds], iron forks and cornbread, the tables were fine renditions of the kind of table that farm workers sit down to. (C.S. 1934:6)

In the same month, the newspaper *O Primeiro de Janeiro* reported a similar occurrence at one of the Porto area's best-known beaches, where a great variety of regional costumes was on display:

> The Regional Costume Ball held today in the Grand Hall of the Espinho Casino was a great social success. . . .

> Among the enormous crowds, especially noticeable for their elegance were the large numbers of ladies wearing a variety of beautiful costumes from the Minho, Trás-os-Montes, Beira and Ovar. (C. 1934:4)[10]

With the arrival of the 1930s, ideologues pursued stripped-down ways of using provincial cultural imagery to inculcate a new national culture. As the newspaper accounts quoted above suggest, in the new political situation it became possible to compel ordinary citizens to represent themselves as inhabitants of the provinces, decked out in costumes that the ethnographers' work of objectification in earlier decades had legitimated as "authentic." As we shall see, the Exhibition attempted to ensure that the ethnographic representation of the metropole was acted out by the metropolitan popular classes, who attended it in response to the summons by representatives of Salazar's new authoritarian government, rather like the "natives" brought from each of the colonies to be exhibited in the Crystal Palace gardens. But it is also true that on the fringes of the official events the exhibition registered some interesting examples of mutual mimesis, encounters, and learning opportunities not found on the program (Taussig 1993). For example, the editor-in-chief of the *Comércio do Porto Colonial* noted: "I even saw a black man turn the most characteristic regional dance of the North into a *batuque* [an Afro-Brazilian dance]" (Rocha 1934:3). There are also frequent expressions of a sexual response, for example, the fugitive (homo)erotic notes of the reporter who enthusiastically describes the bodies of the male dancers from Guinea—"the strange contours of sweating naked bodies" (ibid.). The desire of the Porto middle and working classes is also aroused. Journalists portray this arousal as doing the rounds staring at the bare breasts of the African women in the "native villages" of the exhibition grounds and courting the "slim, comely and beautiful Inez" or the "black Rosinha." (J.R. 1934:4).[11] In the prose of one journalist, "Rosinha," who acquired a certain fame during the exhibition, is figured as a peculiar Portuguese national: "If you were to remove her skin—the blackness of it—and turn her into a white woman, you would see in her movements and the exquisite air she assumes when walking a graceful Minho woman" (Gonçalves 1934:4).

Another of the chance encounters made possible by the Exhibition is particularly surprising for the intensity of the mutual mimetic impulses of the participants:

[T]he famous bass–drum folklore group from Marco de Canavezes . . .
visited the *Comércio do Porto Colonial*'s pavilion and put on a brief
show full of color and sound.

A black man from the Guinean lake-village who happened to
be attending the show improvised a violent, agitated dance among
the Portuguese bass drummers.

For a few moments Guinea and the Douro were fraterniz-
ing . . . the strange dance of the Negro who was moving his hips and
muttering barbaric songs from the African backwoods took place
amid the vivid scarlet, green and black costumes of the Douro girls
and men, whom the sound of the bass drums drove crazy with
enthusiasm. (J.N. 1934:5)[12]

Clearly, however, while the new iconic representations of cultural
spaces created a context for unruly mimesis, a new censorship was also
brought to bear on the icons with the greatest power to incite. A
suggestion by Michael Herzfeld helps clarify the dynamics of the authoritarian censorship of many folk customs especially evident in Portugal of the 1930s and 1940s, when emblematic images of the
metropolitan provincial cultures were being developed. Focusing on the
nationalist discourse of Greece, Herzfeld reveals how fixing icons is a
discursive means of articulating power, a procedure that entails obligatory selection from—or censorship of—the existing array of cultural
forms. Exclusion is inherent in the selection process. Converting provincial cultures into icons may be understood as a development of this
process of censorship. As Herzfeld argues: "The very heterogeneity of
iconicity is what recommends it to the reductionist needs of ideology:
it simplifies the awkward, complicated, messy truths about ethnic and
other kinds of internal diversity that undergird its bland assertions of
homogeneity" (Herzfeld 1997:73).

The Colonial Exhibition represents a pioneering effort in
iconification because it trained its sights not only on a disembodied
provincial "culture," but also on the flesh-and-blood human agents who
made that culture. Newspaper archives from the period also suggest that
the most modest rural visitor to Porto in 1934 appeared as a *sauvage de
l'intérieur* (Certeau et al. 1986), and therefore as part of the Exhibition. In
February 1934, a few months before the opening of the Exhibition, one
news article syncretically packed together some very curious references
in which such overlapping identifications were already clearly affirmed:

During the Colonial Exhibition there will be various visits to the Palace of the Colonies by rural workers from the different counties of Entre-Douro-e-Minho and possibly other provinces of the country.

In Braga, Porto and Viana do Castelo these visits are being actively organized. The groups will parade through the city of Porto, from the Praça da República to the exhibition grounds, dressed in their regional costumes. They will carry their work tools and sing their regional songs . . . along with the Count of Villas Boas' verses, which we shall publish later. During the procession the different groups will sing to the music of the shepherds' chorus from Alfred Keil's opera *A Serrana*. (Author anonymous, "Exposição Colonial Portuguesa," *Ultramar*, February 1, 1934:1)

First staged in 1901, *A Serrana* (Keil 1901) is a good example of efforts to create a national middle-class Portuguese culture at the turn of the century. The "Minho costumes" of the chorus typify bourgeois cultural syncretism: the action was located in the Serra da Estrela, two provinces to the southeast of the Minho. Additionally, in one of the news reports, the Villas Boas verses mentioned are described as "popular in nature" (Author anonymous, "Ecos do cortejo colonial: A representação da lavoura," *Ultramar* 18:2). Such phony accreditation reveals how surprising the modes of legitimation pursued by the new regime could be. The following is an example of Villas Boas' verses:

> Como as tangerinas
> Em que um só fruto tem muitos gomos
> Nossas Províncias Ultramarinas
> São Portuguesas como nós somos.

> Like tangerines
> In which a single piece of fruit has many segments
> Our Overseas Provinces
> Are Portuguese the way we are. (ibid.)

That many of the visitors were simultaneously (hardly voluntary) participants and exhibits in an orchestrated visual demonstration of support for the new regime was most evident with the two processions that were the high points of the whole event: The Entre-Douro-e-Minho Regional Parade on July 15, and the Colonial Procession that closed the Exhibition on September 30, 1934. On these days the greatest numbers of people gathered in Porto.

The massive attendance at the July 15 Regional Parade can be attributed to the power of the dignitaries, old and new, in the various localities
of northern Portugal. Those holding political office under the new regime
were especially able to generate attendance. On many occasions, massive
attendance was the result of compulsion, even apart from special events
such as the processions. Reading between the lines of different accounts,
we can discern the will of large landowners and industrialists to make the
Exhibition a success, stimulating local councils and dignitaries—"the most
representative people in every county," as the *Comércio do Porto* put it
(Author anonymous, "A Exposição Colonial Portuguesa," May 18, 1934:5)—
to bring the greatest number of visitors to Porto.[13]

However, even some of the most influential people working on
this initiative had a seriously limited understanding of what—beyond
the most immediate and obvious political advantages—was at stake in
the newly developed art of summoning and inculcating the masses. A
feeble grasp of the propagandistic potential of exhibitions is expressed
in comments by the Count of Villas Boas, the elderly organizer of the
Entre-Douro-e-Minho Regional Parade and, later, of the homeland
section of the Colonial Procession that closed the Exhibition (as well
as the composer of the faux-popular verses cited earlier):

> Many people think . . . that it [the Parade] is panoramic, picturesque,
> a traveling exhibition limited to the display of customs, dress and
> folklore from regions within Portuguese national boundaries. . . . Yet
> above all it is meant to demonstrate the care and concern felt by our
> province and the Portuguese provinces associated with us, for our
> sister provinces across the sea. . . . (Villas Boas 1934:5)

Villas Boas focused not on an imagistic effect, but on notions of
"care and concern" (ibid.), as if the stress should be on the sort of face-
to-face social interaction found in small rural settlements. In contrast,
Henrique Galvão had a nimble mastery of the new image-based principles of propaganda and the possibilities they offered for effectively
organizing a new mass culture. Years later Galvão would say about the
Procession of the Portuguese World that took place in Lisbon during
the famous exhibition of 1940:

> It truly presented itself as one of the events that could best reflect the
> government's intentions . . . a grand procession displaying past glories,
> present imperial aims and also the kindness, charm and picturesque

colorfulness of the Portuguese people in the twenty-one provinces of
the empire. . . .

A procession is ephemeral by its very nature.

A procession passes. What remains is sometimes just an image
in our mind's eye—a fleeting one, at that—and at other times an
image that touches our soul and stays with us for the rest of our lives.

It was precisely this latter kind of image that we wanted to
conjure up. (Galvão 1940:27–31)

In the Entre-Douro-e-Minho Regional Parade, the first great
ethnographic display mounted by the Estado Novo, there were considerable organizational difficulties. These were the result mainly of the
promoters' inexperience and haste. Particularly important was the goal
of orchestrating a mass demonstration to legitimate the new regime;
accuracy in ethnographic representation was a secondary matter, and
clearly neglected. On various occasions, specialists close to the regime
particularly concerned about the authenticity of representations of
cultures in space (e.g., Abel Viana) would mention the Entre-Douro-e-
Minho Parade as an example of what an ethnographic procession should
not be. The plebeian crowds making up the procession were said to be
disorderly and, with rare exceptions, little concerned with accuracy in
traditional dress or enactment of customs. Rather, they offered up "imitations of foreignness," "insipid, ridiculous artifices" and obvious failures
of "rectitude" (Viana 1953:12–13).

This attempt to emphasize the idea of "historical provinces" in the
context of a "modern" event provides evidence of the parodic or
carnivalesque features of the bourgeois process of nationalizing popular
culture. The processions of the 1934 Exhibition represented distinctive
"provinces" that had been invented only several decades previously by
leading intellectuals (Hobsbawm and Ranger 1983). As noted previously, the process of creating a national Portuguese culture through
distinguishing such spatial and cultural specificities had been intensifying since the end of the nineteenth century. In the hasty, unprecedented
effort to attract the fifteen thousand people present at the procession,
the organizers certainly would have found ethnographic realism a tall
order. Because the great landowners and the captains of industry well-
disposed toward the regime—and the parish priests, mayors, and local
council chairmen they appointed—were the most important recruiters
of participants for the July 15 procession, there was a heavy presence

in the procession of fire brigades, tour groups, choral societies, musical associations, bass drummers, local dignitaries, "women from Viana," and "women with their famous Cabeceiras de Basto bonnets," as well as the occasional "Grupo Ervidense os Estoiras" (Ervidense Firecrackers), and various other groups with equally quirky, homespun names.[14]

Yet though some of these "bizarre" groups (as one of the news reports in O Comércio do Porto called them ["Parada regional de Entre Douro e Minho," July 16:1]) encountered a festive reception in the city's streets, this moment was the death knell for ethnographic processions involving parody.[15] The Colonial Procession closing the Exhibition in September was already more restrained. With Henrique Galvão himself taking charge of the whole procession, it was carried out with "composure," "solemnity," "vibrancy," and "feeling" (Author anonymous, "O grandioso cortejo alegórico que foi a apoteose vibrante da Exposição Colonial," Ultramar 17:4–5). In addition to depictions of industry and business, the especially long allegorical procession included a large African contingent: "Mandinga rulers," "tall, handsome, bare-backed Bijagós and Balantas," a "Kipungo maiden" and "marimba players," "black people with a savage look, primitive Vatuas" (ibid.). There was also an important rural metropolitan component: "farmhands," "boys with Arabic faces" from the Algarve, "peasant women," "corn threshers" from the Minho, etc. The goal was to represent the "21 provinces of the empire" (ibid.). "From the Minho to Timor" was one of the most famous slogans circulated during this period.

CODA

In the 1934 Porto Exhibition the modern development of a discourse of cultural specificity had not yet been achieved, as is obvious with the two most important processions organized for it. Yet this discourse was rapidly and effectively refined and consolidated in the following years: it would appear in a developed form in the Exhibition of the Portuguese World, a 1940 landmark in celebrations of the Salazar regime (Acciaiuoli 1998; Melo 2001).

Apart from these stage-scenery collages produced for processions at a national level, under the Salazar regime the Portuguese state did not allow any teaching about the provinces "for themselves" to be carried out. The authoritarian New State appropriated for its own ideological purposes icons representing specific "provincial" spaces that had been created by leading Portuguese intellectuals only in the late nineteenth and early twentieth centuries. The idea of the "provinces" was distinct from those other spaces within the Portuguese polity that historically had some administrative power (such as counties or parishes). I have suggested in this chapter that processions representing both overseas colonies as well as interior "provinces" central to the Exhibition of 1934 were important media for fusing culture, space, and state power in Salazar's Estado Novo. In closing, one can question how the iconicity reinforced by the motifs arrayed in these kinds of "ethnographic" processions might have created a more powerful lasting effect on people's national identity than images more directly associated with the dictatorship, and more easily rejected following the fall of the regime by virtue of this relatively unmediated connection. For processions meant to represent folkloric differences characterizing specific regions are found today in the largest towns of northern Portugal. Moreover, in rural parishes most distant from their county seats such processions have been put on for the first time only in recent years. In both cases, they very closely resemble the model first produced at the state level in the years between 1934 and 1940.

NOTES

1. Recent historical research on the Estado Novo's first years, which were marked by intense propaganda campaigns, has paid scant attention to the 1934 First Portuguese Colonial Exhibition. Greater attention has been given the Exhibition of the Portuguese World that took place in Lisbon in 1940. The latter initiative had greater resources, registered more visitors and left behind more impressive monuments (see Acciaiuoli 1998, and França 1980, for example).

2. This is based on the most optimistic calculations of Henrique Galvão (1895–1970), the "technical director" of the Colonial Exhibition and the person responsible for some of the Estado Novo's most important propaganda initiatives in the 1930s and 1940s (Galvão 1940:x). Along with António Ferro (1895–1956) and Leitão de Barros (1896–1967), Galvão was one of the regime's most capable and informed propaganda experts. He rose meteorically in the thirties and, of particular note, was appointed the first director of the radio service *Emissora Nacional* (National Transmitter), set up in 1935.

3. In this chapter, I use "ethnographic" because this is a direct translation of the term used by those staging the processions. In this context the word's meaning is close to "folkloric."

4. It was only in 1951 that the colonies were legally constituted as "provinces."

5. See Leal in this volume for an incisive discussion of how the after-image of empire has haunted the representation of Portuguese cultural realities. Parkhurst's chapter in this volume also discusses images inviting imagined community, in his case narrative images generated and directed at the regional level via regional newspapers.

6. I count North American exhibitions as European. As a rule, the imperial features of the great exhibitions were conspicuously maintained until World War II. A baseline was established by the Great Exhibition of London in 1851. After the Exposition Internationale de Paris in 1937, however, the promotion of these great events began to decline. This degeneration was already evident in the New York World's Fair of 1939 (Benedict 1983 and Greenhalg 1988). The First Portuguese Colonial Exhibition was, in the final analysis, the first "great exhibition" in a country with no significant tradition of displaying the nation's identity and wealth. Hence, each of the events in Portugal that emulated the great international occasions as closely as possible—other examples being the Exhibition of the Portuguese World in 1940 (see Acciaiuoli 1998) and Expo '98 in 1998—seem to be late arrivals, marginal to the central tradition of imperial and cosmopolitan exhibition that reached maturity in the nineteenth century.

7. Compare the references to the special prestige and influence that right-wing intellectuals won in the Portuguese society of 1910–1920 in Ramos (1994).

8. Baudelaire's saying is well known: "The street is the school of modern man." In all his writings Galvão shows a very clear understanding of the benefits of façades, processions, and succinct images—in other words, the street and propaganda—as means for implanting a new popular culture among the modern masses. (See, for example, Galvão 1940. Compare, also, the uses of propaganda in authoritarian Germany and Italy analyzed in Eksteins 1990 or Schnapp 1992).

9. Hermann Bausinger notes in relation to Germany: "The dominant influence of the idea of the national on the folk culture of the nineteenth and earlier twentieth centuries can hardly be overestimated" (1990:44). I think the same can be said of Portugal. It is only much later—from the 1920s on—that different provincial motifs were established. For example, at this time the adoption of Minho-style costume throughout the country began to be seen as abusive, though hitherto it had provided the basis for ethnographic representation of Portugal as a whole.

10. These are all provinces or localities in the north of Portugal.

11. These are fictitious names selected at the time for being typically Portuguese, and applied in more or less parodic form to the most popular figures from the colonies in the Exhibition.

12. Marco de Canaveses ("Canavezes" in an older spelling) is a northern Portuguese town near the Douro River about thirty-five miles east of Porto.

13. Most directly involved in recruiting visitors were the great landowners and industrialists, along with corporatist associations (Rosas and Brito 1996:212–24), and figures that they effectively placed in office: parish priests, mayors, local council chairmen, and other unelected authorities. In rural areas, the organizers viewed guaranteeing the cooperation of the local priests as the best means of assuring a continuous stream of visitors to the Exhibition. The following are extracts from a letter written by the president of the Federation of Agricultural Trade Unions in Northern Portugal to the Bishop of Porto, which the prelate forwarded to all the parish priests in his diocese: "The Colonial Exhibition, which should represent a beneficial lesson for all Portuguese people, is proving a complete success. Through this exhibition, the people need to learn about the efforts of Portuguese soldiers, settlers and missionaries. For their part, the clergy can exert great influence on attendance. . . . As for the organization of trains, accommodation, admission, etc., we will take charge of everything in the certainty that morally and materially we are offering an important service to the country and our fellow citizens" (Author anonymous, "Exposição Colonial Portuguesa," *O Comércio do Porto*, July 17, 1934:1).

14. "Firecrackers" approximates the ludic side of *"estoiras,"* but it is important to note that in this context the Portuguese word also denotes "pyrotechnicians."

15. The censorship of carnival festivities, especially their "excesses," is an oft-revisited topic in the Portuguese newspapers of the 1930s and 1940s. The parodic imitations of rural customs and costumes were also notably censored at the time. Commenting on Horkheimer and Adorno, Michael Taussig quite rightly suggests, "Fascism . . . is an accentuated form of modern civilization which is itself to be read as the history of repression of mimesis. . . . But above all, fascism is more than the outright repression of the mimetic; it is a return of the repressed, based on the 'organized control of mimesis' " (Taussig 1993:68).

REFERENCES

Newspapers Consulted

O Comércio do Porto
O Comércio do Porto Colonial
Gazeta das Aldeias
Jornal das Colónias
Notícias de Viana
Portugal Colonial
O Primeiro de Janeiro
Ultramar

Specific References

Acciaiuoli, Margarida. 1998. *Exposições do Estado Novo: 1934–1940.* Lisbon: Horizonte.

Anderson, Benedict. 1991[1983]. *Imagined communities: Reflections on the origin and spread of nationalism.* London: Verso.

Anderson, Perry. 1962. Portugal and the end of ultra-colonialism–2. *New Left Review* 16:88–123.

Bausinger, Hermann. 1990. *Folk culture in a world of technology.* Bloomington: Indiana University Press.

Benedict, Burton. 1983. *The anthropology of world's fairs: San Francisco's Panama Pacific International Exposition of 1915.* London: The Lowie Museum of Anthropology/Scolar Press.

Branco, Jorge Freitas. 1999. Autoritarismo político e folclorização em Portugal: O mensário das Casas do Povo (1946–1971). *Actas del VIII Congresso de Antropologia* 9:29–45. Santiago de Compostela: Asociación Galega de Antropoloxía/Federación de Asociaciones de Antropología del Estado Español.

C. [Note: in older publications of this type, it is not uncommon to find the author's intials listed in abbreviation as opposed to his or her full name]. 1934. O baile de trajes regionais em Espinho. *O Primeiro de Janeiro,* August 26:4.

C. S. [abbreviation]. 1934. De Vizela: Uma festa elegante. *O Comércio do Porto,* August 14:6.

Certeau, Michel de (with Dominique Julia and Jacques Revel). 1986. The beauty of the dead: Nisard. In *Heterologies: Discourse on the other,* trans. Brian Massumi, 119–36. Minneapolis: University of Minnesota Press.

Chabal, Patrick (with David Birmingham, Joshua Forrest, Malyn Newitt, Gerhard Seibert, Elisa Silva). 2002. *A history of postcolonial Lusophone Africa.* Bloomington: Indiana University Press.

Clifford, James. 1988. *The predicament of culture: Twentieth-century ethnography, literature, and art.* Cambridge: Harvard University Press.

Costa Júnior, J.R. 1934. A renascença da vida rural. *Gazeta das Aldeias* No. 1804:468.

Eksteins, Modris. 1990. *Rites of spring: The Great War and the birth of the Modern Age.* New York: Anchor Books.

Ferro, António. 1933. O movimento nacionalista. *Jornal das Colónias* 1, April 13:1.

França, José Augusto. 1974. *A arte em Portugal no século XX.* Lisbon: Bertrand.

———. 1980. 1940: Exposição do Mundo Português. *Colóquio Artes* 45 (second series):24–47.

Galvão, Henrique. 1934. *Ultramar* 18:1.

———. 1935. *Primeira Exposição Colonial Portuguesa. Relatório e contas.*

―――. 1940. *Portugal, 1940; Álbum comemorativo fundação*. Porto: Litografia Nacional.

Gay, Peter. 1968. *Weimar culture. The outsider as insider*. London: Penguin.

Geertz, Clifford. 1973. Deep play: Notes on the Balinese cockfight. In *The interpretation of cultures*, 412–53. New York: Basic Books.

Golan, Remy. 1995. *Modernity and nostalgia: Art and politics in France between the wars*. New Haven: Yale University Press.

Gonçalves, Elísio. 1934. Crónica da tarde. Eis a Rosinha Leitor. *O Comércio do Porto Colonial*, June 19:4.

Greenhalg, Paul. 1988. *Ephemeral vistas: The expositions universelles, great exhibitions, and world's fairs, 1851–1939*. Manchester: Manchester University Press.

Handler, Richard. 1988. *Nationalism and the politics of culture in Quebec*. Madison: University of Wisconsin Press.

Herzfeld, Michael. 1997. *Cultural intimacy*. London: Routledge.

Hobsbawm, Eric, and Terence Ranger, eds. 1983. *The invention of tradition*. Cambridge: Cambridge University Press.

J. N. [abbreviation]. 1934. Exposição Colonial Portuguesa. *O Comércio do Porto*, July 17:5.

J. R. [abbreviation]. 1934. À beira duma aldeia. Tanagra da Guiné. *O Comércio do Porto Colonial*, July 5:4.

Medeiros, António. 2002. The Minho: A 19th-century portrait of a select Portuguese landscape. *Journal of the Society for the Anthropology of Europe* 2, no. 2:18–28.

―――. 2003. *A moda do Minho: Um ensaio antropológico*. Lisbon: Edições Colibri.

Melo, Daniel. 2001. *Salazarismo e cultura popular (1933–1958)*. Lisbon: Imprensa de Ciências Sociais.

O Comércio do Porto Colonial. 1934a. Author anonymous. June 1:3.

―――. 1934b. Author anonymous. Exposição Colonial Portuguesa. July 17:1.

―――. 1934c. Author anonymous. A Exposição Colonial Portuguesa. May 18:5.

O Comércio do Porto. 1934a. Author anonymous. Parada regional de Entre Douro e Minho, July 16:1.

―――. 1934b. Author anonymous. Exposição Colonial Portuguesa, July 17:1.

Ramos, Rui. 1994. *A Segunda Fundação (1890–1926)*. *História de Portugal, Vol. VI*. Ed. José Mattoso. Lisbon: Círculo de Leitores.

Rocha, Hugo. 1934. Crónica da tarde. Vira e Batuqe. *Comércio do Porto Colonial*, July 16:3.

Rosas, Fernando. 1994. *O Estado Novo (1926–1974)*. *História de Portugal, Vol. VII*. Ed. José Mattoso. Lisbon: Círculo de Leitores.

Rosas, Fernando, and J. M. Brandão de Brito, eds. 1996. *Dicionário da história do Estado Novo, Vol. I*. Venda Nova: Bertrand Editora.

Schnapp, Jeffrey. 1992. Epic demonstrations: Fascist modernity and the 1932 Exhibition of the Fascist Revolution. In *Fascism, aesthetics, and culture*, ed. Richard Golsan, 1–36. Hanover: University Press of New England.

Taussig, Michael. 1993. *Mimesis and alterity: A particular history of the senses*. New York: Routledge.

Ultramar. Author anonymous. Ecos do cortejo colonial: A representação da lavoura. *Ultramar* 18:2.

―――. 1934. Author anonymous. O grandioso cortejo alegórico que foi a apoteose vibrante da Exposição Colonial. *Ultramar* 27:4–5.

Viana, Abel. 1953. Ranchos regionais: Da organização e tratamento. *Mensário das Casas do Povo* 85:12–13.

Villas Boas, Conde de. 1934. Exposição Colonial. A parada regional de Entre Douro e Minho. *Notícias de Viana* May 5:5

PART 2

Fascism, Cultural Spaces, and Memory Politics

The following chapters illustrate that the deep-seated reverberations of people's experiences of fascism, dictatorship, and exile shape their memories of space and culture. Susan DiGiacomo analyzes why ambiguous and piercingly satirical treatments of the Franco dictatorship have become so popular in recent years in Catalonia and elsewhere. She explores the politics of remembering fascism via the school classroom—one of the most trenchant spaces of memory for those who lived under the dictatorship. An exhibit in the National Museum of Catalonia contrasts the fascist classroom with the Republican classroom. The memories provoked by this exhibit are rendered even more intense by attending a comic play based on an adaptation of Andrés Sopeña's sophisticated memoir of schooling, *El florido pensil*. Through subversive satire, the audience is transported back to the spaces in which many first felt the full brunt of attempts to inculcate the dictatorship's vision of the "Spanish" nation through rote learning. DiGiacomo argues that humorous representations of the fascist classroom not only employ it as a metonym "of the Franco regime," but also push us to recognize that the National-Catholic education was "absurd to the point of *self*-caricature." Her chapter is an important illustration of how everyday practices such as attending a satirical play can entail a compelling reclamation of Other histories of political violence, and thus a reappropriation of particular periods in one's life. It serves as an examination, as well, of how cultural manipulations such as those outlined in Medeiros's chapter have been challenged. Sharon Roseman's chapter examines the Franco regime's intrusion into Galician rural spaces through the employment of largely urban women working for the Falangist Sección Femenina. Ambulant teams working under the Sección Femenina circulated in the countryside, their routes taking them to villages where they would operate courses and competitions directed at transforming people's bodies,

101

practices, and physical spaces. Unable to dominate the countryside as easily as it did urban public space, the dictatorship relied heavily on the seemingly innocuous "social work" of women volunteers concerned with the purveyance of "modern development" to all of Spain's people. Roseman argues that understanding the "aesthetics of power" during the Franco regime requires focusing attention both on the larger-scale, more elaborate, political displays held in Spanish cities and on the cultural idioms employed in rural areas by agents working on behalf of the state. Like O'Neill's, Oriol Pi-Sunyer's chapter challenges confining the study of particular spaces and cultures within territorial borders. It is an autobiographical analysis of his life as a child in a family of Catalan Republicans forced into exile during the Spanish Civil War. Pi-Sunyer's account of how members of his and other families rearticulated their lives and national identities as Republican refugees from Catalonia in wartime London provides an alternative to accounts of exile that emphasize displacement, uprooting, and dispersal. Rejecting any simplistic binary characterization of immigrants and refugees as either "assimilating" or "resisting assimilation," Pi-Sunyer argues that the "place" where his family's Catalan culture "sat" during World War II was English, this mobile culture being inscribed into the exile environment through the Catalan language, family rituals, memories, food, photographs, books, and other forms of material culture. However, the reconstitution of life in London also involved the selective appropriation and reconstitution of some British practices. This is a vivid account of the distinction that emerged between the restricted physical space of wartime London, in which the Catalans and others from Spain were welcomed but still treated as "aliens," and the open "counterspace" that the families created in their own homes. His analysis of the mid-twentieth-century experience of war and exile parallels the focus on memory, space, and power in the chapters by DiGiacomo and Roseman. All three chapters illustrate that memories do not sit in the past to be examined from a distance: they inform politics and identity into the twenty-first century.

CHAPTER 5

Re-presenting the Fascist Classroom

Education as a Space of Memory in Contemporary Spain

SUSAN M. DiGIACOMO

INTRODUCTION

This chapter explores a space of memory for Spanish citizens now in their forties and older—the fascist schoolroom—as a metonymy of the Franco regime, and its re-presentation in two forms: memoirs of the public schools of the Franco period (Sopeña 1994; Otero 1996 and 2000), one of which (Sopeña) was also adapted into a highly successful comic play; and a museum exhibit in Barcelona's National Museum of Catalan History. I argue that the ambiguities built into the transition to democracy beginning in 1977 had the effect of foreclosing a public conversation on the Civil War of 1936–39 and its consequences. In the midst of an otherwise resounding silence on this period of contemporary Spanish history, it is in playful subversions of the Franco regime in ludic spaces—theatres, literature, and museums—that two generations of Spaniards who grew up and were educated under fascism can confront and disarm their history. My point of observation is situated on the periphery of the Spanish state, in Barcelona, the capital of the autonomous community of Catalonia, where education, history, and democracy intersect in a distinctive way.[1]

Education—especially the teaching of history—is not only a space of memory but a hotly contested political space. The Partido Popular, the right-wing party that dominated Spanish political life from 1996 until 2004, was emboldened by the absolute majority it achieved in 2000 to begin effectively recentralizing the Spanish state. In the summer of 2000, the Spanish minister of education, Pilar del Castillo, appeared on June 20 before the Congress of Deputies in Madrid and subsequently before the Spanish Senate's committee on education and culture to announce plans for a major restructuring of public education, including new requirements for the humanities curriculum. She warned legislators that a "point of equilibrium" would have to be located in order to "balance" the "unitary and centralist" vision of Spain characteristic of education during the Franco period, and the "excessive particularism" of history curricula in the contemporary autonomous communities (AVUI, 21 June 2000, 31).[2]

A week later, on June 27, the Real Academia de la Historia released a report asserting that the history curricula and textbooks of autonomous communities with separate languages—Catalonia, Euskadi (the Basque Country), and Galicia—had "deliberately twisted" the historical record, teaching students a tendentiously nationalistic version of the past in a way that reproduced the worst sins of public education during the Franco regime. The Real Academia reserved its strongest criticism for the Basque *ikastolas* (primary schools that teach all subjects in the Basque language), which were singled out for fomenting a brand of racist and exclusionary nationalism that rejected any notion of a common history shared with all other Spanish citizens (Segura i Mas 2000, 17).

An angry Barcelona resident old enough to remember the character of public schools under the Franco regime wrote in a letter to the editor (Joan Serch, AVUI, 6 July 2000, 4), "Having read the report of the Real Academia de la Historia, I find there's one thing I'm still not sure about. Are students required to sing 'Cara al sol' [the official hymn of the Falange] before their history classes, or afterwards?" Sometime during the 1940s and 1950s, when "Cara al sol" was the obligatory prelude to every new school day, the eminent Catalan historian Jaume Vicens Vives wrote to a colleague, Santiago Sobrequés, with whom he had undertaken the updating of primary and secondary school history textbooks. In his letter, Vicens warned, "Be careful . . . because they [the fascist censors of the Ministry of Education] have a special mania about history, almost a persecution complex" (quoted in Sobrequés, AVUI, 2 July 2000, 20).

CATALAN EDUCATIONAL REFORM IN THE TWENTIETH CENTURY

Catalans have special reasons to be sensitive to attempts by the Spanish government to use the control of education and school curricula as an instrument of political repression. The earliest efforts to create a Catalan-content, Catalan-language public school system in the twentieth century were undertaken by the Barcelona city government and the Diputació (provincial administration), many of whose functions later passed to the Mancomunitat de Catalunya (1914–25), an administrative unification of the four Catalan provinces under the leadership of Enric Prat de la Riba that was the predecessor of the restored Generalitat. There are earlier precedents for modern, secular, rationalist, coeducational, experimental, and progressive schools in the Escola Moderna of the anarchist educator Francesc Ferrer i Guàrdia (see Ferrer Guardia 2002 [1976]). Founded in 1901, the Escola Moderna was intended to function as a normal school, educating middle-class teachers to teach working-class children. But in the short space of five years it inspired more than thirty small schools in Catalonia serving workers desperate for education and dignity on their terms. After the Tragic Week, private secular schools and workers' athenaeums in Barcelona were closed down and Ferrer was arrested, tried by a military court, and executed as the "author and chief of the rebellion" (Ullman 1968:45).

A few years later, in 1916, the Barcelona city government created a cultural commission that took up the legacy of Ferrer in less radical form, and began to introduce Catalan-language instruction and to include in the curriculum activities such as music, art, nature walks, physical education, and health and personal hygiene (Ardit et al. 1980:438). Two years earlier, in 1914, Rosa Sensat created an innovative, child-centered public school, the Escola del Bosc. It emphasized character development, training for citizenship, Catalan patriotism, and direct contact with nature and physical activity as a means of learning (Seminari d'Història de l'Ensenyament 1978:18–19). In the same year both municipal kindergartens and summer schools for teacher education were established by the Diputació de Barcelona, which also, in 1915, opened the first Montessori school in the Spanish state (Maria Montessori herself made a number of extended visits to Barcelona), followed by a teachers' college in 1919. At roughly the same time, the Mancomunitat established professional schools for nurses and librarians, a modern technical/vocational high school, a school of commercial studies, an agricultural studies institute, and the Industrial University, none of which then existed as part of the Spanish state's public education system (Ardit et al. 1980:439).

In 1924 the Primo de Rivera dictatorship closed the Montessori school, and the parents and teachers, led by the pedagogic visionary Alexandre Galí, formed the Mútua Escolar Blanquerna, a progressive and experimental school that educated several prominent members of Catalonia's political and intellectual elite. After 1931 and the transformation of Spain into a decentralized republic, the Catalan autonomous government's Ministry of Culture created, as one of its first acts, a teachers' college and a pilot school, the Institut-Escola,[3] where innovative pedagogical theories based on the formation of the whole person (as opposed to the information-transmission model of education) and techniques could be tested in educational practice (Galí 1979:150–51; Risques et al. 1999:312). The Institut-Escola created a unified, secular, coeducational curriculum from primary school through secondary education. The Patronat Escolar de Barcelona emphasized public primary education, and Rosa Sensat continued to play a prominent role in its development. Her legacy is such that in the mid-1960s, when the Franco regime finally allowed the creation of private schools because it had become clear that the public system was simply unable to meet the educational needs of Spanish citizens, Catalan educators created a private teacher-training institute and named it after her. The "Rosa Sensat" became synonymous with progressive and Catalanist education, and its faculty and graduates have had a major role in the development of educational policy and programs in autonomous Catalonia.

THE FASCIST SCHOOLROOM

When Franco and his rebellious generals finally defeated the Spanish Republic in 1939, life changed for the average Spanish citizen as well as for the Republican soldier, the socialist or communist party member, the anarchist or trade unionist, the Catalan or Basque nationalist, and the feminist. One of the key places in which the Franco regime penetrated the lives of ordinary citizens was in the domain of education. Any teacher suspected of republican or *rojoseparatista* (socialist, communist, or separatist) sympathies was promptly purged and forbidden to exercise his or her profession, and the liberal and secular pedagogies of public schools (now condemned as "foreign to Spain's own educational tradition") under the Republic were quickly dismantled and replaced with repressive curricula dependent on rote memorization and enforced conformity with a strict religious morality and General Franco's backward-looking vision of Spain (see Marquès 2002:47–56). For the fascist victors, "the greatest political mission of our Movement is educational, and in accordance with sound educational principles, it acts upon the heart of childhood and youth. Without this, the Movement would be devoid of meaning, and there would be no way to ensure the permanence of the Regime" (the fascist minister of education in 1942, Ibañez Martín, quoted in Cámara 1994:16). The duty of the teacher was to

> proceed in an *a priori* fashion, choosing facts not only for their objective historical value, but for their value in developing the [Spanish] national patriotism we wish to inculcate. He must take special care to emphasize those facts which show the values of our race, and to consign to oblivion those which do not favor it, or could be subject to twisted interpretations. It is a question, I repeat, of creating Spaniards who feel their history, and not of training men who understand their history fully. (remarks by a once-famous history professor at the University of Valencia whom Cámara [1994:17] declines to name)

A permanent exhibit in Barcelona's National Museum of Catalan History represents this undisguised attempt at ideological domination through *"formación del espíritu nacional"* ("training of the national spirit") in the form of a comparative diorama which visitors may enter and touch. Places known in childhood and revisited in adulthood can seem smaller to us, and this exhibit is a smaller-than-scale model. This has two effects: it returns the visitor in a very personal way to the experiential world of childhood (one may even sit down at the benches); and it situates that experiential world firmly in the past.

What did a public elementary school classroom look like in that lost world of Republican Catalonia? First of all, it was a Catalan-speaking world in which children were taught in their own language as the vehicle for instruction in all subjects, and introduced to their own literary tradition. On the blackboard is written a verse from a poem by one of Catalonia's most famous nineteenth/early-twentieth-century poets, Joan Maragall, *"La vaca cega"* ("The blind cow"). The textbooks on the teacher's desk are also in Catalan: *Geografia de Catalunya, Civisme*, a children's book of songs and a Catalan-language copy of the 1931 Constitution of the Spanish Republic. The children's attention is directed systematically to their own surroundings, as a way of opening them to the wider world. A map of Catalonia hangs on the wall, and there is a globe on the teacher's desk, along with tools for developing a scientific knowledge of the physical world: a ruler, triangle, and a one-meter measuring stick. A notebook on the teacher's desk records daily observations of weather conditions. The day's civics lesson is reinforced by the maxim for the day: "Do nothing you would be ashamed of, either in the presence of others or in private." On the wall hangs a portrait of the first president of the restored Generalitat, Francesc Macià, whose personal integrity was beyond question. A jump rope on one of the benches suggests the importance of physical activity and play as integral components of education. Many of these same elements can be seen in the Spanish film *La lengua de las mariposas* (José Luis Cuerda, dir.,1999; Sogetel, Producciones del Escorpión, Grupo Voz; released in the United States a year later under the title *Butterfly*), which offers both an idealized vision of the liberating effects of secular education under the Republic, and an understanding of the vulnerability of its achievements when people are frightened (as they were by the arrival of fascist troops in 1936) into abandoning their beliefs and values—and their friends—in a wild scramble for self-preservation.

After 1939, an educational system grounded in civil liberty, secularism, and science was replaced by a diametrically opposed set of values: a narrow religious morality inculcated in an authoritarian manner, a nostalgic idealization of rural life, and a highly militarized image of society. On one wall there is a map of the Iberian Peninsula depicted as the Garden of Eden: the world before the Fall. On the wall directly behind the teacher's desk there is a crucifix, flanked by portraits of José Antonio Primo de Rivera (the founder of the Falange) and General Franco. On the schoolmaster's desk is a child's composition (in Castilian, of course, as is everything else) in honor of Franco's birthday, stressing his "glorious life" and personal virtue as examples to be emulated; a book about Catholic missionaries striving to convert the benighted natives of pagan countries; and a textbook open to a lesson on national hymns and patriotic songs which describes the origin of the official Falangist hymn "*Cara al sol*," a militaristic celebration of youthful self-sacrifice to the victorious cause. On the blackboard is written a lesson on one of the many enemies of National Spain, the Jews, stressing their hypocritical character, the threat they posed to the greatness and stability of Spain, and the farsighted wisdom of the Catholic Kings, Ferdinand

and Isabella, who expelled the Jews in 1492. Any child would think at least twice before questioning such wisdom, for discipline was enforced with the cane, displayed prominently on the schoolmaster's desk. Playfulness and spontaneity have no place here. A moralistic illustration from a 1944 textbook (reproduced in Otero 1996:152) suggests that the child who remains at his desk to study during recess embodies the ideal Spanish national character.

A Catalan historian of my acquaintance dismissed this particular exhibit as "caricature," but I think this is precisely the point. National-Catholic education under the Franco regime was absurd to the point of *self*-caricature.

Of course, it could be, and was for many, an alienating and wounding experience; for others it was simply an early experience one grows out of. Class and gender may have something to do with this. Boys and girls were taught in separate classrooms. Girls were educated minimally, with an eye to their destiny in life as wives, mothers and homemakers, and they often shouldered child care, housekeeping and cooking responsibilities from a young age. Families struggled and sacrificed to educate a son, but not a daughter. As one woman recalled, without bitterness, "for a girl to go away to school would have been seen as excessive and unnecessary, but not for a boy" (Roca 2001:131). This woman learned to put aside such ambitions, but this did not stop her from noticing that "Men had their own world, the outside world, and women had the inside world of the home, but even that was scarcely our own . . . I've always said that I'm glad my own three children are boys, because when I was young I found that being a woman meant I couldn't aspire to the many things I wanted to do" (Roca 2001:129–30).

Those girls (and boys) lucky enough to get an education often were sent to religious schools. Another woman interviewed by Maria Mercè Roca remembered being happy at school and getting good grades. She and her classmates studied geography, mathematics, history, Latin (taught by a priest), and music for those who had some talent; and every afternoon they spent an hour doing needlework. "Yes, I was happy . . . but the nuns never taught us how to think, only how to repress our feelings" (Roca 2001:37). This girl noticed from an early age that her parents' world and that of the school were not the same: "Sometimes I'd tell my father what we'd done at school that day, and he'd smile a little sarcastically and say 'Those nuns . . .' " (Roca 2001:37).

One of her most vivid memories of early childhood was of her father, who had been collectivized[4] as a railway worker during the Civil War, saying to her mother that the end of the war had brought no real peace, "because they have trodden on us, they've put their boot on our necks and taken everything from us, culture, education . . ." (Roca 2001:28). She shared with other Catalan children the postwar experience of speaking Catalan at home, and being obliged to speak Castilian at school, "and if sometimes you spoke Catalan with a friend there was always a nun shouting at you, 'Speak Spanish!' And it made me furious" (Roca 2001:37).

An anthropologist friend and colleague, Ignasi Terradas, shared with me his memories of attending a Jesuit secondary school in the early and middle 1960s. One of his teachers was a Catalan Falangist, the only card-carrying member of the Movimiento Nacional at the school. What was striking about him, however, was not the ideology, which he did not seem to care a great deal about, but the authority that it supported, and he enjoyed using it by inventing imaginative punishments. A boy unable to sit still must be in need of exercise, and was sentenced to twenty laps around the classroom. A boy unable to resist talking out of turn must need to be noticed; he would have to spend the next hour standing on top of his desk. But the worst class of all was French. Ignasi's parents sent him to France in the summers, and his excellent French was precisely the problem. Fascist language ideology had it that all other languages were decadent and that the beauty, order, and purity of Castilian made it the only language fit for the expression of great ideas. Accordingly, Ignasi's French teacher taught French by substituting Castilian phonology, and Ignasi received barely passing grades because his pronunciation was so "poor." In order to demonstrate how Castilian reveals the generosity of Spanish national character, the teacher translated *dar un paseo* (to take a walk) into several other languages. The English, for example, "take a walk," the opposite of "giving a walk" (a literal translation of the Castilian): evidence of their grasping and selfish nature.

Lucia Graves, the daughter of the English poet Robert Graves, grew up on the Catalan-speaking island of Mallorca after the Civil War, and as a small child attended the village school in Deià, where the Graves family lived. It was run by Franciscan nuns, and her only memories of it are of catechism and needlework. When she was ten, the family moved to the capital city of Palma so that she could attend a convent school that offered a better education. Run by an order of French nuns, it had a reputation for being slightly more open-minded than other schools in town—"[I]t was the only school that had agreed to admit me without a baptismal certificate" (Graves 1999:62)—and it did provide an acceptable level of instruction, especially in languages (French, Spanish, and Latin) and in mathematics. But as the young Lucia discovered, no school anywhere in Spain was exempt from the national-Catholic educational program: "We wrote endless dictations about the glory of the Spanish flag and the greatness of the Empire, and we were told that democracy was the ruin of a nation . . . ." (Graves 1999:62).

The history teacher, a laywoman, was an active member of the Sección Femenina (ladies' auxiliary) of the Falange, the Spanish fascist movement, and she often stopped in the middle of a lesson to regale her students with stories of *rojos* ("reds"; communists)—"the Enemy"—burning down churches and slaughtering nuns and priests during the war. Her vivid accounts of the air raids she and her family survived in Madrid omitted the fact that those responsible for the bombing were not, in fact, the *rojos* but the fascists, and the children assumed, as they were meant to, that "anything bad . . . was always the work of the Enemy" (Graves 1999:64). The history textbook (*The holy land of Spain: An exaltation of our national history*) was filled with examples of saintly martyrdom in the cause of the National Crusade, starting with José Antonio Primo de Rivera, the founder of the Falange. It took her years to understand that the demonic *rojos* were not invaders from some other country, but Spanish citizens who took up arms in defense of a democratically elected Republican government.

The history teacher's phantasmagoric images of Enemy violence were all mixed up in the young Lucia's school experience with her love and admiration for her closest friend Francisca, a lovely middle-class girl from a pious, right-wing family and adored by her teachers; the diatribes of Sister Valentina concerning the fate of little Protestant girls who did not embrace the Catholic faith; constant exhortations by all the nuns to "speak Christian" (i.e., Spanish) instead of Catalan; and the absurdity of reducing everything to an exercise in loyalty to the fascist regime. When Señorita Mercedes, the gymnastics teacher, began to prepare her girls for a competition organized by the Sección Femenina,

[t]wice a week we put on our dark blue bloomers, white blouses and white plimsolls, and went into the gymnastics room to train like soldiers. In her long pleated skirt and white blouse, she [Señorita Mercedes] looked younger than she did in the classroom, and she instructed us with an almost fanatical fervor. The movements had to convey a military precision: arms up and open, legs apart, one two, open, close, open, close! But we also had to smile, to project the inner joy of living in Franco's Peace.

[At the competition] I remember the thrill of standing in that huge room . . . singing *"Cara al sol,"* the Falange hymn, with hundreds of other girls, our arms firmly outstretched in the Fascist salute. . . . And we won. . . . I remember Señorita Mercedes on the way back to school in the bus, sitting arm in arm with one of the older girls, her eyes brimming with tears of joy. (Graves 1999:66)

But the teachers at the school conspired to take possession of her soul in spite of herself, if necessary. In adulthood Graves still carries the spiritual wound of the psychic pressure brought to bear on her to convert secretly to Catholicism at age twelve, without her parents' knowledge or consent. She found the courage to confess her own desire for baptism to her father, who merely suggested, sensibly, that she wait a year and a half until she turned fourteen, at which point she could become a Catholic with his permission if she still wanted it. His kindly response liberated her from the sense of compulsion under which she had been made to labor, but at a price: the loss of faith (Graves 1999:106–108).

Others can look back on their childhood indoctrination under the Franco regime more dispassionately. The Catalan essayist Josep M. Espinàs, in his book *Inventari de jubilacions* (*An inventory of retirements*), published in 1992 just before his sixty-fifth birthday, begins a chapter on "Being Spanish" (*"Espanyolitat"*), with an evocation of himself as a twelve-year-old schoolboy, quoted from his memoir of childhood, *El nen de la plaça Ballot* (Espinàs 1988:83–84):

One afternoon a week, Saturday I think, a collective ritual of Francoist sentiment took place in the schoolyard. All the classes formed up as if we were soldiers, facing the interior balcony where the three flags were hung—Spanish, Falangist, and Carlist [Carlists had sided with the fascists during the Civil War]—and the school authorities stood along with Father Seguí, or whoever else was there to deliver a fiery speech to us. This was a modest version of all such ceremonies held in other countries governed by totalitarian regimes. And we sang the usual hymns followed by the obligatory rallying cries of "Long live Franco, Long live Spain, Up with Spain!" I shouted these slogans too, along with all the others, and it didn't seem to me that there was anything wrong with this. I even put my heart into it, giving it all the feeling that came so easily to me. I was a boy full of idealistic enthusiasms, and sensitive to political and emotional appeals. I was easy to indoctrinate . . . .

How do we square this with the Josep M. Espinàs who later became a highly visible member of the cultural resistance against the Franco regime? At that young age, Espinàs writes, he had "Spanish emotions," but as a university student he was already "a different person," a change, he believes, that was more like a "biological destiny" than a rational process of rejection (Espinàs 1992:85). Its first "symptom" was a feeling of discomfort at the ease with which certain Catalan and Spanish acquaintances included him in "we Spaniards," and foreigners in "you Spaniards" (Espinàs 1992:85–86). With no intention of giving offense, they had simply used what they thought was a natural category of ascription, never imagining that it could be otherwise. "I think," Espinàs writes (1992:88–89), "that I lost my feeling of being Spanish by traveling in Spain," not because he met with anti-Catalan sentiment there, but because it was like traveling in England, Sicily, or any other country: it was simply Other, often enjoyably so, but he found himself unable to participate in the social and political construction of a state identity that "requires sentimental confirmation of belonging" (Espinàs 1992:88). The problem is one of recognition and self-recognition, and he finds an analog experience in the four years he spent as a practicing lawyer, without ever feeling that this was his true identity. The difference, of course, is that you can always simply take down your shingle and resign your membership in the Lawyers' Guild, but your national identity document will always identify you as "Spanish."

A public statement that one does not feel Spanish is widely taken to be a political statement, and often it is intended to be one; see, for example, several of the essays in the book *Jo no sóc espanyol* (Alexandre 1999). Espinàs' argument, however, is more nuanced. As he points out, such a statement is rendered comprehensible if it is followed by a recitation of Catalan political grievances against the central government and a declaration in favor of Catalan independence. But if such declarations are not forthcoming, people can become, if anything, more disconcerted and even angry. Indifference, it seems, is an even greater offense than overt resistance because it redraws the boundaries of conventional categories of thought, feeling and action. And this, for Espinàs, is where real liberty begins.

El Florido Pensil

Humor is another mechanism for the redrawing of these boundaries. In 1994, Andrés Sopeña published a memoir of fascist national-Catholic education, *El florido pensil*. The book's dust jacket describes the author as one who, having survived such surrealistic early educational experiences, is "now almost normal, and lives in Granada, where he is a professor at the University." The title is drawn from one of the nationalistic hymns—"¡*Patria mía*!"—all Spanish children were required to sing every day in school. The overheated imaginations of Falangist poets and composers produced a mix of blood-drenched images of youthful wartime sacrifice for the fatherland in the crusade against Godless communists and separatists, and a quasi-Biblical fantasy of Spain as God's kingdom on earth and Spaniards as God's chosen people (quoted in Sopeña 1994:222):

> Long live Spain, my luminous Fatherland,
> Peerless mother, compendium of honor.
> Long live Spain! soil from which noble life springs,
> Royal pedestal of Christ the Redeemer.
> You were once a flowering garden of glories
> [the *"florido pensil"* of the book's title]
> That now bloom again with the strength of youth.
> Twenty nations[5] crown your brow:
> Up with Spain! Our unconquered race sustains you.

In the book, Sopeña explains that

> hundreds and hundreds of times . . . I shouted out "You were once a flowering garden of glories" without having the slightest idea what we were bellowing; and, the truth be told, without the slightest

interest in finding out. But that verse, the memory of its silly and mechanical repetition, has nevertheless come to be for me a symbol of that school, the logic behind so much nonsense. It is all there, in the flowering garden of endless repetition. (Sopeña 1994:222)

Seven months after its publication in 1994, a second edition of *El florido pensil* came out, and between 1995 and 1997 there were four subsequent reprintings. A play based on the book was performed in both Basque and Catalan translation as well as in Castilian, and ran in Barcelona for more than a year to packed houses. Catalonia's political leadership, both in the Generalitat and in Barcelona's municipal government, was well represented at the opening night performance, laughing uproariously, and audiences aged forty and older invariably found it side-splittingly funny. A film version was released in March 2002.

Two years after the publication of *El florido pensil*, Luis Otero, a novelist and journalist who grew up in the postwar period and, like Sopeña, suffered through the absurdities of national-Catholic education, published a memoir of his own. The book is dedicated, tongue in cheek, "To the educators, teachers and other adults of the Francoist period who tried so hard to teach me not to write books like this one. We've all failed!" The title, *"Al paso alegre de la paz"* (*"Along the joyful path of peace"*), is another line from a fascist patriotic hymn, *"Cara al sol"* (quoted in Otero 2000:51):

Face turned to the sun, wearing my new shirt
which you embroidered yesterday in red thread;
This is how death will find me, if it takes me,
and I never see you again.

I will fall in beside my comrades
who stand guard above the stars,
insensible of pain, impassive in bearing,
forever present in our labors.

If they tell you that I fell in battle,
I have gone to the place they have prepared for me.

Victorious flags will return
Along the joyful path of peace,

bringing with them five roses,
the embroidered arrows [fascist yoke and arrows] from my shirt.

Laughing spring will return,
eagerly awaited by the land, sea and skies.
Onward, soldiers! We go to conquer!
For in Spain, a new day is dawning.

The overwrought aesthetics of national-Catholic education are the focus and source of the humor: the fascination with death; the militarization of society, of childhood, and of faith; the portrayal of Franco—a tubby, decidedly uncharismatic figure—as a romantically heroic crusader restoring Spain's lost imperial glory; the reduction of even basic arithmetic, grammar, and phonetics lessons to the symbols of the Falange; the crude depictions of racially inferior Others. A subsequent book published by Luis Otero, *Flechas y pelayos* (2000) consists almost entirely of images taken from school textbooks and from a Falangist magazine for children, *Flechas y pelayos*, published between 1938 and 1949 as an attempt to make the Falange a popular movement (which it never became). For Spanish citizens of the right generation, these images require almost no commentary to produce comic effect; it is sufficient simply to point to the obvious. The very obviousness of the absurdity suggests a "structure of feeling" (Williams 1983, cited in Aretxaga 1997:87) that underlies and constitutes a "community of memory" (Malkki 1997:92).[6]

Of course, these cautionary and inspirational images and children's stories were meant to be taken seriously. Lucia Graves recounts one emblematic tale of a brave young boy and his little brother, who were evacuated from the city of Teruel when the Republican army conquered it. Desperate to rejoin the fascist army and help to re-take the city, the two boys made their way through a snowstorm across enemy territory, the older carrying the younger on his back. By the time they reached the fascist lines, the little brother had died of exposure to the elements. Setting aside his grief, the surviving brother hails him as a martyr, and celebrates the eventual fascist reconquest of the city, an event recorded by the author of the story in the most florid terms (quoted in Graves 1999:65; author's translation):

Halleluiah! Our land opened up to receive the seeds of Peace in its womb! Marxism, like the ivy that chokes its prey, had tried to spread all over Europe, beginning with our beloved Spain, but like Islam, like Protestantism, it found its own grave in our country! All the people came out of the churches rejoicing, raising their voices in gratitude to Heaven and chanting Halleluiah!

Luis Otero (1996:272–73) compares two stories of childhood willingness to sacrifice "all for the Fatherland" (*"todo por la Patria,"* the Falangist motto). Inocencio's father tells him he cannot go to the front and kill *rojos* (reds) because the fascist authorities in their wisdom do not allow children to become soldiers. Why, a brave little boy in a city under siege by the *rojos* was shot in the leg; but he didn't cry, that's how brave he was! Inocencio might not prove to be so tough. In reply, Inocencio puts a finger between his teeth and bites down on it until he draws blood. His father, convinced of his son's courage (Otero includes the textbook illustration of the father expressing shock at his son's willingness to shed his blood, and adds his own caption: "I'm not so sure he's brave, but my Inocencio is certainly quite the little joker!"), binds up the wound and promises to enroll him in the military academy.

If Inocencio was deprived of an opportunity for heroism, Otero continues, Martinillo was not. Retelling with considerably more color and verve than Graves the story of the two little brothers, one of whom died of cold on the way back to the fascist lines, Otero then comments,

> In other school textbooks Martinillo is called Vicente, and his heroism takes somewhat different forms, though the plot is essentially the same. . . . He is also called Pepito Vicente—a milksop name inadequate for the degree of bravery involved—and his brother, Luisito. Some writers even called the little warrior Pepico and his dead brother Luisico, names which sound really sissy and girlish for boys giving all, even lies, for the Fatherland and the greater glory of Franco, but you shouldn't let the truth spoil a heroic plot.

Otero (1996:274) then tries out the "sissy" form on a standard Falangist patriotic call-and-response, undercutting the romantic crusader imagery:

> —¡Todico por la Patria! [Every darling little thing for the Fatherland!]
> —¡Todico! [Every darling little thing!]
> —¡Y a mayor glorica de Franco! [And for the sweet little greater glory of Franco!]
> —¡Sea! [So let it be!]

Unable to resist the opportunity to push the joke still farther into the realm of the absurd, Otero (1996:274) applies it to a child's letter to the Three Kings (equivalent to Santa Claus), from the fascist publication *Arriba España* in Pamplona (by that point in the Civil War under fascist control), on December 22, 1938, mocking its inspirational intent:

> Cortes, December 15, 1938, Triumphal Year III [conventional fascist form of dating]

> Dear Three Kings: Since I read in *Arriba España* that this year you are going to bring us toys, though not so many as in other years, I would like you to bring me a bugle so I can learn to fight and go to the front when I'm all grown up [*mocico*], and bring my darling little sister [*hermanica*] a bed and some chocolates. The bed should be 50 centimeters long for the doll. Yours most affectionately, Lucio Uriel del Río, 10 years old. Up with Spain!

Then he invents a textbook-style dialogue based on the letter (Otero 1996:274):

> Good heavens, little Lucio preparing to go to the front when he's all grown up [*cuando fuere mocico*]!

> And only 10 years old!

>> How long did he think the war was going to last?
>> And what the devil was he going to use a bugle for?
>> As an offensive weapon?
>> A defensive weapon?

> Alas, I've no talent for playing the bugle. I've got a sunken chest and very little lung power. I just wasn't cut out for violent activity.

The joke is completed by another textbook illustration showing a soldierly little boy blowing his bugle, from which emanates not music but a grammar lesson on verb forms. Otero adds his own caption: "Bugle boy rehearsing grammar in order to go to the front when he's all grown up [*cuando sea mocico*]."

The satire then turns to the story of Constantino, the timid boy who plays with a wooden sword and toy gun but is so afraid of the dark that even his little sister laughs at him: a negative example for Falangist youth. Otero (1996:276) cites a textbook passage urging boys who see themselves in Constantino to pull themselves together: "Fear, timidity, a tendency to blush, bashfulness, like so many other signs of a weak character, have no reason to exist; you create them yourselves." Otero then takes up the cry: "Constantino! Don't worry, kid! Cowards united shall never be defeated! Through timidity to God! Long live fear!" Otero's meditation on a text explaining how to follow Franco's example and become Caudillo by first attaining mastery of oneself is underlined by an episode from his own childhood: "And just so you won't feel so alone, Constantino, let me tell you how one day the schoolmaster punished me for being a coward" (Otero 1996:278–80).

> "Why did you tear that page?" demanded the schoolmaster, grabbing my right ear and twisting it.
>
> "I didn't mean to. It got caught in the zipper of my sweater," I lied.
>
> "All right, just so you don't get it caught again, for the next two months beginning today, you'll stay in during recess to copy in your notebook the following sentence: 'I will treat books with respect, for they help me to become a useful citizen of tomorrow.' Understood?"
>
> "Yes, sir."
>
> "Repeat!"
>
> "Yes, sir."
>
> "No, you idiot, the sentence . . . . And on Sundays you'll stay home copying out the same sentence. I'll have a word with your parents, understood?"
>
> "I will treat books with respect, for they help me to become a useful citizen of tomorrow."
>
> "No, not that"—the schoolmaster twisted my ear again—"Now you say: 'Yes, sir.' "

At this point, tears begin to roll down the boy Otero's cheeks and the schoolmaster twists his ear hard a third time, making him cry out in pain, and tells him,

> "Brave boys don't cry. . . . The Fatherland and the Caudillo [Franco] demand bravery of you, and you mustn't cry or complain. Be a man, not a chicken."

"Me?"

"Yes, you. Or maybe you're a chicken after all?"

"No."

"Say: 'No, sir.' "

"No, sir."

"Do you want to be a chicken?"

"No, sir."

"Brave boys think about becoming useful citizens. Do you know what chickens think about?"

"No, sir."

The schoolmaster snickered evilly, taking full advantage of his opportunity. "Roosters!"

To Constantino the cowardly boy, who has now become Otero's imaginary companion in resistance, Otero confesses that in fact he did tear the page in his textbook on purpose, after reading something he found insulting:

"Young man, always keep this sentence in mind: 'The entire world belongs to God, but he rents it to the brave.' " . . . Why would I want to be brave, or want God to rent me the world? The tin-pot dignitaries, fake intellectuals, and self-appointed national saviors of history have always had the world rented out. Wait, Constantino, don't leave, let's go rob a bank."

The moving point of view and shifting voice characteristic of this passage from Otero's book can also be found, in a somewhat different form, in Sopeña's *El florido pensil*. In the play, the simultaneity of adult and childhood experience and thought was represented by having the stoutish, middle-aged actors wear schoolboy short pants that exposed their hairy adult legs and smocks whose buttons were strained at the girth, and sit at child-sized school benches. In the book, the adult Sopeña recites his lessons in a voice of childish credulity, reproducing even the mistakes, and the result is broad satire.

CONCLUSIONS: A DISARMING SENSE OF HUMOR

For Spaniards who were born and/or grew up under the Franco regime, the school experience evokes Francoism as a whole, and three generations of schoolchildren had it forced down their throats. One of the many variants of a joke about the stupidly catechistic pedagogy of national-Catholic education (cited in Pi-Sunyer 1977:182) goes as follows:

> Instructor: "Who is your father?"
> Boy: "Franco!"
> Instructor: "And who is your mother?"
> Boy: "The Falange!"
> Instructor: "Excellent, my boy, and what would you like to be when you grow up?"
> Boy (after some thought): "Well, I think I would like to be an orphan."

In 1975 Franco died and Spaniards found themselves happy orphans at last. But the end of the regime did not, of itself, bring relief because the past was never confronted in a way that would allow people to stop gagging on it. The fascist past has not so much been overthrown and consigned to the dustbin of history, as it has been pushed into an unassimilated, undigested background called "*el régimen anterior*" ("the previous regime"). This was a deliberate decision on the part of the political leaders responsible for the transition to democracy across the entire political spectrum from right to left. The rationale for it at the time was that a radical break with the Franco regime would provoke the military into attempting to take control once more and plunge the country into a second civil war. It was a real possibility, and no one was prepared to entertain it.

So a veil was drawn over the previous forty years, and a decision made that there would be no victors or victims, no conquerors or conquered. All political actors were defined as equal participants in the new democratic order, and it was quickly impressed upon people that references to the fascist antecedents of some of the major players were in poor taste. Many institutions and structures of the Franco regime—and the personnel that ran them—survived intact into the restoration of democracy, as did certain aspects of political culture (see Cardús i Ros 2000), while others persisted in attenuated form. The right-wing Partido Popular, which governed Spain from 1996 until 2004, is the third-generation descendent of the Falange, and its immediate predecessor, the Alianza Popular of the late 1970s, made unapologetic use of fascist symbols and styles: rallying cries of "Franco! Franco! Franco!" accompanied by the raised-arm fascist salute; dark blue banners—the color of the Falange—intertwined with the Spanish flag emblazoned with the fascist yoke and arrows. The Franco regime was, paradoxically, present and absent simultaneously. And it still is.

The strategy of collective political amnesia has been responsible for many of the remarkable successes of the transition, which is widely regarded as a model for such transformations in Latin America and elsewhere; but it is not without its costs. The Spanish state is still paying some of these costs in blood: the blood shed both by ETA on one side, and by the quasi-official paramilitary death squads of the 1980s on the other. The nonlethal but still costly debts include continuous legal and political challenges by the central government to any serious attempt by Catalonia or the Basque Country to implement fully the home-rule rights they enjoy—in matters of educational policy, among others—by virtue of both the Spanish Constitution of 1978 and their respective statutes of autonomy. Using the "struggle against terrorism" as an excuse, the Partido Popular has chosen—particularly after 2000, when it achieved an absolute majority in the Spanish parliament, the Cortes—to demonize and criminalize difference, dissent, and even dialogue.

Perhaps it should not surprise us that writers such as Sopeña and Otero began making art out of the aesthetically as well as politically objectionable materials of fascist educational curricula just as the balance of political power in democratic Spain tilted toward the far right. Catalan humorists are also quick to make connections between "the previous regime" and current events. A series of cartoons by "Fer" (J.A. Fernández) in the Catalan daily AVUI lampooning the central government's ongoing efforts to uniformize school curricula throughout the Spanish state includes one (July 10, 2003, 3) of Prime Minister Aznar at the front of a schoolroom dressed as a ruler-wielding priest of the national-Catholic era. On the blackboard to his right are written three essential elements of the Francoist historical narrative—the Catholic Kings Ferdinand and Isabella, Philip V (the absolutist pretender to the Spanish throne who subjugated the Catalans in 1714 after the War of Spanish Succession), and El Caudillo (Franco). To his left, under the portrait of General Franco, a schoolboy being punished for some misdeed is wearing a dunce cap and kneeling on the floor, arms outstretched and palms upturned, each hand supporting two books. "All right, children!" Aznar booms to the class. "Stand up now, we're going to sing 'Montañas nevadas' [a Falangist hymn]: Snowy mountains, flags in the wind/In Spain a new day is beginning to dawn . . ."

"If irony does not play much of a role in the [ethnographic] literature," Michael Herzfeld has written recently (2001:65), "that may largely be because anthropologists have found it descriptively as elusive as the sense of smell." I have made deliberate use of the metaphor of indigestion in order to question the canonical requirements of "taste" in realist ethnographic representation, which privileges the intelligible over the sensible (Stoller 1989:25–27). Focusing instead on the experiential qualities of spaces of memory in the lives of recognizable individuals allows us not so much to explain the complex and paradoxical relations of past and present, but to convey "a *sense* of what it is like to live in other worlds, a taste of ethnographic things" (Stoller 1989:156).

This has been the goal of cultural interpretation at least since Clifford Geertz's famous and much-reprinted essay " 'From the native's point of view': On the nature of anthropological understanding," which concludes with the insight that anthropological understanding is like "catching an allusion" or "seeing a joke" (1983:70), although this has been honored at least as often in the breach as in the observance. And it is worth remembering that in another famous essay, "Thick description" (1973:6–7), Geertz demonstrated how ethnography works by applying it to the problem of differentiating between the wink of an eye as an involuntary twitch, and the same contraction of the eyelid as a conspiratorial signal, a parody of a conspiratorial signal, or a rehearsal of a parody of a conspiratorial signal; that is, between the absence of intention, conspiratorial intention, parodic intention, and the professional intention of the satirist.

Geertz, of course, was fully conscious of the perils of deconstructing the "piled-up structures of inference and implication" (1973:7) embedded in such lighter-than-air moments. As Michael Herzfeld (2001:79–80) points out, irony is "an evasively insubordinate idiom. To specify its properties has . . . deadening effects . . ." And to make matters worse, "the great earnestness with which we currently approach such themes as resistance makes the recognition of irony extremely difficult" (Herzfeld 2001:64).

"Irony," Herzfeld (2001:64) observes, "—the trope most directly associated with critical reflection—threatens absolute power through its evocation of the absurdity of all claims to total transparency, certainty, and referentiality." But is the threat hollow? To what extent can we read irony and satire as resistance? Or—and this is a reading Catalans are all too familiar with (see Ferrater Mora 1972)—is it simply a continuing rehearsal of grievances that perpetuates a claim of victimization? Some pages later, Herzfeld (2001:75) notes that "the problem of whether we can speak of resistance where no obvious, lasting effects are evident is precisely that of irony: its uncertain presence, the recognition of which depends on a willingness to suspend agnostic doubts in favor of recognizing some form of intention."

While satirical and ironic commentary does not, in and of itself, change the balance of political power, it does allow people to confront the historical source of the current state of affairs and deny it the power to define them individually and collectively. The emergence of a comic literary/graphic genre treating the material and visual culture, practices, and ideology of national-Catholic education as a metonymy of the Franco regime recalls James Fernandez's (1986:10) observation that "we are generally inspired to metaphor for purposes of adornment or disparagement." Metonymy, he tells us, is the "performance of metaphor" (Fernandez 1986:46), and metaphors are not just "arresting repositories of feelings" but "strategies taken in respect to feelings" (Fernandez 1986:8). If the Franco jokes of three decades ago represented a "victory of imagination over the reality of a gray and flat personality" (Pi-Sunyer 1977:183)—a form of resistance—the contemporary return to the national-Catholic classroom as humor addresses concerns and conditions that emerged from the deliberately induced political amnesia of the transition to democracy and continue to affect political life a quarter of a century later.

In re-presenting the absurdities of the fascist schoolroom as a metonymy of the Franco regime, Spaniards are re-cognizing themselves: acknowledging a shared experience that marks them generationally, and drawing out of it thoughts and feelings other than those intended either by their teachers or by the architects of the democratic transition. Laughing, audiences and readers can both lay claim to their own experience, and refuse complicity with the regime that imposed that experience upon them.

Notes

1. The Spanish Civil War (1936–39) ended in the defeat of the Second Spanish Republic, under which Catalonia had enjoyed a significant degree of home rule. After the death of General Franco and his nearly forty-year-old dictatorship in 1975, the Spanish state began a transition back to democracy, which for Catalonia also meant the restoration of its historical institutions of

self-government. This took place as part of a general decentralization of the Spanish state which culminated in the creation of seventeen autonomous communities with varying powers. The Catalan Statute of Autonomy was approved by referendum in 1979. For further information, see Gilmour (1985), Balcells (1996), and McRoberts (2001).

2. Unless otherwise noted, all translations are my own.

3. The Institut-Escola also has a Spanish precedent of the same name, the Instituto Escuela de Madrid, created in 1918 and based on the principles of the Institución Libre de Enseñanza, a private initiative founded in 1876 by intellectuals forced out of teaching positions by the reestablishment of the monarchy in 1875 and the subsequent suspension of academic freedom, which had been enshrined in the short-lived 1869 Constitution of the First Republic. For further information, see Boyd (2000:25, 65).

4. Early in the Civil War Catalan industries of all kinds, including the railways and urban public transportation, were taken over and operated cooperatively by anarcho-syndicalist workers' councils. Carles Pi i Sunyer, who served as the mayor of Barcelona and as a minister in both the Generalitat and the government of the Republic, recalled in his memoir *La República y la guerra* (1975:394, 434) that so great was the desire for social transformation that the collectivization extended not only to artisan workshops, tailor shops, and barber shops, but even to bootblacks and urban milk cows (of which there were still great numbers in the city in the 1930s). Thanks to collectivization, the Catalan economy continued to function despite the turbulence of the early days and weeks of the war. A few months later, the Catalan government formalized this ad hoc response in the Collectivization Decree of October 24, 1936, which created, among other things, desperately needed war industries where none had previously existed. For an extended description of the collectivization process, see Payne (1970:245–61). For an eyewitness account of revolutionary Barcelona as George Orwell experienced it in December 1936— "a town where the working class was in the saddle"—see *Homage to Catalonia* (1952), especially pages 4 and 5.

5. This is a rhetorical resuscitation of a Spanish empire that had long since ceased to exist. The "twenty nations" in question are Spain's former overseas colonial possessions in the Americas, the Caribbean, and the Pacific. For further detail, see a recent reprinting of the third edition of the *Catecismo patriótico español* (Menéndez-Reigada 2003:67–70), originally published in 1939. The empire was invoked not only in inspirational ways but in repressive ones as well. Shortly after Catalonia was overrun by the fascist army, posters began to appear on walls commanding people to "Speak the language of the Empire!," or, more insultingly, "Don't bark! Speak Christian!"

6. The evidence for this is negative as well as positive. That "structure of feeling" is not shared by those born too late to have personal memories of

national-Catholic education, who simply don't get the joke; or by those who were born and/or grew up in exile, for whom the satiric remembrance of things past can seem at best like an incomprehensible lapse of taste, and at worst like an equally incomprehensible nostalgia for the Franco regime.

References

Alexandre, Víctor. 1999. *Jo no sóc espanyol*. Barcelona: Proa.

Ardit, Manuel, et al. 1980. *Història dels Països Catalans. Vol. 3: De 1714 a 1975*. Barcelona: EDHASA.

Aretxaga, Begoña. 1997. *Shattering silence: Women, nationalism, and political subjectivity in Northern Ireland*. Princeton: Princeton University Press.

AVUI, 21 June 2000, 31. La ministra d'Educació veu un "excés de particularisme" en l'ensenyament de la història.

———, 2 July 2000, 27. Jordi Pujol titlla d'"injustos" els "atacs" a l'ensenyament de la història a Catalunya.

———, 6 July 2000, 4. Real Academia de la Historia. Letter to the editor by Joan M. Serch.

———, 10 July 2003, 3. Fer (J. A. Fernández). Cartoon.

Balcells, Albert. 1996. *Catalan nationalism past and present*. Trans. Jacqueline Hall with the collaboration of Geoffrey J. Walker. London: Macmillan.

Boyd, Carolyn. 2000. *Historia patria. Política, historia e identidad nacional en España: 1875–1975*. Barcelona: Ediciones Pomares Corredor.

Cámara Villar, Gregorio. 1994. Prólogo. In Andrés Sopeña Monsalve, *El florido pensil*, 13–22. Barcelona: Crítica.

Cardús i Ros, Salvador. 2000. Politics and the invention of memory. For a sociology of the transition to democracy in Spain. In *Disremembering the dictatorship: The politics of memory in the Spanish transition to democracy*, ed. Joan Ramon Resina, 17–28. Amsterdam and Atlanta: Rodopi.

Cuerda, José Luis, dir. 1999. *La lengua de las mariposas*. Sogetel, Producciones del Escorpión, Grupo Voz.

Espinàs, Josep M. 1988. *El nen de la plaça Ballot*. Barcelona: Edicions La Campana.

———. 1992. *Inventari de jubilacions*. Barcelona: Edicions La Campana.

Fernandez, James W. 1986. *Persuasions and performances: The play of tropes in culture*. Bloomington: Indiana University Press.

Ferrater Mora, Joan. 1972. *Les formes de la vida catalana*. Fourth edition. Barcelona: Editorial Selecta.

Ferrer Guardia, Francisco. 2002 [1976]. *La escuela moderna*. Barcelona: Tusquets Editores.

Galí, Alexandre. 1979. *Història de les institucions i del moviment cultural a Catalunya, 1900–1936. Vol. 1*. Barcelona: Fundació Alexandre Galí.

Geertz, Clifford. 1973. Thick description: Toward an interpretive theory of culture. In *The interpretation of cultures*, 3–30. New York: Basic Books.

————. 1983. "From the native's point of view": On the nature of anthropological understanding. In *Local knowledge: Further essays in interpretive anthropology*, 55–70. New York: Basic Books.

Gilmour, David. 1985. *The transformation of Spain: From Franco to the constitutional monarchy*. London: Quartet Books.

Graves, Lucia. 1999. *A woman unknown: Voices from a Spanish life*. Washington: Counterpoint.

Herzfeld, Michael. 2001. Irony and power: Toward a politics of mockery in Greece. In *Irony in action: Anthropology, practice, and the moral imagination*, ed. James W. Fernandez and Mary Taylor Huber, 63–83. Chicago: University of Chicago Press.

Malkki, Liisa H. 1997. News and culture: Transitory phenomena and the fieldwork tradition. In *Anthropological locations: Boundaries and grounds of a field science*, ed. Akhil Gupta and James Ferguson, 86–101. Berkeley: University of California Press.

Marquès, Salomó. 2002. *L'escola a Catalunya durant el segle XX. El testimoni de les germanes Macau Julià*. Girona: Universitat de Girona, Diputació de Girona, Lleure.

McRoberts, Kenneth. 2001. *Catalonia: Nation building without a state*. New York: Oxford University Press.

Menéndez-Reigada, Fray Albino González. 2003. *Catecismo patriótico español [1939]*. Foreword by Hilari Raguer. Barcelona: Ediciones Península.

Orwell, George. 1952. *Homage to Catalonia*. New York: Harcourt, Brace and World.

Otero, Luis. 1996. *Al paso alegre de la paz. Enredo tragicómico sobre la escuela franquista y otras sublimes pedagogías*. Barcelona: Plaza y Janés.

————. 2000. *Flechas y pelayos. Moral y estilo de los niños franquistas que soñaban imperios*. Madrid: EDAF.

Payne, Stanley G. 1970. *The Spanish revolution*. New York: W.W. Norton.

Pi i Sunyer, Carles. 1975. *La República y la guerra*. México, D.F.: Ediciones Oasis.

Pi-Sunyer, Oriol. 1977. Political humor in a dictatorial state: The case of Spain. *Ethnohistory* 24, no. 2:179–90.

Risques, Manuel, et al. 1999. *Història de la Catalunya contemporània*. Barcelona: Pòrtic.

Roca, Maria Mercè. 2001. *El món era a fora. L'educació sentimental de les dones durant el franquisme*. Barcelona: Planeta.

Segura i Mas, Antoni. 2000. D'informes i acadèmies d'història. *AVUI*, 6 July, 17.

Seminari d'història de l'ensenyament i "Rosa Sensat." 1978. *L'ensenyament. Col.lecció "Conèixer Catalunya."* Barcelona: DOPESA.

Sobrequés, Jaume. 2000. La por a la història. *AVUI*, 2 July, 20.

Sopeña Monsalve, Andrés. 1994. *El florido pensil. Memoria de la escuela nacionalcatólica*. Barcelona: Crítica.

Stoller, Paul. 1989. *The taste of ethnographic things: The senses in anthropology*. Philadelphia: University of Pennsylvania Press.

Ullman, Joan Connelly. 1968. *The Tragic Week: A study of anticlericalism in Spain, 1875–1912*. Cambridge: Harvard University Press.

Williams, Raymond. 1983. *Key words: A vocabulary of culture and society*. New York: Oxford University Press.

CHAPTER 6

Cursillos and Concursos in Rural Galicia

The Sección Femenina and the Modernizing Project of the Franco Dictatorship

SHARON R. ROSEMAN

INTRODUCTION

Under the dictatorship of Francisco Franco (1939–75), crowds were not officially permitted to gather publicly at nonsanctioned events and meetings. Nonetheless, mass gatherings for political rallies, folkloric performances, sports events, and Catholic masses were regular occurrences. The authoritarian presence of political leaders, military officers, and the hierarchy of the Roman Catholic Church were glorified in the most "public" of spaces, including squares, stadiums, and cathedrals, as well as mass media venues such as television, radio, and newspapers.

Like other governments, the Franco regime was comprised of various factions that jostled to deploy their power through officially sanctified idioms (e.g., see de Blaye 1976 [1974]; Preston 1995; Rodríguez Jiménez 1997). Citizens from diverse backgrounds reacted variably—and not always consistently—to the technologies of state discipline, sometimes upholding, sometimes contradicting, and other times reconstituting these idioms (after Herzfeld 1997:2; Roseman 1996; also see Foucault 1990 [1978], 1995 [1977]). As Michael Herzfeld (1997:2) has argued, to effectively analyze how political systems work we must "get inside [the] engagement" of citizens in modern states. Part of this analysis must begin with an appreciation of the "common ground" (ibid.) existing between elites or state officials and ordinary citizens. This "common ground" often

129

constitutes shared understandings of particular stereotypes, the employment of similar essentialistic language, and the recognition of meaningful acts of belonging, ironic engagement, or repudiation (Herzfeld 1997; also Fernandez and Huber 2001:5). It is the state's consistent privileging of a hegemonic framework of *commonsense* knowledge against the backdrop of the rule of force and capital that provides a fundamental basis for citizens' participation in the everyday operation of modern European states (Gramsci 1971; also see Comaroff and Comaroff 1997; Foucault 1980), even to the extent that such commonsense understandings can provide the very language of resistance or "insubordination" in cases when citizens overtly reject state actions (after Herzfeld 2001:66; also see Keesing 1994; Mouffe 2000). In some circumstances, such as under authoritarian regimes, state power also often restricts "political expression" to ironic renditions "in circumstances where direct dissent is hard to formulate, risky, or unwise" (Fernandez and Huber 2001:5; also see Scott 1985, 1990).

In this context, I consider how the Sección Femenina (Women's Section, or sometimes translated as "Ladies Auxiliary") of the Falangist political party made claims on defining rural space in the two Galician provinces of A Coruña and Lugo under the Franco regime. I argue that during this period Sección Femenina leaders, the women who carried out their programs, and the rural inhabitants of Galicia all shared a common deeply held stereotype: that Spain had fallen "behind" social developments in other European countries and that rural Galicia was particularly "backward" (*atrasado*). For most rural Galicians, this stereotype fit easily into their commonsense understanding of the world given their personal experiences of poverty and economic differentiation (Gramsci 1971:323–43). The Sección Femenina message was that "modern" hygiene, methods of production, and habits of measurement should be introduced into modes of working the land, operating a household, and raising children so that Spain and the Spanish people might escape lives of "backward" poverty. "Peasant life" should therefore be transformed from "old" ways of working the land into a series of disciplined celebrations of Galician cuisine, folk dance, folk song, and craftwork on special occasions. Alongside this culturally specific discipline, there was also an emphasis on making new "modern" recipes, crafts, décor, and recreational activities part of regular daily experience. Below, I examine how formal instructional and competitive forms of social engagement were used to deploy rural Galicians in activities that constituted a kind of mandated metonymic fulfillment of the purported administrative aim of permanently transforming rural space.

THE SECCIÓN FEMENINA AND ROUTES TO CULTURAL PENETRATION

Most young men received direct lessons in state power as part of conscription into military service under the Franco dictatorship. The Sección Femenina played a major organizational and ideological role in attempting to institute parallel forms of subordination among women and girls who were enjoined in legal documents such as the Fuero de los Españoles (1945) and in school textbooks to serve their country by becoming "angels of the home" (Nash 1991) and valiant mothers to large families (the oft-celebrated *"familias numerosas"*) (ibid.; also see Abella 1996 [1984]:224–27; Alcalde 1996; Folguera-Crespo 1997:535; Gallego Méndez 1983; Morcillo Gómez 1999; relevant examples of textbooks include Sección Femenina 1955, 1961, 1965).

The Sección Femenina of the Falange Española (the Spanish Falange party) was organized in 1934, one year after the institution of the Falange party by José Antonio Primo de Rivera. José Antonio's sister Pilar Primo de Rivera was the founding coordinator of the Sección Femenina and she ended up being its only leader through the Spanish Civil War and during the entire Franco period. Under the Franco dictatorship, the Sección Femenina of what became the official merger party—the Falange Española Tradicionalista y de las Juntas de Ofensiva Nacional-Sindicalista—gained a widespread political visibility in Spain; this women's branch of the merged party secured access to Spanish citizens through such means as incorporating classes in political ideology, domestic science, and physical education into girls' schooling and requiring unmarried women between the ages of eighteen and thirty-five to perform six months of obligatory social service. Three months of this social service constituted a period of *formación* (education or training) which could be integrated into university courses or state-run vocational training. The second half of the social service requirement was termed the period of *prestación* (obligatory service) and demanded direct social involvement such as working in orphanages, day care facilities, hospitals, old age homes, or visiting disabled individuals in their own homes.

Unlike unmarried women from middle-class, urban backgrounds, a large percentage of Galician rural and working-class women did not perform the social service, because they married early, had children, or received exemptions. Others avoided it because they did not require the social service certificate—a compulsory document if one wished to attend university, compete for a civil service job, or obtain state papers such as a driver's license or passport. Similarly, during the first two decades of the dictatorship many rural girls did not attend high school at all or even grade school very regularly, so they were not much exposed to Sección Femenina teachings. From the late 1950s until the mid-1970s, the national departments of the Sección Femenina focused increasingly on ways to mobilize their provincial delegations to penetrate the spaces of everyday life in rural areas. In this chapter, I argue that some of these methods involved targeting regions such as rural Galicia by accentuating the overarching ideological theme of "backwardness." The methods to be detailed are: the teaching of *cursillos* (short courses) in towns and villages by teams of *cátedras ambulantes* (ambulant groups of teachers), and the organization of *concursos* (contests) and closing ceremonies held in conjunction with these courses.

INSTRUCTING "MODERN" PRACTICES IN THE COUNTRYSIDE

The *cátedras ambulantes* went to the remote villages where the women didn't know how to do anything. Even let's say, how to plant . . . leeks! They taught them about hygiene. They went [to the villages] on mules, on donkeys.[1]

—Comment made by María, a former
Sección Femenina teacher

The notion of "backward" rural agriculturalists—articulated in a nonironic tone—that permeates María's description is an example of the predominant idiom of Sección Femenina instructional courses. Not economic and political oppression, but the "ignorance" of peasant agriculturalists and the working class was highlighted as a major cause of various trends, ranging from high levels of infant mortality and "low" crop yields to the lack of female and filial obedience to men's authority. According to Falangist doctrine, one of the most important remedies was education. One of the oft-stated goals of the Sección Femenina was the "complete training" of women citizens to make them most able to contribute to their families, their communities of residence, and thereby to the Spanish "nation" as a whole (e.g., Sección Femenina 1962, ARG, Box 4728; also, Enders 1999; Gallego Méndez 1983). Teams of *cátedras ambulantes*, joined by local collaborators (e.g., teachers, priests, and physicians), gave classes on a wide range of subjects in towns and villages including Falangist political ideology, Catholicism, physical education, folk dance and song, sewing, cooking, nutrition, infant care, and agricultural production. These classes replaced the training given to urban Spanish girls and young women as part of schooling and the social service. For worker-peasant women and girls living in the Galician provinces of A Coruña and Lugo, the concept of receiving formal training similar to that provided to those in the privileged social classes was a new idea in the 1950s and 1960s; it was consonant, moreover, with the notion that rural Galicians were "backward" or "primitive" vis-à-vis other Spaniards, and the idea that Spain was "backward" in relation to other parts of Europe (Roseman 1996; 2002). Even the six women (originally from rural Galicia) I interviewed who vehemently criticized how the Sección Femenina had promoted the political messages of Falangism said that the Sección Femenina did valuable social welfare work and that rural people in Galicia and elsewhere had acquired exposure to "modern" techniques and technology through them. "We didn't know anything" was a phrase I often heard used strategically by agriculturalists when talking about the Franco period. In it we hear a strong echo of the Sección Femenina claim that "the women didn't know how to do anything," a view articulated by María in the interview quotation that opens this section.

When referring to their sweeping educational mission in the context of Galicia and other areas with substantial rural populations, Sección Femenina and other Falangist leaders often emphasized the particular challenge of promoting "appropriate" behaviors and values. Rural Galician women were said to require instruction in a wide array of topics ranging from appropriate submissiveness to authority to "modern" methods of housework, nutrition, hygiene, and childcare. This message was consistently promoted throughout the years of the dictatorship and had not altered in significant ways by the last years of the Franco regime, as can be seen in a 1974 report by the Sección Femenina

Provincial Delegate of A Coruña, in which she notes: "If we consider the case of the province of La Coruña, which is mainly rural and has had, until the awakening that occurred only a few years ago, scarce industrialization in its coastal areas, the neglect of women's preparation for their contributions to communal life was notorious. . . . Therefore, in our province, the work of promoting women requires constant effort and dedication, with the resulting sacrifice and abnegation on the part of those who carry it out . . ." (ARG, Box 4728).[2]

The Sección Femenina characterization of the Galician provinces as requiring particular attention and dedicated effort because of their eminently "rural" character was a discourse unique neither to the Falangist party nor to the Franco period (e.g., see Bauer 1992; Roseman 1996). Like other missionaries who have defined their goals of societal transformation as the making of "modern" subjects, the Sección Femenina characterized the rural poor in Spain as living somehow almost out of "modern" time and out of the reach of "civilization": "[They extend] their mission to all parts of the province, from major cities to the most isolated corners of our geography. It is precisely in these most isolated places where the provincial Sección Femenina carries out their most unknown and effective work, through the Rural Propagators [*Divulgadoras*], the Training Schools (for adults) and the *Cátedras Ambulantes*" (ARG, Box 4728;[3] see Fabian 1983; Herzfeld 1987; and Trouillot 1991 for anthropological treatments of similar rhetorical phenomena; also see Collier 1997).

In an interview with two former members of a Galician provincial delegation of the Sección Femenina, Prudencia and Lucía emphasized to me the importance of the work done by "Rural Instructors" and other members of the *cátedras ambulantes* who traveled throughout rural Galicia: "They [the members of the *cátedras ambulantes*] lived with them [the peasants], gave them classes. Moreover, these [places] were remote." Both women then assured me that this was "The most important work that they did, a great labor." The *cátedra* teachers explained how peasants should "care for children" and the Rural Instructors taught women "things about the land," instruction meant to result in significant changes such as lower infant mortality rates and more "productive" agriculture.

The *cátedras ambulantes* were composed of at least four and as many as six Sección Femenina instructors, including those specializing as rural instructors, as propagators, as teachers of physical education or simply of "youth"; as teachers of household science and/or sewing; as teachers of Falangist politics (referred to as the "Formation of the National Spirit"); and as teachers of folk dance and music (e.g., Lists, 1970s, AHPL, Box 120). The role of the Sección Femenina as part of Falangist modernization came to be well understood among officials, as can be seen in this explanation by a Provincial Chief in 1962 for his office's investment in Sección Femenina courses: "The six female comrades who composed the team were specially prepared by the Sección Femenina through [official] national or provincial courses in those teachings that the Sección Femenina considers basic to women's education; that is, Religion, Familial and Social Training, Households, Rural Industries, General Culture, Hygiene, *Puericultura* [literally Pediatrics but, in practice, Infant Care], regional dances and songs, etc." (ARG, Box 4730).[4] The classes these women were trained to deliver were supplemented with those on religion offered by local parish priests and classes on hygiene and medical matters taught by local physicians. Although the primary purpose of the *cátedras ambulantes* was to give forty-five days of regularly scheduled classes to women (both unmarried and married), these teams also normally gave classes in physical education, dance, and song to children of both genders; in some cases, Rural Instructors delivered classes on agricultural methods to men.

By the end of the dictatorship, these courses were still prevalent. For example, a summary of the *cátedras ambulantes* operating during 1971–73 in the province of A Coruña listed "a total of <u>thirty-two courses</u> under the regimen of ambulant teams with a total of 3,616 [individuals] taking part" (ARG, Box 4728 underlining in original).[5] The objective of "complete training" was taken very seriously in the design of curricula delivered to rural women; for most, it was the first time such an intrusion into the most intimate layers of their family life and work had been effected by agents of the state. As part of the *cátedras ambulantes*, minute aspects of household and personal care were taught in subjects such as Cooking, Household Science, and Infant Care. The naturalization of this level of intrusion was an important aspect of the Movement's approach to making Spain's rural agriculturalists part of a broad social transformation aimed at encompassing family relations and contouring the connections between citizens and the Falangist state (Foucault 1990 [1978]).

Even the style of clothes that women were taught to make, household décor, and food dishes became the target of a serious attempt to introduce "modern" consumerist practices and aesthetics despite economic poverty. Therefore, a priority could be placed on teaching women about "the organization of cupboards," "what one must avoid" in home decoration, and the rules of color combination (AHPL, Box 2).[6] All of the former Sección Femenina teachers I interviewed, as well as other Galician women who said that they were forced against their will to teach some Sección Femenina curricula in state schools, defended the importance of talking to worker-peasant women about how to make their homes more pleasant despite economic adversity. The former Sección Femenina teacher María emphasized that the Christmas courses were "very complete": they taught the peasants "how to decorate a table, how to decorate a house for Christmas, or a door. They did basketry." Specific lessons were designed for instructing girls and women from modest backgrounds on topics such as "the problem with small houses" and particularly how to make the best use of rooms that serve a "double function" (AHPL, Box 2).

The importance of modern timetables and the division of villagers into children, unmarried young women, and married women (or "mothers" as they were often called) were also part of the Falangist cultural idiom introduced in the courses delivered by the *cátedras ambulantes*. Each group was taught separately and according to rigid timetables (compare with Thompson 1967) that were set by the central offices in Madrid and were the subject of reports and inspections. Consider, for example, a letter sent to the provincial delegate of La Coruña from the head of the *Cátedras'* Central Service in 1962. The author clearly conveys the Falangist message about the importance of strict gender, age, and life cycle divisions in "modern" families and communities:

I am writing to tell you that I received your report of March 20th to which was attached the Report about the work achieved in the *Cátedra* of. . . . The Report said that the schedule was the same for married women and the young, unmarried women, as it did not seem opportune to separate them because of the small number of the former. This cannot be. The training classes must be given to them separately. . . (ARG, "Cursos en Plan Cátedra" collection; underlining in original)

Included in this emphasis on separation was the training of *cátedra* members. Since only some of the rural instructors came from agricultural backgrounds, a number of these young women had much to learn. In 1953, for example, the rural instructors in training were taught about raising rabbits and fowl; keeping bees and silkworms; dairy production, including the safe storage of milk, churning butter, and making cheeses; the processing of pork; gardening; and home conservation. They were also taught about flower gardening and arranging; the organization of "the rural house"; and "rural feminine crafts." The level of invasiveness that rural instructors were expected to achieve in their attempts to influence peasant women and girls is clear in these archival documents. The 1953 section on "the rural house," for example, dealt with the "[d]isinfection of rooms, bleach. The hygienic and practical life in laborers' houses" (AHPL, Box 2).[7]

Enders (1999) and others have pointed out that the Sección Femenina goals and approaches were derived from middle-class and urban values and priorities. I would argue, however, that the message that worker-peasant agriculturalists were "ignorant" of these values and priorities was very meaningful to rural women and an important example of a salient cultural idiom widespread before and during the Franco period (compare with Frykman and Löfgren 1987). Many rural women from modest households did not necessarily accept the Falangist teachings on politics, but did absorb information on what might constitute the successful achievement of "modern" ways of living and working. However, a further analytical step is necessary. Rural women's awareness of the disjuncture between the teachings of the Sección Femenina and the possibility that their lives could change in significant ways is an important aspect of their engagement in the state idioms pervasive during this period. It has become clear to me that it was their consciousness of this disjuncture, rather than any differences in knowledge, that constituted the real social differences between the Sección Femenina teachers and their rural students. This awareness can be deduced from women's accounts of the courses they attended, which contain ironic references to the oddity of urban women from more privileged backgrounds coming out to "remote" locations to provide instruction in rural living.

Delfina, an elderly woman who lives on a farm in a part of the province of Lugo characterized by widely dispersed hamlets and holdings, told me about the visit of a Sección Femenina *cátedra ambulante* to her parish in 1966. She remembered being delighted that they came and that she generally enjoyed herself, going to classes each day. However, her descriptions are revealing:

> One day they taught us to make cheese. I brought the milk from here [our farm]. They had the coagulant. Then we heated the milk at thirty-one degrees, which was too high in my view. That way you make the cheese too quickly. It doesn't taste as much like butter. The next day we made chicken but clearly [we knew how to make] that. . . . The next day [laughing], widowed potatoes: [Potatoes] served only with some parsley, without meat or anything.

Furthermore, they were taught how to make "centerpieces for the table. They organized an exhibition. I made a decorated American custard that came out very well but I never made it again." The women were also taught "to embroider, to make the point of the cross. I never made it again. Here the Galician woman is very enslaved. We had to hoe the potatoes. There was only one day to teach [that]. I went [to the course that day] like always. That [the embroidery] I didn't like."

As has been explored by both Rainer Lutz Bauer (1992) and myself (Roseman 1996, 2003, 2006), in different historical periods Galician peasant agriculturalists have strategically drawn upon what have been variously termed urban, bourgeois, elite, and state character-izations of rural Galician "backwardness" in the telling of history as well as in attempts to reclaim their rights to control over land and other resources. Much of the documentary and oral historical evidence on the Sección Femenina indicates that a binary opposition peasant igno-rance/modern knowledge—present in both the verbal and social po-etics suffusing their instructional activities—was an idiom that made sense to the rural inhabitants, who accepted that they were not living "modern" lives (after Collier 1997; also see Fernandez 1986; Herzfeld 1985; Pina-Cabral 1986). I would argue furthermore that it is the shared idiom of rural "backwardness" that led to the Sección Femenina's role in indirect rural governance throughout the Franco period.

In the next section, I turn to how the Sección Femenina em-ployed another idiom—that of rural Galician patron saint festivals or *festas* (in Galician)—to give new meanings to public celebrations in rural areas. Public festivity provided opportunities for participants in the *cátedra* courses to display their achievements to others in their communities in a manner that elicited direct comparisons between different individuals as well as reinforced militaristic images of group formations. These took place during the closing ceremonies of *cátedra* courses, providing opportunities for celebrating disciplined timing, the aesthetics of standardization, and interpersonal competitiveness.

RECASTING FESTIVE SOCIALITY IN RURAL SPACE

Marta, who is overtly anti-Falangist and anti-Franco, a labor union activist, and a Galician nationalist, told me that her husband remembered very clearly the *cátedra ambulante* that spent a month and a half in his school in rural Lugo because the teachers taught the children about new sports and on the last day they had an exciting match in front of spectators from all over the parish. Like the days of patron saint *festas* held in each Galician parish, the courses offered by the Sección Femenina were a unique opportunity to escape from the hard labor of agriculture and animal husbandry as well as to learn something that many children in the cities had already been taught. This was echoed by Lucinda, another professed leftist and Galician nationalist who nevertheless retained some positive memories of her experiences of Sección Femenina–organized events from when she was a young girl: "It was the only possibility for young people's entertainment. Music, theatre, we found it there. The daughter of a doctor of that village was admirable. She painted well. Painting Christmas ornaments. It was a time [of our lives] when . . . we liked very much to walk and to sing and to whistle. There was a little group [of the Sección Femenina]."

The horrors of the war years followed by the censorship and surveillance that ensued afterward had dramatically altered public celebratory practices in Spain. The Sección Femenina co-opted the space of village sociality through its public exhibitions, sports competitions, and other contests. As much as it served to demonstrate Falangist political discipline, the public celebration of "modern" achievements by local women and children (and also men) served to engage rural citizens as participants in "national" agendas. From the early days of the dictatorship onward, there is no doubting the importance of the *concursos* (contests) as part of the Sección Femenina agenda. While some of the other publicly orchestrated events made people fearful ("My father did not let us go," explained one woman when referring to political rallies), many of the cultural, folkloric, or sports events of the Sección Femenina (and of the Juventudes or Youth wing of the party) were described to me as having been "*alegre*" (happy) and as having had little to do with "politics." In the first decade of the dictatorship, the Sección Femenina and other Falangist organizations recognized this state of affairs and emphasized the importance of fostering such occasions, as can be seen in the example of a 1949 memo sent from the Music Department of the National Delegation of the Sección Femenina to all of the provincial delegates: "[T]he difficulties that present themselves [in organizing music and dance contests in particular locales] must be overcome, although in order to achieve this, the Organizer will have to go five or ten times to the same locality, sometimes in order to animate the group that has been constituted, . . . telling them that a great number of Locals reach the Final each year . . ." (AHPL, Box 2).[8] By 1952, the national office emphasized that "[o]ne of the most important labors the Organizers of Culture perform is to arrange for the highest possible number of singing and dance groups and to ensure that all of these have the most important qualities: continuity and authenticity. . . . All of the groups that are formed must participate in the Contests, for that is how [local people] will see their work on a continual basis" (AHPL, Box 2; underlining in original).[9] Prudencia, a former member of one of the Galician provincial delegations, echoed these archival documents when she assured me that "[t]here were prizes in order to motivate the people. There were dance and song contests. They [the provincial winners] went to Madrid, to other countries [to compete]."

Information in the archival sources makes clear how much the contests and *cátedras ambulantes* were intertwined in rural spaces. A report on a *cátedra* held in one village in the province of A Coruña from late August to mid-October 1964 referred to the necessary association between the course for "exemplary mothers" (attended by seventy women) and "hygiene contests" for categories such as streets, houses, public washing spots, and public fountains (ARG, Box 4730).[10] The large number of participants in these contests was also emphasized and careful statistics were registered. For example, "CONTESTS—A Contest of Newspaper Murals and Christmas Cards was held, with 2,075 cards and 1,147 murals competing" (ARG, Box 4728 underlining in original).[11]

Furthermore, the types of contests expanded exponentially during the course of the dictatorship to include almost every kind of activity. Contests were clearly a method used to penetrate as many rural locations as possible and to thereby engage as many women and children as possible in the public celebration of the apparent achievement of social and cultural "improvements." The 1965 report on "Culture" for one locale in A Coruña referred to three contests having been held: (1) making vases, (2) cooking, and (3) ironing (ARG, Box 4730). A report on a *cátedra* held in another location in December 1965, which involved people from seven villages under the heading of "Social Labor," described the following: "Under the pretext of the Christmas Course, we organized a Nativity Scene and home organization contests, offering small prizes purchased with money donated by the Mayor's Office" (ARG, Box 4730).[12] Under the next heading, "Visits made," the following was noted: "We visited the villages of [X, Y, and Z] with the motive of [organizing] the contests" (ibid.).

In two lengthy conversations I had with María, a retired Sección Femenina teacher who gave courses on politics, physical education, and folk dance for several decades, she became very enthusiastic while describing the excitement she experienced as a teenager going to Madrid for national contests in folk dance and singing:

> Each province and each town had its dance and song groups. Each year there would be a provincial contest. They [the winners] went to the annual [national] contest. And then we went to Madrid. . . . It was heady (*Fue de locura*). That was something to make you weep [or to die for] (*Aquello fue de llorar*).

María also emphasized the delight that she took in the disciplinary control she witnessed on these occasions: "This discipline that there was. The outfits, they had to be impeccable when we wore them. You would have to go back and iron them again [if they were wrinkled]. There was one hour to eat . . . At such and such an hour, at such and such an hour . . . I have always liked discipline. It was a very *impressive* discipline!" María talked excitedly about how much she enjoyed training young women and children of both genders to move together with military-like precision: "Do you know what it's like to see hundreds of persons doing the same thing at the same time?" Attempts were made to mirror the excitement of these national events at the provincial and even local levels.

Many of the displays of students' entries in the contests held in villages and towns were associated with the closing ceremonies organized to mark the end of the *cátedras ambulantes*. These closing ceremonies (or *clausuras* in Spanish) tended to bring out a large number of interested spectators and always involved the appearance of local officials. The numerous descriptions of these ceremonies reinforce how important the events were as "festive" occasions and political spectacles. For example,

> The closing ceremony for this *Cátedra* . . . was presided over by the Provincial Subchief of the Movement and was attended by the Provincial Delegate and Secretary of the Sección Femenina, the Provincial Delegate of the Old Guard, the Provincial Delegate of the Syndicates, a Commission for the "Beautifying of the Villages," the Mayor and the Local Chief of [X] and the authorities of this locality. As well, the Parish Priest and the Mayors of [Y] and [Z] attended. The closing ceremony was very emotional and attended by an enormous quantity of people who had come from many kilometers away. It consisted of a description of the work that had been done in all its aspects and almost all of the young women and men and children took part, resulting in a real parade of activities. The children also did a gymnastics routine almost perfectly, taking into account, of course, the [short] length of the course. All of the acts were done in the afternoon and evening. In the morning, there was a Mass . . . after the evening acts, an exhibition of all of the craftwork was inaugurated, which was visited by many. . . . The *Cátedra* team participated with their students in the "*Romería* of St. . . ." celebrated in the nearby village, where young men and young women danced a group of Galician dances prepared during the *Cátedra*. Our closing act led into the award to the Mayor of a prize that the village had won in the contest "The Beautification of Villages" for the past year of 1962. (ARG, Box 4730)[13]

Delfina, whom I quoted earlier remarking somewhat ironically on the young women in the *cátedra ambulante* teaching her and her neighbors how to make cheese, how to cook dishes that they would never make again, and how to do embroidery for which they did not have time, was not at all ironic when describing the excitement of the closing ceremony held at the end of the forty-five-day course: "The journalists came. . . . The people liked it a lot. For one man, it had been more than twenty years since he had played a bagpipe. . . . The people were delighted. Everyone went, just like when there's a *festa*. Especially on the last day. It was like a [local] festival, like the dance that takes place after mass [on a patron saint day]."

According to the Sección Femenina records and people's memories, the explicit purpose of introducing public exhibits and contests was to generate interest among potential participants in the organizations' activities and to draw direct connections between small places and the Nation, even to connect particular households to the Sección Femenina agendas via the display and later transportation of objects such as craftwork and cooked dishes from the schools to home:

> The *Cátedra* must not go to a village and do its work and then have nothing continue after it leaves. There are things that can and must continue. For example: we should not limit ourselves to giving the Physical Education class, gymnastics, but should also work . . . with the teacher to stimulate, excite and motivate her so that when the *Cátedra* leaves she will continue to do it. . . . The same with the decoration of the school, the personal arrangement of the girls and our style of training achieved through contests, murals, theatre, etc. The girls bring what is done and said in the school into their homes. (ARG, Box 4730)[14]

Much more elaborate and imposing "fascist spectacles" (after Falasca-Zamponi 1997) were held in Spanish cities. However, in order to comprehend the "aesthetics of power" (ibid.) during the Franco regime, it is just as important to attend to the less dramatic and smaller-scale public displays held in rural spaces (Foucault 1990 [1978]; 1995 [1977]). On these occasions, the idiom of public festivity and the encouragement of participation-in-the-state-through-contests-and-courses were used to induce a commitment to disciplined modern citizenship practices among people having relatively little previous contact with agents of their national governments.

CONCLUSION

I am not concerned here with drawing a reductionist distinction between the Sección's stated aims, policies, and procedures and any particular discernible effects (or lack of effects) of their activities on specific participants. To highlight such a distinction would be, in my view, to misunderstand the significance—indeed, the overall impact—of the economic and social developmentalist activities of this and related organizations on Spanish citizens and particularly on women. In their ethnographic histories of the particularistic means by which missionaries and others colonized the Tswana people of southern Africa, John and Jean Comaroff remind us that the missionaries from the British Empire were engaged in the fashioning of both colonial subjects and modern consumers:

> As worlds both imagined and realized, they were built not merely on the violence of extraction, not just by brute force, bureaucratic fiat, or bodily exploitation. They also relied heavily on the circulation of stylized objects, on disseminating desire, on manufacturing demand, on conjuring up dependencies . . . that tied peripheries to centers by potent, if barely visible, threads and passions. Indeed, the banality of imperialism, the mundanities that made it so ineffably real, ought not to be underestimated. (Comaroff and Comaroff 1997:219–20)

The archival material and interviews I have done reinforce to what degree the Sección Femenina was heavily engaged in inscribing very explicit messages of state-prescribed maternalism and natalism; women's subservience to the paternalist authority; "modern" hygiene, nutrition, and infant care; a dedication to "modern" schedules and systems of labor and consumption as part of the role of housewife; capitalist agriculture and animal husbandry; folklore; and regular displays of Catholic piety (also see, e.g., Enders 1999; Folguera-Crespo, 1997; Gallego Méndez 1983; Morcillo Gómez 1999; Nash 1991). We also know that many of these messages are not unique to Franco's Spain and Falangism. Attesting to this is comparative material from other European military dictatorships as well as from democratic states heavily invested in the project of "modernizing" their citizens in the nineteenth and twentieth centuries (e.g., de Grazia 1992; Frykman and Löfgren 1987; Horn 1994).

However, one of the most significant impacts of the Sección Femenina's activities in rural Galicia is that it engaged rural women in the state's project of modernization not just through the reinforcement of a message of "backwardness" but through the delivery of this message via courses and competitions. These cultural idioms became increasingly meaningful and naturalized for both worker-peasants and members of the state bureaucracy during the Franco dictatorship. Moreover, after the period ended there was a continued expansion in the types and numbers of training courses available to rural inhabitants of Galicia. Many of these were requested of the state by the first democratically elected local politicians. Today they are pursued by groups of constituents organized in various nonstate organizations such as cultural groups and neighbors' associations (Roseman 2003). Through their organization of formalized instruction and contests, the members of the Sección Femenina were engaged as much in introducing modes of participation in the modern state as in inscribing particular messages about "peasant backwardness" and Falangist modernity. They took on the overall project of mounting an intrusion of the Falange party bureaucracy into all corners of the Spanish state (and its colonies), an intrusion that allowed for an expanding Sección Femenina rhetoric about the production of female citizens who would become engaged political subjects. My argument is that they became engaged not so much as party members and adherents to explicit Falangist ideological notions as they did in becoming used to the very notion of state services and by desiring the privileges that came with "modern" participation in an expanding capitalist economy. The shape that this process took reflects the operation of a shared discourse on rural "backwardness" and public festivity among rural Galician women and the mainly urban, middle-class women working under the direction of the Sección Femenina.

As Foucault (1995 [1977]) reminds his readers in *Discipline and punish*, the systems of surveillance that in some cases supplemented, and in others replaced, public state violence are effective because they became naturalized as a part of the experience of citizenship in "modern" states. I would argue that during the Franco dictatorship citizens (such as Galician worker-peasants) formerly marginalized from most state mechanisms were increasingly enjoined to participate reactively in programmatic activities such as the courses and contests organized by the *cátedras ambulantes*. If the glossy fascist spectacles held throughout the period in and near Spanish cities were about marking the state's control of urban centers alongside political executions and imprisonments, the dedicated disruption of the intimate space of Galician villages was specifically about producing a newly disciplined rural citizenry.

NOTES

Research for this chapter was generously funded by the Social Sciences and Humanities Research Council of Canada. Warmest thanks to all the individuals who agreed to talk to me about their experiences with the Sección Femenina for their openness and interest in the project. Thanks as well to the staff in the Arquivo do Reino de Galicia and the Arquivo Histórico Provincial de Lugo for their superb assistance and permission to use materials for my research. I would also like to thank Wayne Fife, Shawn Parkhurst, Michael Herzfeld, Jim Fernandez, Susan DiGiacomo, and three anonymous reviewers for their helpful comments on earlier drafts of this argument.

1. Translation into English is my own. This is true for all translations of material from the archives, interviews, and cited sources, except when otherwise indicated.

2. Report on "The real situation regarding the advancement of women in this province," the Provincial Delegate of La Coruña writing to the Secretary of the Provincial Council of the Movement, February 20, 1974.

3. Index of Activities and Needs of the Sección Femenina of La Coruña,

4. Report on the Investment of 70,000 pesetas in the Political Action Plan for the Year 1962 in the Work of Rural Propagation by the Sección Femenina, Provincial Chief of the Movement, November 12, 1962.

5. Report on "The real situation regarding the improvement of women in this province," Provincial Delegate of La Coruña, February 20, 1974.

6. Teaching Plan for Social Politics and Household Science according to the Decree of August 7, 1950; memo from the Director General of Primary Education to the principals of Teaching Colleges, March 20, 1952.

7. Central Organizer of Culture, Expansion on Memo No. 533, April 23, 1953.

8. Memo 52, from the Department of Music, National Delegation of the Sección Femenina to the Provincial Delegates, January 28, 1949.

9. Memo No. 1, "On Training in Singing and Dance in Districts and Localities," from the Central Organizer of Culture to the Comrades, Provincial Delegates of the Sección Femenina, February 28, 1952.

10. Propagation and Social-Sanitary Assistance, 1964.

11. Clarification on the statistical data, Provincial Secretary, La Coruña, February 3, 1964. The use of statistical records to profile "accurate" measures of social change was an idiom that, it seems, was shared by many agriculturalists impressed with official accounts of the significant numbers of individuals affected by Sección Femenina campaigns and courses, and who themselves could remember exactly how many individuals from their own families and villages attended health clinics, received educational upgrading or other training, or participated in contests (see a related argument in Urla 1993).

12. Report on a *cátedra*, December 1965.

13. Report on a *cátedra* held in the province of La Coruña, October 23, 1963.

14. Letter from Chief of the Central Service of the *Cátedras* to the Provincial Delegate of the Sección Femenina of La Coruña, March 30, 1962.

REFERENCES

Primary Sources

Acronyms used for the archival collections. Detailed citations of particular documents are included in the endnotes.
ARG—Arquivo do Reino de Galicia (Cidade de A Coruña)
AHPL—Arquivo Histórico Provincial de Lugo (Cidade de Lugo)

Secondary Sources

Abella, Rafael. 1996 [1984]. *La vida cotidiana bajo el régimen de Franco.* Madrid: Ediciones Temas de Hoy.

Alcalde, Carmen. 1996. *Mujeres en el franquismo: Exiliadas, nacionalistas y opositoras.* Barcelona: Flor del Vento Ediciones.

Bauer, Rainer Lutz. 1992. Changing representations of place, community, and character in the Spanish Sierra del Caurel. *American Ethnologist* 19, no. 3:571–588.

Collier, Jane Fishburne. 1997. *From duty to desire: Remaking families in a Spanish village.* Princeton: Princeton University Press.

Comaroff, John L., and Jean Comaroff. 1997. *Of revelation and revolution: The dialectics of modernity on a South African frontier. Volume two.* Chicago and London: The University of Chicago Press.

de Blaye, Edouard. 1976 [1974]. *Franco and the politics of Spain.* Trans. Brian Pearce. Harmondsworth: Penguin Books.

de Grazia, Victoria. 1992. *How fascism ruled women: Italy, 1922–1945.* Berkeley: University of California Press.

Enders, Victoria Lorée. 1999. Problematic portraits: The ambiguous historical role of the *Sección Femenina* of the Falange. In *Constructing Spanish womanhood: Female identity in modern Spain,* ed. Victoria Lorée Enders and Pamela Beth Radcliff, 375–97. Albany: State University of New York Press.

Fabian, Johannes. 1983. *Time and the other: How anthropology makes its object.* New York: Columbia University Press.

Falasca-Zamponi, Simonetta. 1997. *The aesthetics of power in Mussolini's Italy.* Berkeley: University of California Press.

Fernandez, James W. 1986. *Persuasions and performances: The play of tropes in culture.* Bloomington: Indiana University Press.

Fernandez, James W., and Mary Taylor Huber. 2001. Introduction: The anthropology of irony. In *Irony in action: Anthropology, practice, and the moral imagination,* ed. James W. Fernandez and Mary Taylor Huber, 1–37. Chicago: The University of Chicago Press.

Folguera-Crespo, Pilar. 1997. El franquismo. El retorno a la esfera privada (1939–1975). In *Historia de las mujeres en España,* ed. Elisa Garrido González, 527–48. Madrid: Editorial Síntesis.

Foucault, Michel. 1980. *Power/knowledge: Selected interviews and other writings, 1972–1977.* Ed. Colin Gordon. New York: Pantheon Books.

———. 1990 [1978]. *The history of sexuality: An introduction. Volume I.* Trans. Robert Hurley. New York: Vintage Books.

———. 1995 [1977]. *Discipline and punish: The birth of the prison.* Trans. Alan Sheridan. New York: Vintage Books.

Frykman, Jonas, and Orvar Löfgren. 1987. *Culture builders: A historical anthropology of middle-class life.* Trans. Alan Crozier. New Brunswick: Rutgers University Press. First published in Swedish in 1979.

Gallego Méndez, María Teresa. 1983. *Mujer, falange, franquismo.* Madrid: Taurus.

Gramsci, Antonio. 1971. *Selections from the Prison Notebooks of Antonio Gramsci.* Ed. and trans. Quintin Hoare and Geoffrey Nowell Smith. New York: International Publishers.

Herzfeld, Michael. 1985. *The poetics of manhood: Contest and identity in a Cretan mountain village.* Princeton: Princeton University Press.

———. 1987. *Anthropology through the looking-glass: Critical ethnography in the margins of Europe.* Cambridge: Cambridge University Press.

———. 1997. *Cultural intimacy: Social poetics in the nation-state.* London and New York: Routledge.

———. 2001. Irony and power: Toward a politics of mockery in Greece. In *Irony in action: anthropology, practice, and the moral imagination,* ed. James W. Fernandez and Mary Taylor Huber, 63–83. Chicago: The University of Chicago Press.

Horn, David G. 1994. *Social bodies: Science, reproduction, and Italian modernity.* Princeton: Princeton University Press.

Keesing, Roger. 1994. Colonial and counter-colonial discourse in Melanesia. *Critique of Anthropology* 14, no. 1:41–58.

Morcillo Gómez, Aurora. 1999. Shaping true Catholic womanhood: Francoist educational discourse on women. In *Constructing Spanish womanhood: Female identity in modern Spain,* ed. Victoria Lorée Enders and Pamela Beth Radcliff, 51–69. Albany: State University of New York Press.

Mouffe, Chantal. 2000. Hegemony and new political subjects: Toward a new concept of democracy. In *Readings in contemporary political sociology,* ed. Kate Nash, 295–309. Malden: Blackwell Publishers.

Nash, Mary. 1991. Pronatalism and motherhood in Spain. In *Maternity and gender policies: Women and the rise of the European welfare states, 1880s–1950s,* ed. Gisela Bock and Pat Thane, 160–77. New York: Routledge.

Pina-Cabral, João de. 1986. *Sons of Adam, daughters of Eve: The peasant worldview of the Alto Minho.* Oxford: Clarendon Press.

Preston, Paul. 1995 [1990]. *The politics of revenge: Fascism and the military in 20th century Spain*. London and New York: Routledge.

Rodríguez Jiménez, José Luis. 1997. *La extrema derecha española en el siglo XX*. Madrid: Alianza Editorial.

Roseman, Sharon R. 1996. "How we built the road": The politics of memory in rural Galicia. *American Ethnologist* 23, no. 4:836–60.

———. 2002. "Strong women" and "pretty girls": Self-provisioning, gender, and class identity in rural Galicia (Spain). *American Anthropologist* 104, no. 1:22–37.

———. 2003. Poniendo la artesanía gallega y el turismo rural gallego en el mapa global: Políticas administrativas y propuestas locales. In *Las expresiones locales de la globalización: México y España*, coord. Carmen Bueno and Encarnación Aguilar, 381–404. Mexico: Centro de Investigaciónes y Estudios Superiores en Antropología Social, Universidad Iberoamericana, and Miguel Ángel Porrúa.

———. 2006. Reivindicando el paisaje gallego: asociaciones rurales y políticas de desarrollo. In *Galicia & Terranova & Labrador. Comparative Studies on Economic, Political and Socio-cultural Processes. Estudos comparativos das dinámicas económicas, políticas e socio-culturais*, coord. Xaquín S. Rodríguez Campos and Xosé M. Santos Solla, 93–106. Santiago de Compostela, Spain: Santiago de Compostela University Press.

Scott, James C. 1985. *Weapons of the weak: Everyday forms of peasant resistance*. New Haven: Yale University Press.

———. 1990. *Domination and the arts of resistance: Hidden transcripts*. New Haven: Yale University Press.

Sección Femenina de F.E.T. y de las J.O.N.S. 1955. *Economía doméstica*. Madrid: Sección Femenina de F.E.T. y de las J.O.N.S.

———. 1961. *Economía doméstica, Quinto curso y sexto curso*. Madrid: Sección Femenina de F.E.T. y de las J.O.N.S.

———. 1965. *Formación político-social, segundo curso de bachillerato*. Madrid: Sección Femenina de F.E.T. y de las J.O.N.S.

Thompson, E. P. 1967. Time, work–discipline and industrial capitalism. *Past and Present* 38:56–97.

Trouillot, Michel-Rolph. 1991. Anthropology and the savage slot: The poetics and politics of otherness. In *Recapturing anthropology: Working in the present*, ed. Richard G. Fox, 17–44. Santa Fe: School of American Research.

Urla, Jacqueline. 1993. Cultural politics in an age of statistics: Numbers, nations, and the making of Basque identity. *American Ethnologist* 20, no. 4: 818–43.

CHAPTER 7

Crossing Borders, Reconfiguring Lives

A Catalan Exile Family in Wartime London

ORIOL PI-SUNYER

England, great England, England the free, England commanding all the seas—she will understand us and our purpose,

—Theodor Herzl cited in Buruma 1998:177

Memory is life. It is always carried by groups of living people, and therefore it is in permanent evolution.

—Pierre Nora 1984:xix

INTRODUCTION

In what he calls an "Overture," Eric Hobsbawm (1987) opens *The age of empire* by tracing the paths of his future parents: his future mother, recently graduated from an elite Vienna secondary school; his father-to-be, an Englishman working in Egypt for the Egyptian Post and Telegraph Service. The details of the story of the vacationing Viennese and the Englishman making his career in "the East" need not detain us. However, in the author's (1987:2) opinion, the meeting of the young man and his future wife in Egypt took place "where the economics and politics of the Age of Empire, not to mention its social history, brought them together."

Hobsbawm considers it "extremely improbable" that such an encounter would have happened at any other period of history. He also tells us (a matter I shall take up later) that his father's family, who

151

originally came from Russian Poland, "were passionate in the pursuit of English language and culture, and anglicized themselves with enthusiasm" (1987:2). The usually reticent Hobsbawm defends "this autobiographical anecdote" by pointing out that "for all of us there is a twilight zone between history and memory; between the past as general record . . . and the past as a remembered part of, or background to, one's own life" (Hobsbawm 1987:3). Others, including Bourguignon (1996) and Boyarin (1991) have noted this moving space, this twilight zone, and the predicaments of bridging the professional and the personal.

Much as the social forces of the Age of Empire brought Hobsbawm's future parents together, my family and countless others moved through Europe as a consequence of the catastrophes that convulsed the continent in the middle decades of the twentieth century. In our case, we are dealing with the escapes and evacuations that marked the end of the Spanish Civil War (1936–39). More than half a century after these events, and perhaps inevitably, the brutality and ugliness of the period has been overlaid by a certain patina of romance and nostalgia. Another point, implicit only in Hobsbawm's "Overture," is that identities are not only constantly (re)invented, but that the experience of major discontinuities makes available symbolic elements that can be appropriated and incorporated into memory. High on the list of such events are war, displacement, and occupation (Gefou-Madianou 1999; Armstrong 2000; Sutton 1998).

While one may discuss place, time, and memory in the abstract, they are also highly personal, granted that individual memory may become incorporated into what Armstrong (2000:604) terms "the poetics of remembrance." I will be speaking as someone who experienced exile as a child and an adolescent. As such, I form part of an intermediate generation: not yet adult, but old enough to remember, however episodic the memory, the sequence of departures and arrivals; lives left, lives restarted. It is also important to note that I took this route as part of a family—not everyone was so fortunate—and that while I was not fully conscious of it, a society and its forms had already helped to shape me.[1] Time is very important here. Those who were five to ten years older experienced exile as adults; children only five years younger than I grew up with no knowledge of their parents' world.

Exile is both highly personal and distressingly common. The fact that there seems to be no end to "the refugee crisis" (only the geography changes) forces us to discuss it as a phenomenon emblematic of our era, not something aberrant that will sort itself out once exiles and refugees "go home" (Black and Koser 1999; Grimes 1998). Being a refugee also constitutes a particular body of knowledge, so much so that more than sixty years after 1939 I find myself sharing a certain psychology with Cambodian friends who escaped the horrors of the Pol Pot regime. While our cultural backgrounds could hardly be more different, the experience of displacement has marked us in similar ways. Not long ago, I was reading an application essay to our graduate school written by a young woman from Kosovo, a recent refugee. How, she asked, is an identity or a nationality transformed into the "Other," in country of origin or outside it? And, how, she continued, does the intolerable so easily become the unremarkable, part of the "normal" fabric of life? I had no difficulty understanding what she was expressing, and her need to address it.[2]

THINKING ABOUT DIASPORAS

I want to devote a few paragraphs to discussing how I will be approaching the topic of exile. The argument I will be developing is that the manner in which exile and similar situations are discussed and represented typically follows a well-defined narrative and discursive model. This is a model that places considerably greater stress on the pain of displacement, uprooting, and dispersal, than on the ways by which exiles and refugees rearticulate their lives in new, and often quite strange, environments.

The reasons why exile is often approached in this manner are several. Most obviously, the trauma and loss of departure are profoundly felt; exile not only involves drastic changes in personal and collective life, but generally an extreme reduction in rights and statuses (this price is a central element in Ugresic's [2000] memoir, *The museum of unconditional surrender*). To the destruction of critical networks of family, work, and community is added a powerful element of peripheralization. There is, all too often, the drama and danger that accompanies escape: packed trains, dangerous routes, long lines of people struggling to reach safety. Certainly among the most evocative images of the Spanish Civil War are the photographs of fleeing civilians and worn-out soldiers crossing the Pyrenees into France in the winter of 1939.

Displaced people also play an important, though seldom recognized, role for receiving societies. All those refugees escaping vengeance or disorder can be interpreted as powerful evidence of the superiority of the society that gives them shelter. I have seen this with respect to arrivals from the former Yugoslavia (the Balkans portrayed as a region of "ancestral hatreds") and other war-torn lands. Recently, a Colombian colleague explained that when he is asked about the latest crisis or killing in his home country, he often detects a subtext: "Awful things are happening *there*; aren't you fortunate to be *here* where it is safe [and civilized]."

It is not surprising, therefore, that now as in the past, diasporic discourse is strong on disarticulation. But this perception *also* meshes with powerful national myths and the disciplinary and academic division of labor. It fits the way that territory, people, culture, race, and sovereignty have been constructed since early modern times: compartmentalized, slotted into neat spatial and conceptual boxes. Bounded. Furthermore, every major distinction and divide in human experience can be treated as a border, whether separating the present from the past or demarcating life from death. Such frequent figurative language points to the force of the image and helps naturalize a political instrument. Frontiers may be cultural constructs marking the edges of state systems (Anderson 1996), but even in our postmodern and globalized world they have remained remarkably durable—and not just in the imagination.[3]

What I am trying to describe is a multilayered construct of the way that societies are assumed to operate. Often, there is a commingling of popular cultural models with those derived from social science and other disciplines. Thus, from at least the turn of the last century, immigrants and refugees have been conceptualized in simplistic binary terms: they are either achieving assimilation or "resisting" this process. In the United States, this polarity is at the core of a long-running debate on the "melting pot" (Glazer and Moynihan 1963; Varenne 1998), a concept that has traveled back and forth between popular culture and academic discourse.[4] Very similar debates are taking place in Western Europe. I will argue that such approaches are not only simplistic, but reinforce tropes of despair and victimhood.

IMAGINED HOMELANDS AND PORTABLE CULTURES

Discussion of various types of diasporic experience has been facilitated by a series of paradigmatic shifts that have taken place during the last couple of decades. Basically, these approaches have contributed to, or stimulated, novel ways of conceptualizing cultures and societies, and their component membership.[5] An important strand of this reconceptualization reinforces the notion that the subject—society or the individual—is constructed by and in historical discourses and practices. It follows that identities are constantly being reshaped by collective and individual agency. This is linked to an assumption that such a process is ongoing and not the product of some essential psychological or cultural quality transmitted from the recesses of the past. Studies of what has been termed the "invention of tradition" (Hobsbawm and Ranger 1983; also Friedman 1992) have similarly revealed that the past is a surprisingly flexible symbolic resource, one that is constantly being reinterpreted to meet the needs of the present. I do have some reservations concerning what has been termed the "anti-essentialist critique" found in some of this writing: too often, and quite unconsciously, it proceeds to essentialize aspects of the Western intellectual and political tradition (Peabody 2000:176).

Another contemporary social science axis addresses the complexity, uncertainty and contestations of social life, a situation that some observers believe warrants discarding the traditional concept of culture itself (for a sample of the debate, see Clifford and Marcus 1986; Abu-Lughod 1991, 1997; Brumann 1999). However, anthropologists and others discussing human societies would be hard pressed to manage without some concept that addresses the network of shared meanings and symbols—however malleable these may be—that help to articulate social life.

Basically, these approaches should help us problematize social theory, in particular an Enlightenment legacy that all Western societies share and which assumes a high degree of order in the political, cultural, and ideological realms. Of particular significance is the extent to which modern identities have been linked to circumscribed social space within which members of the collectivity are assumed to live and work. This physical grounding is consolidated by symbolic sites, national landscapes, and archetypical objects and scenes celebrated by writers, poets, and artists. Although these symbolic ingredients are continually fought over, the underlying assumption remains that a "proper" nation has—or should have—a well-defined territory, a "homeland," a place of historic memories and associations where territory and people exert mutual and beneficial influences.[6]

The problem with representations of the physical—the "transparent reality" of cartography, landscape painting, and scientific discourse—is that they too easily are rendered transcendental, outside of history. However, it is also beyond question that human beings assign powerful—and complex—meanings and emotions to places and spaces (for some examples, see Kaufmann 1998; Zimmer 1998). Such a sense of attachment is clearly important in Catalan consciousness (Pi i Sunyer 1983:154–56). We must therefore assign proper value to these emotions, recognizing their power and the sense of loss they can engender. In short, the nostalgia, the homesickness of the five senses, could not be more real. The point, however, is that these are facts of culture, not of nature.

If, as has been suggested, identities are culturally constructed and often are associated with quite specific locations and perceptions of the past, how does the exile manage the severance? There are various forms and strategies, but the key element is the degree to which what we term culture is in fact portable, and in some historically important instances, closely linked to the diasporic process.[7] Edward Said (1984:171–72; see also 1990), writing as a contemporary exile, stresses the duality—and the positive elements—of the exile's vision:

> Most people are principally aware of one culture, one setting, one home; exiles are aware of at least two, and this plurality of vision gives rise to an awareness of simultaneous dimensions, an awareness that—to borrow a phrase from music—is contrapuntal. For an exile, habits of life, expression or activity in the new environment inevitably occur against the memory of these things in another environment. Thus both the old and the new environments are vivid, actual, occurring together contrapuntally.

I would push the argument farther. If we agree that all modern nations are, to use the title of Benedict Anderson's (1991:5–6) book, "imagined communities" articulated by what he calls "the image of their communion," it follows that at the core of every culture rests a sense of moral authority. And this sense, I suggest, not only crosses borders but is capable of being redeployed almost anywhere in the world. What I find impressive—and the Civil War displacement constitutes an excellent example—is the tremendous amount of time and energy that exiles spend in the impassioned construction and dissemination of cultural and moral positions. There is a dual audience for this narrative process: the exile community itself—we survive, we endure—

and a host society that needs to be informed, won over. The "contra-puntal" nature of the exile's vision not only makes it possible to exist in two (or more) cultural dimensions, but actually to value the status of refugee as a sign that the displacement is temporary, and that one's cause awaits the proper international attention (Malkki 1992:34–38).

As is evident from the diverse and complex exile experience of Spanish Republicans, such attention is not always forthcoming, and it is also true that confidence may wither. As hope of return and vindi-cation meet the growing realization that such prospects are unlikely to be soon achieved, deep disappointment may well replace initial high expectations. My impression is that for many individuals this was psy-chologically the hardest part of the exile journey. It is also from the late 1940s onward that it becomes harder to treat the Civil War diaspora as a structurally fairly simple phenomenon of war, privation, flight, and sanctuary. Unquestionably, the failure of the Allies to force a regime change in Spain came as a deep disappointment to all Spanish Republi-can refugees. At this juncture, the always-present internal heterogene-ity of exile groups became more marked, while circumstances dictated greater attention to personal strategies of survival. Which brings us to the paradox that many who fled in 1939, and needless to say their children, succeeded as immigrants, but "failed" as exiles: the dictatorship lasted almost forty years.

In summary, I am suggesting that exiles and other uprooted people—I am using the term consciously—may experience tremen-dous, at times insurmountable, difficulties, but that this does not make them handicapped social actors. Even in relatively small groups, they have the capacity—I would say the need—of (re)constructing a life that not only meets individual needs, but communal ones as well. Although obviously related, the culture of place and the culture of mind must be kept separate. While physical space cannot be moved, memories can travel, as can language and a full range of mental constructs, emotional habits, and learned behaviors. In an environment of exile, this salvaged patrimony must be made to mesh with the pragmatic realities of an-other place, another country.

PASSAGES

I have a 1935 photograph of my extended family in Roses, a small seaside village north of Barcelona. It shows twenty-seven people in "family photograph" format: small children seated on the ground, a line of chairs for matriarchs and patriarchs, and a couple of rows of standing people behind. Not all the relatives are present, but for me it functions as a visual marker of a "before" followed by many "afters": the Civil War, dislocation, displacement, exile, another war, the Americas. Obviously, no single picture can express or represent diaspora, but about the same number of kin—although not the identical group—left for France, which for many was the first stop on a much longer journey.

One may reasonably ask how much remains the same, even as one moves, traversing borders and countries. A great deal. But the significance of this "cultural cargo" is reconfigured at each major stopping place, each "home," whether transitory or more permanent. I have argued that culture "travels," and that it consists not only of concepts and beliefs, but of concrete practices that can be rearticulated in specific contexts. Clifford (1997:3) is of the opinion that "practices of displacement might emerge as constitutive of cultural meanings." This seems reasonable if one applies his fable for our times, *Routes* (with the pun on "roots" intended), with some care (Geertz 1998:69).

If part of my argument rests on the mobility of culture, an equally important component is, to use the title of another study, that culture "sits in places" (Escobar 2000). But, obviously, the context—the place—matters, and in the next couple of sections I will be discussing the English one, the formative one for me, and a critically important one for everyone else in my family. The issue I will be addressing is how a collective sense of being is maintained and transformed. Memory, always linking, always constructive, is a crucial element in the maintenance of a sense of integrity. And memory is inseparable from the language that carries it. But we should also include material links, such as family photographs, keepsakes, documents, and books. Typically these are few in number but carry a powerful signification. In our case, they included family pictures, photographs of landscapes, and some small museum reproductions. At a later junction, there may be the correspondence exchanged with those who did not leave and those exiled in other lands.

I have mentioned cultural practices, by which I mean how culturally specific forms are reconstituted and at the same time subtly changed. Food is an excellent example, replete with meanings, tastes, and memories. How hard, yet how important, it is to reproduce foodways in an alien land, particularly a northern country so distant from the Mediterranean. Thus, it should not be a footnote that my mother, and the other women of my family, engaged in a daily task of keeping this link unbroken, even as they were adapting their techniques to available raw materials. More generally, it is of course women—particularly in those days—who, by arranging and organizing, transform domestic tasks into vital cultural practices.

In a discussion of the Greek experience of displacement—the causes are many—Sutton (2001:75; see also Seremetakis 1994) argues for the importance of "cultural sites" that become points of memory and identification. He suggests that "food might be analyzed as just such a cultural site, and is especially useful in understanding . . . Greek experiences of displacement, fragmentation, and the reconstruction of wholeness." I will later explain how, for us at least, food became the most important means of engaging in reciprocity and expressing hospitality in wartime London. In this respect, it is worth noting that Sutton (2001:50) believes that such acts reflect the reality that they are "an important part of the construction of an honorable personal, local or national identity." For my family, it was certainly something that had to be done right, even with a certain degree of solemnity. Consequently, while life in London is remembered in myriad ways, it is often linked to food: the saving of sugar for apple fritters (my favorite dessert), the aroma and anticipation of my mother's slowly simmered beef (as commented on not long ago by my sister-in-law). There is some paradox that in England we pined for the foods of home, and now when most of the nuclear family lives in Barcelona, we talk about the food of exile as something of a triumph. Food was important, particularly in wartime, but I cannot stress too much that the key cultural practice was linguistic. Although we spoke several languages, Catalan remained the language of home, the language of memory.

As for routes, much depends on circumstances. My memories of the Civil War are fragmented, not by privation but by a first—and happy—displacement to the safety of my grandmother's house in La Jonquera, on the French border. This period remains far more vivid in my memory than the whole stay in France, which is remembered chiefly by a sense of impermanence and danger that I must have picked up from the adults. When I recall France, it is in terms of hotels and temporary furnished flats, of movement and trains. We spent a year there and I attended school in Paris and learned French very well, so I am told. But little specific remains, whether of the language or the experience. Expressed differently, this part of the route is for me something like a space on the side of the road: occupied for a moment, but neither origin nor destination. A space that is now both a space of memory and an ethnographic space. I first made use of this "space" concept before having read Kathleen Stewart's *A space on the side of the road* (1996), a "story" on how ideological, aesthetic, and social space can be created on the margins of American capitalism. One does not have to stretch the comparison between political exile and the displacement of Appalachian coal miners: "Picture a world in which there is something wrong with the everyday and an 'Other' world—more real than 'the real,'" because it is the "home place" replete with the "force of a local social imaginary" (Stewart 1996:50). Exactly.

No doubt uncertainty and anxiety conditioned our lives for years to come, but this story would have been very different, and possibly tragic, had we not made the move to England. French people differed in their attitudes to Spanish Republicans, but official France was almost unanimously hostile toward the half-million refugees that crossed the Pyrenean border.[8]

London: Imperial Capital, Bastion of Democracy

In one of the short articles that he wrote in 1940 for the British Ministry of Information, my father (Pi i Sunyer 1996:69) comments on the medley of early wartime London—"a new diversity"—occasioned by the war, and made visible by the forms and details of military uniforms:

> the square caps of the Poles, the *képis* of the French, the broad-brimmed hats of the Australians, the hanging ribbons of the Dutch sailors, the red pompons on the blue caps of the sailors of France. (my translation)

To which might have been added the troops of the British and Imperial services, among them turbaned Indians and kilted Scots. It is an element of multinationalism—even exoticism—that has been commented on by other observers, including the authors of a history of the Battle of Britain (Hough and Richards 1989:186).

Certainly, we were highly conscious of the international dimension of the war, and of the type of experience that, as refugees, we shared with other victims of fascism, whether they had succeeded in crossing the Channel or remained in Nazi-occupied Europe. Psychologically and politically, this association not only permitted us to identify ourselves as part of a grand alliance but, as Spanish Republicans, make the reasonable claim to have been in the vanguard of the fight against the darkness that was engulfing Europe.[9]

But this powerful sense of prior experience, of alliance and comradeship, has to be positioned in the complex, and often contradictory, social and political environment of early World War II London—and by extension Britain. Quite evidently, we lived in a city that was at one and the same time an imperial metropolis and, as it so often seemed to its inhabitants, the very capital of resistance to tyranny. For the outsider, this could be a conceptually difficult combination, but the two elements were inextricably joined, and in common with other refugees, we did our best to "make sense" of a body of strange assumptions and beliefs.

Let me begin with the obvious. The first thing we discovered on arrival in England was that, unlike the situation in France, we lacked a working knowledge of the language, not to mention a sense of how forms of speech encoded an elaborate system of manners, class, and regional differentiation. Certainly, a reasonable control of English was essential, whether we were adults or of school age, whether we had to find ways of earning a living or—as was the case with my mother— run a household on exceedingly limited funds. But, as is true of all *in situ* language learning, proficiency was acquired as part of a comprehensive cultural experience. It now takes something of an intellectual effort to do justice to that period, a time of uncertainty that later becomes more firmly structured in memory and narrative. Our first formal introduction to the English language and things English took place shortly after we settled in the London suburb of Clapham in the spring of 1939, and the location was a small neighborhood school. It was run by two middle-aged (they looked ancient to me) and middle-class "ladies" and consisted of a couple of downstairs rooms of their suburban house. If from the beginning we were exposed to pervasive class markers in speech, dress, and behavior, our most important cultural lesson had to do with the relationship of Britain (England in particular) and the entity referred to as "the Empire"—a term that was always capitalized.

A couple of examples may help recapture time and place. The schoolroom maps of my childhood were, as all maps are, representations of power, but in this case communicating a particularly intricate message. Every member of my generation then growing up in England will remember when one-third or one-quarter of the globe was colored red. A color most obviously associated with the red tunics of the British infantry—the "thin red line" of military legend—but also with such mundane, yet official (all bearing the royal cipher), objects as letterboxes ("pillar-boxes").[10] The maps proclaimed vast stretches of the world as "British," regardless of what the inhabitants of these territories might have felt about the matter. Much of my introduction to geography concerned such matters as the river systems of India, the rice and oil production of Burma, the tin mines of Malaya, and the vast sheep stations of Australia (a Dominion which, of course, counted as part of the Empire). Maps and text pointed to the contrast between a small country off the coast of Europe and the immensity of its possessions. Indeed, it was the smallness, distinctiveness, and separateness of Britain/England that stamped it as privileged, as I was later taught when guided through Shakespeare's *Richard II* (II.i. 40): "This precious stone set in the silver sea, which serves it in the office of a wall."

I am a little ahead of myself, but it would otherwise be difficult to explain *how* most of us learned English: not simply by working through exercises of grammar, but by taking down dictation from long passages of Victorian histories narrating British victories (and occasional gallant defeats). To this day, my sisters and I chuckle at half-remembered passages describing episodes of British history, such as the death of General James Wolfe at the siege of Quebec (1759). I am certain that our tutors did not perceive themselves as engaged in indoctrination, but in a task that matched historical and literary fare with the needs of an adult and literate audience—this writer excepted, needless to say. The aim, I believe, was both linguistic and broadly cultural: an exposure to a particularly English worldview, refracted by the class and generation of our teachers. And, I am equally convinced, an introduction to this cultural universe adapted to a family from a professional background, however impoverished our current condition.[11]

Looking back on the world we were entering—and the long perspective helps—I have become increasingly conscious of how remarkably recent this apparently old—even "timeless"—ideological and institutional system really was. Anthony Sampson (1962:620; see also Hobsbawm and Ranger 1983), has stressed that the society of the first half of the twentieth century was the work of Victorians "who invented so many of the institutions with which we now work—regiments, public schools, the professional civil service, political parties." A good deal of this prewar Britain survives in institutions and in mentality. However, the time I am discussing *was* very different from the present, one in which Britain, and by this I mean the British public as a whole, retained a sense of Victorian entitlement buttressed by an imperial symbology of battleships, plumed colonial governors, ethnically marked colonial regiments, and distinctly British sports (Malcolm 2001). This world that the Victorians built had also suffered a relatively recent tragedy, the costly "Great War," which had caused the death of about one in ten of the country's younger men (Marwick 1965:290). Paradoxically, this devastating loss helps explain both a broad, if hardly universal, support for "appeasement" policies during the 1930s, and a profound distrust of Germany. It is important to keep in mind that the Armistice that had ended World War I was scarcely two decades in the past. When I later attended boarding school, I found that many of my teachers were veterans of World War I; one of them had served in the South African War at the turn of the century.

The England, and particularly the London, I am discussing constituted a symbolic landscape revealing what Anthony Smith (1991:16) describes as "the uniqueness of the nation's moral geography," a geography marked by specific sites as well as more general constructs such as the fantasies associated with the English countryside. Many of these locations can be thought of as "sacred centers" acting as storehouses of common memory, myth, and tradition. Among these would be Buckingham Palace with its linkage to royalty (the fact that the royal family stayed there through the blitz contributed much to its popularity); Westminster Abbey with its amalgam of dead royalty, statesmen, and poets; and the Houses of Parliament, in English eyes the "mother" of democratic institutions (Edensor 1998:38–39; Eade 2000). Some sites, in particular Christopher Wren's St. Paul's Cathedral, would, as the blitz progressed, become symbols of sustained defiance (Hill 1955:91), while London itself—"London can take it"—in a sense constituted one vast symbolic space.

I have been discussing an ideology maintained and reflected in institutions, monuments, memories, and national myths. At an even deeper level we can speak of an understanding and imagery, which, in a totally different context, Michael Taussig (1986:366; see also van de Port 1999) calls "implicit social knowledge." This is presented not as conscious ideology, but rather as a shared sense of

> what moves people without their knowing quite why or quite how. . . . what makes the real real and the normal normal, and above all with what makes ethical distinctions politically powerful.

I would suggest that an unspoken knowledge about the world, about the past, about social and international relations, was very much part of the mentality of the English on the eve of the war. This owed little to the concerns or formulations of politicians or professional historians, but rather to "of course" explanations and assumptions, the central one being the ethical distinction between Britain "alone" and the dangers that faced her. The past offered lessons, or perhaps better said, images, that could be linked to today's experience. This appropriation of the past helps us to understand such matters as the "obstinacy" of the English and the quasi-religious language of many of Churchill's early wartime speeches.

Reconstituting Lives and Hopes

Earlier in this chapter, I made use of Edward Said's metaphor of "contrapuntality," the plurality of vision and experience that characterizes exile life. Other writers have addressed this sense of multiple realities, perhaps most powerfully W. E. B. Du Bois (1989) in the concept he terms "double consciousness."[12] The duality, the painful paradox, which he places at the core of his analysis—two souls, two thoughts, two unreconciled strivings—is, in his opinion, internalized in the collective psyche of Black Americans.

Perhaps the special value of Du Bois's insight for the present essay rests in the fact that double consciousness is held to extend from institutional structures to quotidian experience. Similarly, recent social theory stresses the heterogeneity of space and culture and the importance of what have been called "counterspaces" and "spaces of everyday life" (Lefebvre 1991; de Certeau 1984). I believe that such spaces are—

and in our case definitely were—critically important for the maintenance of a sense of meaning and purpose.

Much of the writing on exiles focuses on *public* representations, public spaces: how exiles collectively define themselves and their cause. This coverage is understandable not only because the practices are by design accessible, but also because they are often documented. Enough exile magazines and newsletters were published in London to keep historians busy for years, as well as titles aimed at a wider audience, such as the *White Book* on Catalonia (Rocamora 1956), and *The case of Catalonia* (Catalan National Council 1945), an appeal to the United Nations.

A detailed discussion of the efforts of Catalans and Spanish Republicans in London to work collectively falls outside the limits of this essay. There is, however, a link between the public and the private, since for exile communities collective structures often emerge out of contacts, plans and discussions initially made in private homes. My father (Pi i Sunyer 1978:30–31) has described how Catalan political and cultural institutions emerged from various meetings in London flats and houses, including ours. For instance, shortly after Britain declared war, Catalans met to draw up a list for the Foreign Office detailing the skills and experience that the community could offer in support of the war effort.

Catalans and other refugees also reformulated or appropriated quite specific English/British cultural practices. From the first Christmas of the war, my family and many others became avid senders and receivers of Christmas cards. One from Christmas 1939 (Vilanova 1995:210) is an excellent example of how English forms were given new meanings. It contains a bilingual (English/Catalan) seasonal greeting, followed by a clearly political message:

THE CATALANS
sheltered by English hospitality,
wish
A MERRY CHRISTMAS
AND A HAPPY NEW YEAR
to you and yours,
FREEDOM
for Catalonia and all the oppressed,
VICTORY
for Great Britain and France,
PEACE
for the World.

I would put into a similar category the incorporation of such English habits as afternoon tea, a repast that could mark formal hospitality without the need for a complex (and expensive) meal.

Much of what I will be discussing is based on the life of my family in London. Many of these observations will be better understood if we take account of the economically precarious situation which we (as so many other exile families) had to contend with. This is not at all evident from the family photographs of the time, which depict clearly middle-class people in appropriate suits, coats, and hats. The camera does not catch—and is not supposed to catch—the concern over clothes: how everything is made to last another month, another season; the consultations with cobblers on the life expectancy of shoes; turned cuffs and collars. If there was little money for clothes, the same was true of other needs or expenses. We virtually never visited the doctor: our medical "coverage" consisted of the local pharmacy and the ministrations of my father. We were not insured against any eventuality. My family loved books, but initially we could afford very few; my father wrote on any bit of white paper he could find, and every pencil was valuable. I had virtually no games or toys, which might account for frequent "experiments" with kitchen utensils. Later on, during the blitz, I collected pieces of bombs and fragments of antiaircraft shells—playthings and items of exchange among children. It is almost inconceivable in today's world that we did not own a radio, but rented one by the month; we lived for a dozen years without a telephone.

I could add further examples, but the important point is that economic difficulties powerfully influenced and reinforced the structure of family life. In many respects, this exile bourgeois family replicated the forms of support and reciprocity that have characterized peasant societies around the world, and that also typify first-generation immigrant households (Abrahams 1991:143–66; Kintz 1990:63–82; Re Cruz 1996). Key features of such kinship units is that all members have rights and obligations, and that the household serves a multiplicity of purposes, most obviously economic, but also emotional, educational, and broadly cultural, in the sense that the family is the chief instrument of cultural reproduction. All such households provide sanctuary from the outside world.

My sisters Carolina and Núria (Pi-Sunyer and Pi-Sunyer 1995:20) have written that "[b]it by bit, in England we learned to live in another way and become accustomed to what we were, for example that we fell into the category of *aliens*" (my translation). Essentially, this is recognition of the powerful authority of a wartime state, even democratic one, to "normalize" its various components, including different types of foreigners. As a case in point, our mobility was restricted, and initially only our father had the necessary permit to be out at night, and then only while on duty as an air raid warden. My sisters also take note of the importance of a psychologically open and secure home environment. It was within this "counterspace" that we most *comfortably* managed our contrapuntal lives.

To say that home functioned as a space of discussion barely scratches the surface. It was also where we—if I may phrase it this way—attempted to "deconstruct" the English. Admirable people in so many ways, but also so strange. The explicit cultural model could be gleaned from everyday life, not to mention novels and the cinema: diffident, self-effacing, steadfast, decent, and middle-class. Bernard Shaw and George Orwell, among others, recognized that there were deeper realities, and we soon became aware of dissonance. The truth of the matter is that while we could all be counted as anglophiles, this fabled land of common sense, good manners, and fairness was not without its darker side. For example, this was a country that had—and still has—a royal society for the prevention of cruelty to animals. We were initially struck by the concern and affection that our hosts lavished on dogs and cats; later in the war, the lighter side of the news often included stories of brave firemen rescuing pets from bomb-damaged buildings. But at the same time we were aware that the education of the young, particularly in boarding schools, was accompanied by the systematic use of corporal punishment. My point here is not simply that the management of children and animals differed substantially, but that the way that children were treated was not congruent with the stated, and strongly believed in, values of fairness and respect. The English, it seemed to us, were unconscious of this contradiction—and of several others.

What I am suggesting is that not only did we have to learn to live within the structure of English society, but that we were constantly engaged in a task of analysis. Why did so many English feel superior to everyone else—and not just refugees? Why, with their empire and their commerce, were they so ignorant of the world beyond the Channel? How did a functioning democracy continue to enshrine such deep and obvious structures of class privilege? It may appear that we ran a graduate seminar around the dining room table, but this is simply my way of expressing our need to make sense of a complex, and at times contradictory, world. It was my mother, hardly trained as a sociologist, who first noticed a feature common among the English: their terrible teeth, discolored, often crooked or missing. I know now that she had spotted a complex health problem, in part attributable to poverty, in part to major dietary changes dating back to the Industrial Revolution.

It was also at home that we made the outside world more manageable by naming, categorizing, incorporating. Although we had very little (and possibly because we had very little), we were a remarkably hospitable family. Looking back on this, it seems to me that hospitality is pivotally important for exiles, for it provides them with a quasi-homeland of memories, sounds, images, and tastes; a little replica of the one lost, and into which strangers may be invited. Hospitality and reciprocity obviously reinforce the bonds of the exile community. But I think we can develop the argument farther. For example, inviting English people to dinner in wartime London not only allowed us to show gratitude for British protection, but by the act of sharing our food and our home, we also made an implicit statement of reciprocity, dignity, and equality.

This inner space was also by definition a hybrid space. The outside was brought in, transmuted. Our normal language was Catalan, but with numerous accretions of English terms and concepts. A comparable diversity was evident in our reading: English and Catalan, but also Castilian and French. Some of this, no doubt, reflected the educational experience of my elders, but only the context explains why, to greater or lesser degree, we all became enthusiasts of the English detective novel, and especially of the eccentric Sherlock Holmes. If this "outside" was brought "in," we also engaged in a process of giving Catalan meanings and names to matters important and trivial. Certainly, we fitted British political leaders (and later Russian and American ones) into a body of understanding based on prior experience, a shift that also applied to the mundane. Hence, a neighbor who claimed aristocratic descent was soon dubbed *el blueblood*, and will forever remain so in our memory.

Our most central concern was the progress of the war, and for some of us—certainly for me—the war became a defining experience. Again, I want to stress that this was something we lived together, much of it at home. We religiously listened to the BBC nine o'clock news— the major source of official information—from before the declaration of war, until long after it was over. We read and commented on the editorials in the papers, and chuckled at the Low political cartoons, particularly his depictions of Franco. My point is that we did not experience this conflict as outsiders, but as a particular category of participant, and that much of this sense of belonging was rooted in family dynamics. We had brought with us not only language, culture and memory, but also our own models, our own "implicit social knowledge." It was because these understandings were flexible enough, open enough, that we went through this conflict (on top of the previous one) remarkably well. Of course, we were also remarkably lucky.

ENDNOTE

Exile in England not only influenced us, but I believe changed us for the rest of our lives. We can think of it as a powerful "situated experience." Our sense of place has to be contextualized: England as a place of the imagination that, as Ian Buruma (1998) points out, had a particular appeal for sectors of the European bourgeoisie, perhaps especially people from smaller countries and those who liked their liberalism with an element of stability. Also, a heroic England, fighting for her life and haven for refugees from throughout Europe. In the introduction to a book he wrote on London parks (his favorite place to write), my father (Pi i Sunyer 1977:9) comments that it was in London that he again found peace, even in the midst of war. He goes on to say, that "from the very beginning I felt a kind of spiritual affinity with the English people which," he continues, "came from their ability to manage things well without resort to extremes of passion" (my translation).

Undoubtedly, we all shared similar, even romantic, perceptions. But it would be erroneous to assume that we were seduced by the power of illusion. England was also a very concrete place where we led real lives. We saw and learned a lot in England, but this also reinforced key elements of our collective identity. Thus, if we identified as Catalans, we also identified as Spanish Republicans, and have continued to do so long after most contemporary Spaniards associate the Republic with a distant and fratricidal conflict. The link here is one between our experiences in England and our sense of loss for democracy in Spain. It was also in England that we broadened our horizons, making friendships— some of which have lasted more than a half-century—which simply would never have been possible had we remained in Spain. Finally, we never constructed our experience of exile as that of "survivors," but as something more empowering: participants in a war which, we felt, was also our struggle.

Shifting to a more (self) analytical mode, I will endeavor to explain why Britain and its empire had such a profound effect on me. The war and my age no doubt had a lot to do with it, but the context itself is worth revisiting. The British Empire between the 1850s and the 1950s can be conceptualized as a vast interconnected world with forms, institutions, and even sentiments in common. It was hardly one vast democracy, but certainly something more complex than the product of a rush to conquer or subdue; or, as one sometimes reads, a reflection of deep-seated racism. It is remarkable, for example, that during World War I Mahatma Gandhi worked to recruit soldiers for the Indian Army because he believed that this would facilitate Home Rule for India within the imperial order, a status comparable to that of Canada or Australia. Also, what we can think of as the imperial core was more diverse than is often recognized. This is essentially the point made by the historian Simon Schama (2002:553) in his discussion of "those who have shared the fate of empire," counting among them "Jews from remote places . . . like my father."

In a formal sense, almost all of this world has disappeared, and with it a certain recognition of the transnational dimension of empires. It was the diversity of this universe that appealed to me, and perhaps I began to formulate an anthropological voice out of the experience of disjunctures, strong cultural contrasts, and an environment that fostered extended analyses.

NOTES

1. I am thinking here especially of the fifteen thousand Basque children who were evacuated beginning in May 1937, at that juncture probably the largest organized evacuation of children in modern times (Castresana 1969; Legarreta 1984).

2. What refugees have in common is a condition of relative powerlessness combined with strangerhood, an official and legal "alienness." All exiles and refugees are—or have been—"people at risk."

3. As Sahlins (1989) has discussed in detail with respect to the Pyrenean frontier, the seventeenth-century French state based its territorial claims not only on power but on a cultural cartography of "natural frontiers." The French "hexagon" is a particularly well-internalized concept, but no different from similar constructs.

4. Other metaphors have been "crucible" and "cauldron"; more recently, newspaper editorialists speak of an American "mosaic" in the making. The term derives from Israel Zangwill's paradigmatic play *The melting pot* (1909), describing, in positive terms, immigrant life in turn-of-the-century New York. Since then, it has been the vehicle for myth, metaphor, and performance in literature and political rhetoric (Sollors 1986).

5. These are interpretive frameworks, still very open, and far from mutually consistent. The approaches borrow from a variety of disciplines besides anthropology, including history (particularly that of women and subaltern groups), cultural studies, feminism, political economy, critical geography, and research on identity. Not surprisingly, it has been described as ushering in an era of "blurred genres" (Geertz 1980), although it can be thought of more positively as a space for intellectual exchange.

6. No one should doubt that such a territorialized model is alive and well in Catalonia. One need only remember the Generalitat's 1992 exercise in creative cartography in the world press which posed the question, "In which country would you place this spot (Barcelona)?," answering in the following page, "In Catalonia, of course." Catalonia is depicted in Western Europe, but unencumbered by state boundaries (Pi-Sunyer 1995:46).

7. This is particularly true of Jewish experience and of an African diaspora that goes back a half-thousand years. Gilroy (1993:205) notes that the very term *diaspora* enters the vocabulary of Black Studies and politics from Jewish thought: "The themes of escape and suffering, tradition, temporality, and the social organization of memory have special significance in the history of Jewish responses to modernity."

8. Most refugees crossed during January and February 1939. About 270,000 were soldiers, the rest civilians. Virtually all the soldiers, and some civilians as well, were incarcerated in French concentration camps, some of these in North Africa. My family was fortunate: my brother and his cousins of military age crossed the Pyrenees and, through luck and various stratagems, escaped the camps. "Politically dangerous" internees were sent to "hard" or "punishment" camps and prisons. Hundreds died of hunger, sickness, and abuse.

9. Ways of marking this relationship were many: personal, political, literary. One small example—the booklet is tiny—is my father's tribute to the Poles (Pi i Sunyer 1940) in which the Virgin of Montserrat, patron of Catalonia, dialogues with the Virgin of Czestochowa, explaining to the Polish patron that her voice "[c]omes from a small country, like yours worthy; from a land conquered, but not lost." (1940:2, my translation). While we applauded the courage of the Poles, we were well aware that prewar Poland had been governed by an authoritarian right-wing regime.

10. The symbolic language was extensive, if at times discrete. Thus, the postage stamps of the period are basically a bust of George VI. However, a

small floral emblem graces each corner: English rose, Scottish thistle, Irish shamrock, Welsh leek.

11. My father managed to place me in two successive boarding schools by outlining our economic circumstances and family background. In one letter he explains to the headmaster that "I am a Spanish refugee" who works for the BBC (he offers income and expenditure information) and comes from a "Catalan family of professors and teachers since some generations." For these reasons, he is "resolved to make an effort and sacrifice" in order that his son may also enjoy a good education, but that this is impossible on his salary. The result is that I became the recipient of a bursary, without which my prospects would have been very different. Even as a refugee, class counts.

12. Paul Gilroy (1993:89) writes of Du Bois's "polyphonic montage technique" and links it to the songs of the Fisk Jubilee Singers, which he describes as being both Black and American.

References

Abrahams, Ray. 1991. *A place of their own*. Cambridge: Cambridge University Press.

Abu-Lughod, Lila. 1991. Writing against culture. In *Recapturing anthropology: Working in the present*, ed. Richard G. Fox, 137–62. Santa Fe: School of American Research Press.

———. 1997. The interpretation of culture(s) after television. *Representations* 59:109–34.

Anderson, Benedict. 1991 [1983]. *Imagined communities*. London: Verso.

Anderson, Malcolm. 1996. *Frontiers: Territory and state formation in the modern world*. London: Polity Press.

Armstrong, Karen. 2000. Ambiguity and remembrance: Individual and collective memory in Finland. *American Ethnologist* 27, no. 3:591–608.

Black, Richard, and Khalid Koser, eds. 1999. *The end of the refugee cycle?* Oxford: Berghahn.

Bourguignon, Erika. 1996. Vienna and memory: Anthropology and experience. *Ethos* 24, no. 2:374–87.

Boyarin, Jonathan. 1991. *Polish Jews in Paris: The ethnography of memory*. Bloomington: Indiana University Press.

Brumann, Christoph. 1999. Writing for culture. *Current Anthropology* 40:S1–S27.

Buruma, Ian. 1998. *Anglomania: A European love affair*. New York: Random House.

Castresana, Luis de. 1969. *El otro arbol de Gernika*. Bilbao: Biblioteca de la Gran Encyclopedia Vasca.

Catalan National Council. 1945. *The case of Catalonia*. New York: Catalan National Council.

Clifford, James. 1997. *Routes: Travel and translation in the late twentieth century*. Cambridge: Harvard University Press.

Clifford, James, and George E. Marcus, eds. 1986. *Writing culture: The poetics and politics of ethnography*. Berkeley: The University of California Press.

de Certeau, Michel. 1984. *The practice of everyday life*. Trans. Steven Rendall. Berkeley: University of California Press.

Du Bois, W. E. B. 1989. *The souls of black folk*. New York: Penguin Books.

Eade, John, ed. 2000. *Placing London*. Oxford and Providence: Berghahn Books

Edensor, Tim. 1998. *Tourists at the Taj*. London and New York: Routledge.

Escobar, Arturo. 2000. Culture sits in places: Anthropological reflections of globalism and subaltern strategies of localization. Paper prepared for Globalization, Postdevelopment and Environmentalism. Five College Faculty Symposium. Hampshire College, Amherst, MA, June 1–3.

Friedman, Jonathan. 1992. The past in the future: History and the politics of identity. *American Anthropologist* 94, no. 4:837–59.

Geertz, Clifford. 1980. Blurred genres: The refiguration of social thought. *American Scholar* 49, no. 2:165–79.

———. 1998. Deep hanging out. *The New York Review of Books*, October 22, 69–72.

Gefou-Madianou, Dimitra. 1999. Cultural polyphony and identity formation: Negotiating tradition in Attica. *American Ethnologist* 26, no. 2:412–39.

Gilroy, Paul. 1993. *The Black Atlantic*. Cambridge: Harvard University Press.

Glazer, Nathan, and Daniel Moynihan. 1963. *Beyond the melting pot: The Negroes, Puerto Ricans, Jews, Italians, and Irish of New York City*. Cambridge: MIT Press.

Grimes, Kimberly M. 1998. *Crossing borders: Changing social identities in Southern Mexico*. Tucson: University of Arizona Press.

Hill, William Thompson. 1955. *Buried London*. London: Phoenix House.

Hobsbawm, Eric J. 1987. *The age of empire 1875–1914*. New York: Pantheon Books.

Hobsbawm, Eric, and Terence Ranger, eds. 1983. *The invention of tradition*. Cambridge: Cambridge University Press.

Hough, Richard, and Denis Richards. 1989. *The Battle of Britain*. London and New York: W.W. Norton.

Kaufmann, Eric. 1998. "Naturalizing the nation": The rise of naturalistic nationalism in the United States and Canada. *Comparative Studies in Society and History* 40, no. 4:660–95.

Kintz, Ellen R. 1990. *Life under the tropical canopy*. Fort Worth: Holt, Rinehart and Winston.

Lefebvre, Henri. 1991 [1974]. *The production of space*. Oxford: Blackwell Publishers.

Legarreta, Dorothy. 1984. *The Guernica generation: Basque refugee children of the Spanish Civil War*. Reno: University of Nevada Press.

Malcolm, Dominic. 2001. "It's not cricket": Colonial legacies and contemporary inequalities. *Journal of Historical Sociology* 14, no. 3:253–75.

Malkki, Liisa. 1992. National Geographic: The rooting of peoples and the territorialization of national identity among scholars and refugees. *Current Anthropology* 7, no. 1:24–44.

Marwick, Arthur. 1965. *The deluge*. Boston and Toronto: Little Brown.

Nora, Pierre. 1983. *Les lieux de la mémoire. Vol 1: La République*. Paris: Gallimard.

Peabody, Norbert. 2000. Collective violence in our time. *American Ethnologist* 27, no. 1:169–78.

Pi i Sunyer, Carles. 1940. *Montserrat i Czestochowa*. Barranquilla, Colombia: Tipografia Escofet.

———. 1977. *Aquell verd anglès*. Barcelona: Editorial Pòrtic.

———. 1978. *El Consell Nacional de Catalunya, 1940–1945*. Barcelona: Curial.

———. 1983 [1927]. *L'aptitut económica de Catalunya*. Barcelona: Edicions La Magrana.

———. 1996. *La guerra des de Londres. Articles per al Ministeri d'Informació britànic (1940–1941)*. Edició a cura de Francesc Vilanova. Barcelona: Fundació Carles Pi i Sunyer.

Pi-Sunyer, Carolina, and Núria Pi-Sunyer. 1995. L'entorn familiar. In *Carles Pi i Sunyer*, coord. Francesc Vilanova, 11–26. Barcelona: Ajuntament de Barcelona.

Pi-Sunyer, Oriol. 1995. Under four flags: The politics of national identity in the Barcelona Olympics. *Political and Legal Anthropology Review* 18, no. 1:35–56.

Re Cruz, Alicia. 1996. *The two milpas of Chan Kom*. New York: State University of New York Press.

Rocamora, Joan, dir. 1956. *White Book of Catalonia*. Buenos Aires: Ediciones de la Revista Catalunya.

Sahlins, Peter. 1989. *Boundaries: The making of France and Spain in the Pyrenees*. Berkeley and Los Angeles: University of California Press.

Said, Edward. 1984. Reflections on exile. *Granta* 13:159–72.

———. 1990. Third World intellectuals and metropolitan culture. *Raritan* 9, no. 3:27–50.

Sampson, Anthony. 1962. *Anatomy of Britain*. New York: Harper and Row.

Schama, Simon. 2002. *A history of Britain, Vol. 3, The fate of empire 1776–2000*. New York: Miramax.

Seremetakis, Nadia. 1994. *The senses still: Perception and memory as material culture in modernity*. Boulder: Westview Press.

Smith, Anthony. 1991. *National identity*. London: Penguin Books.

Sollors, Werner. 1986. *Beyond ethnicity: Consent and descent in American culture.* New York: Oxford University Press.

Stewart, Kathleen. 1996. *A space on the side of the road.* Princeton: Princeton University Press.

Sutton, David E. 1998. *Memories cast in stone: The relevance of the past in everyday life.* Oxford: Berg.

———. 2001. *Remembrance of repasts.* Oxford: Berg.

Taussig, Michael. 1986. *Shamanism, colonialism, and the wild man.* Chicago: University of Chicago Press.

Ugresic, Dubravka. 2000. *The museum of unconditional surrender.* Trans. Celia Hawksworth. New York: New Directions.

van de Port, Mattijs. 1999. "It takes a Serb to know a Serb." *Critique of Anthropology* 19, no. 1:7–30.

Varenne, Hervé. 1998. Diversity as American cultural category. In *Democracy and ethnography*, ed. Carol J. Greenhouse, 27–49. Albany: State University of New York Press.

Vilanova, Francesc. 1995. Aproximació al primer exili de Carles Pi i Sunyer (1939–1946). In *Carles Pi i Sunyer*, coord. Francesc Vilanova, 191–233. Barcelona: Ajuntament de Barcelona.

Zangwill, Israel. 1975 [1909]. *The melting pot: Drama in four acts.* New York: Arno Press.

Zimmer, Oliver. 1998. In search of natural identity: Alpine landscape and the reconstruction of the Swiss nation. *Comparative Studies in Society and History* 40, no. 4:637–65.

PART 3

Regionality and Space

The meanings attached to the concept of "region" have varied from its usage to refer to broad geographical landscapes that incorporate more than one country and even entire continents to the scale of the supralocal, subnational spaces discussed in the chapters in this part of the book. Like the chapter by Roseman in Part 2, María Cátedra's chapter deals with urban/rural distinctions. Cátedra explores how the precedence often given to urban interests is reflected in the history of spatial politics by concentrating on contested spaces and history in the context of the cult of the Virgin of Sonsoles. While the Virgin is invoked as a key religious patron and protector of the city of Ávila, her sanctuary is located five kilometers from the city. Although an important destination for urbanites' religious *excursionismo*, the Virgin of Sonsoles is also a patron saint of rural agriculturalists who carry the image of the saint into the city when appealing for rain. Cátedra explains how Sonsoles reveals longstanding rivalries over space and power in Ávila. During the 1980s, the Association (*Patronato*) of the Virgin of Sonsoles was involved in a legal case with the Bishop of Ávila, who attempted to appropriate the property and administration of the sanctuary from the members of the *patronato* on behalf of the Catholic Church. The 1989 decision of a Supreme Plenary of Cardinals that the rights of the *patronato* should be upheld on the basis of a 1526 Papal Bull underlines how twentieth-century struggles over religious space reverberate with various lines of historical conflict. The control by urban males of the *patronato* of the sanctuary "in the countryside" does not diminish the centrality of the Virgin for rural inhabitants or for women. In fact, it demonstrates that city dwellers have to "go beyond the city" to fully recognize the myriad connections between Ávila and the landscape that surrounds it and gives it life. The chapter by José Manuel Sobral traces the intellectual history that partly underlay the revival of debates over the contested notion of a north/south divide in postrevolutionary (1974–75) Portugal. Sobral argues that stereotypes of northern Portuguese space as "Aryan" and southern Portuguese space as "Semitic," championed at the turn of the twentieth century by influential thinkers such as Basílio Teles, were deeply influenced by racialist arguments developed in other parts of Europe in the nineteenth century, but were also accented heavily by Portuguese national particularities. For one thing, the discourse of the north was purveyed in a context of relative domination: Lisbon, associated with southern Portugal, is clearly the political heart of Portugal. Over time this fact seems partly to have defused the racial radicalism of northern intellectuals, generally residing in and around the coastal city of Porto (Portugal's second city), as they were taken to task by racial "centrists"—who viewed Portugal more as a place of racial blending—aligned with the real power of Lisbon. Still, the argument by Teles and others that it was necessary to colonize the south from the north in order to prevent a "decay of the Portuguese nation" continues to have implications for current-day Portugal, though mainly at the level of discourse developed among non-elites in the northern parts of the country. Parkhurst's chapter provides a counterpoint to studies that emphasize culture—imperial, national, or provincial—as the result of representational processes orchestrated through the writings or stagecraft of urban elites. It shows how regional newspapers convey symbolic regional homogeneity by emphasizing the regional reach of the political and economic core of the region: region-wide depictions of the Alto Douro region—Portugal's famous zone of port wine production—emanate from Peso da Régua, the region's urban center and the locus of port wine regulation. Yet the Alto Douro is like other regions in that depictions of regional cultural homogeneity require interest on the part of a readership residing in peripheral regional localities to work their homogenizing magic. This interest depends, paradoxically, on the provision of space in regional papers for depictions of local distinctiveness. The local depictions of village writers work to produce a sense of regionality in villages while focusing on seemingly aregional matters. Parkhurst shows that the village author Onésimo Azevedo used different genres in the course of assigning different kinds of "essence" to his village: a male essence, an upper-class essence, a progressive essence, an essence as political center to its parish. Parkhurst also outlines the logic by which Azevedo imagined specific types of readership—more regional or more local—depending on the genre he used, and grapples with how Azevedo's social location as both inside and outside of village space contributes to the local logic of regional cultural production. The chapter argues for detailed analyses of processes of cultural regionalization (and, by extension, nationalism) via local rhetoric in Portugal, Spain, and the rest of the world.

CHAPTER 8

The City and the Countryside

The Virgin of Sonsoles

MARÍA CÁTEDRA

This Saint's Image is so old, and people are so devoted [to it] that there is no memory of her beginning . . . she has a happy face, a brown one, holding baby Jesus, and she is greatly venerated and adored. The Lord allows many miracles through her mediation, and so she is very much visited by many people from the city of Ávila and from the land. . . . They offer many alms to ask for remedies for their needs. To bring about the most urgent of their requests, like relief from epidemics or droughts, they bring the very image of the Saint by a general procession to the city, and leave her at the Parish praying novenas and she grants their needs. For that reason they make rich offerings. So she is embellished and decorated with many valued dresses and jewels. . . . Her temple has three spaces, the main chapel is closed with a beautiful grate . . . a beautiful house for pilgrims, another for the caretakers . . . the place is agreeable, with trees and fountains.[1]

—Ariz 1978 [1607]:85–86

In this chapter I provide an analysis of the significance of the cult of the Virgin of Sonsoles, an important Catholic image (or icon) for the city of Ávila (Spain).[2] Much less known by outsiders than the more famous Teresa de Ávila, the Virgin of Sonsoles is nonetheless the religious figure to which the city devotes itself the most. She is the patroness, defender, and advocate of the region of Ávila, shield of the city and patroness of the Amblés Valley. Despite her importance for the city, she

181

is a peasant Virgin; more appropriately, she is the link between Ávila and its surroundings, between the city and the countryside. The Sanctuary of Sonsoles is found at the top of a small hill five kilometers to the southeast of the city, in the middle of the Amblés Valley. Farmers and cattle ranchers have made a living in this fertile valley by supplying the city market with their goods. The Virgin is also called the Divine Highlander (*Divina Serrana*) and she is considered to represent the peasantry, to be the patroness of the highlands. This image of the saint is loosely associated with the city's most crucial historical events:[3] its early Christianization or the conquest of the territory from the Moors in the twelfth century. The more elite version of history considers that the name *Sonsoles* may have originated during the time when a committee passed through the region transporting the remains of Saint Zoilo from Córdoba to the north of Spain in the year 1080. However, according to a local and more popular history, the name comes from the appearance of the image of the Virgin to some shepherds; there was such brightness around both the mother and child that they shouted: "They are suns!" ("¡Son soles!").

In fact, the origin of the sanctuary is not known. Its name is first mentioned in a document from 1303.[4] The primitive building almost collapsed in 1480; in that year, the farrier Andrés Díaz from the city of Ávila asked for permission to restore it with alms collected from the city and the countryside. Then he built up the shrine, the bell tower, a fountain, the caretaker's house, and the shelter for pilgrims and poor travelers. The sanctuary was raised and the brotherhood organized around the year 1500.

The Statutes (*Ordenanzas*) of the Brotherhood from the year 1526 assigned rights and duties to the brothers as well as specified their concerns and needs, fulfilling many functions: they (the *Ordenanzas*) functioned as a court to mediate differences among brothers; the statutes also outlined rules of behavior and good manners. Mainly, they were concerned with organizing the collective attention that would be paid to the sickness and death of the brothers, assisting them and their families with prayers, company, burial, and attendance at anniversary masses. A very important chapter dealt with regulating occasions on which commensality would be practiced among the members of the brotherhood. All the celebrations would end with lavish meals of veal, fruit, and wine; this abundance led to strong criticism from members of the clergy. On the other hand, in the statutes there are careful rules as to the constant care and exhaustive control that should be maintained over the brotherhood's possessions, with details about how to exercise a strict vigilance over the accounts and the care of its objects, properties, and other types of corporately held wealth. The different appointments to offices in the brotherhood and their specific functions were also to be carefully controlled. Offerings in kind (animals and grains) were frequently given to the brotherhood and then sold at public auctions to raise funds for its activities.[5]

The brotherhood located its seat in Ávila. Later, three rural confraternities were created: those of the Amblés Valley, the Sierrecilla, and La Colilla. Despite the brotherhood's humble origins, it soon began to enlist members of the nobility, powerful personages, and authorities whose influence over time transformed it into an elitist committee of patrons (*Patronato*). The friendly and deferential invitation to the knights (*cavalleros*) to belong to the brotherhood in 1526 became a right by 1600, the year in which they came to control half of the board of directors, a change that occurred as a result of much tension and many quarrels.

Also in 1526, a bull from Pope Clemente VII was issued. It was called "protective" (*protectora*) since it defended the rights of the brotherhood against different ecclesiastical suspicions about the brotherhood's wealth. In the middle of the eighteenth century the sanctuary maintained a huge amount of goods and properties. However, in 1801 the sanctuary became a powder storehouse and the Virgin's image was transferred to another place. Soon after, in the War for Independence, the French army confiscated the sanctuary and turned it into an ox stable. This lamentable situation repeated history from four centuries prior: in 1812 a neighbor (or legal resident) of Ávila asked permission to collect alms in order to restore the sanctuary, and he accomplished the task within a couple of years. The brotherhood recovered at the time that the sanctuary was restored, and the image of the Virgin was transferred back to her home.

The nineteenth century brought many improvements (a new altarpiece, a new crown for the Virgin, two large murals in the main chapel). The Virgin was solemnly and canonically crowned in 1934. Later, during the Spanish Civil War, explosives were kept in the altar of Sonsoles. In 1956 Sonsoles became a *Santuario Diocesano*. But the struggles did not end. In the 1980s, the sanctuary endured a major crisis as a result of a dispute between the bishop of the city and the *patronato*. I will elaborate on this later in this chapter.

The eager restoration of the Sanctuary in 1480, and its subsequent popularity, is still considered to have been due to the many miracles believed to have been performed by the Virgin,[6] some of them very impressive. Proof of one such miracle hangs from the shrine's ceiling: the remains of a *cayman* (or crocodile) from whom a devotee of Sonsoles was saved when he invoked the Virgin's name in the "Indies." But most of the miracles involve daily problems such as illness (especially epidemics) and drought (a situation often repeated over the centuries). In these situations, the Virgin journeys from her rustic shrine to the city. Her path follows the landmarks and borderlands between city and countryside. One by one, during the days she spends there, the most important and significant people of the city file by the Virgin in order of precedence: the bishop and the cathedral chapter, the convent and religious order representatives, the municipal government, brotherhoods, highborn ladies, artisans, the humble people, outsiders and countryfolk, etc. The Virgin spends the night in different parishes and thus symbolically "takes" the city. Finally, she leaves the city—once the hospitals are empty because everyone is cured, or in the middle of a heavy shower ending a drought—and is accompanied back to her rural Sanctuary.[7]

TERESA AND SONSOLES

The Virgin of Sonsoles, patroness of the district of Ávila and its land, is in competition with the patroness of the city, Saint Teresa of Ávila. Residents comment that *la Santa*[8] appears as the representative image for the city to the outside world, while Sonsoles remains a local and insider cult that does not have fame outside of the area. But the main difference between the two is the human nature of Teresa and the divine nature of Sonsoles. People say that *la Santa* is "a woman" perhaps the most distinguished countrywoman from Ávila, but still human. About the Virgin they say that she "is the Virgin." Some comment that *la Santa* was "saintly but not a virgin" (*santa pero no virgen*), suggesting the possibility of not very honorable behavior before entering the convent as well as afterward. Saints, after all, have human weaknesses too. This competition between both images is carried out in a conscious manner, and people wonder about how some families choose to name their girls with one or the other name. Both names appear quite frequently. The name of Saint Teresa is employed with great familiarity in Ávila in various businesses (a flour factory, garage, electric company, a confectioners, etc.) and it is a very common name among the working class. Without a doubt, Sonsoles is associated with the high-class women of "well-rooted" old families. And while *la Santa* is associated with civil authority and ecclesiastical hierarchy, Sonsoles is associated with the home and family. So *la Santa* looks like a daughter or a sister, an urban neighbor, while Sonsoles is the mother who takes care of her sick children and worries about the youngsters' exams—two tasks for which she is often invoked. The Virgin is often considered the miraculous one, the *Santa* an intercessor, a kind of ambassador.

Some beliefs about the Virgin of Sonsoles highlight this rivalry for divine territory and competencies. At the sanctuary there are two images of Sonsoles: the Large One and the Small One (*la Grande y la Chica*). The first is the principal image, the most visible at the main altar, the one that goes on processions. The small one, *la Chica*, is almost hidden by a glass screen above an altar in the sacristy. To many people, this small one is the "authentic" image that originally appeared to the shepherds. The fact that there are two images, a public one and a private one, one in the main altar and the other hidden in the sacristy, corresponds with very distinct behaviors: while *la Grande* goes to the city, *la Chica* does not and, despite her small size, when one attempts to pick her up she becomes so heavy that it is impossible to move her. It would be impossible to cross the limits of Ávila with her in tow, and even a cart would be broken by her weight. Some comment: "Since Saint Teresa was named the patroness of Ávila . . . she [Sonsoles] does not want to go to Ávila," or, "The Virgin of Sonsoles is angry because Saint Teresa was named patroness of Ávila and so she does not like to go to Ávila." Each image retains her respective jurisdiction and distinct rules regarding separate spatial realms.

The devotion to Sonsoles is due to her fame in connection with various miracles that have occurred in the distant as well as the recent past. Frequently, she is mentioned in association with the Spanish Civil War.[9] The Virgin was the patroness of the airfield adjoining the sanctuary, which was miraculously spared during the intense bombing of the immediate area. A miniature of a light airplane hangs in the rustic shrine in remembrance of this miracle. It seems that the Virgin of Sonsoles has something to do with this "miracle" in more ways than one. The Virgin appeared in the shape of an old country woman to the "red" (or Republican) troops and told them that the city was heavily defended and to try to conquer the city would amount to sure defeat. The "Marxist hordes" (*hordas marxistas*) rapidly retreated in the face of this news. The story is well known in Ávila and is retold with a profusion of details. Juan Costa, a local artist, made a painting of this miracle with the Virgin dressed as a peasant woman atop a small donkey. Still, there are people who think that the woman was not the Virgin but the *Santa*, and others who point out the political repression that took place in the city at this time. ("Here there was repression . . . but the war didn't come . . . [said ironically]. A miracle from the Virgin of Sonsoles, they said—there was a poster at the door of the sanctuary saying that the Virgin of Sonsoles prevented the entry of the "Marxist hordes" into Ávila. Being a capital in which there wasn't a war—it didn't get here—there was much repression; on the first of September, thirty-two of the so-called 'red people' were killed.").

The sanctuary has a small room full of very diverse ex-votos (for example, bridal gowns, soldiers' uniforms, small written documents, crutches, and especially limbs and other body parts made from wax) that some ironically refer to as the "orthopedic ward" (*sala de ortopedia*). To attempt to ensure that their requests are granted, the Virgin's devotees offer gifts ranging greatly in value, from a humble plant cared for with great conscientiousness to a luxurious mantle. There are three situations in which Sonsoles is most invoked, and each situation corresponds with a distinct demographic group. Children and young people frequent the Sanctuary with their school groups in May, the season in which they study for exams, and solicit the Virgin to "illuminate" (*les ilumine*) them. Their mothers go and make the same requests. Adults fondly recall Sonsoles in association with their worries about exams in their youth. But for youngsters, more than anything, the visit to Sonsoles has traditionally been an excursion full of adventure. For the smallest ones, the sanctuary held a certain halo of mystery owing to the ex-votos that hung from the ceiling of the shrine: a boat, an airplane, and the remains of the crocodile that all at once frightened and fascinated the children. Older people recall this imagery when they want to describe a place full of rare and unusual things, a hodgepodge ("in there you'll find the crocodile of the Virgin of Sonsoles").

When one is older, Sonsoles is invoked primarily during one's illnesses or that of one's children. The Virgin in these cases is solicited as a mother. Traditionally, when the patient cannot go to the sanctuary the Virgin's mantle is taken to his or her home. But Sonsoles cares for the health of her devotees in more than one way. These days, the sanctuary is visited frequently during fine weather *by the urbanites*. The footpath to Sonsoles has become a hiking trail that some trek in devotion—for example, the Mass of the Pilgrim, which is attended almost solely by men—and others use the trail for exercise. Some humorously refer to Sonsoles as the "Virgin of Cholesterol" (*La Virgen del Colesterol*).

On the other hand, the people of the countryside count on Sonsoles for very basic and practical agricultural necessities. The Virgin attracts the rain, with all certainty, if she is taken to the city and a novena is performed for her. Indeed, this is a paradox. When the laborers need rain for their fields, they transport an icon from the countryside to the city. Some say that the Virgin is transported to the city so she can view the dry lands along the way and bless them as she goes along. This transfer of the Virgin forms part of an elaborate ritual and follows a strict route on her way to and from the cathedral or the Parish of San Pedro. Civil and ecclesiastical authorities (the municipal corporation, the Catholic council) take their charge of the icon in a very formal manner in exchange for a wax gift. They organize the triduums and novenas in her honor even though during her time in the city, her "residence" offers her constant service from a caretaker of the sanctuary who leaves her only to sleep. The language used to refer to the icon when she is transported to the city is very anthropomorphic. The Virgin "sleeps" in a church, she visits another at "lunchtime," she "greets" other icons, and has a "preference" for being placed on the highest altar. One of the most anthropomorphizing facets is the way her garments are looked after. For any fiesta or other occasion when she goes out, the Virgin needs to go "well dressed" and "beautiful." The Virgin of Sonsoles has beautiful vestments (given to her by an ancient queen) and a select group of ladies in waiting (selected from the best families of the city) at her service that dedicate themselves to every detail of her appearance.

The Cult and Its Fiestas:
The *Patronato* and the Brotherhoods

In recent times, owing to the proliferation of automobiles, the number of visits to Sonsoles has gone up considerably. Mass, for example, occurs daily and includes three on Sundays whereas in the years prior only one occurred on Sunday. Before, devotees would travel by carriage, on horseback, or even on foot; later on, they went in taxis or on passenger buses. The increased number of people who own automobiles has diminished the numbers that attend on fiesta days, but overall attendance during the rest of the year has increased and created greater prosperity for the sanctuary. Moreover, it has become a place for specific celebrations (first communions, guild reunions), thanks to the restaurant that the patrons of Sonsoles constructed nearby in the last decade, although the ancient pilgrimage practice—whereby the families ate a meal on the sanctuary's esplanade—has been reduced. There are diverse religious activities throughout the year. For example, in May, when "a day is made for the Virgin" (*se hace un día a la Virgen*), the local schools organize field trips for the children. Different pious organizations also make pilgrimages. These are the major celebrations:

First Sunday in July, Fiesta of the *Patronato*
First Sunday in October, Small Offering, Brotherhood of Sierrecilla (*Ofrenda Chica, Cofradía de la Sierrecilla*)
Second Sunday in October, Large Offering, Brotherhood of the Amblés Valley (*Ofrenda Grande, Cofradía del Valle Amblés*)
Third Sunday in October, Offering of La Colilla (*Ofrenda de La Colilla*)

Of these four fiestas, the first typically is a fiesta of the city people while the other three, the Offerings, are fiestas of the countryside, taking place after the harvest. The fiesta of the *patronato* begins on the prior evening with a variety of functions. On Sunday, the ringing of the bells announces the Mass of the Pilgrim, when there is an offering to the Virgin of a bough of flowers from the mayor, or representatives of the city, the naming of the Brother Patron of Honor, and the awarding of medals to certain brothers. After this ceremony follows the Major Mass (sometimes presided over by the bishop), which often includes a choir, a procession through the area surrounding the sanctuary, and an auction of offerings. In some years, a formation of horses and carriages is organized to travel to the sanctuary. Diverse activities (competitions, displays, children's games, romances or sacraments to the Virgin, performances of musicals and "bullfights" using calves [*vaquillas*]) occur throughout the day. The brotherhood convenes for a luncheon on Sunday, and sometimes for an apéritif at mid-morning and a lemonade in the morning or afternoon. The fiesta ends, like all fiestas of the Ávila region, with fireworks. The following day, or one week later, a mass is read for the deceased.[10]

One of the obligations of the members of the *patronato* requires attendance at the first Mass for Pilgrims every Sunday of the year, and they must hike the trail by foot no matter what the weather, though the attendence seems to be greatest during the sunny days of spring and summer. Every year the most assiduous members win a medal. The winners are usually men, with a few exceptions here and there. The leadership of the *patronato* is largely male as well, with the posts of president and vice president rotating from clerical to secular every four years. One exception, however, occurs with the ladies in waiting of the Virgin, who are always women. One woman indicated, with a degree of humor: "They are all men, until now there have not been any women . . . the women are left to only dress the Virgin [laughter]; they really discriminate against us women."[11]

The Offerings take place during the first three Sundays in October. The Brotherhood of the Amblés Valley consists of fourteen villages, the Brotherhood of Sierrecilla consists of another fourteen villages, and the Brotherhood of La Colilla consists of only one village.[12] The Amblés Valley harbors the most important brotherhood on account of the vitality of its villages and their participation. They are in charge of the ritual known as the Large Offering. If the fiesta of the *Patronato* is, as is often said, the "most distinguished" (*más señorial*), official, and urban, the Large Offering is the largest, most popular, and is of the countryside. In contrast to the vitality of the Large Offering, the Small Offering is much more modest and less organized, and that of La Colilla is the smallest. The Offerings are considered to provide an index of the relative standing of the villages concerned, with respect to the villages of the plains and those small villages of the highland areas with small populations. A farmer from the Amblés Valley ironically calls these villages the "United States" (*los Estados Unidos*). All of the celebrations, including the urban-sited *patronato*, contain strong resonances with the countryside. However, the objects that are auctioned by different brotherhoods demonstrate some differences; items of the *patronato* are often city products: liquors, artwork, or potted plants. The Offerings auction products that are more closely associated with agriculture (sheep, doves, rabbits, fruit, chickpeas, beans, grains).

The relationship between the two collectivities associated with Sonsoles and their respective fiestas—the urban population and the fiesta of the *patronato*, the rural population and their Offerings—do not exactly conform to a simple correspondence. For one thing, though it is said that anyone can belong to the *patronato*, not everyone agrees once one considers its enduring elitism, even if, as some say, "it's not what it used to be." This elitist reputation finds its root in the wealth of the *patronato* and its consequent ability to offer many alms ("It's that there are devoted people who come from money, right? That is to say, things are better at the *Patronato* fiesta, it's in July, and they get lots of dough"). The official membership of the *Patronato* of Sonsoles carries a certain social weight; it is considered one of the key associations connected with the distinguished social set in Ávila, the group "that endures" (*los de siempre*).[13] Moreover, the rural brotherhoods do not complain as much as dissemble about the control the city maintains over them and the city's association with wealthy families, despite its humble origin: "People who live in the city of Ávila gain the most power . . . it was always controlled by the city . . . and the ones who take everything are the people from the city. . . . But this *always belonged to* . . . the best parish of Ávila, the wealthiest . . ." However, despite this control, it is the rural brotherhoods that supply the grandeur of Sonsoles and the major part of her wealth: "We, with our fiesta, which is the Large Offering, have the biggest fiesta, and raise the most money for the Virgin on that day and there is no other fiesta that earns more money."

It is interesting to detail how a single cult functions as both a city-based *patronato* and a rural Brotherhood. Two metaphors attempt to describe this duality: one is a plant metaphor that emerges from the nature-based rural icon ("It is like a tree with branches, it's the same. The Brotherhoods are the tree's branches, the tree is the *Patronato* . . . it was born like that, more or less") and the other, rather humorously, comes from the precinct of religion: "We are Father, Son, and Holy Spirit, to help you better understand. . . . The Father is the *Patronato* . . . then you have these Brotherhoods, that is the Son, and it is separate from the *Patronato* . . . we all belong to the Virgin but each Brotherhood is distinct from the *Patronato*. . . . And the Holy Spirit is *La Colilla* [laughter]."

The Offerings are organized into squadrons that each take charge of certain celebrations, and these are decided by means of a draw, vows, or an auction. There is a Major Squadron, and charge of it rotates annually among the different villages. In the past, at least, this naming was considered an honor and it was celebrated with festive meals and drinks in the area nearby the sanctuary. Among the three Offerings there are also the Mass of the Pilgrim, the Major Mass, and the procession; in the first two, there are auctions of donations. One of the flashiest customs during the Large Offering is the dance of the standard performed in front of the Virgin. This game consists of a series of showy exercises performed by the squadrons. The standard represents all the villages of the valley and includes other "insignias"—the halberd and the baton—equally distributing rights and duties and symbolically unifying all the villages that comprise it. The Virgin represents the collectivity; she is the standard of collectivity. That is how a president of the Brotherhood of the Amblés Valley explains it: "Well look, the standard is like . . . the standard represents all the Brotherhoods of the Amblés Valley, as if the Virgin were equal to the Spanish flag. It is like a standard, it can advance like a soldier who is protecting the flag, a standard-bearer, and the command baton is what Sonsoles commands, the baton represents the command of all the Brotherhoods every year."

During the Large Offering, the fourteen villages get together and organize the accounts and shifts for the coming year. In the annual accounting the villages enter into some competition, carried out by means of the number of members of each respective brotherhood, a number that at times is increased, or "padded," with a small trick—including some children or infants in the calculations in order to surpass the number of members in a neighboring village. Food has always been an important ingredient of the pilgrimage. Until very recently, there were groups of families who took their own food in baskets and ate in the esplanade of the sanctuary, but these days the practice is less frequent. In the past, there was a special menu for the occasion and families took care to organize the ingredients and consume the dishes together. This included the sacrifice of the best rooster of a household corral and other food, accompanied with measures (arrobas) of wine. Those who held annual positions of responsibility displayed especially generous spreads. The president of the brotherhood distributed wine among his assistants. This gift resulted in return trips to the village that were less dignified than the original departures for the celebration: "Was there wine left over? Well, on the road you will see, in that direction everyone went on foot, but to get here—that was when no one had yet drank any wine—and many came mounted on burros, mounted they came [laughs]" (*muchos venían atravesados en los burros, atravesados venían* [*ríe*]).

A Raucous Lawsuit

In February 1988, I attended the General Assembly of Sonsoles. It was a cold and disagreeable day, with the ground covered in snow. Owing to that, the attendance was especially scarce—not even a twentieth of the 1,855 members of the brotherhood appeared. It started with a prayer, as happened in almost all of the meetings. Among other things, the discussion concerned the construction of a bar and restaurant at Sonsoles and the work was assigned to a contractor and one of the brotherhood members. Authorization was requested for a former altar boy to recite for the Virgin his experiences in verse form. Various commentaries were made and some information delivered; the last item concerned expenditures and revenue. The most interesting part of this meeting revolved around the dispute the *patronato* had with the bishop of the city. At this time, the president was a priest and he used warm and admiring language about the brotherhoods as lay organizations that had successfully and valiantly survived for up to five centuries in some cases. There were also, from all directions, many criticisms of the bishop, with whom the brotherhood maintained a raucous dispute. It goes without saying that these commentaries in this very Catholic town of Ávila left me astonished.

I will explain this recent dispute, which has its origin in the 1980s. The *patronato* published a pamphlet (Patronato 1989) that detailed the process to be followed by the Bishop of the city and the *Patronato* of Sonsoles, which I will summarize as I continue. On September 14, 1981, the Bishop of Ávila issued a decree establishing the separation of both of the properties as well as the administration of the sanctuary and the *patronato*, and naming by his appointment a new rector of the Sanctuary. The *patronato* called the decree into question and refused to follow it, citing the Bull of Clemente VII of 1526, and called for a ruling from the Spanish civil and ecclesiastical tribunals who, in turn, recused themselves from making any rulings over the dispute; in light of this outcome, the members of the *patronato* went to the Roman Congregation of Clerics. On July 18, 1984, a decree from this assembly ruled in favor of the bishop. Significantly, the Bishop of Ávila signed this decree. One month later, the president of the *patronato* (the priest referred to before) appealed this decree and asked for its nullification and the suspension of its execution by the *Signatura Apostólica* (a branch of the Supreme Court of the Papacy). On February 14, 1985, the execution of the decree was suspended. Nevertheless, the bishop did not accept the suspension. An attempt was made once again to newly ratify the suspension (March 1, 1985) but the bishop once again did not suspend the execution. Then a solicitation was made to declare the decree of the bishop and the congregation illegal. The Plenary of Cardinals of the Supreme Court gave the definitive sentence on April 15, 1989, ruling in favor of the *patronato* and declaring the decree of the congregation illegal for contradicting the Bull of 1526. The pamphlet of the *patronato* briefly covers the history of the creation and evolution of the brotherhood and narrates the early attempts of the parish priests and monks to take control of the sanctuary and the possessions and duties granted by the Bull. The Bull outlines a perpetual union, annexation, and incorporation of the shrine with the hospital sharing their properties and rents, and governed by two patrons and two other individuals selected by and from among the brotherhood, the ability to edit and change statutes, the obligation to repair the shrine, and the concession of indulgences. It expressly declares null the transfer of properties or rents to other entities.

This conflict basically involved a conflict of economic interests between the bishop and the *Patronato*. The Bull of 1526 had unified the *patronato*, the shrine, and the administration of properties in a way that only the Pope could revoke. The bishop tried to separate the properties of the sanctuary from those of the *patronato* so each could be managed separately: the sanctuary's by a rector named by the bishop and the *patronato*'s by the patrons. The bishopric would name a commission that would follow the directive of the brotherhood and carry out the division of properties. This definitely involved an attempt to control the properties of the *patronato*. The allegations of the bishop leap from the text: these are ecclesiastical matters and one cannot leave the care of a sanctuary in lay hands. The reply states that this is not a question of ecclesiastical matters but, rather, a question of justice and that there is no assurance gained in merely placing the sanctuary in ecclesiastical hands, as this paragraph expresses: "The truth is that in the diocese there have been other sanctuaries in the hands of the clergy.

Now, for whatever reason, they have become eagle's nests, abandoned with their masonry falling apart and into piles of gravel. This one has not only escaped disintegration, but because its caretakers converted it, it has served as a Marian Sanctuary of pilgrimage and adoration for centuries. . . . We believe that it is a model institution" (Patronato 1989:9).

Nevertheless, it must be said that this is not only a conflict between the bishop and the *patronato*, but also a struggle between two ecclesiastical lines. A short time after the ruling in favor of the *patronato*, its president died, this president being the priest who was credited as having been "the mind behind the great triumph of the lawsuit that in the twentieth century sustained the *patronato*."[14] As for the bishop, he was transferred to another seat a short time after the definitive verdict. There are those who are certain that this dispute over Sonsoles cost the bishop his post.

The dispute and news related to it are much discussed in Ávila and, at every turn, details about each stage of the dispute and its eventual resolution have filled the pages of the local press. It has also dominated many private conversations as well as public ones, even including portions of sermons from some pulpits. On the whole, the people of Ávila took the side of the *patronato* and became well versed in history, ecclesiastical law, and bulls. Shortly after I arrived at Ávila I spoke with a devotee of Sonsoles who held a post in the *patronato*. One does not usually speak of these types of conflicts with someone outside of the brotherhood, but in this case I timidly alluded to the fact that I had heard that there was "a little confrontation with the bishop" and I received this blunt reply:

> No, not a little one, no . . . a big one! Quite a big confrontation! Quite big, quite big, to the point that we almost have had the misfortune of excommunication [laughter]. . . . He imposed a decree naming a rector and a director and then, well . . . he said he wanted to separate the properties of the shrine from the properties of the *patronato* and we believe that there is not a separation between the properties of the shrine and the properties of the *Patronato* because if we separate the properties of the shrine what is left for us, what do we want the *Patronato* for? [¿ pa que queremos el Patronato nosotros, qué pintamos nosotros?].

The brothers often emphasize that the sanctuary exists thanks to the humble blacksmith and the group that reconstructed it in the past as well as the dedication and control of the following generations. They are certain that the popularity and prosperity of the sanctuary depends on their organization and relative independence from ecclesiastical control. They also often refer to the many alms and pious gifts that the brotherhood has accumulated, from the ancient hospital for pilgrims to the alms that are distributed to the needy today. These are alms that, once the dispute was settled, the bishop refused to accept. This decision was something much commented upon and for which people felt very hurt.

The principal motives behind the dispute can be reduced to two, the brotherhood's independence and its economic means, which are best summed up by the following phrase "The clergy wants control over her because she [Sonsoles] is so wealthy... since she has always been independent of the Church..." According to the brothers,[15] the *patronato* wanted to construct a parking lot to facilitate the pilgrims' access and an agreement was reached with the bishop, who managed the lands adjacent to the sanctuary, to purchase nearly two hectares of land. Money was deposited and when time came to sign the deed, the bishop declared that he would only sell the land to the sanctuary, and not to the *patronato*. At this point someone observed "He'll sell it to himself, he's clever" ("*Se lo vendía a él mismo, mira que listo*"). But there is something else; the real source of the dispute can be attributed to the moment when plans to construct a bar–restaurant, and even a hotel, in addition to the parking lot were revealed. Some said that "the Bishop later commented that if this was a tavern... it was a lie because it is really a legalized *Patronato*." This old complaint on behalf of the clergy in regard to the brotherhoods' consumption of lavish meals and beverages combined with the existing tensions between laypeople and the ecclesiastics over money, is something observable in this confidence shared with me by a member of the rural Brotherhood of Sonsoles: "I have here the remaining money; it's what I have from the Brotherhood. Whatever is left over from the accounts here I gave it to the Virgin, if there are ten thousand pesetas or twelve thousand pesetas... they're for the *Patronato*, for the Virgin. I never keep any money here, I don't like to keep money, that's why what happened with *Patronato*... [clerics] they were money hungry [*olían a perras*], ... that's where it all started... they were money hungry, you understand? And they would clean you out, understand? That's why now there isn't any more money, and there's no more war, understand? That war was there [with the *Patronato*], and now that has retreated..."

The people themselves affirm that tensions have existed for a long time between the laypersons and the clergy: "This is something found throughout history, even though this is a very religious city, where the Church has a strong presence, every time the Church has sought to escape the bounds, there have been problems, I don't know if you have the most recent documentation in regard to Sonsoles, it hasn't reached the public yet . . . I already have a photocopy of the decision, a pitched battle . . ."

CONCLUSION

A person from Ávila would say that in the series of observations that I have presented here, one could find everything, even the crocodile of the Virgin of Sonsoles. Two images: *Sonsoles* and *La Santa*, a crocodile hanging in a shrine next to a light airplane, belief in an image that refuses to enter the city, divine jealousies, squadrons dancing with standards, and the Virgin of Sonsoles dressed as an elderly woman. I have attempted to offer a vision of how an important symbol of identity is situated in physical space and over time, a symbol that ironically represents an insider identity in Ávila but which is located outside the city's boundaries in space. The most important Virgin of the city, with the most extensive and historically rooted cult, signifies volumes despite her origins in the countryside and the fact that most people from outside the area remain unaware of her existence.

The association of close identity that is normally drawn between Ávila and *La Santa* is incomplete (or one-sided) and must be seen in the context of the history of the city and its surrounding countryside: in contemplating both sacred figures at once, *La Santa* and Sonsoles actually complement one another, despite the history of divine jealousies and human suspicions. The intensity that exists between devotees of Teresa and Sonsoles demonstrates the hierarchies that place divine figures vis-à-vis each other and these two saints' respective jurisdictions and competences. They also show the susceptibility of divine figures' reputations and characterizations being impacted by human sentiments and behaviors.

Sonsoles serves as a symbol for the new society as well as the old. The history of the brotherhood reflects the efforts by the people of Ávila to organize themselves according to distinct categories; in this case, in connection with a cult. The Statutes (*"Ordenanzas"*) of the Brotherhood demonstrate the importance of the culture and social values that these institutions sustain. In sum, all indications point toward the possibility of smoother relations among the humans involved in the future and a related effort to create more harmonious divine relations, ones less burdened with conflict. Although the principal functions of Sonsoles deal with illness and death, the needs of the living and the healthy also come to the fore with her fiestas, meals, and beverages; a certain joy for life and perhaps, as well, an endemic spiritual and social hunger is sated with these celebrations. To judge the outcome from the ruling in favor of the brotherhood, after very few years, it seems that the union benefits everyone. This can be concluded from a careful examination of the accounts, the fiscal security, and care that is taken over its collective properties. The simple fact of these institutions' survival over the centuries offers the best proof of their competence; this is a good strategy to protect properties from the voracity of ecclesiastical demands.

Confrontations between laypeople and the clergy appear throughout the long history of Sonsoles. Some commentaries indicate the criticisms of priests and friars about the supposed "excesses" that, today as yesterday, relate to commensality. In 1526 one of the statutes prohibited descriptions of the brothers as "eaters or drinkers or destroyers" (*comedores o bebedores o destruydores*); the construction of the bar-restaurant was the source of the confrontation of 1981. Proclamations of clerical religious purity are long-standing and enduring; the goal of separating the sacred from the profane (as if it were even possible!) seems to constitute an effort to peremptorily distinguish communion from commensality. Behind these prescriptive behaviors and ancient, as well as modern, confrontations, one can see the ecclesiastical establishment's motivations to gain control over lay organizations; therefore, one also sees a reaction when the determined brothers make subsequent declarations about their independence and autonomy. And the fundamental issue lies ultimately with fiscal control over these institutions. The history of the brotherhood can be traced along the path of these innumerable conflicts, jurisdictional disputes, and reclamation of rights that are waged with a variety of authorities (friars, clerics, chaplains, bishop) up to the highest levels of the Roman Catholic Church hierarchy. The Bull of 1526 is necessarily "protective." At issue is the abundance of alms collected at the sanctuary, especially in regard to their use and how the surpluses are deployed.

However, this cannot be considered a simple or neat opposition between a group of poor brothers and a group of covetous clerics. Not all the brothers are rich, nor do the clerics form one undivided bloc. In the late sixteenth century, a shift occurred with respect to the class affiliation of the majority of the patrons of Sonsoles, resulting in those of "the enduring class" having most of the control over the brotherhood, in a similar manner to what happened with other urban contexts. By the same token, there were also clerics, chaplains, and ecclesiastical lawyers who pertained to the brotherhood itself, as can be seen in the solicitous nature of the Papal Bull as well as in the recent dispute with the bishop. The practice of rotating the positions of president and vice president each year between laypeople and the clergy also serves to create, in a routine manner, a regular mix in the brotherhood of those from these two parts of Ávila society.

Perhaps the biggest contrast does not occur between the two distinct collectivities of laypeople and clergy within the city, but instead between the city and its countryside; that is, between the noble and urban *patronato* and the more modest rural brotherhoods. Sonsoles offers a symbolic perspective of the hierarchal relations that exist between the countryside and the city, and the way that the countryside sustains and supports the city. The countryside becomes the mediator between a Virgin who is, paradoxically, a peasant and her devoted farmers who, in praying for relief from drought, carry their Virgin to the cathedral in the city. It is not from her rural vantage point but rather from her journey to the city that the Virgin can observe the drought-stricken territories. Perhaps, after all, despite its connection with a social hierarchy, one can also recognize in a symbolic manner, via Sonsoles, a dependency—like that the city has relative to its countryside—in the opposite direction. The city sustains its countryside, and in such a realization, perhaps those of the city also recognize their intrinsically rural nature and recall that their ancestors were once rural as well. Or, perhaps, simply, they each see that together they exist. The most enclosed plaza in Ávila, *el Mercado Chico*, the major plaza that houses the mayoral offices, is filled every Friday with a fruit and vegetable market; the Virgin travels to the city when she visits and spends the night in the cathedral. The peasants must go to the city to sell their products, but the city also relies upon the peasants for their survival. Power is found in the city, in the mayoral offices and the cathedral; this is an expression of culture and social organization. Sonsoles, like the fruit and vegetables, is a peasant "product," an expression of the power of nature.

Sonsoles succeeds in unifying distinct bioregions: the city, the valley, the highlands, and even a small village. In turn, this image engagingly attracts a confederation of communities unified by their Offerings and their common struggle for survival. Note the way that these villages are proximate but not intermixed, and how each entity retains its own fiesta and conserves its own characteristics. It is not in vain that the rural fraternities perform the dance of the standard, for its performance serves to reinforce each village's individual identity, whether these be villages from the highlands or from the valley. In addition, the offerings themselves symbolically represent the villages' products and modes of life.

These divisions among different rural communities are disrupted by the new ways in which the countryside and rurality are now put to use. The image of Sonsoles offers the city a way of understanding and expressing all at once its distance from the countryside as much as its return to the land. The attentions paid to Sonsoles, her vitality and the continued affluence of her devotees, are associated with new meanings being given to the urban and the rural: these include a deliberate search for the rural in the urban, and a process of an urbanization in the countryside, which is becoming a major movement. The peasants have been emigrating to the city for years, some for employment, others to spend the harsh winters of this region in comfortable city dwellings. At the same time, city dwellers have traveled the reverse path in gentrifying old rural lodgings to make them into permanent homes or vacation and weekend retreats. The Virgin of Sonsoles personifies so many rural mothers who have witnessed their children's abandonment of the lands to which they eventually return. The location of the sanctuary in the countryside shows the urban population the necessity to travel "beyond" the city, to escape the medieval city walls, to reunite with nature and recognize the interconnections Ávila maintains with its countryside. Even the ironic label of "Virgin of Cholesterol" seems to indicate the absence of human health without the connection with nature.

The largely male administration of the sanctuary in both the past and the present, and the almost exclusively male attendance at the Mass of the Pilgrims, exists despite the usual association of the Church (or attendance at the church) with the feminine. Perhaps this is a reproduction of the historic model of the relationship between the city and its surroundings. The man traveled beyond the city to conquer territories while the woman stayed behind within the city walls. A legend tells of Ximena Blazquez, a noblewoman of Ávila, who protected the city from an invasion of Moors (at a time when the men were in battle in other places) by strategically placing women dressed in men's hats on the city walls. At the sight of such a well-defended city, the Moors retreated, fearing defeat. The Virgin of Sonsoles is reputed to have carried out a similar ploy in the last civil war when she appeared as an old woman to the Republican troops and instructed them not to march in the direction of Ávila since it was well fortified. The "Marxist hordes," apparently in fear, did not approach the city. The halo of the warrior reflects Sonsoles' eventful history, in the frequency of the disasters that destroyed the sanctuary and the struggles to rise from its ashes. It is also associated with a particular ideological heritage. Some progressive residents of Ávila (laypeople and clergy) protest the conservatism of these institutions such as the brotherhood and, in recent years, they have attempted to remove the ex-votos or signs that reflect associations such as those connected with the Spanish Civil War, called for the inclusion of women in positions of authority, and requested that the sanctuary be made available to different groups aside from the brotherhood. In a certain manner, the sanctuary remains close to traditions of the past, but it also adapts to new social orders, reflects shifts in modes of living, and performs new ways of defining the city. The pilgrimages to Sonsoles and the celebration of this icon not only stimulate a movement of peoples, groups, and communities but above all play a role in the development of significations, powers, ideals, weaknesses, and worlds in conflict. Through the ritual invocation of the past, the present can be better understood and this process of discovering new meanings can even lead to major shifts in people's cultural paradigms.

NOTES

1. "Es tan antigua esta Santa Imagen, y la mucha devoción que con ella se tiene, que no ay memoria de su principio . . . es de . . . rostro alegre, y morena, con el niño Iesus en una mano, de gradissima veneración, y devoción, por cuya intercessión obra el Señor grandes milagros, y assi es frecuentada de muchas gentes de la Ciudad de Ávila, y de toda su tierra . . . que con grandes

limosnas acuden a pedir remedio en sus necessidades. Y en las más urgentes como son pestilencias, faltas de agua, se han visto encomendándose traer a esta Santísima Imagen, traerla con prucisión general a la Ciudad, y ponerla en una Perrochia, teniéndola sus novenas, socorriéndoles en las necessidades. Por lo qual se le hazen ricas ofrendas. Y assi está adornada de muchos vestidos, joyas, y preseas, de mucho valor, muy bien hornamentada. . . . Su templo de tres nabes, la capilla mayor cerrada con una hermosa reja, dorada . . . una muy hermosa casa . . . para peregrinos . . . y sus santeros en otra casa. . . . Su sitio es muy ameno, con arboledas, y Fuentes." (Ariz 1978 [1607]:85–86). Translations into English here and throughout are mine.

2. A much more extended initial version of this essay was published in 2001. About Ávila see Cátedra (1995, 1997). I would like to thank, here, the historian Serafín de Tapia for his suggestions and comments concerning the manuscript as well as Bill Christian, a specialist in the subject (1990, 1991), and Sharon Roseman and Shawn Parkhurst for their invitation to participate in this book. This essay was translated by Priscilla Ybarra and revised by Carlos Valdés and Susana Castillo. Ávila is a small Castilian city of around fifty thousand inhabitants, well known for its medieval walls and its saints (it is called "la ciudad de cantos y santos" or "the city of stones and saints"). Both of these characteristics are found to be integral to key moments in the history of this city: the walls that shaped the external structure of the city formed a defense against the Moors after the first millennium. When the border moved south, the internal structure of the city was gradually developed so that by the sixteenth century one could find the characteristic pattern of churches, palaces, and convents that still characterize Ávila today. In that century, which marks both the climax of the city's power and the beginning of its decline, its most well-known saints were born in Ávila: Saint John of the Cross and, perhaps the best known of all, Saint Teresa of Ávila.

3. There is information about the saint's origin in the book, *Historia de Nª Sª de Sonsoles*, published in 1930 by the *patronato* and signed by its president, the presbyter Vicente López González. The book contains diverse historical information and includes details about the miracles that begin to be recounted in the seventeenth century. It is copied from the 1686 manuscript of Fernández Valencia—the first extensive history about the Virgin. The manuscript is kept in the sanctuary.

4. Specifically, from the *Becerro de Visitaciones de Casas y Heredades* of the cathedral. This is cited in Belmonte (1986:122) to whom I extend my appreciation for loaning me documents regarding Sonsoles.

5. In the seventeenth century the Virgin is offered the weight of an individual in grain or wax. Sabe Andreu (2000:120).

6. Twenty-three miracles are listed in López's libretto, 1930.

7. One verse (*coplilla*) reads:

> Virgin of Sonsoles
> You who have the power
> Remove the lock from the clouds
> So that it will begin to rain.

8. That is the way the people from Ávila refer to their most famous saint, called as well the "saint of the race" ("*santa de la raza*") in the Franco era and who, ironically, research shows to have had Jewish ancestry. There are traces of Teresa de Ávila practically throughout the old city, from the church built on the site of her birthplace to the different convents where she studied, entered as a nun, or founded (for more information, see Bilinkoff 1989).

9. A *Novena a la Santísima Virgen de Sonsoles* that was published in 1939 uses an eloquent subtitle of *At work thanks to the definitive triumph of our troops* (*En acción de gracias por el triunfo definitivo de nuestro ejercito*). The wording of the novena abounds in phrases that allude to the Civil War, such as: "the offensive initiatives, insults, and grave actions committed . . . by the enemies of the Religion and the State . . . proclaiming a State Without God . . . the assassinations committed against our Bishops, Priests, the Religious, and other Catholics . . . profanities committed with Sacred images." The Virgin of Sonsoles defended the city in these moments via *La Santa*: "You, from your Sanctuary . . . have constantly stood vigil over your children and now, in the middle of eminent danger, made even more solicitations that Ávila not fall into the abyss. You heard, without a doubt, the fervent supplications that your favored daughter, Saint Teresa of Jesus, sent you from the skies above."

10. Distinct significant entities of the city collaborate on these celebrations, including the Junta de Castilla y León, the provincial Diputación and Ayuntamiento (mayoralty) of Ávila, local banks (Cajas de Ahorro), the Clubhouse Abulense and the Restaurant of the Sanctuary, the Peña Taurina (Bullfight Club), those who pertain to the Junta of Holy Week, in addition to some private businesses such as bar proprietors.

11. The humor of the phrase comes from the old expression "left to dress the saints" (*quedarse para vestir santos*) which was employed to designate with a negative connotation a single woman who kept herself busy with pious duties, not having anything better to do.

12. The Brotherhood of the Sierrecilla is formed by the villages of La Venta, Tolbaños, La Alameda, Cortos, Gallegos, Saornil, Los Patos, Berrocalejo, Mediana, Bernuy Salinero, Vicolozano, Urraca Miguel, Brieva, and Escalonilla. The villages of the Brotherhood of the Amblés Valley are: El Fresno, Aldea del

Rey, Gemuño, Cabañas, Niharra, La Serrada, Muñopepe, Padiernos, Muñogalindo, Santa María del Arroyo, Duruelo, Martiherrero, Tornadizos, and Narrillos de San Leonardo. The Brotherhood of La Colilla consists only of the small locality of the same name. There is also a group in Madrid called Sonsoles that visits Ávila every year.

13. This is the term commonly used in Ávila to designate the elite of the city and is also the title of a book by Eduardo Cabezas (2000) about powerful groups during the Restoration.

14. Angel Córcoles Bordera. *El Diario de Ávila*, 24 de marzo de 1991.

15. "The issue really started because so many people attended and we didn't have anywhere for them to park and that was a problem; and then the bishop controls so much land surrounding the sanctuary—that certainly was at one time long ago, maybe before Sonsoles . . . and surely the people granted the lands to Sonsoles . . . but fair enough, the bishop controls them now. And then we made the proposal to the bishopric for the sale of the land and they agreed, they told us in writing that they approved the sale of many meters, I think close to two hectares of land to make into parking space. We took up a collection and gave them a million pesetas, not in its entirety, they sold it to us at what rate I cannot exactly remember—it was an amount of money that they needed to fix the Seminary roof—I don't remember if it was two or three—and we gave them a million and then the other million we were going to give them when we signed the deeds. And then the bishop arrives and says he will not sell to the *patronato*; rather he would sell it to the sanctuary."

References

Ariz, Luys. 1978 [1607]. *Historia de las Grandezas de la Ciudad de Ávila*. Fascimile edition. Alcalá de Henares: Caja de Ahorros de Ávila.

Belmote, Díaz, José. 1986. *La ciudad de Ávila*. Ávila: Caja de Ahorros de Ávila

Bilinkoff, Jodi Ellen. 1989. *The Ávila of St. Teresa: Religious reform in a 16th century city*. Ithaca: Cornell University Press.

Cabezas, Eduardo. 2000. *Los de siempre. Poder, familia y ciudad (Avila 1875–1923)*. Madrid: CIS-Siglo XXI.

Cátedra, María. 1995. *L'invention* d'un saint. Symbolisme et pouvoir en Castille. In *La Fabrication des Saints Terrain* (Mars) 24:15–32.

———. 1997. *Un santo para una ciudad. Ensayo de antropología urbana*. Barcelona: Ariel.

———. 2001. La ciudad y su tierra: la Virgen de Sonsoles. *Revista de Antropología Social* 10:71–121.

Christian, William, Jr. 1990. *Apariciones en Castilla y Cataluña (Siglos XIV–XVI)*. Madrid: Nerea.

————. 1991. *Religiosidad local en la España de Felipe II.* Madrid: Nerea.

Fernández Valencia, B. 1686. *La divina serrana de Sonsoles.* Manuscrito. Archivo Patronato de Sonsoles.

López González, Vicente. 1930. *Historia de Nuestra Señora de Sonsoles.* (Varias ediciones). Patronato de Nuestra Señora de Sonsoles.

Novena a la Santísima Virgen de Sonsoles en acción de gracias por el triunfo definitivo de nuestro ejército. 1939. Imp. Católica y Enc. Sigiriano Diaz.

Ordenanzas. 1526. *Libro de las ordenanças de la cofradía de Nuestra Señora de S. Soles llamada de la Buena muerte hechas y confirmadas con Bula Apostólica, Año del Señor MDXXVI.* Manuscrito.

Patronato de la ermita y hospital de peregrinos Nª Sª de Sonsoles, Ávila. 1989. *Decretos para una sentencia 1981–1989.* Ávila.

Sabe Andreu, Ana María. 2000. *Las cofradías de Ávila en la Edad Moderna.* Ávila: DPDA, IGDDA.

CHAPTER 9

Race and Space in Interpretations of Portugal

The North-South Division and Representations of
Portuguese National Identity in the Nineteenth
and Twentieth Centuries

José Manuel Sobral

INTRODUCTION

There is substantial evidence that a north-south division is one of the key, durable models of sociocultural difference in Europe (Fernandez 1997). That division played a large role in cultural representations of Portuguese national identity in the nineteenth and early twentieth centuries. In this chapter I am most concerned with revealing the racial ideology connected with claims of north-south division as these emerged in the nineteenth century and were transformed into the twentieth. I also discuss how such representations, which were mainly developed by northern Portuguese intellectuals, were discarded over time by most of the Portuguese intellectual elite, but circulate currently in the popular discourse about the north.

RECENT IMAGES OF THE NORTH-SOUTH DIVIDE

It is, above all, recent incarnations of the divide that prompt this historical examination. These have a strongly political coloring. After the institution of a liberal-democratic regime in Portugal in 1974, many political analysts stressed the existence of a north-south divide. With the fall of the authoritarian regime, various conflicting political proposals

205

emerged, particularly following the summer months of 1974. Partisans of more conservative political ideologies proposed solutions similar to those of other European liberal democracies. Radical and socialist proposals abounded, as well. In 1975, the socialization of important sectors of the economy coincided with the dismantling of the Portuguese colonial apparatus, creating an explosive situation. The revolutionary Left, including the Communist Party, sought to avoid elections that year. The right and the Socialist Party successfully pursued elections as part of democratic reform and garnered an electoral majority, with the Socialists pulling in the greatest number of votes.

These first truly free elections in Portugal since the early 1920s gave Portuguese voters a sense of the country's political cartography. The more conservative parties were most successful in the north and center of the country; the south was the stronghold of left-wing forces. The industrial periphery of Lisbon—the country's capital, and generally treated as southern—was a hotbed of revolutionary activity, while Porto— the country's second metropolis, located in the north—evinced a conservative reaction. In the south, landless workers began occupying land in 1975, and were followed by a government-led agrarian reform that redistributed the great landholdings of the southern latifundists to the poor. During the so-called Hot Summer of 1975 conflicts became so serious that they verged on civil war. In the northern part of Portugal many of the local offices of the Communist Party and of other revolutionary organizations were attacked and destroyed; there were also a number of bomb attacks. In most of the south, public demonstrations of right-wing and even Socialist Party sympathies were often suppressed by Communist Party members and sympathizers. These more acute conflicts seemed to give a clear spatial configuration to the political and ideological divides found in the country.

Over time, elections demonstrated an enduring rift, with left-wing parties remaining strong in the south, and right-wing parties being dominant in the north. Two interconnected explanations were generally offered by political commentators and the mass media for the contrast. In the south, the concentration of property in a few hands had generated a rural proletariat while heavy industry had created an industrial working class. Large numbers of both agricultural and industrial workers holding no landed property provided a voting base favorable to the Left. The more evenly distributed small-holdings of the agricultural north served as an infrastructure for conservatism. Also, the social impact of industrialization was lesser, and many more industrial workers held land. Religious practice also differed regionally, with church attendance markedly higher in the north than in the south, particularly the Alentejo, where few people attended church (França 1980). A well-known Portuguese sociologist has tried to explain these differences as expressions of two distinct—northern and southern—cultures (while claiming that the cultural difference is slowly fading away) (Cabral 1992).

This north-south division has ongoing political and cultural reverberations. A recent referendum on abortion (1998) saw the division between those who opposed and those who favored it matching with the north-south division. It can be found in daily conversation, when people from Porto refer to Lisbon and the south as *Mourolândia* (Land of the Moors), often in the context of the rivalry between the Porto Soccer Club and Lisbon soccer teams (Seabra 1999). It is easy, in fact, to consider ethnic representations of the north-south divide as an essentialism that has become widespread among the general public. As Doyle (2002:79) puts it, "Ethnic . . . stereotypes [give] people a language with which to describe regional differences" (Doyle 2002:79). Often, however, popular essentialism is hard to disentangle from the essentialism promulgated by intellectual elites. I will now attempt to uncover how such elites accorded racial meanings to North and South.

Developing Theories of National Identity in Portugal between Late Nineteenth and Early Twentieth Centuries

Two of the most influential representations of Portuguese national space[1] in the twentieth century were produced by a geographer, Orlando Ribeiro, and an anthropologist, Jorge Dias. Both Ribeiro and Dias cast the difference between northern and southern regions as significant, but valorized the regions differently. Ribeiro's *Portugal, o Mediterrâneo e o Atlântico* (1967 [1945]), is one of the most influential books ever published on Portuguese geography. Ribeiro discovered a split within Portugal between Atlantic and Mediterranean influences. The former, particularly strong in the northwestern part of the country, resulted from relatively high rainfall levels (similar to those of northern Europe), pastures for cattle, and irrigated valleys, which led to a relatively high population density (the latter increasing significantly after the introduction of maize). In the south, a Mediterranean kind of landscape predominated, with wheat, olive trees, holm oak, cork oak, sheep, goats, and a sparse human population scattered across flat lands. Medieval documents from Atlantic Portugal registered the importance of serfs working small plots, while in Mediterranean Portugal large estates had predominated since the Roman occupation. Although Ribeiro further divided the north into a more Atlantic northwest and a more "central European" northeast, he viewed the opposition between north and south to be a significant one.[2] More recently, another geographer (Daveau 1995), called attention to broad topographical, climatic, and cultural differences (among others) between north and south; she also delineated contrasts in religious and political practices and affiliations. Most of the Catholic faithful and political conservatives were found in the north, and their opposite numbers in the south.

Jorge Dias, a contemporary of Ribeiro, was influenced by the geographer's regional views, but added ethnological details, emphasizing cultural and social differences between north and south. For Dias, in the north people were more religious and the extended family prevailed. In the south religious observance was weak and the nuclear family was the predominant form of domestic group (Dias 1961:121–43).

While geographer and anthropologist elaborated regional differences according to their different disciplinary foci—space (landscape) for Ribeiro and social life for Dias—they shared an emphasis on ethnicized characterizations of the areas. They valorized the ethnic groups differently, however. Under the variations he noted, Ribeiro considered Portugal's geocultural base to be Mediterranean (Leal 1999:13), and the Mediterranean influence to register the positive impact of Romans and Arabs on the early formation of Portuguese culture (Leal 1999:27). Dias, on the other hand, viewed the Portuguese national personality to entail deep antinomies because of the diverse ethnic origins of the Portuguese. In the north there was a greater impact of Celtic and Germanic Peoples, and in the south Mediterranean populations and Berbers were dominant (Dias 1961:103; Leal 2000:98). Despite the portrayed complexity, Dias identified with what he considered the "collectivist" feelings and the harmonious attitude toward the natural world found in the north. These he considered rooted in the European ethnic origins of the northerners (Leal 1999:18, 23). That Dias came from the northern city of Porto may well have contributed to this sense of affinity (Leal 1999:23). It should be evident then, that regional depictions apparently focused on geographical and economic factors may be linked to ethnic or even racial presuppositions. Yet these presuppositions do not simply appear of their own accord. Instead, they are constructed. To understand their construction requires an intellectual history, and this is what I endeavor to provide in the remainder of this chapter.

In the nineteenth century, Portugal joined other European countries in the theorization and promotion of nationalism in modern terms. Since the fifteenth century the formation of Portugal as a nation had been viewed as rooted in a tribal group known as the Lusitani (Albuquerque 1974). This group was emphasized as a forebear of the Portuguese. In nineteenth-century Portugal, theories developed to challenge this older form of national identification. In his *História de Portugal* (1846), Alexandre Herculano, the most important figure in Portuguese historiography, claimed that the Portuguese nation is a product of politics: it resulted, he argued, from the formation of a state in the twelfth century by an aristocracy and clergy based in the northwestern zone of the Iberian Peninsula. For Herculano, the main port of this zone, Portucale, gave the state its name. (The port city became the current-day Porto.) The northern aristocracy, along with religious and military orders based in the region, conquered extensive territories in a south populated by "Mozarabs" and "Moors," many of whom continued living there. Colonists from the north settled in the south. In the course of this process, the center of government moved south. In the thirteenth century, the city of Lisbon, with a dense Islamic population and an unequalled seaport open to the Mediterranean south, was conquered, and became the enduring center of the Portuguese state's political and economic life. Herculano challenged the Lusitanian thesis radically. The Portuguese nation was formed as a by-product of the state and was not the result of the action of any preexistent ethnic group.

Herculano's account of Portuguese nation formation, although very influential (even today), would be challenged, particularly by accounts which emphasized the concept of race that was becoming so central to nineteenth-century thinking. For example, Oliveira Martins, the second most prominent Portuguese historian of the nineteenth century, and part of the intellectually influential "1870s generation," kept to Herculano's thesis in his *História de Portugal*: Portugal was formed through the political action of the medieval aristocracy. Yet Oliveira Martins added that certain features of the Portuguese national character were *Celtic* (Oliveira Martins 1917 [1879]:3–4). That the concept of race played an important role in history for Oliveira Martins, is clear from his claim that European (or "standard") civilization was based in an Aryan race or ethnic group. Coming from the east, the Aryans lay at the origin of a civilization that would culminate with the worldwide hegemony of Europeans.[3] The people of the Iberian Peninsula had played a major role in the Aryan epic by leading the "Discoveries" and the conquest of the East and the New World. Oliveira Martins saw the north–south divide within Portugal as at least partially a racial one: the purportedly Celtic women of the north were seen as having a dominant role in local social life, while the supposedly Semitic women of the south were entirely subordinate to their husbands. In his own words: "In the Minho [a province in the north], as in all the Celtic regions, the wife governs the home and her husband. . . . She is not the near-serf that one finds in the Semitic-influenced customs of the south . . ." (Oliveira Martins 1979 [1881]:151–52).

Intellectuals of the 1870s generation developed an influential ethnic/racial argument that was aimed at explaining the trajectory of Portuguese history as one of ascent and decay. Portuguese ascension to empire in the sixteenth century was followed by a decline to a virtually colonized status in the nineteenth century. An influential member of this generation, Teófilo Braga, ratcheted up Oliveira Martins's emphasis on race in his account of the history of Portugal. He was joined in this interpretative enterprise by Francisco Barata and Júlio de Vilhena.

For Braga, race was the "light which submits social facts to natural laws" (Braga 1894:132). Thus, the separation between Portugal and Spain, for example, was caused by a greater convergence of the Iberians in the eastern Iberian Peninsula and a greater prevalence of the maritime Celt in the west (Braga 1894:150–51).[4] The notion that race served as the building material of social and political Portugal can be seen very clearly in three of Braga's works (Braga 1871, 1995 [1885], 1894). In *Epopeias da raça moçárabe* Braga sees two social groups forming Portuguese society: the Mozarab—or "Gothic-Arab"—and the "Gothic-Roman." Braga sees them as forming two antagonistic social classes: the first were serfs who lived in close contact with the Arabs of western Iberia; the second were aristocratic Goths who lost their "natural qualities" through contact with Roman civilization. For Braga, the Mozarabs kept the Germanic traditions alive, and were key in forming local communities—known as municipalities—free from feudal dues. In *O povo português,* Braga argues that the various races that had settled in the

Iberian Peninsula could be detected through physiognomy, settlement organization, institutions, language, and folk traditions. In this book Braga claims that racial Iberians mixed in northern Portugal with Aryans and in southern Portugal with Semites. This mixing resulted in the Mozarab, who became the future Portuguese—the source of national identity (Braga 1995 [1885]:57–74). In *A pátria portuguesa*, the emphasis on a pre-Aryan Iberian racial group wanes, as Braga develops the notion that the populations of the Iberian Peninsula are a mix of Aryans and Arabs, and argues explicitly that ethnic blending is proof of civilizational superiority in the Portuguese case, as in the Ionian one (Braga 1894:26–27, 150). Though some of the details are altered, Braga's claims were consistently founded in racialist conceptions.

Braga's conceptions were not developed within a social vacuum: he was influenced by writers from northern Europe. Braga follows the French romantic historian Augustin Thierry (e.g., 1842) in claiming that social classes in France were expressions of different races, with the nobility rooted in the race of Frankish (Germanic) conquerors and the commoners stemming from the Gauls, the group conquered by the Franks.[5] Braga also cited William Edwards as an influence. Edwards, one of the founders of the *Société Ethnologique de Paris*, saw ancient races persisting in the present and forming the base of nations.[6]

As Braga was influenced by northern European writers, he was also challenged by Portuguese interpreters of national history.[7] His critics, however, provide a sense of how pervasive the racialist interpretation of Portuguese history had become. Let us take two important critics as examples. Francisco Barata (1872) took Braga to task for his notion that the Mozarabs were a race, claiming, as had Alexandre Herculano, that they were to be defined as Christian populations living under Islamic rule who had adopted the Arabic language and Arab cultural practices while maintaining their Christian belief system. At the same time, however, he viewed the main features of Iberian society and culture to be explainable as the outcomes of a union of Aryan and Semitic peoples, with the Aryans—represented by Greek, Roman, Germanic peoples—as dominant. Vilhena's (1873) criticism of Braga centered on the claim that Braga overvalued the Germanic strain in the Portuguese population. For Vilhena, Romanization was the decisive factor. He emphasized the Aryan character of the Roman people, however, and so produced an interpretation of Portuguese history also based in racialist argumentation. Vilhena echoed Barata (and Oliveira Martins, moreover) in claiming that despite the durable presence of Semitic "blood" in Portugal (with an emphasis on Phoenicians and Carthaginians), the Aryan element would always prevail.

ARYANS, SEMITES, AND THE NORTH-SOUTH DIVISION IN PORTUGAL

The notion of Aryan superiority in late-nineteenth-century Portugal is not surprising, as such a notion was common in many European countries of the time. Its implantation within Portugal was, however, not a smooth, homogeneous, procedure, but a complicated social process. Symbolic struggles over its implications within Portuguese national space were informed by the regional locations of the writers promoting it.

At the end of the eighteenth century, the British scholar William Jones emphasized the linguistic connections between Sanskrit, Greek, and Latin. In the early nineteenth century the German linguist Franz Bopp established the scientific reality of the Indo-European language family (embracing Celtic, Germanic, Romance, Slavic, Greek, and Albanian languages). The German poet Friedrich Schlegel meanwhile deduced racial affinity from linguistic genealogy (Poliakov 1974 [1971]:168–71). This construction of race was tied strongly to nationalism, both in Germany and elsewhere. Since the second half of the nineteenth century, notions of an Aryan race depended for meaning on the construction of an opposite and inferior "Semitic race" (Poliakov 1974 [1971]; Olender 1989).[8] The genealogy of praise for "the Aryan" as bearer of civilization and its accompanying stigmatization of "the Semite" as culturally stagnant are well established.[9] In nineteenth-century northern Europe the discourse of science, the development of industrialism, and the exercise of social power found a convincing stalking horse in the ideology of Aryanism. Nationalism was an attempt to promote cultural homogeneity as a means for resolving class and cultural contradictions within states, and a notion of race as something settled and based in fate could contribute ideologically to nationalization.[10] As Marvin Harris put it, "Racism could be invoked to overcome the class and ethnic diversities of the nation. . . .The racial interpretation of nationhood imparted to the physical, cultural, and linguistic hodgepodges known as England, France, Germany, etc., a sense of community based on the illusion of a common origin and the mirage of a common destiny" (Harris 1968:106). Oliveira Martins, Braga, Barata, and Vilhena endeavored to use race to accomplish these outcomes.

Could the notion of Aryan superiority actually work the magical spell it was meant to?[11] The example of Basílio Teles helps provide us with an answer to this question.

Teles was an important writer on the topics of economic reform within Portugal at the turn of the twentieth century. Through him, we get a glimpse of how the geographical identification of the writer often conditions strongly the concepts s/he deploys in making interventions within the public sphere. Teles's writing was heavily influenced by the Portuguese social and political conjuncture of the turn of the century. His specific response to that conjuncture seems to have been sparked significantly by his identification as a northerner.

At this time, Portugal was a parliamentary monarchy controlled by an oligarchy based in patron–client relationships. Its main product of value was wine: wheat production was insufficient for the national market, and industrial production was negligible. There was massive migration from the northern and central parts of the country to Brazil. The remittances of emigrants kept the country's balance of payments even. Portugal was a highly subordinate ally of the British Empire, and a very weak actor on the European stage.

Like other intellectuals of the era, Teles witnessed various national crises, one of the most acute occurring in 1890 and 1891.[12] Portuguese colonialism dreamt of occupying the territory between its colonies on the west coast (Angola) and the east coast (Mozambique) of the African continent. Britain, however, successfully brought political and military pressure against the country to make it abandon its designs. Meanwhile, an interruption in remittances from Portuguese emigrants in Brazil spurred an acute economic crisis in Portugal. These crises led to intensely nationalist political agitation. In 1891 Republicans channeled this agitation into an attempted revolution against the monarchy in Porto. Teles took a prominent role in the Republican efforts. The revolution failed, and beginning in the late 1890s Teles dedicated himself to diagnosing the causes of Portuguese decline and to proposing national reforms.

Teles's proposals can be viewed as deriving from his political commitments. They stemmed also from his geographical positioning. Raised in Porto, Teles rarely left the area. For Teles, Portugal was divided between the highly productive small farms of the north, and a scandalously underproductive southern agriculture. The low productivity of the south was caused by the concentration of land in the hands of a small group of absentee landowners allied with the monarchy and averse to capital investments in agriculture. For Teles, the best solution was to promote the colonization of the south by the small, progressive, overcrowded farmers of the north, if necessary through expropriating property from large landowners. This proposal promised to solve a number of problems: it would render wheat production sufficient for the national market; emigration could be channeled within the country instead of outside of Portugal; and the growing population of the interior would increase the country's military, and thus political, power. Teles's proposals seem to have been structured by his regional affiliations, and this is indicated by the fact that Oliveira Martins had years earlier made similar proposals (Oliveira Martins 1956 [1887]), while Ezequiel de Campos, a friend of Teles's, sought to impose a similar agrarian policy while a Republican minister. Campos, like Teles, was from the north. Oliveira Martins, although born in Lisbon, lived in the north for a long time as an adult and was even a member of parliament representing a northern constituency. At the time Teles was writing, it was not, moreover, only northerners defending regional interests; economic writers from the south promoted the utility of the large holdings found there (Bourdon 1991).

While the rationale for Teles's proposals might have been economic, the rhetorical force behind them was a combination of historical and racialized images. In *O problema agrícola* (1899), Teles exposes his view that there was an opposition between the warriors and farmers of the Portuguese north, where trade had a subordinate role and where the state had historically formed, and the southerners, who gave a prominent role to trade and imperial adventure (Teles 1899:140–48). His racial reasoning: the inhabitants of the north were productive *Aryans*; the north's Roman-Hispanic population being almost untouched by *foreign* (such as Arab and Berber) populations (Teles 1901:19–20). The south Teles saw dominated by trade, seafaring adventures, and mercantilism.[13] He linked the south's activities to the fact that there was a significant *Semitic* ascendancy in the south, due to the important presence of Arabs and Berbers whose descendants stayed in the region after the Christian *Reconquista*. Lisbon could be compared with Arab cities: "Say Cairo or Baghdad instead of Lisbon and camels instead of ships and we can see the fit is perfect: . . . the same rapid victories and the same thundering downfall, the same religious spirit and the same weakness for trade" (Teles 1899:145–46). The Portuguese Seaborne Empire, considered by most Portuguese the highest moment in national history—its Golden Age—although praised as "epic" is seen foremost as a consequence of the excessive love of trade, luxury, and adventure of the "Semitic."[14] There is, for Teles, a "Semitic" hegemony in Portugal based in the development of Lisbon as a port and cosmopolitan city. He portrays Lisbon's growth as a consequence of the Revolution of 1383 against the high aristocracy and Castilian sympathizers: "If [anyone] scrutinizes the true meaning of this great historic fact, he will conclude that it was the first strong expression of the south's *Semitic* spirit . . . more erudite, lively and imaginative, flexible, political, and, therefore, apparently more progressive and broad-minded . . . against the *Aryan* populations of the north, . . . which at first sight are slower and more limited but which [are] actually ingenuous, poetic and reflective, full of love for nature . . ." (Teles 1901:19–20). In the aftermath of the 1383 revolution, "southern Portugal relegates *Aryan*, warrior, farmer, nationalist, serious, traditionally supportive northern Portugal to a subaltern position (Teles 1901:29–30).[15]

While his views echoed the emphasis on the purported racial factor found in the works of Oliveira Martins, Braga, Vilhena, and Barata, Teles heightens the conflict found between what he considers northern and southern "races."[16] This increased sense of struggle would seem to derive, moreover, from the regional position from which he writes. Not only does he share the bias of his fellow northerner Ezequiel de Campos in emphasizing northern superiority in agriculture; he differs from Braga, Vilhena, and Barata in emphasizing the opposition of the races, their inability to blend. In this he shares much with another northern writer, the influential historian Alberto Sampaio, whom he singles out for high praise. In *Ontem e hoje*, a piece from 1892, Sampaio (1923 [1892]:431) describes Portugal as a country of "two unfriendly races." To inhabitants north of the Vouga River, Sampaio attributes the impulse to conquer and colonize the rest of the territory, peopled by those of other non–European "ethnic stock" (Sampaio 1923 [1892]:430). For Sampaio the work of the first Portuguese royal (Henriquean) dynasty (twelfth to fourteenth centuries) was interrupted, and the transition to the Avis dynasty (fourteenth to sixteenth centuries) prevented the north's colonization of the south and the formation of a "homogeneous race" (Sampaio 1923 [1892]:429–46).

Thus, Teles produced the most militant images of northern racial superiority over the south, but there were other writers who shared in his notions and promoted them, albeit in softer language. It is perhaps significant that these writers were generally northerners. At the end of the 1920s, the great writer Raúl Brandão depicted yet another Portuguese crisis as the result of a "racial" problem. For Brandão, in Portugal the pure blood of the Aryan *race* (broken down into Celtic and Nordic components), which predominated in the aristocracy of the early (and glorious) years of the Portuguese state, became polluted with the blood of the "Semitic" and "Negro" *races*. Brandão located Aryans in the north and Semites in the south (Brandão 1969).

Another writer from the North, the poet Teixeira de Pascoaes, employed a more coded presentation of region-based races within Portugal. In outlining what he considered the *essence* of the Portuguese nation—cognizance of which was necessary for the rebirth of Portugal—in his *Arte de ser português*, Pascoaes emphasizes *permanent* features of Portugueseness (Pascoaes 1978 [1920]). These are revealed, for example, in untranslatable aspects of the language. In a chapter significantly entitled "Blood," Pascoaes ignores the anthropology of the era, and its height and head measurements. For Pascoaes, because there was one Portuguese language, one art, one literature, one history, etc., there was one Portuguese "race," which he designated, the Lusitanian (Pascoaes 1978:25). Race was the equivalent of the nation (Pascoaes 1978 [1920]:18), and in Portugal it was a blend of Aryans (Celts, Greeks and Romans, Goths) and Semites (Phoenicians, Jews, and Arabs). This blending entailed a fusion of pagan naturalism (the Aryan legacy) and spiritualism (the legacy of the Bible)—a fusion that gave the "race" its "own superior qualities" (Pascoaes 1978 [1920]:72–75). Pascoaes also saw in *saudade* (a bittersweet sense of nostalgia) the essential trait of the Portuguese "soul," and "the only perfect synthesis of Aryan and Semite blood" (Pascoaes 1988:45–47; Leal 2000:91–92).

Although he praised the Semitic legacy and the racial hybridism he thought characterized Portugal, Pascoaes located the spiritual core of the nation in the Entre Douro and Minho regional landscape of northwestern Portugal (his ancestral home), which he opposed both to the Alentejo of southern Portugal, which he followed popular notions in linking to the "Moors," and a northeast characterized by what he called in anti-Semitic terms a "hostile and yellow Jewish aridity" (Pascoaes 1978 [1920]:70).[17]

The topic of the north-south division was already portrayed to be a venerable theme in Teles's time, transmitted from Greek, Hellenistic, and Latin authors via Jean Bodin, Montesquieu, or David Hume, to list only a few of the influential political thinkers taken with it. And, according to a recent study, the division was linked in some writers to behavioral, and even racial, differences (Isaac 2004:55–109). By the second half of the nineteenth century, the division was fully racialized.[18]

Thus, the writing of authors such as Teles, Sampaio, Brandão, and Pascoaes has a family resemblance to writing racializing a north-south divide in other European countries. In France, for example, there was a perceived difference between Aryan and Semite (Sternhell 1978:153), often rendered as a difference between the north and south (Boas 1962 [1928]:63), with the former treating the latter as enemy "Moors" (Juaristi 2000:285–86). In northern Spain there is an emphasis on the greater purity of noble lineages, and Germanic blood, which would have resisted the Muslim settlements beginning in 711 (Caro Baroja 1990 [1956]:154–68). While in the Basque Country Germanic blood is not invoked, an old, autochthonous "race" is counterposed to "races" that mix with Jews and Moors (Chillida 2002:229–36; Wulff 2003:157). The same emphasis on northern purity, this time "Aryan," can be found in Catalonia (Wulff 2003:167–81; Chillida 2002:240–59), and especially in Galicia. For Manuel Murguía, an important Galician writer of the nineteenth century, Galicians were Celts (Aryans, that is), and thus superior to the "Semitic" people of southern Spain (Murguía 2000 [1889], 1865). Strong continuities can be found with Italian anthropologists writing at the end of the nineteenth century. In Italy, the north-south contrast has roots in a contrast between industrialization in the north and a particularly "inefficient" agriculture in the south. Economic contrasts were often treated as based in racial difference, with Aryans (Germans) predominating in the north, and Semites in the south (Gibson 1998).

Within Portugal, the north-south racial division depicted by the northern writers would meet a cool reception. One reason: while it was apparently attractive to many northerners, often identifying themselves with the city of Porto, the division was not acceptable to residents of Lisbon (the metropole of the south and the national capital, significantly bigger than Porto) and the greater south. There were other important reasons. In examining these I will focus on the case of Basílio Teles.

In echoing the north-south division emphasized in other national intellectual traditions, Teles ran up against an established institutional reality that weakened the charge of his rhetoric. While his discourse divided the country, there had never been any institutional legitimation of this division in Portugal. The Portuguese state developed relatively early, and with it the idea of the Portuguese as a homogeneous ethnonational group. Conceiving of the country as divided into two races implicitly questioned the existence of a united nation, assumed by most intellectuals, and spurred even unexpected antagonists to respond quite negatively. Thus, the southerner royalist writer António Sardinha, who shared in Teles's ideas of local autonomy and the preeminence of agriculture in his representation of national history and promotion of anti-Semitism, accused Teles of incitement to civil war (Sardinha 1961 [1927]).

Racially preoccupied intellectuals more influential than Teles argued that the Portuguese population resulted from a union of peoples among whom there were branches of the Aryan and Semitic "races" that had inhabited the Iberian Peninsula (Oliveira Martins 1954 [1879]; Severo 1924 [1911]; Corrêa 1919). By denying a shared ethnic identity among the Portuguese, Teles also put in question the national myth linking the Portuguese to the Lusitani, an idea that had experienced a revival since the last decades of the nineteenth century. This myth was adopted by many influential intellectuals, from Martins Sarmento in the nineteenth century to Jorge Dias in the twentieth century (Leal 2000; Sarmento 1884). Corrêa, in particular, defended the continuity between Lusitani and Portuguese: "With the war between the Lusitani and Romans, with the heroic deeds of Viriato, the Portuguese epic is born and the Nation appears" (Corrêa 1919:75; see also Corrêa 1928).[19] As a university professor, anthropologist, and archaeologist, Corrêa was considered an academic authority. Though highly regarded by many, Teles did not have a postsecondary degree, and was not viewed as an academic authority, particularly in physical anthropology. Corrêa promoted the idea that race played a role in conditioning the behavior of people, but he relied on "scientific," or physical, metrics—color, stature, cephalic index, head measurements, etc. (Corrêa 1919)—totally absent from the writings of Teles. He also criticized the idea of a primitive Aryan race.

Another critique of Teles came from the most influential intellectual in the liberal-democratic opposition to the authoritarian regime (1926–74) in Portugal: António Sérgio. Although he recognized the existence of a north-south division in Portugal, linked to differences in behavior, in geography and social features, Sérgio denied the racial factor any explanatory value. He explained the historical differences

portrayed by Teles in his depiction of a nation that shifted from agriculture to overseas trade not as the product of the action of races but
as outcomes of different economic policies (Sérgio 1977 [1925]).

In Salazar's pro-fascist New State, which strictly controlled the
teaching of history for four decades, two main representational schemas
of Portuguese national history and identity coexisted: a political schema,
deriving from Herculano, and an ethnic schema. The latter emphasized
the positive contributions of different ethnic groups in making up the
Portuguese, with special stress on the Lusitani contribution. The terms
Aryan and *Semite* virtually disappeared from discourse, probably because
of stigmatization linked to the racial policies of Nazis and Fascists. But
we still find them in a work of the 1960s that emphasizes Portuguese
identity as a harmonious fusion of the two (Langhans 1968).

Conclusion

Whatever it was about the 1970s that led to a stress on the difference
between north and south, there was some continuity with the constructions dating from the turn of the twentieth century. The idea of
a north-south division is still evoked in discussions by influential scholars, as well as in media depictions of behavioral and attitudinal differences within Portugal. What has generated these kinds of spatialized
accounts? Examining the intellectual constructs in Portugal of the notion
of north versus south as one of essential difference, we should recall that
the founding proponents of the division around the turn of the century
hailed mainly from the north—Teles, Sampaio, Brandão, and Pascoaes.
Even Oliveira Martins was closely linked to the north. It would be
simple enough to argue that this division was an invention of people
disillusioned with power located in the south, and it would not be
wrong: the invocation by northern writers was part of the construction
of a northern identity, centered in its main city, Porto, in opposition to
the "Significant Other" (Triandafyllidou 1998:593–612) the south, where
Lisbon is the dominant city.

However, any account of north-south differences would be incomplete without an examination of the real territorial differences at
play, and the historical conjunctures leading to an emphasis on the
difference between areas of the country in some historical moments
and a waning of such emphasis in others. So, we must remember that
there are broad differences in climate, physical features, patterns of land

ownership, and sociocultural patterns between northern and southern Portugal. Moreover, the idea of some kind of political north–south divide seems to endure over time, as the electoral results show.[20] But we must keep in mind that distinctions corresponding to different geographical spaces are contextually constructed and reproduced spatial representations. Also important is an effort to trace the social-class circuits of how racialized meanings get attached to spatialized cultural descriptions through time. Nowadays the ethno-racial factor, which was in an earlier period so important in the work of writers based in the north, has disappeared from political and intellectual discourse and from the media. It shows up often, however, in the everyday discourse of lower-class northerners who call southerners "Moors."[21] Therefore, in the late twentieth and early twenty-first centuries we find a racialized discourse not in the world of the intellectual elite, but in the realm of subaltern experience, not in writing but in the oral register. This discourse encodes the resentment of people who think the north, and its capital (Porto), are unjustly dominated by Lisbon and its surrounding region.

NOTES

1. When they refer to Portugal, most of the authors with which this essay is concerned are referring to the continental territory; therefore, I will not be referring to the case of the Atlantic islands (Azores and Madeira) that are also part of Portugal.

2. He further divided the country into twenty-three units of landscape (Ribeiro 1967 [1945]:145–55, 174–75).

3. Oliveria Martins (1957:19). Quoted in Catroga (1998:167–78).

4. In another work (Braga 1995 [1885]:72–73), he places the Celtic element from the North against the greater number of "Semites" in the "Spanish race."

5. A genealogy of the conception of the population of France as divided into two races, from the seventeenth century, is found in Poliakov (1974:16–28) and Foucault (1997:37–74). See Thierry, *Lettres sur l'histoire de France*, "Lettre XII," Paris, 1842.

6. Braga (1894:132) and (1995 [1885]:43, 58–59). Braga referred to other much later theories on race, which already correspond to an era of development of physical anthropology and the impact of Darwinism. But his basic outline is that of Thierry and Edwards. See Blanckaert (1988).

7. On the discussion of the proposals of Teófilo Braga see Matos (1998:324–32) and Catroga (1998:120–24).

8. On the beginnings of the "Aryan myth" and of modern anti-Semitism, see Poliakov (1974 [1971]:161–95), and Mosse (1978:35–127). The necessarily brief assertions made here about the various aspects of the Aryan theme come from this work and other fundamental works on racism: Snyder (1962:39–53); Hannaford (1996); Banton (1998). Also see Augstein (1996).

9. It is found in detail in the works quoted in the previous note, starting before European Romanticism.

10. Certainly there are several meanings attached to the word "race," even when used by the same author in the same work. See Mosse (1978:45) on the growing identification of the terms "people," "nation" and "race" in the second half of the nineteenth century.

11. It is worth emphasizing that the ideological trajectory of the notion of race was as follows: an emphasis on an Indo-European language morphed into a stress on biological Indo-Europeans, and from there to the celebration of national identities. See Thiesse (1999:172–79).

12. On this crisis see Cabral (1979).

13. The south is ambiguously defined as being the region which is below the Mondego River, or below the Tejo River. But unambiguously it was said by Teles to be populated by people "polluted" with "Semite blood." See Teles (1901:19).

14. Teles excepts Brazil from condemnation because, according to him, in Brazil agricultural colonization was carried out by northerners (Teles 1899:144).

15. The italics in both quotations from Teles are mine.

16. Teles (1968 [1905]:35) claimed explicitly that the Portuguese from the north belonged to the "great family of people, the Aryans or the Indo-Europeans."

17. With less rainfall, the landscapes of both the Alentejo and of the northeast contrast with the green that characterizes Pascoaes's home region even in summertime, and are associated here with the stereotypical traits of landscapes of the Middle East.

18. See Hannaford (1996:235–368). The topic of the north-south division surfaces in this work, which harbors a different interpretation of ethnic prejudice in Antiquity than that of Isaac (2004).

19. Viriato was a local leader who successfully resisted Roman domination for some time. He can be viewed as a Portuguese or an Iberian equivalent of the nationalist and mythical heroes Vercingectorix or Arminius.

20. The results of the last elections for the presidency (January 2006) show a clear division between north and south; the winner, the right-wing candidate, got the majority of his votes in the north (above the river Tejo). See the newspaper O público (23 Feb. 06, "Eleições presidenciais: resultados finais," 4).

21. Although in the Alentejo (the largest southern region of Portugal) northerners are called "galegos" (Galicians), there seems to be no equivalent in

the oral register of Lisbon subalterns for the dismissive "Moors" that is current in Porto. Neither is there an equivalent in the discourse of the elites for the popular one found among northerners.

REFERENCES

Albuquerque, Martim. 1974. *A consciência nacional portuguesa*. Lisbon: Ed. do Autor.

Augstein, Hannah Franziska. 1996. Introduction. In *Race, the origins of an idea, 1760–1850*, ed. Hannah Franziska Augstein, ix–xxxiii. Bristol: Thoemmes Press.

Banton, Michael. 1998 [1987]. *Racial theories*. Cambridge: Cambridge University Press.

———. 2000 [1980]. The idiom of race. In *Theories of race and racism*, ed. Les Back and John Solomos, 51–63. London: Routledge.

Barata, Francisco A. Corrêa. 1872. *As raças históricas da Península Ibérica*. Coimbra: Imprensa da Universidade.

Blanckaert, Claude. 1988. On the origins of French ethnology: William Edwards and the doctrine of race. In *Bones, bodies, behavior: essays on biological anthropology, history of anthropology*, ed. George W. Stocking Jr., 18–55. Madison: The University of Wisconsin Press.

Boas, Franz. 1962 [1928]. *Anthropology and modern life*. New York: W. W. Norton.

Bourdon, Albert-Alain. 1991. Économistes et régionalismes au Portugal au début du XX siècle. In *L'identité régionale: L'idée de région dans l'Europe du sud-ouest*, ed. Centre d'Études Nord du Portugal-Aquitaine (CENPA), 301–12. Paris: Éditions du Centre National de la Recherche Scientifique.

Braga, Teófilo. 1871. *Epopeias da raça Moçárabe*. Porto: Imprensa Portuguesa.

———1894. *A pátria portuguesa: o território e a raça*. Porto: Livraria Chardron.

———1995 [1885]. *O povo português nos seus costumes, crenças e tradições*, vol. I. Lisbon: Publicações Dom Quixote.

Brandão, Raúl. 1969. *Memórias*. Lisbon: Jornal do Foro.

Cabral, Manuel Villaverde. 1979. *Portugal na alvorada do século XX: Forças sociais, poder político e crescimento económico*. Lisbon: A Regra do Jogo.

———. 1992. Portugal e a Europa. Diferenças e semelhanças. *Análise Social* 118–119 (XXVII): 943–54.

Caro Baroja, Julio. 1990 [1956]. Sobre ideas raciales en España. In *Razas, pueblos y linajes*. Murcia: Universidad de Murcia.

Catroga, Fernando, et al. 1998. *História da história em Portugal, sécs. XIX–XX*. Lisbon: Temas & Debates.

Chillida, Gonzalo Álvarez. 2002. *El antisemitismo en España*. Madrid: Marcial Pons.

Corrêa, A. A. Mendes. 1919. *Raça e nacionalidade*. Porto: Renascença Portuguesa.

———. 1928. A Lusitânia pré-Romana. In *História de Portugal. Vol. 1*, ed. Damião Peres, 79–214. Barcelos: Portucalense Editora.

Daveau, Suzanne. 1995. *Portugal geográfico*. Lisbon: Edições João Sá da Costa.

Dias, Jorge. 1961. *Ensaios etnológicos*. Lisbon: Junta de Investigações do Ultramar.

Doyle, Don H. 2002. *Nations divided: America, Italy, and the Southern Question*. Athens: University of Georgia Press.

Fernandez, James W. 1997. The north-south axis in European popular cosmologies and the dynamic of the categorical. *American Anthropologist* 99, no. 4:725–28.

Foucault, Michel. 1997 [1976]. *Il faut défendre la société*. Paris: Hautes Études/Gallimard-Seuil.

França, Luís de. 1980. *O comportamento religioso da população portuguesa*. Lisbon: Moraes Editores, I.E.D.

Gibson, Mary. 1998. Biology or environment? Race and southern "deviance" in the writings of Italian criminologists, 1880–1920. In *Italy's Southern Question: Orientalism in one country*, ed. Jane Schneider, 99–115. Oxford: Berg.

Hannaford, Ivan. 1996. *Race: The history of an idea in the West*. Washington and Baltimore: The Woodrow Wilson Center Press/The Johns Hopkins University Press.

Harris, Marvin. 1968. *The rise of anthropological theory*. New York: HarperCollins.

Herculano, Alexandre. 1980–81 [1846]. História de Portugal, vol. I. Lisbon: Livraria Bertrand.

Isaac, Benjamin. 2004. *The invention of racism in classical antiquity*. Princeton and Oxford: Oxford University Press.

Juaristi, Jon. 2000. *El bosque imaginario: Genealogías míticas de los pueblos de Europa*. Madrid: Taurus.

Langhans, Almeida. 1968. *Antropologia luso-atlântica*. Lisbon: Parceria A. M. Pereira.

Leal, João. 1999. Mapping Mediterranean Portugal: Pastoral and counter-pastoral. *Nar. Umjet* 36, no. 1:9–31.

———. 2000. *Etnografias portuguesas (1870–1970): Cultura popular e identidade nacional*. Lisbon: Publicações Dom Quixote.

Matos, Sérgio Campos. 1998. *Historiografia e memória nacional no Portugal do século XIX (1846–1898)*. Lisbon: Edições Colibri.

Mosse, Georg L. 1978. *Toward the final solution: A history of European racism*. London: J. M. Dent & Sons.

Murguía, Manuel. 1865–66. *Historia de Galicia, I, II*. Lugo: Soto Freire.

———. 2000 [1889]. *El regionalismo gallego*. Santiago de Compostela: Librería Follas Novas.

O Público. 2006. January 23, "Presidenciais 2006 : resultados finais," 4.

Olender, Maurice. 1989. *Les langues du paradis. Aryens et Sémites: Un couple providentiel*. Paris: Gallimard-Le Seuil.

Oliveira Martins, Joaquim P. 1954 [1879]. *História da civilização ibérica*. Lisbon: Guimarães Editores.

———. 1917 [1879]. *História de Portugal, vol. I*. Lisbon: Parceria António Maria Pereira.

———. 1956 [1887]. *Fomento rural e emigração*. Lisbon: Guimarães Editores.

———. 1957. *Política e história, vol. II*. Lisbon: Guimarães Editores.

———. 1979 [1881]. *Portugal contemporâneo, vol. II*. Lisbon: Guimarães Editores.

Pascoaes, Teixeira de. 1978 [1920]. *Arte de ser português*. Lisbon: Delraux.

———. 1988 [1912] O espírito lusitano ou o saudosismo. In *Teixeira de Pascoaes. A saudade e o saudosismo*. Lisbon: Assírio & Alvim.

Poliakov, Léon. 1974 [1971]. *O mito ariano*. São Paulo: Editora Perspectiva.

Ribeiro, Orlando. 1967 [1945]. *Portugal, o Mediterrâneo e o Atlântico*. Lisbon: Livraria Sá da Costa Editora.

Sampaio, Alberto. 1923 [1892]. Ontem e hoje. In *Estudos históricos e económicos, vol. 1*, 429–46. Porto: Livraria Chardron.

Sardinha, António. 1961 [1927]. O sul contra o norte. In *À Sombra dos Pórticos*, 3–48. Lisbon: Editorial Restauração.

Sarmento, Francisco Martins.1884. Les lusitaniens. In *Congrès International d'Anthropologie et d'Archéologie Préhistoriques—compte rendu de la neuvième session à Lisbonne*, 393–431. Lisbon : Tip. da Academia Real das Ciências.

Seabra, Daniel. 1999. *Mágico Porto, vence por nós*. Masters thesis, University of Minho. Braga: Universidade do Minho.

Sérgio, António. 1977 [1925]. *Ensaios, vol. II*. Lisbon: Livraria Sá da Costa Editora.

Severo, Ricardo. 1924 [1911]. *Origens da nacionalidade portuguesa*. Coimbra: Imprensa da Universidade.

Snyder, Louis L. 1962. *The idea of racialism*. Princeton: Van Nostrand.

Sternhell, Zeev. 1978. *La droite révolutionnaire 1885–1914: Les origines françaises du fascisme*. Paris: Éditions du Seuil.

Teles, Basílio. 1899. *O problema agrícola*. Porto: Livraria Chardron.

———. 1901. *Estudos históricos e económicos*. Porto: Livraria Chardron.

———. 1916. *A Inglaterra pacifista*. Porto: Livraria Figueirinhas.

———. 1968 [1905]. *Do Ultimatum ao 31 de Janeiro*. Lisbon: Portugália.

Thierry, Augustin. 1842. *Lettres sur l'histoire de France* (7 ed.). Paris: Just Tessier.

Thiesse, Anne-Marie. 1999. *La création des identités nationales*. Paris: Éditions du Seuil.

Triandafyllidou, Anna. 1998. National identity and the "other." *Ethnic and Racial Studies* 21, no. 4:593–612.

Vilhena, Júlio de. 1873. *As raças históricas da península ibérica e a sua influência no direito português*. Coimbra: Imprensa da Universidade.

Wulff, Fernando. 2003. *Las esencias patrias*. Barcelona: Crítica.

CHAPTER 10

Local Correspondence

A Village Writer's Contribution to the Cultural Production of Regionality in the Alto Douro of Northern Portugal

SHAWN S. PARKHURST

INTRODUCTION

The spatial problematic in the contemporary social sciences has a tendency to congeal into a litany of "the global," "the national," and "the local," with the mediate levels of reality favored by anthropologists—Herzfeld's "militant middle ground," for example (Herzfeld 2001:10)—left out of the mix. A premise of this chapter is that "the regional" is good to think with, not only because of its sociocultural reality but also because it can loosen the welds joining the terms of the conventional theoretical recitative (Soja 1989; Entrikin 1991). It also offers a usefully dislocated understanding of circulation, "the basis of all culture" (Urban 1996:xiii).

The ethnographic context in which I will elaborate on regional considerations is the Alto Douro region of northern Portugal, a small area, even in Portuguese terms.[1] The zone of port wine production, the Alto Douro was the first effective demarcated wine region in the world (Pereira 1996:182). In 1756, the Portuguese state set off the area and began regulating wine production there as a way of securing a reliable source of foreign exchange. After a series of dissolutions and redemarcations, from the 1930s until the 1990s the state monitored production of grapes within the region through the Casa do Douro (House of the Douro), the winegrowers association in the city of Peso da Régua. Régua lies along a sweeping bend of the Douro River below

225

the plunging, terraced slopes that make the Alto Douro the most to-pographically boxed-in wine region in the world (Guichard 1992:332). The city's population is about 10,000.[2] Like many cities of a similar size in Portugal, Régua serves as a regional administrative and economic core. Through the 1990s, the institution decided yearly on each grower's *benefício*—a document certifying how many of a grower's grapes could be sold for port wine prices.[3] Régua is also a regional center of wine storage, and the key point of wine transport to Porto, the wine's name-sake, and Portugal's second-largest city, on the northern Atlantic coast. (Vila Nova de Gaia, just across the Douro River south of Porto, is now the main entrepôt for port wine.)

The importance of Régua makes it tempting to ignore the re-gional periphery—villages nestled high above the river among vine terraces dynamited out of fractured schist. From a distance, such villages appear identically inserted into the vineyard landscape. Up close, though, we see that, within, they harbor dramatic social (most importantly, class and gender) division, and that between villages there is significant eco-logical variation and social conflict. Consider, for example, Socalcos,[4] a village of three hundred where I spent most of my time during fifteen months of fieldwork in the Alto Douro, distributed across the years 1993, '94, '96, and '99. In much of the Alto Douro, economic polar-ization, and accompanying social domination, approach that of the Alentejo region of southern Portugal, the ground zero of rural Portu-guese social inequality (Bennema 1992:249; 1996; Costa 1997). Socalcos shares fully in this regionally characteristic social inequality. In Socalcos, male predominance in the gendered balance of power is also notewor-thy (Parkhurst 1999, 2000), especially in a broader northwestern Iberian social landscape reputed to manifest considerable gender equality (Brøgger and Gilmore 1997; for a forceful critique, see Roseman and Kelley 1999). Between villages there is conflict. The villages of Socalcos and Cimo illustrate this. Both villages lie fully within the Douro Demar-cated Zone, within the same parish, only a mile from each other. Both have about three hundred residents. But they differ in that Cimo is five hundred feet higher than Socalcos. This downgrades the quality as-signed its vineyards by the Casa do Douro.[5] Related to this difference, Socalcos growers own, on average, more vineyard (exchange-oriented) land than do Cimo growers, who own more subsistence-oriented land and are thus considered comparatively "rustic" (by Socalcans). Though Cimans consider themselves the equals of Socalcans, Socalcos' ecological features and its role as parish seat put the Cimans on the defensive. Despite this division, however, the concrete public signs traveling a regional circuit from Socalcos tend to represent social placidity.

My task in this chapter is to examine how the signs representing regional culture are generated in their local context. This should take us a good distance toward a fuller grasp of "regionality"—which I define as a sense of regional identification and difference felt, thought, and acted, with variable haziness and precision, by local actors (see Pina-Cabral 1989, 1991). Regionality is structured in significant part by regional culture, but not reducible to it. Many of the signs forming regional culture come in the form of written discourse. While it is common now (Clifford and Marcus 1986) to reflect on how anthropologists use writing in constructing their units of analysis, it is worth emphasizing that more locally oriented social actors also often use writing in cultural production. Print, in particular, has significant regional importance, and in focusing attention on it I have been influenced by Benedict Anderson's now classic (1991 [1983]) analysis of the role of "print capitalism" in the formation of nationalism, and by Roseman's important (1997) recasting of Anderson in her analysis of a "non-state nation." I aim in part to determine how print is equipped to do cultural work in social spaces other than—if generally dependent on—the national. As regional theorist Anssi Paasi has emphasized, regional newspapers help define the experience of regional commonalities by circulating stereotypes designed to attract the largest number of readers possible (Paasi 1986:129). While here I concentrate mainly on the written word, my analysis is consistent with the approach to rhetorical movement—involving transformations between writing, speech, and action—developed by Michael Herzfeld (1985) and James Fernandez (1986).[6]

In the first part of the chapter, I describe the work done by regional newspapers in representing the Alto Douro region as a cultural entity. In the second, longer, part, I read the village of Socalcos through the regional newspapers as a way of conveying how localities fit themselves to the region, and the region to themselves, through the representations moving to and from the regional core.

THE REGIONAL PRESS AND REPRESENTATION

Since 1863, Régua has been the home of at least nineteen different newspapers, ten of which have, judging from their titles, been explicitly pitched at representing the Alto Douro Region (Tóro 1946: unpaginated).[7] Currently there are two important newspapers published in Régua that address the interests of the region, *Notícias do Douro* and *O Arrais*. *Notícias do Douro* is by far the older paper, founded in 1934. (*O Arrais* was founded in 1978.) Both papers sport titles printed in red, and next to these images of *barcos rabelos*—the long-ruddered boats essential until the turn of the twentieth century for the transport of wine to Porto, and an icon of the Alto Douro. While below its title *Notícias do Douro* proclaims itself "The Weekly of the Demarcated Region of the Douro," *O Arrais* trumpets that it is "An Independent Weekly for the Defense of the Alto Douro."

The regional newspapers are systematic defenders of the political and economic operations of the Casa do Douro, the Alto Douro's core regional institution. As these operations depend on political leadership and staffing drawn largely from the Baixo Corgo subregion, this means a de facto support for the political dominance of one subregion over the other in the key economic regulatory apparatus.[8] The other cities with core-like functions in the Alto Douro—namely Lamego and Vila Real—are located in, or on the edge of, the Baixo Corgo.

Though the regional newspapers focus attention on the politics of the Alto Douro economy, they also portray the Alto Douro as a region with a distinctive culture. To do so, the papers abstract greatly, ignoring local differentiation. As the images used are often developed by writers based in Régua or the Baixo Corgo, the newspapers work to produce a sense of the region as culturally homogeneous, while reproducing Régua's importance as the site of regional hegemony.

Nearly every issue of *O Arrais* or *Notícias do Douro* contains portraits of the Alto Douro dedicated to interpreting the human meaning of the regional landscape. The article "Douro: Landscape of Abundance" (Monteiro 1998) is a good example. Here we read that the author has always been moved by "the Herculean grandeur of the Douro." The terraces "erected by the hands of men and women . . . frame a landscape of abundance" and "resemble altars" to a classical pagan god. The whole landscape, with its terraces and "traditional *quintas* [wine estates]" of an "unmistakable architectural type" is a "reality of the permanent confrontation between man, . . . schist, . . . the weather, . . . and . . . the markets," but it is also a "dream" landscape illumined by "Mediterranean light." In the latter part of the essay we learn that

[t]he cultural ties uniting generations through the centuries adapt themselves to the realities of today. But the Douro[9] remains faithful to the roots of time and its solitary love of the land.

And the wine—Noble Wine—as noble as the sweat which produces it, remains the most valuable piece of art in the museum of [the region's] memories. (ibid.)

The animating idea of Monteiro's essay seems to be that landscape and wine underpin the culture of the Alto Douro region. Yet clearly Monteiro acknowledges that these very material realities are cultural, as well. In a sense, then, there seem to be two levels of culture: one deposited in time immemorial, and based in the transmutation of human body, soil, and grape; the other located closer to the surface current of change. Monteiro stresses the former level: in his depiction of the Alto Douro we see the remains of work done (estate houses, briefly, but above all the river, and wine), but no villages, working people, or subregional differences to disturb this peacefully monolithic region.

Representations of the region as a cultural entity work systematically not just to mirror the region, but to fashion it as well, in a process deriving from what Clifford Geertz long ago specified as culture's dual orientation: that is, culture is always a model *of* reality *and* a model *for* reality. For Geertz such modeling worked via "public symbols." Journalists contribute to this proactive modeling by abstracting certain elements from a varied regional reality, ennobling them and handing them back as a mirror to a self-satisfied (largely bourgeois) regional public. The imagery comes laden with an overarching spatial order of regional core and periphery. Such mediated homogenization and domination cannot hope to work, however, without a reverse circulation of cultural materials from periphery to core.

LOCAL STORIES

For cultural "regionalization" to work, the Régua newspapers must establish and maintain a readership in the various subregions of the Alto Douro. This occurs through a sophisticated interpellation—or textual "hailing" (Althusser 1971:127–86; Silverman 1983:219–22)—of the readers from these communities as "regional people." In order for this interpellation to work, acknowledgment of and appeal to local interests is imperative.

In this section I examine a set of stories that speak to how a peripheralized locality can use the core media to make itself appear more authentically regional. For nearly fifteen years a local correspondent contributed articles on Socalcos parish to *O Arrais* and *Notícias do Douro*. The author, Onésimo Azevedo, is a slender elderly man with smooth, delicate skin, thick glasses, and a taste for subdued suits and trilby-style hats. After a few meetings he presented me with sixteen articles published between 1980 and 1992, bound together under a transparent plastic cover, tinted blue, with the title "Guide-Book to Socalcos." Because the articles make few explicit references to Socalcos' regional context, they prompt questions about how intensely local representation can work to produce regionality from the periphery.

Article 1, published in 1980, is a notice about the fortieth anniversary of the opening of the road that inaugurated motorized transport between Socalcos and the town of Pinhão, some four miles away. The improvement, which ended "the people's isolation" and linked "their land . . . to the rest of the country," was the doing of the "local patriot" José Teixeira.[10] While the article refers to Socalcos in the context of the "rest of the country," the closest thing to an explicit reference to the region is the fleeting mention of "port wine." Article 2, also from 1980, is a transcription of a description of Socalcos parish originally published in a 1758 geographical dictionary. Mr. Azevedo considers the entry important for indicating sites in Socalcos of archaeological interest because they were occupied by Romans and Moors. The article includes no spatial framing of the transcription, regional or otherwise.

The next article, published in 1986, is about the celebration of the fiftieth anniversary of the Casa do Povo (the town hall). Such Casas, promoted by former dictator António Salazar, were built in nearly all Portuguese parishes in the 1930s to provide medical services, unemployment relief, and recreation, and thus served as the local mainstays of Salazar's corporatist regime. Mr. Azevedo claims that it is time to pay homage to the men—and he capitalizes "MEN"—responsible for the installation of the "health, sports and cultural" center that contributed to the development of Socalcos.

In 1987, three articles were published. Article 4 is a brief report on the pollution of the water issuing from the main fountain in Socalcos, constructed in 1874, and a call to the parish government to solve the problem. No reference to the region is made, but the national minister for public works in 1874 is named. Article 5 is a criticism of the vandalism that destroyed the parish's train stop after the Portuguese Railroad removed all employees from the site in the early 1980s, and an appeal to the railroad to rebuild the station for the "poor rural workers" who must wait for the train in bad weather. The first emphatic reference to the locality's regional context is found in this article, where we read: "[T]he vandalism which has spread across the country like a cursed plague could not fail to reach this region, which God seems to have blessed by endowing it with fertile land which produces that nectar, worthy of gods, called port wine." Article 6 is a call to Socalcos villagers to reject the parish council's decision to build a stairway in the village that would, in Mr. Azevedo's view, be detrimental to the community. It makes no reference that could be construed as regional.

Article 7, published in 1989, is a notice about the fiftieth anniversary of the introduction of electricity in the village and the thirtieth anniversary of the remodeling of the primary school. Mr. Azevedo uses these occasions to remind Socalcos readers to vote in the upcoming local elections for the candidates representing "the path of progress," defined by their attention to water and sewage systems, along with other infrastructure improvements. While the "European" frame is invoked, the region is not.

1990 saw a spate of six articles. Article 8 is a reminiscence about a Galician man who settled in Socalcos parish after bringing "various Galego workers" to the area at the turn of the century. The Galicians helped rebuild the vineyards destroyed by phylloxera, a vine infestation that seriously harmed "the winegrowers not only of the region, but of the whole of Europe." Article 9 is a centennial biography of the important nineteenth-century writer Camilo Castelo Branco, who stayed for some days in Socalcos in 1848. Only the "north of Portugal" is invoked as an extra-local reference. Article 10 is a call for the parish council of Socalcos to demand the parish's due from the Municipality of Altasparedes in preparing to be "a part of [the] Europe" to be constructed according to the convergence criteria of the Maastricht treaty. Article 11, published in June, is a reflection on the upcoming "popular saints" festivals (those for Saint Anthony, Saint John, and Saint Peter). Mr. Azevedo anticipates that the youth of 1990 will avoid traditional revelry, because they are as closed to "cultural expressions" or "traditions" as the youth of his generation were open to them. Socalcos' amateur theatre, band, and traditional dances have disappeared. Mr. Azevedo evinces no concern with regional or other levels beyond the local and the national. Article 12 is a recollection of the Socalcos Shoemaker's Shop between 1934 and 1945, at the time a "social center of the parish" and the "seat of local 'wisdom.' " Here the local "scholars" (Mr. Azevedo's quotation marks) met to discuss the contents of the newspaper delivered daily to the shop. The men would discuss "any subject, from the problems of the community to international politics." Regional subjects would presumably count among these, but are not mentioned. Article 13, published in December, is a notice about the fiftieth anniversary of the death of José Teixeira (mentioned in article 1), an "illustrious" local figure to whom Socalcos, a "land . . . blessed by God," "owes so much." Teixeira, we read, was noteworthy for his work on behalf of the region. This included joining other winegrowers in the mid-1920s to petition the minister of agriculture for the creation of the entrepôt for port wine in Vila Nova de Gaia, across the river from Porto. Also important were his work for the locality, including the founding of the Casa do Povo, for which, Mr. Azevedo says, the residents of Socalcos should pay him homage.

The three final articles in the collection are from 1992. Article 14 recounts the history of the locality over the last 2, 500 years. It opens by describing Socalcos as lying in the center of the Douro. The village is described as aesthetically beautiful, and very old. The description serves as a preamble to the complete transcription of the charter of rights and duties granted to Socalcos in the 1160s by powerful political figures, making it the recipient of one of the "first charters of local rights granted in the ancient county of *Portucale*."[11] Following the transcription, Mr. Azevedo conveys his sense of the charter's importance in a few short lines: "There are already innumerable reasons to have pride in being from Socalcos. However, these further traces of the past retrieved from the dust of time reinforce the pride we feel in having been born in this old and beautiful part of Portugal." Article 15 is a retrospective complaint about the visit to Socalcos in 1988 of Mário Soares, at the time president of Portugal. The "land of the Douro," "which for long years has been watered by the Portuguese sweat of those who draw their sustenance from it, thus contributing humbly, but nobly, to the enrichment of the country," is used to frame the complaint that Socalcos did not get the chance to greet Soares properly, and wants, as a good Portuguese community, to erect a plaque commemorating the visit. The final article in the collection, number 16, is an excursion into the past comparable to article 14 in being composed mostly of an expanded transcription of the document transcribed in article 2. Mr. Azevedo ends this last article by emphasizing that the document demonstrates very well how "the history of Socalcos stretches back into the dust of time," and is an "old noble land in the corner of the world that is Portugal."

How are relations of regional periphery and core illuminated by this local writing? Because regional references are comparatively scarce, and national references relatively abundant, it might seem that Mr. Azevedo considered a regional identity for Socalcos less important than the village's national identity.[12] The issue of regionality is far from laid to rest with this, however. To get a fuller sense of how written periphery-core relations work in constituting regionality we must consider both the rhetorical character of the articles and the full meaning of their publication in newspapers that trumpet their regional identities on the front page of every issue. I will take up these matters in turn.

Of crucial importance is that articles submitted *from* peripheral localities are always *about* the localities, not about regional matters labeled as such, which are the province of writers from the regional core towns of Régua, Lamego, or Vila Real. Such local-regional slippage is part of the regional hegemony of the core. Being about Socalcos does not mean that articles manifest no thematic variation, however. The theme can be Historical Socalcos or Political Socalcos, and these themes can be further divided. The importance of such variation: thematizing Socalcos differently can have implications for the "regionality" of an article. What Terence Turner has argued about genre—that "the essential cultural information coded in different genres of narrative expression . . . relates to different levels or modes of social consciousness" (Turner 1988:273)—seems to apply to Socalcos. But while Turner views the spatial constitution of distinctive societies to lead to different forms of historical consciousness, I view it as at least equally important to ask how representing time differently can inflect a sense of social space.

Historical Socalcos is the theme of eleven articles, which are divided between what I call "commemorative" and "historicist" emphases. I choose these rubrics for their ability to convey a sense of temporally informed social function.[13] Articles 1, 3, 7, 9, and 13 are commemorative articles, focusing on cyclical anniversaries such as the opening of the Socalcos-Pinhão road and the Casa do Povo. The historicist articles, in contrast, stress not the recycling of important historical events but the ephemerality of the irretrievable past. An example of an historicist article is article number 2 (the transcription of an entry in an old geographical dictionary). Others in this vein are 8, 11, 12, 14, and 16. Quite different from articles on Historical Socalcos are those concerned with Political Socalcos. These focus on politics in the here and now. Number 6, for example, calls on the parish government to halt plans for a new public stairway. There are four others: 4, 5, 10, and 15.

These classifications help us read the articles for their "local regionality," (1) in terms of the audiences being presupposed, and (2) in terms of the writer's intended effect. The easiest to grasp in such terms are the political articles. As unvarnished attempts to intervene directly in current local political issues, these address a local audience. In contrast, the historical articles appear to be directed at a more diffuse audience. It makes sense that degree of audience diffuseness would vary with the degree of distance from the here and now of the particular historical topic. Thus, as commemorative articles emphasize the continuing presence of the past, they aim at a more locally delimited audience, calling for local people to engage in the commemorations being noted: in article 3, Mr. Azevedo writes that "[t]he people of Socalcos should show gratitude by not letting [the founding of the Casa do Povo] pass without notice." By contrast, in historicist articles the here and now dissolves. Here, a further dispersion of the imagined audience is suggested, with the limit set at the bounds of the region. Articles focusing on the age of Socalcos (16) and disappeared practices (11) should be read as attempts to establish Socalcos' distinction from (in the case of the former) and similarity to (in the case of the latter) its wider regional surround.

Arguably, Mr. Azevedo did indeed imagine a regional audience for at least some of his articles. On a number of visits to his home I consulted Mr. Azevedo's personal archive, where I found copies of letters he had sent to both regional and national papers thanking them for printing his articles. His attention to the spatial orientations of the newspapers to which he was writing is clear from the letters: their phrasing is identical except for one word. To the national papers he writes, "Your publication of the articles is all the more praiseworthy when it is considered that this remains the only way for the small communities [terras] of the interior to get their voices heard." In the letters to O Arrais, "interior" is replaced with "Region" [sic]. The word change suggests that Mr. Azevedo operated with one sense of region— "the interior"—in the national media context and another sense in the regional media context. Most importantly, it is in the letter to *O Arrais* that the term *region* is used, which suggests a clear sense of membership in the particular named region that *O Arrais* explicitly addresses. Also to the point is that after 1980, the archive only holds letters to *O Arrais*. Since the national papers had been willing to publish his articles, this shift suggests that Mr. Azevedo decided to focus his attention entirely on a Duriense readership. There is also reason to believe that Mr. Azevedo understood the Alto Douro to be culturally anchored in Régua. During the 1980s a number of other newspapers were headquartered near the Alto Douro and sometimes distributed into the region; these included *Notícias da Beira, Repórter do Marão, Voz do Nordeste,* and *Mensageiro* (Pedrosa 1991:260), as well as *Voz de Trás-os-Montes*. Still, Mr. Azevedo devoted himself to the Alto Douro papers, published in Régua. There is good reason to believe, then, that Mr. Azevedo dispenses with explicit invocations of the region because he can assume a regional audience. Yet note that different themes imply different imagined audiences, as I have suggested. Moreover, it stands to reason that the audiences are imagined not just by the author, but also by particular readers of the articles.

The dominant audience for the historicist articles would appear to be regional. These articles have the least direct relationship with current local political developments.[14] Assuming a regional readership, it makes local sense to emphasize the distinction Socalcos has by virtue of its special relationship with national history: Socalcos can claim one of the oldest "national charters" in the region, as well as an entry in a venerable national geographical dictionary; for these reasons Mr. Azevedo can claim a prestigious kind of regional specificity for his locality. Local distinctiveness in national terms cannot fail to be distinctiveness in regional terms—if this distinctiveness has a largely regional audience. Whatever pride the Socalcos audience took in the articles would have depended on imagining a regional readership learning about the village's distinction.

The imagined readership for the commemorative articles would seem more clearly split between regional and local audiences. Here, local distinction is depicted for clearly local, and fairly immediate, reasons. At the same time, there is no mistaking that the local figures behind the events commemorated—especially Mr. Teixeira—are portrayed as figures worthy of the respect of the entire readership, which is potentially a regional one.

Finally, with the articles on local politics the primary imagined audience can only be the local one: the calls to local action can only be answered by local actors, especially in voting. Yet the articles can only work their desired effects of shaming local people into action before a (secondary) regional audience if the (primary) local audience feels it is under scrutiny by a wider world. Local knowledge of the writer's involvement in an apparatus for regional representation raises important issues about how Socalcos is positioned within the regionality constructed by publication.

To this point the focus has been the writing, first as a representation *of* the region from the core and then as a representation from locality *to* the region. But this is not enough. In the pages that follow I attempt to show how writing can be understood as informed by the divisions, mediations, movements, and relations found in and around the village.

To portray how local relations are regionalized in Mr. Azevedo's writing, we must comprehend his social position, as this provided him with the form of literacy required for access to newspapers, and contoured his selection of topics in fashioning his depictions of Socalcos. In what follows, I begin with Mr. Azevedo's alignment in the local class division, followed by gender position, family linkage, and place in local politics. After describing his "location," I explore the representational consequences of Mr. Azevedo's placement in all of these social-spatial levels. That is, I interpret his representations of Socalcos as cultural selections grounded by his particular social footing.

The Writer's Divisions

In Portugal, literacy was a particularly potent means of domination until the 1974 Revolution (Mónica 1978). Even today, the rule of thumb in the Alto Douro is that if you are over fifty and can read and write you likely come from a landowning background and are male.[15] Mr. Azevedo conforms to this rule.

Throughout his adult life, Mr. Azevedo has been a medium landholder in Socalcos. In the early 1960s his vineyard holdings were already fairly large, totaling some three and one half hectares.[16] Additionally, he was an *ajuntador*—a man who organizes the delivery of grapes from smallholders to wine firms for a commission paid by the firm—from the

1950s into the 1980s, when he began to turn his land and some of his work as *ajuntador* over to his son, Raul. He is from an "old" family, and related through sundry consanguineous, affinal, and spiritual kinship ties to various families of high standing in Socalcos. In 1994 he was the symbolic, though not the practical, head of Socalcos' second largest land-holding family. Mr. Azevedo treasures the age of his family's association with Socalcos village, and has gone to great lengths to document the kinship ties between his ancestral *casa* (house) and most of the other historically important *casas* in Socalcos. Mr. Azevedo likes to stress the antiquity of his family's physical house, claiming that it was built in the sixteenth century. It seems that the first family members to own it were aunts of his mother's mother, in whose names it was registered in 1875. Mr. Azevedo enlarged the house significantly, and resided in it at regular intervals. While there, he and his wife were always attended by local servant girls. Currently, Mr. Azevedo's grandson resides in the house.[17]

When Mr. Azevedo was born (in 1915), the economic standing of his family was in significant decline. This helps explain some of the fuzziness around Mr. Azevedo's "belonging to" Socalcos. He was born near Porto, where his mother had gone to work as a household servant, and he spent a significant portion of his life outside of Socalcos, working his way up socially through clerkships in various large Portuguese enterprises, and his way around northern Portugal in doing so. His profession provided him with significant writing skills in Socalcos terms. That the Socalcos context remained significant to him can be inferred from the pattern of his movements through the years. His mother took him as an infant to Socalcos, and he lived in the ancestral home until the age of six, when he returned with his mother to live in the Porto area for two years. At eight he returned to Socalcos with his mother, where he lived in the family home until he was about thirteen. At this age he moved to Régua, and then to Porto, working as a clerk and, in the latter city, attending Commercial School. At about twenty he returned to Socalcos, worked the family holdings he inherited after his mother's death for a number of years, married a young woman from Socalcos, and after four years in the village returned to Porto as an administrator for a large construction company. He worked up the ranks in this company. At a certain point he hired servant girls from Socalcos to attend to his Porto residence, thus adding further social links between his Porto and Socalcos identities.

Mr. Azevedo retained his property in Socalcos in the meantime, and used his salary—ample for the time—to purchase more. He contracted with caretakers on a half-share basis to maintain his vineyards and his other agricultural holdings, often returning to Socalcos on the weekends to inspect the work and issue instructions. On his typewriter Mr. Azevedo produced densely detailed instructions for vineyard work. He must have delivered these verbally, however, for his two most enduring caretakers were illiterate.

Mr. Azevedo's location in the social structure of Socalcos and his somewhat "ex-centric" relation to the locality were further accented by his role in local politics. With the toppling of the fifty-year-old authoritarian regime in 1974, parish governments were dissolved, and "Administrative Commissions" put in their place. In Socalcos the administrative commission governed until 1977, when the first fully democratically elected local government began operating.[18] Mr. Azevedo was the president of the administrative commission. Then his Socialist Party list was elected three times in succession over the Social Democrats' lists to run the Socalcos parish government. To come to power and maintain it, Mr. Azevedo needed a certain cachet. His gender gave him one basic component of electability, but successful candidates needed a prominence that came with class position, dense familial interconnections, and "cultivation." Mr. Azevedo had these. In the eyes of the local electorate, his "cultivation" was exemplified by the literacy required by his managerial positions.[19]

His kin connections worked to locate Mr. Azevedo clearly on one side of a local political divide, which crosscut the social class divide between large and small vineyard owners and which fractured kinship ties.[20] The political divide set those critical of the old regime against those who had supported it and had taken local office under its tutelage. Mr. Azevedo was tied by both "real" and spiritual kinship to the most prominent local figure in the national fight against the Salazar-Caetano regime, and benefited from this figure's popularity. Moreover, Mr. Azevedo's running mates included a large number of kin. In addition to himself, the administrative commission included two members from Cimo and two from Socalcos proper. The latter were second cousins of the president. In the first election, in 1977, there were six members elected to the parish assembly—which has nominal approval/veto power over council initiatives—in addition to Mr. Azevedo:[21] three from Cimo and three from Socalcos. Each of the latter three was related to Mr. Azevedo through kinship, either as second cousin or more closely. It is not surprising, then, that the member from Socalcos elected to one of the two positions on the parish council was a relative. In the 1980 election, there seems to have been a shift, measurable in terms of the residence, the familial ties, and the political alignment of the assembly members. In this year three members of the assembly were from Socalcos, two from Cimo, and two from elsewhere in the parish. Apparently there was a need to appeal more than previously to parish voters from outside of the settlement of Socalcos. At least as significant, though, is that two of the Socalcos men on the assembly list were not related to the council president, and were, moreover, linked to the pre-1974 local political regime. Still, in 1980 Mr. Azevedo retained a kinsman and political ally on the list. In Mr. Azevedo's last term in office, there seems to have been a settling down after the threatened political shift. The assembly had more members, and there was a very even distribution of members across the parish's localities: three from Socalcos, three from Cimo, and three from the hamlet of Vale. Social adversaries disappeared from among the Socalcos members.

By the mid-1980s, when he decided not to run again, Mr. Azevedo had enjoyed twelve years in local office and a parish council composed of significant numbers of Socalcos villagers who were also kin and political allies. In negotiating local social divisions he had operated from a position on the strong side of the political fracture through the mobilization of familial ties. It would be surprising if those divisions failed to show up in his representations of the locality, but equally unlikely that they could be read off from the articles in a straightforward way. In fact the divisive character of the writer's local backdrop leads him to foreground particular kinds of unity, so strongly that the backdrop is effectively erased.

PAPER-THIN UNITIES

In analyzing Mr. Azevedo's representations of Socalcos, it is useful to recall the different genres he employs. It is precisely in the explicitly political writings that the reader gets the strongest sense of division. But what kind of division is this? No names are mentioned, no local social conflicts detailed at all. It is as if the sense of immediacy generating the articles leads Mr. Azevedo to veil the divisions in vagueness, so as not to generate recriminations. Thus, in article 4, the people of Socalcos are characterized sweepingly as "hard-working," and therefore meriting decent treatment by the parish council, which is left undescribed. In article 5, the only social referents are "vandals" and people who use the ruined railway station, "the majority of which are rural workers." In article 6 there is a highly generic division invoked between "those who only look out for themselves"—found on the parish council—and the collective social body made up of those "who work for the land, giving it their whole life, pouring their sweat into it."

The rest of the political articles make similarly abstract distinctions between "the people of the village" and some kind of force or intent that works against "the people." It is likely, of course, that this division refigures an enduring concrete political division found in the village. Mr. Azevedo's political battles in the village confirm this: there was an "old-guard" political faction aligned with the Salazar-Caetano regime that his own faction challenged successfully after the Revolution and that challenged him in turn a few years later by, for instance, publicly accusing him of appealing to the Casa do Douro to cut the *benefício* of Socalcos' winegrowers. These factions were contoured by class and gender divisions in the village, and the divisions between Socalcos and Cimo (see Parkhurst 2000:97–131; 216–46). Yet Mr. Azevedo's political articles—all of which he wrote after leaving office—disguise these factions, while depending on them for their meaning. This suggests the simultaneous volatility and durability of the factionalism.

Precisely because they are less engaged with immediate political circumstances, the historical articles offer a clearer optic on Socalcos' social divisions. Not surprisingly (given Mr. Azevedo's high social standing) the big landowners are represented as the durable, defining elements of Socalcos. In article 3, Mr. Azevedo invokes the memory of a Mr. Teixeira, "great landowner" and patron of Socalcos, José Pimentel, a renowned local medical doctor, another Mr. Teixeira (a cousin of the first), who occupied a place in the national government during and after the Salazar regime, two of Socalcos' past priests, and Dr. Passos, prominent in the national government. The reader is told that Socalcos owes a great deal to these men who "contributed much toward the realization of this work [the Casa do Povo] 50 years ago." The same sort of lionization, concentrated mainly on Mr. Teixeira, can be found in other articles. Nearly all of the commemorative articles share a focus on the great men (the wealthy or the nationally noteworthy) associated with Socalcos and providing it with durable cultural value.[22]

Representatives from the lower side of the class divide are not completely absent, but they inhabit a kind of oblivion from which Mr. Azevedo retrieves them as representatives of ephemerality. In article 8, for example, Mr. Azevedo singles out a Galician immigrant for becoming a true "Socalcan" by being absorbed by the locality. In article 11 the author draws attention to Socalcos' long-dissolved theatre group. Among those named are men and women from both sides of the class divide, but particular attention is paid two men of scanty means who worked respectively as festival auctioneer and fireworks specialist, both activities that Mr. Azevedo feels have disappeared or declined in quality. In article 12, which describes Mr. Azevedo's memory of the "intellectual" (his quotation marks) center of the village, the reader learns that the shoemaker was an "autodidact," and thus typical of the village, that the mail carrier who brought the newspaper to the shop was a woman, and that a group of men—small landowners, caretakers for larger owners, and local employees of the Portuguese Railroad—frequented the shop. The scene is described with a sort of ironic affection for things past, never to return. Especially noteworthy is the absence from the scene of each and every one of the notable figures extolled in article 3. Engaged as they were in the works that define the durable heart of Socalcos' lastingly distinctive character, these latter men were, we can infer, not given to the frivolous sociability of those common folk. The best illustration of the difference in the social meanings attributed to people on either side of the class divide comes in article 1, which combines commemorative and historicist themes. In this article, "the great landowner," Mr. Teixeira, is commemorated for his "progressiveness" in organizing the construction of Socalcos' first road for automobile traffic. Later in the article, various oxcart drivers are invoked as the ephemeral incarnations of "primitiveness": "As progress does not agree with primitivism," we read, "its advent meant the end of the oxcart era."

Thus, in the rhetorical world we are examining, the upper class is characterized by both its durable contributions and the progress it spearheads, while the lower is presented as primitive and ephemeral. Mr. Azevedo's position on one side of the divide cannot be neutralized by what he considers his dispassionate view on the local facts. Further exploration of his biases requires a consideration of gender division in his articles, and of his position as a type of migrant returned to Socalcos.

The gendered division of Socalcos is indeed expressed in Mr. Azevedo's writing, but, like class division, this expression is by no means straightforward. Once again, in fact, it varies with the genre of the article. In the political articles, gender is even less visible than class as a concrete referent. In the historical articles, it is more obviously present, but, like class, represented differently in commemorative and historicist articles; women are mentioned only in the historicist articles. Consider the article commemorating the founding of the Casa do Povo. We read, "The house which 50 years ago a dedicated group of MEN, lovers of their land, built. MEN who have already left us. MEN who physically no longer exist! Only the CASA DO POVO remains, our house, that they bequeathed us." For Mr. Azevedo, just as the upper class embodies progress and Socalcos' essence, so does the MALE side of the gender division.[23]

Like the lower classes, women are found exclusively in the articles focused on the ephemeral. "The wife and children" of the Galician immigrant of article 8 is the first mention of a woman. A more extensive comment on women and their role in local life comes in article 11: the long defunct theatre group seems to have been made up of as many women as men, but it is a local feature defined mainly by its absence. In the same article, women are mentioned again only as participants in traditional dances, which have long disappeared. Finally, the mail carrier who delivered the newspaper that fueled the discussion of the local "intellectuals" (all men) was "a likable old woman," Senhora Olívia. The female owner of the land overseen by one of the "intellectuals" is also mentioned by name. At the time of writing both women were long deceased, and the old-style mail carrier job had disappeared (turned over to men with cars). This is the last mention of women.

Mr. Azevedo's depictions of local life were influenced not only by his class and gender positions, but also by his footing simultaneously inside and outside the locale. He could be said to be as much of Porto and other large northern towns as of Socalcos and the Alto Douro. His experience outside of Socalcos is often viewed by villagers as the source of his ability—in terms of literacy and widespread social contacts—to represent Socalcos in the regional papers. Mr. Azevedo pointed out to me that, as he was not born in Socalcos and spent much time outside of it, he was not really "of" the village. In his articles, however, the perspective is that of the most firmly rooted village dweller. Clearly, he is negotiating a balance of urban and village identity, with actual experience of the former intensifying the attractiveness of the latter.

Though his formation as a Socalcan was ambiguous, the conflict between Socalcos and Cimo compelled Mr. Azevedo to align himself with one or the other. The conflict intensified during his tenure as president of the parish, and led him to seek a posture that transcended that old division. This helps explain a key absence in his writing. Though Cimo was very much on Mr. Azevedo's mind in the early 1980s, there are no substantial references to it. The vandalized train station and the hamlet of Vale make one appearance apiece. The absence of Cimo is all the more curious because its conflictual relations with Socalcos reached a climax at the time Mr. Azevedo wrote his early articles. In 1980, Cimo had begun to agitate for the formation of its own parish. Success would have meant both a material loss for Socalcos villagers and a symbolic victory for their old adversaries. Signatures in support of separation were gathered in Cimo (along with the thumbprints of dozens unable to sign their names), and a leader emerged who took the case for separation over Mr. Azevedo's head to national administrators. Mr. Azevedo was forced to consult with a number of political allies, and work through piles of legal documentation in his attempt to prevent the separation. To say that it was "village patriotism" that led Mr. Azevedo to take the position he did would not be entirely fair. His main concern was maintaining stability. Also, though, he could not alienate the Socalcos voters who had put him in office and whose houses were pressed up close to his home and to the office he occupied as president of the parish council. The Socalcos Old Guard portrayed him as too weak to hold Cimo, partly because he was not really "from" Socalcos. He was intent on dispelling doubt in his abilities. In the end, Cimo's effort to separate failed.

Because mention of Cimo held the potential of drawing unfavorable regional attention to the conflict between the villages, Mr. Azevedo's silences made political sense. The elision of Cimo reminds us, moreover, that one of Mr. Azevedo's literary strategies was to "paper over" conflicts. Just as he represents the upper class and men as the essence of a socially seamless village, he represents Socalcos as the unchallenged center of an unconflicted parish unit. Read in the context of the parish political crisis, one of Mr. Azevedo's historicist texts reveals a political rhetoric with regional consequences. The transcription of Socalcos' charter was first publicized in an address by Mr. Azevedo to members of the parish to remind them that the parish boundaries had been in place for more than eight hundred years. Such an enduring unity should not be broken, he insinuated. The article based on this politically generated documentation was published twelve years after the speech, however, and with a different purpose in mind: demonstrating the regional distinctiveness of Socalcos parish.

Such examples indicate how strongly mediated are representations of Socalcos before they circulate through the regional media. This prior mediation shows up in the representational strategy Mr. Azevedo uses in different articles. Underlying this strategy are social divisions that work on the writer as he works on his prose, crafting it to represent the locality in a selective fashion. All of this recalls the process of hegemony described by Raymond Williams. For Williams, with hegemony, "selectivity is the point; the way in which from a whole possible area of past and present, certain meanings and practices are chosen for emphasis, [and] certain other meanings and practices are neglected and excluded" (Williams 1980:39).[24]

CONCLUSION

The Alto Douro has a clear cultural core, parallel to the economic and political core, and located in the same place: the town of Peso da Régua. The fact that the newspapers are issued from Régua does not mean that representations of the region are only developed there. It does mean, however, that the papers will try to present a view of the region as a whole. In their representations of politics and economics, the newspapers take the core to be what is important about the Douro. This is clear from the meager coverage beyond the Baixo Corgo sub-region. When representing the region as a cultural entity, however, the papers represent it in more abstract terms, implying that it is rooted in some kind of accessible shared essence embodied most completely by Régua. These portrayals purport to be models *of* a regional cultural reality, but actually help *forge* regional commonality by circulating certain generic images of the Alto Douro throughout the region's villages on a weekly basis.

The residents of these localities do not passively conform to these images, however, and in fact demand space in the newspapers to convey their own sense of local realities. While it is to be expected that local stories would focus on political issues of immediate concern or on local history, the dearth of discussion of grapes, wine, and regional membership is surprising. So is the lack of obviously delineated regionalism. Yet, as I have attempted to show, such articles appeal to a regional audience by issuing claims to local distinction and local unity. Localism lacking divisive content and undue pretentions can work to create a powerful, subtle regionality.

Hegemonic (selected) representations circulate through Duriense regional newspapers, distributing signs from the periphery throughout the region. In the end, these selections make their way back to villages such as Socalcos. Here, they are not necessarily accepted at face value. They might, in fact, exacerbate existing local social divisions. In the local responses to Mr. Azevedo's political articles, for example, one Socalcos political faction would gloat, the other smoulder. Even some of Mr. Azevedo's kinsmen complained that he was misrepresenting the village. These conflictual responses did not stop the ongoing production of a picture of local unity spoiled only by egotists in the local government. Meanwhile, in Socalcos' central square people animatedly discussed Mr. Azevedo's articles even if they had not read them or would never be able to do so. Though print is important for regionality in contemporary Portugal, it is talked as much as it is read. The region finding its way into the village is the village finding itself mediated to itself—circuitously and in modalities as hybridized as a rebus.

Notes

Thanks to Sharon Roseman and James W. Fernandez for helping me improve this chapter.

1. To provide some sense of scale: there are single counties in California with more than twenty times the territory of the Alto Douro (965 square miles).

2. The 1990s serve as the ethnographic present for this chapter.

3. The *Instituto do Vinho do Porto* (Port Wine Institute) decided how much *benefício* to offer, but the Casa do Douro determined how it would be distributed. By the end of the 1990s, important institutional changes were afoot, separating port wine regulation from table wine regulation, but the Casa do Douro is still a major, if embattled, player in the regulation of wine production. By law, all Duriense wine growers must still belong to the Casa do Douro ("Reforma Institucional do Douro Entra em Vigor," *O Arrais*, December 4, 2003, 3).

4. The village names Socalcos and Cimo, the town name Altasparedes, and all personal names of residents and former residents of Socalcos, including "Onésimo Azevedo," are pseudonyms.

5. Some Cimo growers have vineyards close to the Douro River, and thus have high quality grapes, just as some Socalcos growers have grapes high above the river, and thus of lower quality. The tendency is, however, for

growers to own vineyards close to their settlements, and thus, by and large, Socalcos growers have higher-ranked vineyards.

6. The chapters in this volume by Leal, Medeiros, and Sobral have a particular resonance with what I am attempting here because of their attention to the relations between text, stereotype, and cultural work. They differ from my chapter in focusing mainly on notions of nation, empire, and regions constructed in the metropoles of Lisbon and Porto.

7. Tóro only offers data on newspapers published up to 1946. Further archival work may well reveal important newspapers founded between that date and 1978.

8. The Alto Douro is conventionally divided into three subregions: from west to east (or downriver to upriver, wetter to dryer, and older vineyards to newer vineyards) these are the Baixo Corgo, the Cima Corgo, and the Douro Superior. The Baixo Corgo is the subregional center of political and economic gravity in the Alto Douro.

9. "Douro" here, as elsewhere, refers to the Alto Douro. In this case it is used to refer to the society of the area.

10. In the interests of maintaining the anonymity of the village I work in, I have dispensed with bibliographic references.

11. The county of *Portucale* expanded southward and gave its name to the nation. It is of some interest that the first such charters of local rights granted in what would become Portuguese national space were issued in the Alto Douro (Mattoso 1991:92; Reis 1991).

12. There are six references to the region (though rarely named—articles 1, 5, 8, 13, 14, 15), and 11 references to Portugal (articles 1, 3, 4, 5, 6, 7, 10, 11, 14, 15, 16). It is worth noting that there are four references to Europe— 7, 8, 10, 12.

13. They are close in character and function to Turner's (1988) "major" and "minor" history, which represent different balances of "myth" (codifying a sense of timelessness) and "history" (indexing change).

14. Some may, as we shall see, have had their original impetus in "interlocal" struggles.

15. Ramos (1988) shows how prior to 1960 men in the north of Portugal were more likely than men in the south to be literate. He links this difference to property holding. The north had many small landholders, and their property both enabled and motivated their literacy. The south's comparative lack of literacy was an effect of the concentration there of landless rural laborers. However, northern women were less likely to be literate than southern women. Again this is linked to landowning, in a roundabout way. The Alto Douro seems to interrupt this schema somewhat, with literacy rates tending toward the southern figures. If landlessness was indeed linked as strongly to illiteracy as Ramos holds, then the long-standing proletarianization of the Alto Douro would help explain this regional interruption.

16. In statistics collected for the early 1970s, the average size of vineyard holdings in the Alto Douro was one hectare, and in the Cima Corgo, where Socalcos is located, nine-tenths of one hectare (Martins 1990:429).

17. For an insightful analysis of houses as durable sites/sights of status in northern Portugal, see Brettell (1999).

18. During authoritarian rule, the three members of the parish council were elected by heads of households meeting property/tax qualifications from a list of candidates nominated by the president of the municipal government. With the end of the regime came universal suffrage. (See Reed 1989:76–77.)

19. Cutileiro's observations on "Vila Velha," in the Alentejo, from the 1960s were applicable in Socalcos of the 1990s, and certainly also during Mr. Azevedo's heyday as political player: "The world of literacy is . . . not only mysterious but also powerful. The entire structure of the administration and the formal organization of political control by locally powerful individuals is channeled through the written word" (Cutileiro 1971:196).

20. The social class divide is conceived locally as the point setting off those who can survive without selling their labor from those who must sell their labor to survive. For an analysis, see Parkhurst (2000, chapter 4).

21. As head of the victorious list Mr. Azevedo was automatically the president of the parish council.

22. It is worth noting that one article commemorates a writer from outside of the locality who brought fame to Socalcos by writing of his experience there. Camilo Castelo Branco is implicitly likened to the indigenous Socalcos notables in the durability of his contribution to the locality, and differentiated from the local toiling classes, absent from the article.

23. The term used is *homens*. Judging from the local discursive practice I became familiar with, had there been any significant gender doubt, the term used would have been *pessoas* (people) or *indivíduos* (individuals). Of course, Mr. Azevedo also lists only men in the article.

24. Williams's notion of hegemony has more recently been applied to the construction of tradition in an "inscribed" Iberian space by Maddox (1993:8–11). See Medeiros, this volume, for a look at how icons can be involved in hegemonic representations of regions in Portugal.

References

Althusser, Louis. 1971. Ideology and ideological state apparatuses. In *Lenin and philosophy and other essays*, 127–86. New York: Monthly Review Press.

Anderson, Benedict. 1991 [1983]. *Imagined communities: Reflections on the origin and spread of nationalism*. London: Verso.

Bennema, Jan. 1992. *Port, kerk en arbeidsvrede: Economische en politieke verhoudingen in Alto Douro, Portugal*. Proefschrift, Katholieke Universiteit Nijmegen.

————. 1996. A paz social na agricultura do Alto Douro. *Douro: Estudos & Documentos* 2:287–92.

Brettell, Caroline. 1999. The casa of José dos Santos Caldas: Family and household in a northwestern Portuguese village, 1850–1993. In *House Life: Space, place, and family in Europe*, ed. Donna Birdwell-Pheasant and Denise Lawrence-Zúñiga, 39–72. Oxford: Berg.

Brøgger, Jan, and David Gilmore. 1997. The matrifocal family in Iberia: Spain and Portugal compared. *Ethnology* 36:12–30.

Clifford, James, and George E. Marcus, eds. 1986. *Writing culture: The poetics and politics of ethnography*. Berkeley: University of California Press.

Costa, António Luís Pinto da. 1997. O abandono da prática religiosa como protesto social: O caso dos jornaleiros alto-durienses no primeiro terço do século XX. *Douro—Estudos & Documentos* 4:287–96.

Cutileiro, José. 1971. *A Portuguese rural society*. Oxford: Oxford University Press.

Entrikin, J. Nicholas. 1991. *The betweenness of place: Towards a geography of modernity*. Baltimore: The Johns Hopkins University Press.

Fernandez, James W. 1986. *Persuasions and performances: The play of tropes in culture*. Bloomington: Indiana University Press.

Guichard, François. 1992. *Porto, la ville dans sa région: Contribution à l'étude de l'organisation de l'espace dans le Portugal du Nord, Volume 1*. Paris: Fondation Calouste Gulbenkian.

Herzfeld, Michael. 1985. *The poetics of manhood: Contest and identity in a Cretan mountain village*. Princeton: Princeton University Press.

————. 2001. *Anthropology: Theoretical practice in culture and society*. Malden: UNESCO/Blackwell.

Maddox, Richard. 1993. *El Castillo: The politics of tradition in an Andalusian town*. Urbana: University of Illinois Press.

Martins, Conceição Andrade. 1990. *Memória do vinho do Porto*. Lisbon: Instituto de Ciências Sociais.

Mattoso, José. 1991. *Identificação de um país: Ensaio sobre as origens de Portugal. Volume 1—Oposição*. Lisbon: Editorial Estampa.

Mónica, Maria Filomena. 1978. *Educação e sociedade no Portugal de Salazar: A escola primária salazarista, 1926–1939*. Lisbon: Editorial Presença.

Monteiro, J. Gonçalves. 1998. Crónica da semana: Douro: Paisagem de abundância. *O Arrais*, 5 de Fevereiro.

Paasi, Anssi. 1986. The institutionalization of regions: A theoretical framework for understanding the emergence of regions and the constitution of regional identity. *Fennia* 164, no. 1:105–46.

Parkhurst, Shawn. 1999. In the middle of the myth: The problem of power in gender relations and the Alto Douro region of northern Portugal. *Anthropologica* XLI:103–15.

————. 2000. *The region in the village: An ethnography of the local production of regionality in the Alto Douro of northern Portugal.* Unpublished PhD dissertation, University of California, Berkeley.

Pedrosa, Fantina Tedim. 1991. La presse et l'identité régionale: Contribution et reflet. In *L'identité régionale: L'idée de région dans l'Europe du sud-ouest*, ed. Centre d'Études Nord du Portugal-Aquitaine (CENPA), 253–61. Paris: Éditions du Centre National de la Recherche Scientifique.

Pereira, Gaspar Martins. 1996. A região do vinho do Porto—Origem e evolução de uma demarcação pioneira. *Douro—Estudos & Documentos* 1, no. 1:177–94.

Pina-Cabral, João de. 1989. Sociocultural differentiation and regional identity in Portugal. In *Iberian identity*, ed. Richard Herr and J. R. Polt, 3–18. Berkeley: Institute of International Studies, University of California.

————. 1991. *Os contextos da antropologia.* Lisbon: Difel.

Ramos, Rui. 1988. Culturas da alfabetização e culturas do analfabetismo em Portugal: Uma introdução à história da alfabetização no Portugal contemporâneo. *Análise Social* XXIV, no. 103–104:1067–1145.

Reed, Robert Roy. 1989. *Managing the revolution: Revolutionary promise and political reality in rural Portugal.* Unpublished PhD dissertation, Indiana University.

Reis, António Matos. 1991. *Origens dos municípios portugueses.* Lisbon: Livros Horizonte.

Roseman, Sharon R. 1997. Celebrating silenced words: The "reimagining" of a feminist nation in late-twentieth-century Galicia. *Feminist Studies* 23, no. 1:43–71.

Roseman, Sharon R., and Heidi Kelley. 1999. Introduction. *Anthropologica* XLI:89–101.

Silverman, Kaja. 1983. *The subject of semiotics.* Oxford: Oxford University Press.

Soja, Edward. 1989. *Postmodern geographies: The reassertion of space in critical social theory.* London: Verso.

Tóro, Bandeira de. 1946. *O concelho do Pêso da Régua.* Lisbon: Imprensa Baroeth.

Turner, Terence. 1988. Ethno-ethnohistory: Myth and history in native South American representations of contact with western society. In *Rethinking history and myth: Indigenous South American perspectives on the past*, ed. Jonathan D. Hill, 235–81. Urbana: University of Illinois Press.

Urban, Greg. 1996. *Metaphysical community: The interplay of the senses and the intellect.* Austin: University of Texas Press.

Williams, Raymond. 1980. Base and superstructure in Marxist cultural theory. In *Problems in materialism and culture*, 31–49. London: Verso.

PART 4

Cultural Politics and the Global

The chapter in this part of the volume moves readers right into the late twentieth- and early twenty-first-century contested cosmo-politanism of cityscapes such as the Basque city of Bilbao. Jacqueline Urla writes about how in the Basque Country the "street" has for decades been identified as a site of barricade and *borroka* (conflict), yet has in recent years been reinscribed by language activists as a space in which public celebrations of ludic boundary-crossing activity can also be promoted. She introduces us to Bilbao's Kafe Antzokia which she argues is likely the best example of a new kind of cultural space and new mode of activism in the landscape of Basque language revival of the post-Franco era. Unlike the Guggenheim Museum, however, the Kafe Antzokia was created by a grassroots community association called Zenbat Gara—one of many such associations that emerged during the 1990s. Urla argues that the concentration on remaking the physical space of Kafe Antzokia and other public sites dedicated to promoting Basque language and culture reveals a new activist politics. Instead of reproducing "Basque-only" spaces, by promoting locations such as Kafe Antzokia, associations such as Zenbat Gara are engaging in an impor-tant "experiment in expanding notions of global citizenship." The lead-ers of this remaking of spaces for Basque action tell Urla that they were inspired by the ideas of the nomadic scholar José María Sánchez Carrión (nicknamed "Txepetx" in Basque). Txepetx's important book *Un futuro para nuestro pasado* (*A future for our past*) (1987) advances an ecological argument for the protection of multiple "natural habitats or spaces" of linguistic diversity. Urla contends that the popularity of this argument may be based in part in the fact that it appeals to long-standing ide-ologies of the boundedness of "language, territory, and identity." But she also observes that it opens the door to a new ethics of pluralism, interconnectedness, and "globalization from below."

CHAPTER 11

Kafe Antzokia

The Global meets the Local in Basque Cultural Politics

JACQUELINE URLA

DESTINATION BILBAO

"We hope to be the second stop tourists make when they visit Bilbao: first the Guggenheim, then Kafe Antzokia." With these words Jose Angel Irigaray ushered me out of his office above the performance space of Kafe Antzokia, a Basque café-theatre that had recently opened in the heart of this predominantly Spanish-speaking city. We had just concluded a lengthy interview on the goals behind this project, which had rapidly gained much attention in the world of Basque language revival. As I transcribe the cassette tape back in the United States, the frequent interruption of the telephone, Jose Angel's seamless transition among various languages, an incoming Fax, salsa music, and church bells evoke the busy and interconnected world this writer, doctor, and advocate of the Basque language inhabits.

It was the spring of 1998, a moment of hope in the Basque Autonomous Community. ETA was about to announce a cease fire and a peace process seemed on the horizon. I was on my own circuitous path, tracking activists,[1] a language movement, and, as I'll suggest, a concept of culture on the move. In fact, the Guggenheim *had* been my first stop that morning, as I too had wanted to see for myself the glinting titanium structure, visible testament, at least in one author's view, to the seduction of Basque ministers to the wiles of Thomas Krens and the allure of world-class art (Zulaika 1997). At first glance, Kafe Antzokia and Guggenheim Bilbao would appear to be very dif-

253

ferent kinds of endeavors: the first is an effort by concerned Basques to create a haven for a "local" language and culture. The second is a project of national elites gambling on an as-yet-untried transnational museum franchise. But before we rush to proclaim one project *local* (rooted, bounded) and the other *global* (deracinated, cosmopolitan), indeed, before we even accept the terms of this contrast—local *versus* global—we need to look more closely. Both are in fact cultural projects that engage global cultural currents but of very different sorts and with very different goals. While Guggenheim Bilbao imports a more or less North American vision of "universal" art into Basque society, Kafe Antzokia tries to bring the global and the local together attempting to create a space of transcultural encounter that asserts, to use James Clifford's phrase, both roots and routes (Clifford 1997).[2]

URBAN COSMOPOLITANISM

Bilbao's Kafe Antzokia's air of urban cosmopolitanism is a far cry from the folkloric or provincial images that have tended to circulate about "regional" language movements in Europe. It also signals important shifts that had begun to take place within the world of nongovernmental Basque language revival after nearly two decades of rocky, yet nevertheless official, recognition. The creation of the regional Basque government in 1979 gave Basque language revival, once a clandestine activity under Franco, resources and governmental support. Though still far from fully normalized, Basque, like Catalan and Galician, is now being taught in the public schools, it has some media usage on television and radio, and subsidies are allocated to support Basque-medium cultural activities. Kafe Antzokia, however, is explicitly nongovernmental. It was created by Zenbat Gara, one of a number of grassroots community language associations that had been appearing in the Basque Country in the course of the nineties.

These community-based associations are testament to the continued vitality of popular nongovernmental activism in Basque language politics. Their existence speaks to a keen sense among its members that language revival cannot be abandoned to government planners and schools. As Irigaray told me, Zenbat Gara was formed by a group of self-denominated *euskaltzaleak* (Basque language advocates) teaching at or associated with one of the largest adult Basque language schools of

Bilbao. Such adult language schools, known as *euskaltegiak*, have been key instruments of the language revival movement, not only teaching the Basque language, but also, at least in their origins, operating as mobilizing forces in the social movement challenging the marginalization of Basque in public life. By the nineties, however, language teachers and advocates were despairing over the effectiveness of their strategies and the future of Basque revival. Language advocates I had been interviewing in 1998 told very similar stories of their movement having reached an impasse. They saw themselves in a losing battle: teaching Basque grammar, trying to motivate speakers to use it, and having to depend on the ups and downs of electoral politics that control the largesse of government subsidies. They were also frustrated over the political divisions amongst Basques and searching for ways to overcome the divisive effects of nationalist politics that blocked the formation of coalitions among *euskaltzaleak* and hobbled the movement.

Zenbat Gara is a result of these frustrations. It is one of many community-based associations that formed in the nineties with the goal of finding new ways of promoting Basque language use by creating a new kind of space and operating according to a new set of strategies. It is part of a rather profound transformation in Basque language activism that takes place when the momentum of popular involvement begins to slow down and the grassroots organizations that had been at the forefront of language revival were finding the rhetorical strategies of the past—strategies that relied on evocations of patriotism—less persuasive with younger generations. As the discussion below will hopefully make apparent, their spatial and cultural politics redefine the look and meaning of language "normalization," as Basque language revival is typically called by language advocates. Normalization is generally seen as the process of making Basque into the "normal," habitual, or customary language of life. For all intents and purposes, normalization was understood within the framework of the modern nation-state. Basque had to become a language of the state and its institutions of governance over a particular specific bounded territory. This goal has been pursued in large part via normativization—the creation of standardized Basque, and regulations for its teaching and use in the public sphere. As we will see, however, normalization as pursued by this newer generation involves putting Basque onto a global stage, in affinity with the cultural productions of other minoritized groups and social movements.[3] It is this expansion of the Basque cultural universe to a world forum that is key to this generation's sense of what it means to have a normal language and culture.

The group's method hinged from the beginning on creating a new kind of physical space for cultural activities. The group raised funds to purchase an old theatre and renovated it to accommodate multiple uses. At the core is the performance space of the theatre with a stage and tables. In addition to viewing nightly musical or theatrical performances, patrons come for mid-day meals and drinks at the bar. These activities bring in a clientele from throughout the city and generate the bulk of the income for the association. In the upstairs space the association has its offices, offers adult language classes, organizes activities for youth, runs a low-power radio station, a small publishing house, and had plans for creating a travel agency.

When I visited, there was very little about the physical place that would identify it as "Basque." Absent were any of the ubiquitous political insignia that have tended to mark a space as Basque nationalist: there were no posters of political prisoners and no Basque flag (*ikurrina*). Nor were there any of the usual slogans *Euskalerrian Euskaraz* (Basque in the Basqueland), *Euskaraz badakigu* (we speak Basque), *Euskaraz eta Kitto!*, (Basque is enough!) by which *euskaltzales* had been accustomed to literally inscribe their pro-Basque politics onto the physical environment. Absent as well were any emblems of Basque folklore that might be found in tourist shops marketing Basque culture (no nostalgic images of farmhouses, rustic furniture, busts of farmers, or traditional costume). The aesthetic of the furniture and design is a kind of modernism and the acoustic environment is nothing if not eclectic.[4] There is indeed nothing remarkable to mark this space as Basque, except, of course, that all the staff speak Basque as well as one or two other languages.

Jose Angel Irigaray is in charge of programming at the theatre, lining up music groups, theatre performances, debates, and events. He is no stranger to this world, having been a founding member of the legendary Ez Dok Amairu, an innovative performance collective of artists, writers, and musicians that launched the Basque New Song Movement of the sixties. A chalkboard located at the entrance to Kafe Antzokia contained a list of the month's events ranging from theatre, live bands, to political/cultural debates. Book parties are held, press conferences, roundtable discussions, and lectures. And they have ac-

quired a Web site for their younger patrons who surf the net.[5] In
contrast to the Guggeheim, Kafe Antzokia gives prominence to *euskaldun*
(Basque-speaking) artists and music, but their stage is also host to groups
that don't sing in Basque and are from elsewhere. The musical selections
as noted above are eclectic, varying widely from any number of Basque
musical varieties (balladeers, rock, heavy metal, Basque accordion [*trikitixa*]
and its many new fusion styles), to the sounds of Kid Frost, Bill Evans,
the indie Mexican bands Tijuana No and Molotov, as well as representatives of alternative *"rock en español"* from elsewhere on the peninsula
or Latin America. Kafe Antzokia had also recently hosted, said Irigaray,
a musical group from France whose members were of Berber, African,
and Caribbean descent. And what was perhaps an even more dramatic
indicator of a new cultural politics: a band playing flamenco fusion
from Andalucía had performed the night before I had arrived.

Ten years ago the presence of a flamenco band or the sounds of
sevillanas in a space of Basque cultural activism would have been almost
inconceivable—requiring at the very least a bit of satire—so identified
was this music with the Spanish state and its cultural hegemony. Within
Basque cultural activism, affirming Basque identity had been premised
on defending oneself from the hegemony of Spanish and French language and culture through their exclusion and denial. The identities
and languages were routinely posed by both language loyalists as well
as their detractors as oppositional and mutually exclusive. The slogan
Euskaraz eta Kitto! (Basque is enough!) frequently used in the Basque
revival movement, succinctly conveys the essence of what has been
until recently the prevalent strategy of grassroots cultural/linguistic
resistance in the Basque Country and indeed in many other language
revival movements. This strategy obeys what we might call a protec-
tionist logic, which aims to save the minoritized language by sheltering
it, creating spaces that can serve as a refuge away from the majority
languages and culture. It is a strategy common in many liberation
movements. One thinks, for example, of the creation of woman-only
spaces in the early feminist movement. Woman-only space was seen by
many feminists as a necessary component in a struggle that aimed not
only at attaining legal rights, but at overcoming a dominated subjectivity and habits of subservience ingrained from childhood. In many respects, language loyalists also seek to challenge a certain kind of dominated
or "minority" subjectivity. *"Euskaraz eta Kitto!"*, a key slogan of the

movement for many years, for example, asserts the capacity of Euskara to be a medium for all aspects of life. As a slogan it addressed the pervasive belief for much of the twentieth century that Basque, like other minority languages, was deficient, supplementary at best, but ultimately inadequate to performing all the tasks of a real "Language." Zenbat Gara and the strategies of the many other local cultural associations that were emerging in the nineties were shifting this discourse and calling for something new. While giving prominence to the Basque language and culture, Kafe Antzokia rejects the deleterious effects of a fortress mentality and plunges ahead creating a new soundscape and cultural imaginary in which Basque culture and language participate in transnational cultural flows, crossing even that most politically problematic of boundaries: the one between Basques and Spain.

Most of my interview with Irigaray that afternoon revolved around a discussion of Zenbat Gara's strategy, goals, and methods. What follows is a synthesis of that original conversation and as well a few followup exchanges in 2003 in which we discussed further the context of political strife that has motivated this innovative project. Readers should be aware that the Spanish state's position toward Basque cultural activities became increasingly hostile since the original interview, marked in particular by the government ordered closing of the Basque language newspaper *Egunkaria* in February 2003 and arrests of key figures in Basque journalism and publishing. The account I provide here does not address the impact of this shift in climate nor does it try to account for the evolution of the project in the subsequent years. How and to what degree language loyalists have been able to realize the goals professed here in this new context remains a topic for further investigation.

EX-CENTRIC THEORY AND SPACES OF LANGUAGE

Kafe Antzokia, as noted, represents a qualitatively new approach to language normalization oriented not toward drawing boundaries and confrontation, but rather toward expanding the *euskaldun* (Basque-speaking) cultural universe and attracting people to it. Irigaray explained:

> In the past, activist groups like Basque in the Basqueland and others have practiced a certain kind of militancy, demanding rights, laws, and subsidies to teach Basque. These are all important, but we should be

working not just for the survival of Euskara—of course we want that. But we also want to create a language for *living*.

The people who came up with the idea saw that there was a need for something else beside schools, rights, and planning. We wanted to make a place here in Bilbao that would not feel like a ghetto, but rather a place for living in Basque; a place where there is cultural development, performances, humor. Open to everyone: Basque speakers, semi speakers, people who want to get closer to this world . . . everyone. People who come here know that they come to a place that is a kind of temple of Basque, but not closed. They begin to have respect. They see that there is life here—that interesting things happen here. And they start to have a new attitude.

A team of sociologists exploring new forms of civic participation and associational life that were appearing at this time in the Basque Country, identified Kafe Antzokia as one of the most innovative attempts to create a new kind of pluralist civil society in Basque (Abad et al. 1999). As part of their study, they conducted a focus group interview with founding members of the Kafe, many of whom, like Irigaray, have had long histories of involvement in the Basque language and cultural movement extending, in some cases, to the Franco era. In the words of one of the participants in the interview, a member of the Kafe's board of directors: "Kafe Antzokia is an attempt to create a *gune* [space] to live Basque and also to live the ludic and the cultural in a different way, and for us to grow in our own internal relations as a collective and as individuals" (quoted in Abad et al. 1999:7). Key to the overall vision of the project is this sense of an urgent need for new spaces of usage—spaces that are less associated with the political community and more linked to the quotidian and intimate relations of everyday life. The Basque term *gune* appeared frequently in the vocabulary of these activists to refer specifically to the creation of new kinds of noninstitutional spaces of Basque usage.

Irigaray, like most of the members in the community language associations, including the interviewees in the aforementioned study, traced an important part of the inspiration for this shift in strategy to the work of José María Sánchez Carrión and his influential book, *Un futuro para nuestro pasado* [A future for our past] (1987). Born in Cartagena, Sánchez Carrión, affectionately nicknamed "Txepetx," has lived the life of a nomadic scholar residing in Britain, the Canary Islands, and the

Balearic Islands. He is neither a permanent resident of the Basque Country nor ethnically Basque. Yet he has become one of the foremost scholars of Basque sociolinguistics.[6] His works were widely read and interviews and short articles by him regularly appeared in the press in the eighties and nineties. In the world of Basque language studies, especially among grassroots advocates, his work is respected. At the same time he occupies a position of geographic and political excentricity. This has afforded him a kind of neutrality that few "local" intellectuals are able to enjoy in the current political climate of the Basque Country.[7]

Written as his doctoral thesis, *A future for our past* is a huge and eclectic tome about the nature of language and identity, language acquisition, and a blueprint for reversing Basque language shift. Central to the book is the notion of ecology as an ethical framework for grounding the value of language diversity. Sánchez Carrión thus legitimates Basque and other language revival struggles not principally in terms of national sovereignty claims, but rather in terms of the planetary good of biodiversity as the principle on which one should defend linguistic diversity. Related to this, it presents an elaborate theory of the factors that govern linguistic reproduction, which places emphasis on the maintenance, as he calls it, of natural habitats or spaces of usage. Each "language" must have its spheres of hegemonic usage in order to develop and survive. In Jose Angel's words:

> *A future for our past* offers a framework that is valid for human language—for *all* languages—and it also provides for us the ethical principles for relations between nations and languages of the world . . . based on equality, mutual respect, and a recognition of our common humanity, but not uniformity.

Txepetx's ecological discourse is an example (albeit somewhat idiosyncratic) of the growing trend in popular and scientific literature to link linguistic and biological diversity. This linkage is signaled by the increasing use of the term *endangered* languages.[8] Part of the appeal of this discourse to Basque language advocates may have come from the fact that ecology is a movement that historically has been quite popular. But perhaps more significantly, I would argue, is that the discourse of "nature" that it mobilizes (evoking natural habitats, discrete language communities) leaves intact bounded ways of thinking about language, territory, and identity that are deeply rooted in European language ideology and entirely consistent with the national imaginary that underwrites it (Dorian 1998). It leaves these fundamental imaginings comfortably in place, but it accomplishes other discursive tasks, other strategic reorientations to language revival that were tremendously exciting and useful to Basque advocates.

Kafe Antzokia, of course, was not simply an application of Txepetx's ideas. But his work offered something some loyalists felt they lacked: a theoretical model for language revival based on principles derived from the study of language contact and language acquisition. For Irigaray and other long-time language advocates with whom I spoke, *A future for our past* rescued language revival from the alienated state into which it had fallen and invested it with a method and universal values that transcended nationalist politics. In the context of tremendous polarization and political impasse that had come to color all forms of cultural politics in the southern Basque Country today, this shift in discursive footing was of no small significance.

In my discussions with grassroots language activists about the past two decades, they frequently described a sense that their movement had become paralyzed. This paralysis was not solely attributed to antagonism from the Spanish state, though that was a factor particularly after the electoral victory of the right-wing party of José María Aznar in 1996. It was also, they explained, due to the hardening of oppositions among moderate and radical Basque nationalists that took shape in the transition to democracy and the acquisition of regional autonomy. The end of authoritarian rule in Spain signaled an end to the unity that had characterized language revival efforts and indeed much of Basque nationalism during and immediately after Franco's death. A deep and as yet unresolved split amongst Basque nationalists emerged over the Statute of Autonomy of 1979 between those who saw its limited form of self-rule as a viable compromise and others who considered it unacceptable.[9]

This split reverberated throughout Basque civil society and affected all cultural initiatives in the post-Franco era, including the language movement. As one long-time member of AEK, the largest adult language teaching organization, told me in an interview, for the better part of a decade virtually all language revival initiatives became caught up in the polarization and were inevitably categorized as belonging to one camp or particular party or another. Those initiatives not specifically promoted by the Basque Government's Department of Language

Policy were frequently suspected or outright accused of belonging to the oppositional nationalist Left and consequently marginalized.[10] During the eighties and nineties, it was quite apparent in daily newspapers that relations between grassroots language organizations such as AEK or EKB (Euskal Kultur Batzarra/the Basque Cultural Association) and the Basque Autonomous Government had become strained and often antagonistic. Many of the extra-institutional language advocates I spoke with in the spring of 1998 made reference to the damaging effects of this climate of paralysis and polarization for the progress of language normalization. A situation of crisis had developed.

For Irigaray and other representatives of community-based language associations, Txepetx's work was the catalyst to something new: new attitudes and new methods. Among other things, Txepetx's work, as Irigaray explained, turned their attention from "saving the life of the language" to creating "a language of life" (*biziaren hizkuntza*). Indeed, this terminology comes directly from Txepetx and signaled for language advocates a new imaginary. *A future for our past* offered a distinct ethics, practice, and focus. The discourse of ecological diversity and balance, as we noted, provided what Erving Goffman (1979) might call a new "footing" on which to argue for language revival. For language revival to succeed, Txepetx argued, it required unity and an ethics of mutual respect and individual responsibility. The agent of linguistic revival could not be any single political party or group, but rather what he called "the linguistic community" in all its political and ideological diversity. Basques had to come together. Firstly, this would require tolerance for ideological pluralism and differences amongst Basques. Secondly, language revival could not be left up to institutions, experts, or planners. Every individual has a role to play in it, as speaker, learner, or advocate. Thirdly, and very importantly, it directed concerned language advocates to focus their efforts on cultivating the motivation to learn and speak Basque by increasing the spaces of usage beyond the classroom or government office.

It was clear to me, having read the book and talked to participants in the grassroots language movement, that Kafe Antzokia and other community-based activities were not simply following the instructions of *A future for our past*. The idea of Kafe Antzokia as a space of pluralist coexistence was their own bold creation, based in part on concepts derived from the book, to be sure. But it was also drawing lessons from recent history, like the community-based language association in Arrasate,

AED (Arrasate Euskaldun Dezagun), which had been experimenting for some time with creating more neutral community-wide social activities in Basque—cooking classes, weekend excursions, after-school play groups, local media. Working at a community level, AED already had been having some success at disengaging language revival from the polarization that beset party politics and experimenting with alternatives to the hitherto routine modes of language advocacy via media campaigns and demonstrations.

Notable in my interview with Jose Angel was his insistence on the break this represented with the more confrontational forms of language advocacy of the past.

> [W]ith these language associations, AED, and so on, the change is qualitative because there is a completely different attitude. There is . . . an attitude of wanting to draw together, to integrate, to develop a more integrative policy. Because there is a broader, clearer idea of reality and how complex it is, and the factors that are at work in languages. . . . [There is a desire] to create cultural activities that reinforce all the creativity of living in Euskara but not by closing the door, but opening it, trying to integrate.

While grassroots language advocates of the past might have used images of the barricade to describe their form of militancy, Zenbat Gara uses the image of Bilbao's *jaiak* (holidays, festivities)—such as midwinter carnival and the *aste nagusia* (the "big week" or annual patron saint celebrations) of August—and the *comparsa*,[11] as metaphors for the kind of cultural politics the group seeks to advance. Zenbat Gara, for example, has formed its own *comparsa* for these festivities. Sounding very much like an anthropologist, Jose Angel described *jaiak*, and carnival in particular, as populist, democratic modes of communal celebration that have a long tradition in the Basque Country. *Jaiak*, he explained, are based on the ludic principle, chaos, reversals; they equalize and unify, serving thereby as counterpoint to what he called the divisive, masculine, hierarchizing tendencies of political and social life.[12] Our own Basque traditions, Jose Angel, suggested, provide us with alternate values and kinds of associational life that can be profoundly therapeutic. It is our goal, he said to insert this feeling of *jaiak* into everyday life.

Thus, in the symbolism of the *comparsa*, one finds yet another example of these language loyalists' attempt to reorient their methods and metaphors. Comparsa celebrants perform a reinscription of space by inserting the ludic principle of *jolas* (play) into "the street," the heretofore archetypical space of public expression that in Spain had for so long been dominated by the rubber bullet, the barricade, and political *borroka* (conflict).[13]

In addition to new metaphors, members of Kafe Antzokia could also be seen as introducing a distinctive chronotope. In focus group discussions with members of Zenbat Gara, Abad et al. (1999) found participants describing their strategy as committed to the principle of "*orain eta hemen*," here and now. This presentist practice and ethics contrast with the temporality implied in so many narratives of national liberation or language revival, for that matter. Such narratives, like parallel narratives of Catholic redemption (an equally important influence on the Basque nationalist imaginary), promise the full realization of freedom, the wholeness of the nation, and the salvation of the language, as something that is always on the horizon, that will come into being *after* the battle has been won. For Zenbat Gara, however, the *euskaldun* community is made in the here and now. Thus, we find Kafe Antzokia attempting to break not only with some features that had previously characterized Basque nationalist rhetoric and imagery, but also the nationalist temporality of promised utopias.

LOCAL LANGUAGES IN A GLOBAL WORLD

Kafe Antzokia represents a new strategy of cultural politics, a new scripting of space by Basque language advocates in post-Franco Spain. The pluralist ludic space crafted through eclectic programming unsettles the implicit notion that majority languages—English in particular—are the inevitable vehicle of global flows, while minority language groups are often made to appear hermetically closed—claustrophobic even. The space imagined is not a battlefield, not a fortress or a place of retrenchment, but rather of experimentation and engagement with other cultural currents and social issues. But it is an engagement attentive to power and inequality. "We carry out our lives in Euskara," says Jose Angel. "If you feel secure in Basque, you are open to exchange. You aren't worried about other languages. There aren't problems as long as it is clear that like all human relationships whether these be relations of love, friendship, or among peoples/communities, you have to have reciprocity or else it becomes a situation of domination."

Kafe Antzokia is no postmodern celebration of hybridity for hybidity's sake. Nor is it only a site of the passive consumption of entertainment, though it is to be sure entertaining. For Jose Angel, the larger project of Kafe Antzokia is to create a space of encounter between Basques and cultural/musical others, but also a space of encounter of Basques with other Basques. This encounter, he and other language loyalists feel, is quite urgently needed in the current climate of division. It is a site of communication and partial coalition building with other struggles for social justice. As Jose Angel recounted:

> We just had a visit from a woman from Ecuador talking to us about a foundation for Amerindians that she works for. It was incredible. . . . She described the situation there for indigenous people . . . the subhuman conditions that we the Western world have subjected more than one hundred million people. It is painful. We raised money for schools and sent some books. We gave her a copy of Txepetx's book to take back. He has been there for a conference. I, myself, just came back from a conference in Bosnia. . . . When you are rooted it is not difficult to be open. On the contrary. The more a tree has solid roots, the more it opens upward. And the more it rises, the more it opens itself to the four winds.

Kafe Antzokia, as a cultural project, is consciously about much more than language revival. We might say it is a site for the creation of alternate routes to roots: routes that engage other social movements and incorporate a diverse array of cultural and musical expressions into this project's affirmation of a distinctive *euskaldun* cultural life. In it we find a site for thinking "beyond the nation" (Appadurai 1996) without surrendering the specificities of place, language, and identity. One of the key texts of this movement, *A future for our past*, is itself an example of how "the global" is mobilized in defense of "the local" for the theoretical tool kit Txepetx uses draws from European philosophy, linguistics, Native American traditions, psychology, and anticolonial theory, and its overarching framework—ecology—is itself planetary in scope.

As Anna Tsing (2000) has argued, interconnection is everything in the new globalisms. Some of what makes Kafe Antzokia a different kind of globalism than Guggenheim Bilbao is precisely the kinds of interconnections that it seeks to create: respectful interconnections among Basques and between Basques and other "Others." As a particular instance of globalism, Kafe Antzokia bears some resemblance to the phenomenon Brecher et al. (1993) have called "globalization from below." If globalization from above can be taken to refer to the processes, technologies, and organizations through which capital is being consolidated by elites worldwide, globalization from below refers to non-aligned transnational formations, social movements, or alliances that make use of global technologies and resources. Such social movements, writes Evelina Dagnino, have the potential to give rise to new conceptions of citizenship, democracy, and an enlarged understanding of multiple forms of inequality—economic, social, and cultural—that curtail the formation of a truly democratic society (Dagnino 1993:244). As she and others have argued, locally based social movements grounded in cultural specificity are not necessarily the enemy of planetary community as is so often asserted; rather, they may in fact offer us some of the most promising examples of how such a community might work.

In a phrase echoing the sentiment of so many sexual, cultural, and gendered minorities, Jose Angel said to me at the close of our interview: "I refuse to choose. I am both Basque and a citizen of the world." The project to which he dedicates his time, Kafe Antzokia, is an experiment in expanding notions of global citizenship, of pluralist coexistence, and reanimating a language movement paralyzed by political conflict. It is a reminder that language diversity is and must be a key part of any democratic project of global community. As an example of cultural expression, Kafe Antzokia provides us with insight into some of the changing ways in which locality and local languages are produced under conditions of globalization as well as national strife.

It is somehow fitting that this experiment in *euskaldun* cosmopolitanism should have emerged in Bilbao, once the industrial heart of the Basque financial and industrial elite and the birthplace of Basque nationalism. The early Basque nationalists—like so many other nationalisms of the early twentieth century—romanticized the rural life and looked with suspicion on its urban centers, specifically Bilbao, as impure, resolutely liberal, and *españolista*. This early nationalism located the authentic Basque nation, Euskal Herria, in the rural lifeways of farmers, the *baserritarra*, and fishing villages, while life in the cities, and especially *this* port city, teeming with immigrant labor, was seen as lost to Euskara, if not an enemy. Not only did such an opposition seem to doom Basque culture to a fading past, it also seemed to imply that Basque language and culture could not be reconciled with or be a part of the ethnic and cultural mixing that inevitably characterizes urban life. Kafe Antzokia is one of a number of cultural projects that continue to disrupt this long-standing opposition between the rural and the urban and at the same time carve out a more pluralist understanding of Basque culture and identity.[14] It is a project of not only finding Basque a place in the city, but more importantly, making Basque culture and language its own form of crossroads and encounter with difference. To borrow a play on words by the writer Bernardo Atxaga, it is a project in rethinking Euskal *Herria*, as Euskal *Hiria* (the Basque City) (Martín 2003). This is an ongoing project. Or, in the words of Jose Angel, "We are trying not to repeat old schemas or illusory utopias, but rather to build something real and coherent first of all with our lives and consequently with life. We know it is never perfect. It is something that can always be improved." It remains to be seen how Kafe Antzokia will fare and what impact it and projects like it will have. It will be especially interesting to see whether it will be able to foster alliances with other emerging spaces of alterity in Bilbao where the new immigrants to Spain, North Africans and others, are attempting to forge cultural projects of their own.[15]

NOTES

A warm thanks to Jose Angel Irigaray for graciously sharing his time and views with me. Irigaray reviewed this manuscript suggesting many valuable revisions only some of which I have been able to incorporate. Responsibility for any errors remains my own.

1. I use the term *activist* here in a generic way to refer to people who take part in language revival activities or associations. In the Basque Country, however, the preferred term is *euskaltzale*, which might be best translated as Basque language loyalist or language advocate. The term *activist*, by contrast, tends to have a narrower usage referring to people who are militants in political organizations. Language loyalism, as we will see, is regarded as very distinct from conventional forms of political activism.

2. This analysis focuses on Kafe Antzokia's mode of globalism. For a penetrating analysis of the nature of the Guggenheim's ways of linking the global with the local, see Martín (2003).

3. The terminology used to refer to non-state languages has been a frequent topic of political commentary. Basque language loyalists prefer to speak of theirs as a 'minoritized' language, rather than a *minority* language.

In this way, they seek to underscore that the marginalized status of the language is the result not just of low numbers of speakers, but of specific policies of exclusion and discrimination on the part of the state, elites, and cultural institutions. Irigaray also explicitly rejects the term *minority language speaker* as a subjectivity. "We do not think of ourselves as a minority," he explained in a postinterview commentary.

4. Other important cultural antecedents to this aesthetic and cultural politics include the novels of Bernardo Atxaga, the music of Mikel Laboa, or the poetry of Joxe Antonio Artze. A fuller treatment of cosmopolitanism in Basque cultural discourse would need to examine this longer genealogy as a counter mode of expression to the ruralist, nostalgic notion of Basque culture.

5. www.kafeantzokia.com.

6. Sánchez Carrión's biography and concept of language revival are elaborated on in an extended interview with him by Jon Sarasua (1997). The interview was one of the first books to be published by Zenbat Gara's publishing house, Gara. On the reception of Txepetx, see also the special issue of *Bat: Soziolinguistika Aldizkaria* No. 18 (June 1996) commemorating the tenth anniversary of the publication of *Un futuro para nuestro pasado*.

7. Not to be underestimated according to one long-time sociologist/activist was the fact that Txepetx's work provided them with a "theory" to guide language revival. Theory provided a kind of symbolic capital that the social movement lacked. Here in Euskal Herria, he said, we have a lot of will and energy, but very little theory.

8. For an example of the marriage of biodiversity and language endangerment see the Web site of Terralingua, a nongovernmental organization dedicated to the preservation of language diversity (www.terralingua.org).

9. The sector that has been willing to work within the terms of the existing Statute of Autonomy is largely identified with the Partido Nacionalista Vasco, PNV. The main dissenting nationalists, commonly referred to as the radical nationalist Left (*izquierda abertzale*), reject the autonomy statute and also advocate a more working-class and nonethnic definition of Basque identity (see Kasmir 2002). Throughout the eighties and nineties the *izquierda abertzale* was represented by the political coalition Herri Batasuna. However, whether the nationalist Left will have any political representation is currently very much in question as a result of 2002 Law of Political Parties that effectively makes Herri Batasuna and its subsequent incarnation Batasuna illegal on grounds that their pro-independence goals violate the principles of the Spanish Constitution.

10. At the time of these interviews, when language loyalists were referring to accusations of affinities between grassroots language organizations and the nationalist Left, they were referring to perceived affinities in their political ideologies. Today, however, for any cultural organization to be accused of linkage to the nationalist Left has come to imply a direct tie to ETA. It is an

accusation that now, if made by the Spanish courts, carries very serious consequences that may result in incarceration and the dissolution of an organization. This began to be noted in 1998 with the closing of the newspaper EGIN and can be traced to shifts in the antiterrorist campaign. At about this time Spain's Central Criminal Court (Audiencia Nacional), chiefly responsible for prosecution of terrorists, began to argue that a wide gamut of Basque nationalist social movements, including some language advocacy groups, constitute part of the social and financial infrastructure of ETA. As I have noted, this kind of linkage is not what my interviewees were referring to in 1998; however, since the writing of this essay, this theory has resulted in many arrests, including among them professionals and well-respected members of the Basque intelligentsia. This is now a factor that deeply colors the political climate of grassroots cultural activism today.

11. The *comparsa* is a group formed usually by an association, club, or religious group, to specifically represent that association in *jaiak*. The *comparsa* typically will dance, wear costumes, and often play some musical instruments as it moves through the streets. For a fuller discussion of the linkages of urban space and festivities that brings gender into the analysis, see del Valle (1997).

12. On the significance of *borroka* as a model of political conflict see the seminal work by Zulaika (1988). See Urla (1999) for a fuller development of the contrast between *borroka* and *jaiak* or *jolas* (play) as contrasting strategies of resistance in the language movement.

13. See Abad et al. (1999) on the symbolic significance of the street in Basque politics.

14. See Urla (1997; 2001) for further discussions of cultural crossing in music and radio.

15. One example is the North African bar/cultural center Bere-Bar.

REFERENCES

Abad, Begoña, Javier Cerrato, Gabriel Gatti, Iñaki Martínez de Albéniz, Alfonso Pérez-Agote, and Benjamín Tejerina. 1999. *Institutionalización política y reencantamiento de la socialidad. Las transformaciones en el mundo nacionalista.* Soziologiazko Euskal Koadernoak/Cuadernos Sociológicos Vascos. Eusko Jaurlaritza.

Appadurai, Arjun. 1996. *Modernity at large: Cultural dimensions of globalization.* Minneapolis: University of Minnesota Press.

Brecher, Jeremy, John Brown Childs, and Jill Cutler. eds. 1993. *Global visions: Beyond the new world order.* Boston: South End Press.

Clifford, James. 1997. *Routes: Travel and translation in the late twentieth century.* Cambridge: Harvard University Press.

Dagnino, Evelina. 1993. An alternative world order and the meaning of democracy. In *Global visions: Beyond the new world order*, ed. Jeremy Brecher, John Brown Childs and Jill Cutler, 239–46. Boston: South End Press.

del Valle, Teresa. 1997. *Andamios para una nueva ciudad: Lecturas desde la antropología*. Madrid: Ediciones Cátedra.

Dorian, Nancy. 1998. Western language ideologies and small language prospects. In *Endangered languages*, ed. Lenore Grenoble and Lindsay Whaley, 3–21. Cambridge: Cambridge University Press.

Goffman, Erving. 1979. Footing. *Semiotica* 25:1–29.

Kasmir, Sharryn. 2002. "More Basque than you!" Class, youth, and identity in an industrial Basque town. *Identities: Global Studies in Culture and Power* 9:39–68

Martín, Annabel. 2003. A corpse in the garden: Bilbao's postmodern wrapping of high culture consumer architecture. *Arizona Journal of Hispanic Cultural Studies* 7:213–30.

Sánchez Carrión, José María.[Txepetx]. 1987. *Un futuro para nuestro pasado: Claves de la recuperación del euskara y teoría de las lenguas*. San Sebastián: Elkar.

Sarasua, Jon. 1997. *Txepetxekin solasean. Biziaren hizkuntzaz*. Bilbo: Gara.

Tsing, Anna. 2000. The global situation. *Cultural Anthropology* 15, no. 3:327–60.

Urla, Jacqueline. 1997. Outlaw language: Creating alternative public spheres in Basque free radio. In *The politics of culture in the shadow of capital*, ed. Lisa Lowe and David Lloyd, 280–300. Durham: Duke University Press.

———. 1999. Basque language revival and popular culture. In *Basque cultural studies*, ed. William Douglass, Carmelo Urza, Linda White, and Joseba Zulaika, 44–62. Reno: University of Nevada Press.

———. 2001. "We are all Malcolm X!" Negu Gorriak, hip-hop, and the Basque political imaginary. In *Global noise: Rap and hip-hop outside the USA*, ed. Tony Mitchell, 171–93. Middletown: Wesleyan University Press.

Zulaika, Joseba. 1988. *Basque violence: Metaphor and sacrament*. Reno: University of Nevada Press.

———. 1997. *Crónica de una seducción: El Museo Guggenheim Bilbao*. Madrid: Nerea.

Displacements

The Experience of Vectored Spaces in Peninsular Places

JAMES W. FERNANDEZ

SPACES AND PLACES

What is the place of the author of an afterword, such as I seek to occupy here in respect to this collection of essays? Of course, I appreciate the honor being done in being offered a final space of reflection. It is the penultimate space, really, as the very final space of reflection, at least in the Anglo American tradition, is the Index.[1] In other scholarly traditions, often in the Spanish, such a space is not recognized as something available for that last act of scholarly commitment; that ultimate and arduous construction of parsimonious reference to what has gone before. There is no place for that last indication of scholarly concern. The space for enabling the construction of reflective thought to take place, we see, is handled differently from culture to culture. Still, ultimate or penultimate, I want to make of this space offered to me here a place for indicating how much I have learned from this rich collection of ethnographic essays and at the same time to offer several tools for understanding Culture and Space!

As we see from the start, then, we must be clear about the distinction we will make between a space and a place. The literature, to be sure, offers many different ways of distinguishing between space and place, and often enough no distinction is made at all. Here, however, we will treat a space to be any bounded and self-contained subject of thought, such as a book, or a geophysical part of the world, such as the Iberian Peninsula which is itself subject to geometric dimensioning, that is, to distributive or cartographic measurement and collocation of

271

parts. A place is more than that! It is a space that is culturally constructed and invested with particular meanings in more than a diagrammatic or collocational sense. The Iberian Peninsula, a space, for example, can be constructed, as it is by some, as a bridge to the North African world and Islamic Culture. Spanish Culture, hence, is seen as a mediating culture between conflicting civilizations. Or it can be constructed by others, as it is by the EU, as a farthest outpost of European civilization and a bulwark of defense against African and Islamic incursion and emigration into Europe! There are, of course, various intermediate cultural constructions of any space, although the construction of contrast in culture and civilization is frequent. In any event, we will be attentive to the cultural construction of space as (1) a major transformation of the inchoate in human experience, for, in the end, space is inchoate until given meaning by culture,[2] and as (2) an aid in understanding the complexities of the frequent social experience of living differently in the same space. In our ethnographic experience Spanish villagers, as we see below, living in the same village space put quite different cultural constructions on that space. That is to say they are differently placed in that space and this differential placement makes both for differences in their experience of village life and for complex challenges to any adequate ethnography of that life.[3]

Because of the work of culture we argue that places are spaces constructed by culture in such a way as to be in tension with one another. We argue, therefore, that spaces can through the work and weight of culture become vectored as the tension characterizing their relation can be unstable and vectored in movement. Some places are expansive in relation to other spaces, for example, as Spain and Portugal were in the reconquest and exploration and settlement of the New World during the Imperial Centuries, or contractive and inward looking upon themselves, as they became in later centuries and as Ortega y Gasset and the generation of ninety-eight frequently lamented. In any event, in this penultimate essay we will, as we reflect upon the essays that have gone before, be exploring both what may be revealed in the distinction between space and place and, at once, seeking to understand how some elemental vectors of space play out in the various parts of Iberia where the contributors' ethnography have taken place. The spatial trope is ubiquitous in thought. What this collection of essays is about, as I understand it or seek to understand it, is its conversion into better understanding of the place of culture.

Some Commonplace Vectors in
Ethnographically Identified Places

If the reader will bear with me I am going to proceed deductively from some very general principles, or vectors, of spatial dynamics, and work toward the particular enrichments offered by the various ethnographers' content-rich experience of place, as conveyed in their individual chapters. As an ethnographer myself I ought to say, however, as I first proceed deductively through the several vectored spaces I evoke—the north-south, the imperial or colonizing-colonized, and the city-country—that they were all first experienced in the various places of my ethnographic experience. The vectors adduced, therefore, are ultimately only inductively, that is to say, ethnographically intelligible.

Independent of my field experiences and in another more enduring sense these vectored spaces and the characteristic displacements of action and imagination characteristic of them are old and enduring. The country and the city, for example, as two vectored and interactive spaces, are, as we recognize, ancient and are seen in the dialectics of the pastoral mode in the classical world. As Julio Caro Baroja (1963) has pointed out, "the town and the country" as interactive spaces are "ancient commonplaces," and as Raymond Williams (1973) further points out in *The country and the city*, the Roman rhetorician Quintilian makes these contrasting spaces his first example of a stock thesis or trope of argument which the *rhetor* can bring to bear when proclaiming about and identifying greed and/or innocence, complexity and/or simplicity, knowledge (intellectual virtue) and/or wisdom (moral virtue), alienation and/or incorporation, etc.[4] We employ the term *vectored spaces* in that dynamic sense to indicate at once the constant tension and sense of opposition in spaces as a consequence of their cultural construction into places with sets of contrasting associations, as well as the interactive movement back and forth between these association-rich places over historical time. It is Williams's (1973) main argument in his classic study of the relation between "the country and the city" that these spaces are not to be seen in the end as stable entities in constant and fixed tension with each other but rather as existing historically in vital and dynamic, that is to say cultural, interrelation.[5]

As far as North-South as vectored spaces, Levine and Campbell (1972) have pointed out not only how enduring but how widespread in the world and how very similar in the associated meanings this interactive differentiation of places has been. As far as the Imperial and Imperialized or Colonizing/Colonized Places, very much an interest in this collection of essays, we recognize these in the earliest empires of the classical and ancient mideast. One of the enduring battles for autochthony and self-actualization of the ancient Greeks was fought against imperial domination by the Middle Eastern empires, particularly the Persian.

Early on here, then, I will mainly make reference to deductions about spatial dynamics in culture that have arisen in my own ethnographic experience over the many decades, going on six now, with the placements of space, or more accurately with the *displacements* that have taken place, in the various cultures I have studied in Africa and northern Spain. Displacement is an important word for us. For it is in *displacement* that culturally meaningful experience of different spaces is most clearly accentuated, a fact demonstrated particularly convincingly and forcefully in Oriol Pi-Sunyer's account of his and his family's exile, because of the Spanish Civil War, from Spain to England, and from Barcelona and Roses to London.

Though I will at first here mainly deal with my own deductions about vectored spaces I have investigated, it would be illuminating to consider an elemental vector present in our very last chapter, that of Jacqueline Urla in her comment on that place of Basque language learning, speaking, and revival, "Kafe Antzokia: The Global Meets the Local in Basque Cultural Politics." Urla points out that in contrast to previous Basque places of language, learning, speaking, and revival, which were inward looking, self-isolating, and self-protective, Kafe Antzokia's effort is to open up to multicultural, indeed global, influences in an effort to project the Basque language onto an international stage. The principal vector of displacement is from the local to the global. Urla makes reference here to the work of the Basque anthropologist, Joseba Zulaika (1997), and his treatment of the now-famous Guggenheim Museum in Bilbao, *Crónica de una seducción*.[6] Zulaika's is a book on the coming into Bilbao of the international art world, in the form of the multinational Guggenheim Museum. Without attending to all the subtleties of that displacement of the New York art world to a Basque locality and the accompanying displacement or marginalization of Basque art, which Zulaika details, let us simply point up the contrast in vectors between Kafe Antzokia moving from the local to the global, the Basque nation to the international, and "El Museo Bilbao Guggenheim" moving from the global to the local, the international art world into the national and the local. Though the vectors are different in direction, in both cases we see the making of a local space into a global place and vice versa. In a first case the vector of communication is from the local culture below to the overarching global culture above and in the second case from an international art culture above into a local art culture below.

SOME VECTORED SPACES OF AFRICAN AND IBERIAN ETHNOGRAPHY

Now let me move to some vectors in my own ethnography. This is not quite that movement through the twilight zone between history and memory of which Hobsbawn and Pi–Sunyer speak because much of which I refer to here briefly is contained in the more complex form of ethnographic fieldnotes taken and ethnography written and published as directly as possible after the fieldwork itself. I ask the reader's forbearance, therefore, as I briefly return to recast these former ethnographic experiences in order to find a perspective upon the spatial vectors manifest in them. I will be mainly interested in some dominant vectors with the hope of showing how the materials in this collection give detail and thickness to such schematic understanding.

Our[7] first several years of fieldwork were spent among the Fang of Gabon, Western Equatorial Africa. They were, in my first year among them, a colonized people, and then at the end of our second year, with the granting by the French of independence they passed into the state of an early post–colony. In that condition they still are found, although with their wealth of resources, in contrast to most African countries, they have come to have a much greater international presence. With all its relative wealth, however, Gabon is still a place of peripherality and subordinance to the great world centers of politics and commerce.

My main object of study in Gabon and among the Fang was a religious movement, Bwiti, which, amidst the subordinance of colonial peripherality and subsequent dictatorial government, sought out by self–isolation to gain access to the very centers of spiritual power, of spiritual self–actualization, and of spiritual self–sufficiency. They did this by syncretizing a mostly abandoned but nostalgically recalled ancestor worship with important elements from missionary Christianity. Because of its isolationist yet creative tendency I spoke of this movement as a microcosm and of their creativity in thought and action as "micro-cosmogony." That is, they sought to create an absorbing and assuaging self-sufficient religious universe of belief and action for their member-ship. Their religious activity was centripetal, designed to bind the mem-bership tightly together through the gravitational discipline and attraction of their night-long rituals into a sheltered and spiritually uplifting cen-tral place. In elemental spatial terms I spoke of the predominant vector of movement in Bwiti as endocentric in nature (cf. Fernandez 1969, 1978, 1979, 1982).

In subsequent years, throughout the sixties, I worked with a half-dozen other religious movements in Sub Saharan Africa. Some of them like The Hlabazahlangana Movement or the Old Man's Church, or the Zionists among the Zulu in peri-urban Durban, Natal, were also endocentric and centripetal seeking to gather in members into a central healing place of isolated spiritual and corporeal tranquility achieved through vertiginous involuting rituals. They promised this ultimate tran-quility of spirit and wellness of body amidst the many external afflic-tions, harassments, and subordinations of Apartheid South Africa (Fernandez 1967, 1973).

But other movements studied in those years, particularly those in West Africa, were evangelical in their nature and calling. In a centrifugal manner they sought to expand their presence in the landscape in num-bers of congregations and church membership and in places of worship (Fernandez 1970). They had a different relation to the social and po-litical spaces in which they lived, and rather than escape it into the comforts of a ritual vortex, they saw themselves in competition with other religious groups, seeking by various forms of evangelization to increase their presence in the space of the colonial and postcolonial world made available to them. The relationships to space, we see, whether given by the extant political economy or created more or less whole cloth, were quite different in these different movements (Fernandez 1984, 1986). Accordingly there was a different kind of "taking place" characteristic of them.

In the nineteen seventies my wife and I shifted our ethnographic research out of Africa to rural villagers of northern Spain in the Prov-ince of Asturias. In this displacement we at first worked among cattle keepers become or becoming miners and, more recently, rural tourist-dependent hotel, bar, and vacation house proprietors and innkeepers.

That marked shift in the space of ethnography from Africa to Europe brought to our attention many cultural differences: one thing was the contrast between difficult tonal African languages, Fang, Zulu, and Ewe to one of the easier, for English speakers at least, romance languages in the Indo-European tradition, Castilian Spanish. It was a shift from a formerly and still quite recently autochthonous people living in the subordinance and dependency of colonialism and the post-colony to rural people living in the subordinance and dependency of those never fully dichotomous and often interacting poles of a continuum, variously labeled the folk-urban, the Great Tradition-Little Tradition, or to employ that "ancient commonplace" in Mediterranean Europe, the city and the country (Caro Baroja 1963).

In the European case there was a millenniums-old literate tradition. Though the villagers as a whole, until well toward the end of the nineteenth century, were nonliterate there had been for many centuries the presence, particularly in the priesthood and the Church, of the Great Tradition and of that tradition of literacy. Over the centuries the parishes studied had become, mainly by the church, well-documented places. They were an abundant presence of information and commentary in both parish church and in the administrative archives of the bishopric. This was a substantial challenge to an ethnographer with any interest in historical contexts. Places differ obviously in the amount of information about them contained in them that is available to inform the ethnographic task as derived from the presence or absence of literacy. In this regard we had moved from an information-sparse to an information-rich place. I am referring to things written and to the fact that our understanding of a place in the literate world is in important part based on what has been written about it. After the brevity of the archival record of our African years I found that ethnography in this long literate previously written-up, written-about space in some ways quite daunting.[8]

To be sure many if not most villagers until very recently had been barely literate. The control by certain villagers and village residents, the priest, the schoolteacher, the doctor, local administrators, of the written record in its various forms gave them a certain hegemony and was the basis of a rural class system based in important part on literacy, also not found in the African ethnographies. In any event, we came to recognize the degree to which through the work of culture African and European places differed in the amount of information contained in them relevant to ethnographic interests and the way that that information could be used in class and caste formation and in the hegemonies of everyday life. These were spaces vectored in terms of top-down, superiority-inferiority relations usually anchored in the tools of literacy.

Let me now say a word about the historical place of the mountainous enclave province of Asturias in which our work is still ongoing, in relation to the geopolitical space of Iberia generally. And also let me say something more about the placements, the different occupancy of village space, experienced by the different social-economic formations with which we have been preoccupied and which we have been comparing: agro-pastoralists, miners, and finally tourist-oriented small business people.

Asturias as a space is a seaside province; it is also its own region. It lies behind the ramparts of the Peaks of Europe and the last high mountain extension of the West Cantabrian Range. Its productive agricultural and grazing lands are found in the valleys of the piedmont running from fifty to one hundred kilometers in width from sea to mountain uplands. Travelers coming up from the central Iberian plateau of Castille and Leon to the mountain passes and entering down into Asturias, knowing as yet nothing about its culture, cannot fail, however, to note that they are entering into a much different ecological space. Humidity and rainfall alone, quite besides the very rugged deeply cut valleys the traveler encounters before he may have had any contact with Asturian culture, will convince him or her of a significant if not drastic spatial displacement.

This isolation behind the bulwark of the mountains enabled the inhabitants of Asturias to effectively resist the Moorish conquest and from the eighth well on into the tenth century Asturias and the Asturian Kingdom was the capital of earliest medieval Spain and the seat of the reconquest. Then authority and centrality passed over to Leon and to Castile and finally on to central Iberia. In this displacement in Spanish geopolitics Asturias, once a central Spanish place, became a peripheral place. And though claims to centrality persist, as in the old saw and compensatory claim "Asturias is Spain and the rest of the peninsula reconquered land," in point of fact awareness of having become a peripheral place is ever-present and heavy in Asturian thinking about themselves. The dynamic of centrality-peripherality is probably ever-present in the constructions of most cultures everywhere, but it is as present in Asturias as anywhere in Spain.

While this historical sense of peripheralization in space, of displacement and loss of place, is an ever-present backdrop to work in Asturias, our own work has been among Asturian country people who in the past hundred years, at least in the case of our research focused in the south central Asturian mining valleys, have been in transition from agro-pastoralism to bituminous coal mining to increasing focus on tourism as the mines play out. A space-in-culture and culture-in-space awareness such as put forth in this collection, or as reformulated in terms of displacement and the cultural vicissitudes of place, provides important perspective on this historical dynamic. The agro-pastoralist of annual short-range transhumance is a man or woman of locality, very centered in the day-in and day-out care of his or her animals and his and her crops, a kind of "slavery" of endless tasks and obligations as they frequently call it. He and she and their family know their place. One emphasizes man and woman because agro-pastoralism and herding is work for the entire family.

It is also in these mountains a lifeway oriented up-valley and generally upward in space, to the annual adventure of short-range transhumance to the upland pastures and mountain passes, the "*paramos.*" There is a strong attraction to the congenial and relatively free from village obligation life in the upland *cabañas* (huts) from late spring through early fall. These summer pastures and life there are, as a consequence, places of nostalgia. In contrast, the miner is a man whose lifeway is daily oriented down-valley and downward into that radically different milieu of the deep shaft and gallery mines. The countryman gone into mining must also displace himself daily from the agro-pastoral village to the highly industrial and urban milieu of the downriver mining towns. The agro-pastoralist and cattle keeper, however distant his transhumance may take him into the nearby mountains, remains centered in village life and village resources from which he re-supplies himself. His in the end is a centripetal life. The daily displacements of the miner makes him much more a centrifugal man, much more a man of the world and characteristically a man susceptible to ideological politics, as the mining towns to which he daily journeys have long been full of radical left-wing politics, as the villages are not.

As the mines have tailed out, and mining employment much reduced, men have either returned to agro-pastoralism or to the setting up, together with their families, of various tourist establishments, bars and restaurants, inns, commerce featuring local products or providing for the supply of summer and winter visitors, hikers and skiers predominantly. This lifeway, though very local, and exploiting the environmental attractions of this mountainous rural locality in which these people live, has also become quite global. This is so because, among other reasons, as tourists come from relatively far away those increasingly catering to and dependent on their tourism have to take a much wider social horizon into account. Indeed, many of these recent establishments in the last decade or more have created and uploaded their own Web sites, thus displacing themselves, or representations of themselves, to the wide world, in a way their congeners could not previously have imagined.

Ostensibly, it would be a commonplace to maintain that there is a common culture and a common language[9] in these villages, on the basis of the common space all villagers occupy in a general way. But in point of fact the three lifeways identified have different life worlds based on significantly different placements in that space. That is to say that cattle keepers, miners' families, and tourist families, through their respective subcultures, experience significantly different kinds of daily cycle, seasonal cycle, and life cycle. That is to say also that they experience different displacements within their common space and significantly different ways of exploiting that common space. Their lives are differently vectored. Any general ethnographic cultural description of village life that would appeal only to some very general set of vectors and ignore these "space and subculture" differences, the different placements and displacements of the different interacting lifeways, would miss the full complexity of the vitalizing coordination and the devitalizing discord in village life.

POPULAR COSMOLOGY AND RACIAL IDEOLOGY: THE NORTH AND THE SOUTH IN THE BUILDING OF NATIONAL IDENTITIES

Among the predominant vectors in European space is the north–south one. It is found from Norway to Iberia and it is an ancient vector of spatial understanding[10] and sense of identity. This has been so at least since the turbulent and uncivilized northern Keltoi were identified by the Greeks, and whose challenging incursions into the heart of the classical world in the first millennium BC, conquering Athens and

Rome at various times, made for an enduring historical nightmare, that of the "barbarians at the gates." The Celts, until finally conquered by Caesar, were, in fact, the classic barbarians. In those classical times and through the Renaissance perhaps, the north was barbarous and the south civilized until a kind of sea change in the moral frontier, as it might be called, caused this frontier of respect and accomplishment to reverse itself, as first the Reformation and the Protestant Ethic and then invention and industrialization made the north more powerful and ostensibly more civilized, at least more modern, displacing the now-to-be-understood undisciplined yet anciently civilized south. The latter became mainly an object of the culture of learned curiosity as in the *bildungsroman* of the Grand Tour.

Sobral's chapter on "Race and Space in Interpretations of Portugal: The North-South Division and Representations of Portuguese National Identity in the Nineteenth and Twentieth Centuries" carries forward our understanding of that vector of relationships. He makes clear how ever-present in the nineteenth and twentieth centuries in Iberia has been this spatial vectoring of civilization and backwardness, of power and weakness, and particularly of dominance and subordinance of racial identity. Within the general north-south vector of the peninsula Sobral sees a distinction in the north between the northeast and northwest of Iberia. But the prevailing spatial distinction is that between the North and the South. The former is readily placed as Aryan in nature, while the south, principally Moorish descended, is identified as the place of Semitic influence and culture. Sobral is interested in the way that a racial ideology has taken place in relation to these spatial divisions. Within the north itself Sobral, as noted, remarks the division between the Celtic northwest and the Iberian northeast, a division that is relevant in explaining Portugal's sense of separation from Spain, a separation rather more subtly racial than the gross Aryan–Semitic, north-south divisions of the past two centuries.

Sobral's reading of the north-south division in Portugal and Iberia generally and the associated racial ideologies that energize these divisions with invidious content enriches our understanding of the, on the face of it, too gross differentiation we have been making between northern and southern spaces and northern and southern identities. We learn additional things; of the way, for example, that that sense of division is associated with corporeal and cultural racism, and of how it is mainly energized, which is to say vectored, from the north reacting to southern and Semitic, that is to say, Moorish influences. This sense of northern resistance to southern influence is further complicated by a moral resistance to the fleshpots and corrupted politics of Lisbon. While it is the capital of the Portuguese nation it is yet a "southern" Portuguese city. Above all, Sobral alerts us to the way that the idea of national identity is in constant, ongoing negotiation between differently vectored spaces, each with their particular values and sets of association. North-south racism may be a way of overcoming class and ethnic divisions in nation building but it is also a challenge to the taking place of a unitary Portuguese nation.

THE VECTORS OF IMPERIAL PLACES AND THE RE-SHAPING OF SPACE IN THE DE-COLONIZING AND POST COLONIAL WORLD

Recall the shift we have mentioned in the moral frontier in Europe between northern and southern cultures. The long-time imperial dominance of southern Europe over the uncivilized and pagan north, largely Graeco-Roman and then Roman Catholic in origin, locus, and exercise, changes over by reason of a religious and an industrial revolution into the dominance of the north over the south, the latter left, as it were, to live among the ruins of the "glories that were Greece and the grandeur that was Rome." It is a shift that raises the issue of the Imperial vector, subspecie cultural colonization, in the relation of national places. That is to say that there has long been in Europe an imperial context of domination-subordination and a vector of "colonization of" and "colonization by" in the interest of the civilizing and mercantile mission. The politics of culture and civilization worked to define the geographical spaces identified with nations as expansive and impositional places, on the one hand, and contractive and imposed-upon places, on the other. The experience of Spain and Portugal over the centuries, virtually until Europeanization in the European Union, from imperial centers to relative backwaters, illustrates that change of vectors.

A number of the essays in this collection make clear that the space that nations occupy and the places their cultures construct are possessed of this vectoral dynamic of civilization and mercantile domination and subordination. The ever-presence of this imperial dynamic and the positive or negative sense of place that derives from it is trenchantly discussed in João Leal's "The Hidden Empire: Peasants, Nation Building, and the Empire in Portuguese Anthropology." The background presence of a once-glorious imperial history and the subsequent fate of the Portuguese empire not only is present among the elite in thinking about their nation's place among nations, and about the nationality of one's self, but is something experienced as well by the peasantry. For the nostalgic (*saudade*) sense of loss of empire and an accompanying sense of decadence and degeneration affects them too. One would think such feelings to be primarily the emotions of the political and religious elites directly associated with imperial expansion and contraction. But it is ethnographically observable among the peasantry as well. The peasants too, Leal observes, have that historical sense of "we are small but once we were great," a sense, that is, of loss of place in the affairs of nations, and an affect-laden decline from a former well placed imperial state of having occupied a much greater space in the world.

This comparative historical–nostalgic sense of loss of place from formerly occupying much greater imperial space is surely present everywhere in Iberia. The peninsula was the one-time metropole, after all, of two great empires upon which, indeed, and antecedent to the British claim, "the sun never set." This sense of claim on a once worldwide imperial space and the desire to revive its actuality if only symbolically is convincingly demonstrated in Medeiros's study of the colonial exhibitions characteristic of the early Estado Novo dictatorship under Salazar. This was a regime proclaiming an imperialist ideology invested in "*Ultramar*" politics. The same kind of exhibitions were offered in Spain by the Franco dictatorship, although on a minor scale compared to the Portuguese. Francoism invested its imperialist ideology primarily in various diplomatic-educational institutions of "*Cultura Hispanica*," which reached out assiduously to the former colonies and their common and unifying and worldwide "*hispanidad*," a cultural replica in its way of the geopolitical empire that originally energized it.

Susan DiGiacomo in her illuminating essay shows the presence of that imperialist ideology, or as she aptly names it, the "memory politics" in the cartographic representations of Spain's place in the world and in the history teachings taking place in the Francoist fascist classroom in Catalonia. The contrast is with the classrooms of the Republic where the Crusade trope of fascism was absent and, also, the exaggerated accoutrements of Imperialist nostalgia.

In its way, also, Brian O'Neill in his study of the Malacca Portuguese shows their cultural displacement back, primarily in the folklore of food, music, and dance, from their actual "nondescript" situation in

Malaysia, to a revitalized and recollected identification with the disappeared Portuguese empire, the empire that brought them to Malaysia in the first place. The efforts of the Malaccan Portuguese to preserve or revive commercializable aspects of Portuguese culture not only creates a gratifying memory space redolent with a former empire but leverages their peripherality in the Malaysian scene into a more centered and profitable place.

THE CITY AND THE COUNTRY

Both Caro Baroja (1963) and Williams (1973), as we have seen, show how enduring and dynamic in Western literature and thought from earliest times these contrasting spaces of the town (city) and country have been. At the same time the values associated with these contrasts have been, in various places at various times, variable and in complex relations. In this collection two chapters particularly make this point: that of Roseman, on the action of the Francoist Sección Femenina through its *cursillos* in the countryside and that of María Cátedra on the Virgin of Sonsoles of Ávila. The Virgin studied by Cátedra is a rural divinity whose *patronato* of country people is in tension and occasionally in conflict with the urban religious authorities of Ávila interested in appropriating the sacred power and pecuniary possibilities of Her Shrine. So there is a city-country tension in this religious institution. Yet the Virgin's annual displacements into the city establish a crucial interrelationship of complementarity between the rural and the urban. It is of interest that the crucial vector of interaction and integration here runs from country to city, although the urban authorities in a contrary vector repeatedly seek to appropriate and urbanize the Virgin.

The countryside *cursillos* of the Sección Femenina, discussed by Roseman, we see, were largely undertaken by urban educated young people anxious to establish "common ground" in the fascist state by conveying fascist values and principles of disciplined good order, productiveness, and propriety to the backwardness of the countryside. There is some irony, as Roseman points out, in this attempt by the fascist political elite to establish "common ground," which is to say a mutually agreed upon set of "common places," when their political vision, typically hierarchical and top-down, was heavily influenced by the stereotypic rhetoric of country backwardness. Roseman's essay provides another instructive analysis of the interaction between town and country, the vector here running from the city and its authoritarian ideas of productive citizenship to the backward countryside. And like DiGiacomo's study of the fascist classroom it enriches our sense of the authoritarian version of imperial history as regards these vectored spaces.

In the countryside itself, town and country distinctions are also at play as Parkhurst's analysis of the subregional and interlocal differences in the Douro of Portugal details. Hierarchical in nature following the hierarchical differentiation in the wines of the Douro itself, as classified by the Casa do Douro, Parkhurst examines the rhetorical work of a local newspaper columnist, Onésimo Azevedo, in confirming hierarchies of locality, of culture and class, and of quality of production. The stereotypes of core and periphery, civilized center and rural periphery of his "rhetorical world," and confirmed in his newspaper writings, resonate on a small scale with the enduring town-country differentiations to which we refer.

It is important to observe that our ethnographic task is not unaffected by the vectored spaces in which we undertake it. An ethnographer from a culturally constructed northern place, or a place with a widely recognized imperial or colonizing mission, or a place plainly urban in culture will have, to say the least, distinctly different opportunities and impediments to understanding than one from a space differently vectored. To adapt an important phrase in Roseman's essay, a phrase reminiscent with Michael Herzfeld's (2005) work on "cultural intimacy," while the ethnographer must inevitably be seeking the "common ground of ethnography," he or she cannot ignore the vectored spaces that converge on or in that "common ground" and the "displacements" that, though the ethnographer might prefer to ignore or downplay them, are ever active in his or her ethnography.

In Final Place: The Vectors of Quality Space and the Place of Ethnography

We may conclude by reflecting on some things we have learned from the various essays, all of which in their way have been seeking to understand in their particular ethnographic materials the relation between space and culture. More particularly I find in them also testimony to the dynamic of displacement as revelatory in one's experience of culture. Exemplary here is Oriol Pi-Sunyer's insightful essay, which is preeminently an ethnography of displacement. Pi-Sunyer reflects on his family's exile to England because of the Spanish Civil War and the deepened sense of culture, or rather the "contrapuntal" sense of two cultural spaces, Catalonia and England, Barcelona and London, that that displacement provided for him. In the English classroom he came to understand the meaning of imperial space and the centrality of empire in the British sense of identity. Had he remained in Spain, of course, the fascist classroom that would have been imposed upon him, as detailed by DiGiacomo, would have had its own pointed lessons of respect toward and nostalgia for the languishing patrimony of Spanish imperialism. But the point is that Pi-Sunyer's percipience in the presence of "contrapuntal cultures" is, in the end, the product of the forced displacements that he and his family had undergone. The point we have been making is that it is not placement in space as much as displacement between spaces in which cultural insight arises. Few anthropologists, I hazard, by profession displaced persons, would deny that argument or would deny that the vectors of going out to and coming back from another culture, from north to south and vice versa, from metropole to colony and vice versa and from city to country and vice versa, are or can be a principal source of anthropological insight.

As Iberianists, for our part, we will all recognize these vectors, I am sure. Also, the space–place dialectic we have focused upon will resonate with our experience in the peninsula. For contemporaneously we are witness to the many displacements brought about by Spain's 1978 "ethnogenetic constitution" in Davydd Greenwood's (1985, 1988) phrasing, a constitution that fosters the development of claims to autonomy based on distinct cultural identity. In effect, what we witness is a panorama of displacements as the developing autonomous governments seek to separate their identity from the national identity and centrality of Madrid by focusing on their own place in the peninsula, thus reconstructing the realities of their own cultures and polities. We are seeing emerge before us a Spain that is a space of many essential places. This is a debate, incidentally, prefigured already for Mediterraneanists in the 1980s arguments over the Mediterranean itself as properly a place or, to the contrary, only a space of many places.

As to our own argument here, we have anchored it primarily in the vectoring of space by first of all being attentive, to some enduring, indeed ancient, commonplaces and the vectored spaces that they describe and encompass, north–south, colonizer–colonized, urbanity–rusticity. We argue, however, that it is not from the cultural contrasts of their associations alone that we learn but rather from their vectored interaction and attempted integration, their search for common ground, across the boundaries and frontiers suggested or required by their separate cultures.

But we have also wanted to suggest that the description of cultural space as a quality space or a set of vectors—three were suggested in the original formulation[11]—while it is one viable simplicity to be recognized beyond the complexity of cultural contact and interaction, it is not an adequate resting place for anthropological inquiry. For that inquiry normally is based upon a long-lasting presence and participation "in place" and is characterized by as detailed description of local activity and belief as may be possible. For the anthropologist primarily "the devil is in the details" and not in a coordinate system of vectors of activity, goodness, and power or vectors of north-southness, imperial or colonial domination and subordination, or urbaneness and rusticity. These vectors may provide us a framework of spatial understanding, as suggested, but they do not in the end very deeply instruct our understanding of interacting places. It is in the ethnographic detail of the series of essays in this collection that that instruction lies!

Recalling, finally, Bachelard's (1964) stimulating and insightful book *The poetics of space*, we might observe that what we have been specially focused upon here in this after essay is the kinesthetics of space and not upon the synesthetics or synesthesia of space as pursued by Bachelard, a synesthesia, I think we can argue, that is a characteristic of any attentive ethnography. But in the end, culture is never quiescent and the constancy of kinesthesia inevitably conditions all synesthetic achievements. And it has a certain primacy in those achievements so that though they always take place, as this collection of essays argues, in space, they take place in a space desirous of the construction of meaning. Culture, in respect to space, we might say, "abhors a vacuum"!

NOTES

1. The index is that final space of consultation and of scholarly commitment in which the entire contents of the proceeding work is reflected in a reduced and consultable way. It very often has no place and is a missing space in continental and particularly southern European works to the frustration of many an English-speaking reader.

2. For a foundational statement of a theory of culture as the predication of meaning, mainly figurative, on the fundamental inchoateness of human

experience, among which is surely the experience of space and time, see Fernandez (1974).

3. In this regard see the observation by Yaeger in note 1 of the introduction to this volume that "in a global economy where multiple places converge in a single space . . . the space/place binary becomes porous and provisional" (and) "we need to destabilize . . . the integrity that place-centered analysis sometimes assumes" (Yaeger 1996:5). I would stress the point that the different places of village space and life do indeed have different porosities. The boundaries of a rural bed and breakfast owner or a village innkeeper are much more porous than those of a cattle keeper.

4. Williams (1973:46). Williams shows the reader the complex of opposing values associated with the country and the city in the literature: luxury-penury, production-craftsmanship, greed-contentment, private property-the commons, hustle-retreat, etc. For Williams the particular contrast is between the alienations of exploitative capitalism and the mutuality and sharing of socialism! For him, as for Marx, European rural space has been extensively colonized by capitalism.

5. Ibid., 297. Though Williams spends much time in this book working out the contrasting values with which City and Country are associated, greed versus innocence for example, in the end he argues that "we must not limit ourselves to their contrast but go on to see their interrelations and through these the real shape of the underlying crisis." He is referring to the crisis in his contemporary England of the devaluation and urbanization of the countryside and the proletarianizing of its inhabitants.

6. Joseba Zulaika (1997). Zulaika's paper, "Asymmetries in the Politics of Global Culture: The Bilbao Guggenheim Museum," was originally a part of our symposium and the reader would have been able to directly compare these vectors. Unfortunately, forces beyond editorial control prevented its inclusion.

7. Except for the first four months among the Fang in 1958 and in my 1965 research among the Zulu in South Africa, my research has been undertaken with the participation of my co-ethnographer Renate Lellep.

8. We should be careful not to denigrate all that cultures without writing have to teach and all that can be learned in non-literature milieus. After all, that learning has been amply demonstrated by anthropology and anthropological history over and over again and over many many decades. I simply wish to indicate that the amount of local information committed in writing to the archives in our Spanish research was a challenge to inquiry that was not present in my African work.

9. We will not address the differences in allegiance and use of Castilian and/or Asturian influenced registers in local speech. Different allegiances to these language ways are found in different "barrios" (or corrrales) of the village. See J. W. Fernandez (1996).

10. The East-West vector of spatial opposition, of such importance in central and eastern Europe, which has been its battleground, is of little consequence in Iberia, certainly when compared to the North-South vector of cultural opposition that prevails in the peninsula. O'Neill in his essay on the Malacca Portuguese does touch on the East-West vector as these Easterners of many generations make claims on a Western, that is Portuguese, identity. The northeast Iberia-northwest Iberia is also touched upon in Sobral's essay.

11. Cf J. W. Fernandez (1974). The original three-dimensioned quality space of culture, an idea influenced by the work of the social psychology of Osgood, Tannebaum, and others, was a space of three dynamic vectors, variations, that is, in goodness, power, and activity!

References

Bachelard, Gaston. 1964. *The poetics of space*. Boston: Beacon Press.

Caro Baroja, Julio. 1963. The city and the country: Reflexions on some ancient commonplaces. In *Mediterranean countrymen: Essays in the social anthropology of the Mediterranean*, ed. Julian Pitt-Rivers, 27–40. The Hague: Mouton.

Fernandez, James W. 1967. *Revitalized words from the parrot's egg and the bull who crashes in the krall*. In *Proceedings of the American Ethnological Society for 1966*, 53–64.

———. 1969. *Microcosmogony and modernization in African religious movements*. Occasional Papers, Center for Developing Area Studies, 35 pp. Montreal: McGill University.

———. 1970. Rededication and prophetism in Ghana. Monograph on the Apostle's Revelation Society. In *Cahiers d'Études Africaines* X, no. 2 (June):228–305.

———. 1973. Zulu Zionism. In *Man's many ways, natural history reader in anthropology*, ed. Richard A. Gould, 326–35. New York: Harper and Row.

———. 1974. The mission of metaphor in expressive culture. *Current Anthropology* 15, no. 2:119–45.

———. 1978. African religious movements. *Annual Review of Anthropology* VII: 195–234.

———. 1979. On the notion of religious movement. *Social Research* 46, no. 1:36–62.

———. 1982. *Bwiti: An ethnography of the religious imagination in Africa*. Princeton: Princeton University Press.

———. 1984. Emergence and convergence in some African sacred places. In *Place: Experience and symbol*, ed. Miles Richardson, vol. 24 in *Geoscience and Man*, 31–42. Baton Rouge: Geoscience Publications, Louisiana State University.

————. 1986. Location and direction in African religious movements: Some deictic contours of religious conversion. *History of Religions* 25, no. 4:352–67.

————. 1996. *Campos léxicos y vida cultural n'Asturies.* Uviéu: Academia de la Llingua Asturiana.

Greenwood, Davydd J. 1985. Castilians, Basques, and Andalusians: An historical comparison of nationalism, "true" ethnicity, and "false" ethnicity. In *Ethnic groups and the state*, ed. Paul Brass, 204–27. London: Croom Helm.

————. 1988. Anthropology and ethnogenesis in Spain. Paper delivered as part of the symposium "Post-transitional Iberia," Annual Meetings of the American Anthropological Association. Phoenix, Arizona.

Herzfeld, Michael. 2005. *Cultural intimacy: Social poetics in the nation state.* New York: Routledge, rev. ed.

Levine, Robert, and Donald T. Campbell. 1972. *Ethnocentrism: Theories of conflict, ethnic attitudes, and group behavior.* New York: Wiley.

Williams, Raymond. 1973. *The country and the city.* New York: Oxford University Press.

Yaeger, Patricia. 1996. Introduction: Narrating space. In *The geography of identity*, ed. Patricia Yaeger, 1–38. Ann Arbor: University of Michigan Press.

Zulaika, Joseba. 1997. *Crónica de una seducción: El Museo Bilbao Guggenheim.* Madrid: Nerea.

Contributors

María Cátedra is Professor of Social and Cultural Anthropology at the Universidad Complutense of Madrid. Her books include *This world, other worlds* (1992), *Un santo para una ciudad* (1997), and as editor, *Los españoles vistos por los antropólogos* (1991) and *La mirada cruzada en la península ibérica* (2001).

Susan M. DiGiacomo is a faculty member in the anthropology departments of the Universitat Rovira i Virgili in Tarragona (Catalonia), and the University of Massachusetts at Amherst. Her publications on contemporary Catalonia include several articles and book chapters on a variety of interrelated themes: nationalism, language politics and ideology, political violence, and historical memory.

James W. Fernandez is Professor Emeritus of Anthropology at the University of Chicago. Since the early seventies he and his co-ethnographer Renate Lellep have been working on revitalization processes in the mining valleys of south central Asturias. Most recently UNED has published a collection of his articles in Castilian, *En el dominio del tropo: Imaginación figurativa y vida social en España.*

João Leal is Associate Professor at the Department of Anthropology of Universidade Nova de Lisboa. His books include *Etnografias portuguesas (1870–1970). Cultura popular e identidade nacional (Portuguese ethnographies 1870–1970. Folk culture and national identity)*, published in 2000, and *Antropologia em Portugal. Mestres percursos, transições (Anthropology in Portugal. Founding fathers, pathways, transitions)*, published in 2006. He is currently working on Portuguese immigration to Brazil and to the United States.

António Medeiros is Assistant Professor of Anthropology at ISCTE (Instituto Superior de Ciências do Trabalho e da Empresa) in Lisbon. He has published two books and numerous articles on the relations between anthropology and literary history in Portugal. He is currently working on an English version of the book *Dois lados de um rio: Nacionalismo e etnografias na Galiza e em Portugal*, published in 2006 in both Portugal and Spain.

Brian Juan O'Neill is Professor of Anthropology at ISCTE (Instituto Superior de Ciências do Trabalho e da Empresa) in Lisbon, and author of *Social inequality in a Portuguese hamlet* (1987) and *Antropologia Social—Sociedades complexas* (2006). He has conducted fieldwork in Galicia, Portugal, and Malaysia (Malacca). His recent research interests include life-histories, action-centred and processual theories, Gypsies, and critical analysis of multicultural Portuguese Creole communities in Southeast Asia.

Shawn S. Parkhurst is Assistant Professor of Anthropology and Director of the Portuguese Studies Program at the University of Louisville (Kentucky). He has published on gender relations, kinship, and marriage in Portugal. Currently he is working on a manuscript on spatial structure, political economy, and culture in the Alto Douro region of northern Portugal.

Oriol Pi-Sunyer is Professor of Anthropology at the University of Massachusetts, Amherst. He has written extensively on Spanish political economy, identity, migration, and exile. His current research focuses on the uses of historical memory, particularly in Catalonia.

Sharon R. Roseman is Associate Professor of Anthropology at Memorial University of Newfoundland. She is co-editor (with Ellen Badone) of *Intersecting journeys: The anthropology of pilgrimage and tourism* (2004). The majority of her publications have focused on memory, gender, language politics, political economy, and rurality. Her current research focuses on rural rights claims in Galicia and the historical anthropology of the Franco dictatorship.

José Manuel Sobral is an anthropologist and historian, Senior Research Fellow at the Institute of Social Sciences, University of Lisbon.

He has done research on Portuguese rural society, social memory, heritage, nationalism, and ethnicity. He is the author of several articles on those subjects and a book: *Trajectos: O passado e o presente na vida de uma freguesia da Beira* (*Trajectories: The past and the present in the life of a parish of Beira*).

Jacqueline Urla is Associate Professor of Anthropology and Director of the Modern European Studies Program at the University of Massachusetts Amherst. She has dedicated most of her research to the study of the Basque language revival movement, youth culture, and music.

Index

A Coruña, 130, 133, 134, 135, 136, 140, 141, 146n2–3, 146n5, 146n11, 146n13–14
Abu-Lughod, Lila, 155
Adorno, Theodor, 96n15
aesthetic, 19, 38, 60–61, 64–65, 74n5, 85, 102, 116, 122, 136, 139, 160, 232, 256, 268n4; "aesthetics of power," 102, 143; avant-garde, 85
Africa, 63, 171n7, 275–78; colonized, 20n3, 34, 36, 39, 144, 213; immigrants from, 12–13, 267, 272; northern Africa, 41, 171n8, 269n15, 272; "otherness" and, 36, 88–89, 93
agency, 155; agents of the state, 65, 70, 72, 102, 135, 143; social agents, 58, 60, 70, 85, 89, 262
agriculture, 134, 137, 139, 144, 189, 213–15, 219; agro-pastoralism, 279; land and agrarian reform, 206; landless workers, 206; large landowners, 91, 214; phylloxera, 231; small-holdings, 206; subsistence land, 226; vineyard holding size, 236, 238, 247n16; vineyard land, 226
Albuquerque, Alfonso de, 40, 49n5, 56
Alentejo, 17, 86, 207, 216, 221n17, 221n21, 226, 247n19
Algarve, 6, 10, 86, 93

Alianza Popular, 121
Almeida, Miguel Vale de, 11, 17, 48, 49
alterity, 267; *alterofobia,* 12. *See also* San Román, Teresa; racism
Alto Douro, 3, 178, 225–29, 235–36, 242, 244, 245n1, 246n8–16
amnesia, 49; political amnesia, 122, 124. *See also* hyperamnesia
Amselle, Jean-Loup, 68
anarchism, 23, 105, 106; anarcho-syndicalist, 125n4
Andalusia, 6, 12, 13, 16, 20n3, 257; Alfaya valley, 13; Andalusian, 12, 13, 16, 17
Anderson, Benedict, 74n3, 84, 156, 227
Andorra, 8, 13
Angola, 213
"anthropologies of empire building," 35, 46. See also *völkerkunde*
"anthropologies of nation building," 35, 46. See also *volkskunde*
anticlericalism, 14
antiracism, 12
anti-Semitism, 218, 221n8
Arabs, 208, 209–11, 214, 216
Aracena, 16. *See also* Maddox, Richard
aristocracy, 209; aristocratic, 168, 210; aristocrats, 17; Portuguese aristocracy, 215–16

Armstrong, Karen, 152
Arrasate, 262
Artze, Joxe Antonio, 268n4
assimilation, 33, 43, 44, 59, 62, 102, 154
Asturias, 15, 19, 20n3, 276, 278–79;
    Asturian, 19, 278–79, 288n9
Atlantic, 11, 44, 208, 220n1, 226;
    Atlantic/Mediterranean dichoto-
    mization, 10–11, 207; Atlantic
    Portugal, 207–8, 226
Atxaga, Bernardo, 267, 268n4
Australia, 162, 170; Australians, 58, 160
authenticity, notions of, 64–65, 88,
    92, 140, 185, 230, 266
authoritarian government, 1, 2,
    74n3, 81, 83, 84, 88, 96, 130,
    171n9, 205, 218, 238, 247n18,
    261; mass culture, authoritarian
    ideology in, 86
Autonomous Communities
    (*Comunidades Autónomas*), of Spain,
    10, 20n3, 103, 104, 106, 125n1,
    253, 262, 286; statutes of au-
    tonomy, 9, 122, 261, 268n9
Ávila, City of, 177–200, 200n1,
    201n2, 202n8–9, 203n12, 284
Azores, 8, 46, 47, 220n1

Bachelard, Gaston, 287
Barata, Francisco A. Corrêa, 210,
    211, 212, 215
Barcelona, 3, 16, 103, 104, 105, 106,
    107, 115, 125n4, 157, 159, 171n6,
    274, 286
Barrio de la Celsa, 12
Barros, Leitão de, 94n1
Basque, 13, 17, 106, 115, 170n1,
    251, 253, 254, 255–67, 267n3,
    268n4, 268n9, 269n13, 274–75;
    Arrasate Euskaldun Dezagun, 263;
    Basque identity, 257, 260–61, 265,
    267; Basque language revival, 13,

251, 253–70, 267n1; Basque
    nationalism, 261, 264, 266,
    269n10; Basque New Song
    Movement, 256; *euskaldun*
    (Basque-speaking), 257, 258, 264,
    265, 266; Euskal Kultur Batzarra
    (Basque Cultural Association),
    262; *euskaltegiak* (adult language
    schools), 255; *euskaltzaleak* (Basque
    language advocates), 254–55,
    267n1; *ikastolas* (Basque schools),
    104. *See also* Irigaray, Jose Angel;
    Kafe Antzokia
Basque Country, 10, 20n3, 104, 122,
    217, 251, 254, 257, 259–61, 263,
    267n1; Euskal Herria, 9, 13, 266,
    267, 268n7
Baudelaire, Charles, 87, 95n8
Bauer, Rainer Lutz, 134, 138
Bausinger, Hermann, 95n9
Behar, Ruth, 15
Beira Alta, 86
Beira Baixa, 86
Benedict, Burton, 83
Benedict, Ruth, 42
benefício, 226, 240, 245n3
Bentley, G. Carter, 61
Berbers, 208, 214, 257
Berdahl, Daphne, 2, 6
Bilbao, 3, 17, 251, 253–55, 259, 263,
    266, 267; Guggenheim Bilbao,
    251, 253–54, 265, 274–75, 288n6
biodiversity and language, 260,
    268n8
"blurred genres," 171. *See also*
    Geertz, Clifford
Bodin, Jean, 217
Bopp, Franz, 212
borders, 2, 8, 9, 12, 13–14, 20,
    21n6, 75, 102, 151, 154, 156,
    158–60, 201n2; border country, 8,
    13; borderlands, 13, 184

boundaries, 12, 13–14, 16, 46, 91, 114, 171, 196, 234, 243, 251, 258, 287, 288n3; boundary culture, 48; boundedness, 12; social boundaries, 16

Bourdieu, Pierre, 74n3

bourgeois, 6, 36, 85, 90, 92, 138, 166, 169, 229

Bourguignon, Erika, 152

Boyarin, Jonathan, 152

Braga, 90

Braga, Teófilo, 42–43, 210–11, 212, 215, 220n4, 220n6–7

Brandão, Raul, 216, 217, 219

Brandes, Stanley H., 12, 16–17

Brazil, 41, 75n8, 213, 221n14; Afro-Brazilian dance, 88

Brecher, Jeremy, 266

Brettell, Caroline B., 10, 11, 14, 15, 18, 20n5, 247n17

brotherhoods (*cofradías*), 16, 182–83, 184, 187, 188–98, 200; Brotherhood of the Ambles Valley, 189, 202n12; Brotherhood of la Colilla, 189, 202n12; Brotherhood of Sierrecilla, 189, 202n12; brotherhoods and fiestas, 187–89

Brumann, Christoph, 155

Bruner, Edward, 64

bullfighting, 7, 85, 188

Buruma, Ian, 151, 169

Bwiti, 275–76; compared and contrasted with other religions, 276. *See also* Fang; "microcosmogony."

Cabeceiras de Basto, 93

Caetano, Marcelo, 66

cafés, 1, 17; café-theatre and Basque language revival, 253. *See also* Kafe Antzokia

Caldas de Vizela, 87

Camões, Luís de, 44, 48

Campbell, Donald T., 273

Campos, Ezequiel de, agrarian policy of, 214–15

Cape Verde, 56

capitalism, 3, 4, 5, 130, 145, 266, 288n4; agriculture and, 144, 214; "print capitalism," 227 (*see also* Anderson, Benedict); space and, 3–5, 160; symbolic capital, 268n7

Carlist, 112–13

Caro Baroja, Julio, 7, 8, 10, 11, 217, 273, 277, 284

Carthaginians, 7, 212

cartography, 156, 171n6, 271; cultural, 170n3; political, 206, 283; religious, 207. *See also* maps; memory

casa, 201, 237; Casa do Douro, 225, 226, 228, 240, 245n3, 285; Casa do Povo, 230, 232–34, 240, 242; social and symbolic meanings of, 15

Castelo Branco, Camilo, 231, 247n22

Castile, 18, 278

Castilian,11, 201n2, 215; language, 12, 108, 110, 115, 168, 277, 288n9

Catalan, 3, 9, 21n6, 104, 105, 110–15, 125n4, 151, 156, 165; Catalan left, 9; language and culture, maintaining, 102, 107, 159, 168; education, 104–6, 254; provinces, 105. *See also* National Museum of Catalan History

Catalonia, 9, 10, 15, 18, 20n3, 101, 103–4, 106, 122, 125n4–5, 171n6, 124–25n1; education in, 104–8, 115, 254, 283; in exile from, 102, 151–75, 285–86

Cátedra, María, x, xi, 14, 177, 181, 201n2, 284

Catholicism, 9, 14, 16, 18, 33, 56, 61, 69, 111–12, 117, 177, 181–202, 208, 264, 282; and authority,

Catholicism *(continued)*
129, 187; conversion to, 67, 182;
and creole identity, 74n4; hierarchy in, 129; in Malacca, 33, 61,
74n4; Papal Bull, 177, 194; Pope
Clemente II, Bull of, 183, 192–
94, 197–98; in Portugal, 208; and
the Sección Femenina, 133, 144;
in Spain, 14; *See also* Christianity;
icons; saints
Celts, 216–17, 281
Chan, Kok Eng, 71
childhood, 110, 120, 162, 257;
indoctrination during, 112, 117,
119; militarization of, 116;
recollections of, 82, 107, 110, 112
children, 63, 74n6, 110, 116, 117,
122, 130, 132, 134, 136, 141–42,
167, 186, 199, 202n9; in exile,
152, 157, 166, 170n1; gender
difference and, 109; satire in
children's books and stories, 116–
20; in schools, 105, 107–9, 111,
114, 120, 135, 139, 188. *See also*
humor
Childs, John Brown, 266
Chinese ethnicity in Malaysia, 58–
59, 63, 70, 71, 74n4
Chitties (Malay speaking Hindus),
58, 70
Christian, William A., 12, 14, 201n2
Christianity, 14, 63, 214;
Christianization, 182; *cristão*, 56;
and ethnicity, 211; to speak
"Christian," 56, 111, 125n5. *See
also* Catholicism; Protestantism
circulation: of material objects, 144;
of representations, 1, 225, 229
city, 16, 18, 85, 116, 181, 215, 219;
and Basque cultural revival, 266–
67; cityscapes, 251; countryside
and, 181–204, 273, 277, 284–86,

288n4–5; neighborhoods in, 19.
See also space; spatiality; urban
class, 14, 18, 161, 162, 172n11, 226,
238, 277, 282; divisions, 16, 236,
240–41; in education system, 105,
109; and gender, 132; and literacy,
277–78; middle class, 34, 57, 71,
84, 87, 90, 137, 145, 166–67;
"racialization of class relations,"
13, 210–12, 220; upper class, 178,
185, 241–43; and the Virgin of
Sonsoles, 185, 190, 198; working
class, 15, 16, 38, 88, 90, 125n4,
132, 206, 220, 231, 240, 242,
246n15, 268n9, 279–80. *See also*
bourgeois
Clifford, James, 2, 19, 62, 69, 85,
155, 158, 227, 254
Coelho, Adolfo, 37–40, 42, 43, 46, 49n3
Cohen, Anthony, 74n3
Collier, Jane Fishburne, 16, 134, 138
colonialism, 2, 5, 20, 36–37, 39–40,
73, 206, 213, 275–77; anticolonial
theory, 265; colonial, 82, 125, 163;
Colonial Act of 1933, 81, 83;
colonial settlement, 3; colonialist
categories, 60; colonized space or
places, 3, 5, 72, 276; colonized
subjects, 144; de-colonization, 35,
282; domination, 61, 287; and
empires, 35, 57, 66; "others," 34,
36, 73, 88–90; Portuguese and the
Estado Novo, 81–99;
postcolonialism, 48, 73n1, 275,
276, 282; power, 1, 36, 48, 61, 71,
81, 84. *See also* exhibitions; space
Comaroff, Jean, 130, 144
Comaroff, John, 130, 144
Comas d'Argemir, Dolors, 13
common sense, 167; commonsense
understanding, 130. *See also*
Gramsci, Antonio

communism, 21, 106, 111, 114, 206
concursos (contests or competitions),
  65, 75n8, 101, 111, 112, 129, 132,
  139–43, 144, 145, 146n11, 188,
  276; competitiveness, 139
cooking, 109, 133, 135, 141, 263.
  See also cuisine; food
Corrêa, A. A. Mendes, 218
Correia, Vergílio, 87
cosmology, 280
cosmopolitan, 43, 50n15, 215;
  "cosmopolitan anthropology," 46;
  contested cosmopolitanism, 251;
  euskaldun cosmopolitanism, 266,
  268; urban cosmopolitanism, 254
county, 91, 94, 232, 246n11. *See also*
  parish
Creole, 74n4. *See also* identity;
  Kristang; Malacca
Cuerda, José Luis, 108
cuisine: creole, 74n4, 75n9; Galician,
  130; Kristang, 61; Portuguese, 61.
  See also cooking; food
culture: "Cultura Hispanica," 283;
  cultural activism, 257; Cultural
  Capital of Europe, 16; cultural
  colonization, 282; cultural difference, 4, 5; cultural domination, 8;
  cultural histories, 4; cultural
  idioms, 1, 102, 136, 137, 144;
  cultural imaginary, 258, 264;
  "cultural intimacy," 285 (*see also*
  Herzfeld, Michael); "cultural
  literacy," 49; cultural politics, 1, 20,
  251, 253–61; "cultural sites," 159
  (*see also* Sutton, David E.); culture
  area, 5, 6, 42; multicultural, 55, 66,
  274; subculture, 280; transcultural
  encounter, 254
cursillos (short courses), 132, 284
Cutileiro, José, 247n19
Cutler, Jill, 266

Dagnino, Evelina, 266
Damão, 72
dance, 19, 58, 63, 64, 65, 72, 74n2,
  75n8n11, 269n11, 283; and loss of
  tradition, 231, 242; Makonde, 36;
  national contests, 141; regional
  dance, 88–89; of the standard,
  191, 199; and Sección Femenina
  training in Galicia, 130, 133, 135,
  140, 142, 143, 146n9
de Certeau, Michel, 164
decadence, 39, 283; Portuguese
  decadence, 39, 41, 42; Western
  decadence, 39
del Valle, Teresa, 13, 17, 269n11
Delgado Ruiz, Manuel, 14, 19
democracy, 10, 103, 111, 160, 167,
  169, 170, 266; Spanish transition
  to, 103, 121, 124, 124n1, 261
Dias, Jorge, 20n4, 36, 42–43, 44–45,
  47–48, 50n7, 207, 208, 218
diaspora, 19, 62, 63, 70, 153–58,
  171n7; consciousness of, 62;
  diasporic discourse, 154; diasporic
  process, 156. *See also* Said,
  Edward
dictatorship, 2, 19, 83, 94, 106, 157,
  283; and gender, 131, 132, 133;
  and the Sección Femenina, 139–
  41, 144. *See also* Franco dictatorship; Sección Femenina
DiGiacomo, Susan M., ix–x, 9, 10,
  101, 102, 103, 146, 283, 285, 286
discourse, 154–55; everyday discourse, 3, 37, 49, 220; modernist,
  86; on national and cultural
  identity, 7, 33, 37, 46–49, 89,
  268n4; public discourse and
  "cultural literacy," 49; on social
  characteristics, 89, 93, 134, 145,
  220, 222n21, 260–62. *See also*
  diaspora

displacement, 57, 59, 63, 67–70, 102, 152–53, 158, 156–59, 160, 273–74, 276–80, 283, 284–86
Diu, 72
Donostia, (San Sebastián), 17
double consciousness, 164
Douglass, Carrie B., 7, 15
Douro River Valley: Baixo Corgo subregion, 228, 244; Cima Corgo subregion, 246n8, 247n16; Douro Demarcated Zone (wine region), 226; Douro Superior subregion, 246n8; Duriense, 235, 245, 245n3. *See also* Alto Douro
Du Bois, W. E. B., 164, 172

East Timor, 48, 72
education, 103; curricula, 48, 104–6, 122; and discipline, 109, 119–20; Escola del Bosc, 105; Escola Moderna, 105; *euskaltegiak* (adult language schools), 255; *ikastolas* (Basque schools), 104; Industrial University, 105; Institut-Escola, 106, 125n3; instructor, 121; instructors of the Sección Femenina, 134–35, 137; language and, 76n13; Latin, studying, 56, 212, 217; Montessori schools, 105–6; national-Catholic, 101, 109, 111, 114–16, 121, 124, 125–26n6; and political oppression, 104–5; as political space, 103–4; Rosa Sensat, influence of, 105–6; schoolmasters, 108; teachers, 105, 106, 110, 112, 115, 124, 132–37, 139, 162–63, 172n11, 255. *See also* Sección Femenina
Edwards, William, 211, 220n6
1870s generation (in Portugal), 209–10
elite, 16, 86, 106, 129, 138, 178, 183, 203n13, 222n21, 254, 266,

268n3, 283, 284; intellectual, 106, 205, 207, 220
emigration, 18, 214, 272; emigrants, 16, 213
empire, 1, 20, 33, 57, 64, 85, 111, 151–52, 170, 246n6, 282–83, 286; British, 144, 161–62, 167, 170, 213; colonial empire, 35; "empire-building" anthropology, 46; "hidden empire," 33–50; imperial, 33, 37, 41, 60, 116, 144, 160–61, 163, 178, 272–74, 282–83, 285–87; imperialist ideology, 34, 85, 283; Portuguese Empire, 35–50, 60, 63, 66–67, 74n3, 75n12, 81–84, 93, 210, 214, 282–83, 284; Portuguese imperialism, 34–50, 83–99; Portuguese national identity and empire, 37, 44, 46–50, 67; Portuguese Seaborne Empire, 214; representations of the Portuguese empire, 35, 37, 40–48, 92, 95n5; representations of the Spanish empire, 125n5. *See also* Fifth Empire
enclave, 20n3, 278; cultural enclave, 60, 68, 73
Encomendação das almas, 47, 50n13
Enders, Victoria Lorée, 133, 137, 144
Entre-Douro-e-Minho, 82, 90–92. *See also* Minho (region)
Escobar, Arturo, 158
Espinàs, Josep M., 112–14
Espinho, 87
Esquerra Republicana de Catalunya, 9
Estado Novo (New State), Portuguese, 34, 57, 60, 65–66, 70, 72, 74n3, 75n8, 81, 86, 92–94, 94n1–2, 219, 283. *See also* Salazar, António de Oliveira
Estremadura, 86

ETA, 122, 253, 268–69n10
ethnic, 6, 10, 12, 39, 61, 89, 163, 260, 267, 282; "ethnogenetic constitution," 286 (*see also* Greenwood, Davydd); habitus, 61; homogeneity, 10; "psychology," 41–43, 45–48, 50n6; stereotypes, 207–10
ethnicity, 6, 33, 44; discourses on the origins of Portuguese ethnicity, 208–10, 211, 215, 218–19; ethnicity and racism, 210, 212, 221; Kristang ethnicity, 55–73, 74n3–4, 75n9–10; pluriethnicity, 55
Eurasians, 60, 64, 71, 74n5–6; in colonial administration, 71; "Portuguese Eurasians," 33, 55–60, 70, 74n6, 75n10, 76n13
European Union, 9, 83, 272, 282
Euskal Herria, 9, 13, 266, 267, 268n7
ex-centric, 1, 238, 258; excentricity, 260
exhibitions, 75n8, 83; Exhibition of the Portuguese World (Lisbon, 1940), 91; exhibitions of colonialism and empire, 65, 73, 81, 82–86, 94n1–2, 96n13; Expo '98, 16, 95n6; expositions, 83, 95n6; First Portuguese Colonial Exhibition (Porto, 1934), 34, 65, 81–84, 86–94; imperialist ideology in, 85, 92, 94; Seville '92 Expo, 21n7. *See also* parades
exile, 1, 3, 8, 68–69, 101, 102, 125–26n6, 151–70, 170n2, 274, 286
exotic, 12–13, 44; exotic imagery, 55, 82, 85; exoticism, 160
exposition (*see* exhibition)

Falange, 104, 108, 111–12, 116, 121–22, 145; Falange Española Tradicionalista y de las Juntas de Ofensiva Nacional-Sindicalista, emergence of, 131; Falangist, 110, 112, 114, 134, 139, 140; Falangist messages and Sección Femenina, 101, 129–49; propaganda in schools, 116–19, 122. *See also* Movimiento Nacional; Franco
Falasca-Zamponi, Simonetta, 143
Fang, 275, 277, 288n7
fascism, 2, 60, 65, 73, 96, 101, 103–28, 161, 219, 283, 284, 285, 286; "fascist spectacles," 143, 145
feminism, 106, 257; feminist anthropology, 4; feminist theory, 4, 5, 171n5
Ferdinand II of Aragon, King, 108, 122
Ferguson, James, 4–5
Fernandez, James W., ix, 2, 6, 13, 15, 19, 20, 64, 122, 124, 130, 138, 146, 205, 227, 245, 271, 276, 287–88n2, 288n9, 289n11
Fernandez, Renate Lellep, 17, 288n7
Ferrer i Guàrdia, Francesc, 105
fiestas or *festas*, 75, 138, 139, 143, 187–89, 190, 197, 199
Fifth Empire: myth of the Fifth Empire, 50n14; Portuguese dream of the Fifth Empire, 48
folk culture: art, 37, 45; Basque folklore, 256; ethno-folkloric characteristics, 65; festivals, 34; folk literature, 37, 42, 43; folklore, 15, 65, 72, 91, 144, 283; folkloric dance, 19; folkloric representations, 64, 74n5, 82–83, 86, 94, 94n3, 129, 140, 254; folkloric troupes, 61, 63, 65, 67, 75n11, 89; material culture, 37; music, 41, 61, 135; Portuguese folk culture, 33, 36–45, 47–48, 49n4, 66, 82, 95n9; Portuguese national character and

folk culture (continued)
  folk culture, ideas about, 39,
    41–45; religion, 43; ritual, 47;
    transplantation of Portuguese
    folklore, 57, 60, 63–65
food, 74, 102, 136–38, 142, 143,
  158–59, 166, 168, 182, 191, 283.
  See also cooking; cuisine
Foucault, Michel, 3–4, 145, 220n5
Franco, Francisco, 2, 106–8, 112, 113,
  116–17, 119, 121–22, 124n1, 129,
  144, 169, 254, 261; Franco
  dictatorship, 10, 101–2, 124n1, 129,
  131, 134–35, 144, 145, 283;
  Franco period, 10, 103–4, 131,
  133–34, 137–38, 202n8, 259;
  Franco regime, 11, 101–4, 106,
  109, 112, 113, 120–22, 124, 125–
  26n6, 129–30, 133, 143; Francoist,
  112, 115, 120, 122, 283, 284; post-
  Franco period, 251, 261, 264. See
  also Falange; Movimiento Nacional
frontier, 5, 154, 170n3, 287; "frontier spaces," 13; moral frontier,
  281–82
Frykman, Jonas, 137, 144

Galicia, x, 3, 9–11, 15, 20n3, 101,
  104, 130, 132, 133, 134, 145, 217;
  galegos in Portugal, 221n21, 231;
  Galician language, 56, 254;
  Galicians, 130, 133, 217, 231,
  241–42; rural Galicia and the
  Sección Femenina, 132–45
Gallop, Rodney, 64
Galvão, Henrique, 34, 84, 86, 91–92,
  93, 94n2, 95n8
García Martí, Victoriano, 11
Gay, Peter, 85
Geertz, Clifford, 83, 123, 158,
  171n5, 229
gender, 4, 16–17, 135, 210, 226,
  236, 238, 242, 247n23, 269n11;
  differentiation, 6, 109, 136, 159,
  226, 240–42; "hegemonic masculinity," 17; and land ownership,
  242, 246n15; male privilege, 226,
  236; masculinity, 263; maternalism,
  131, 144; "metaphors of masculinity," 16 (see also Brandes, Stanley);
  natalism, 131, 144; producing
  women citizens, 133, 145; and
  residence patterns, 15, 18; and the
  Sección Femenina, 101–2, 130–45;
  and the Virgin of Sonsoles, 177,
  189, 199; women as "angels of
  the home" 131; women's power,
  17; women's social service, 129–
  45; women's subordination to
  men, 17, 131–32; women's
  training in urban and rural
  contexts, 132–33, 146n2
Generalitat de Catalunya, 105, 108,
  115, 125n4, 171n6
geography, 162; and exile, 152;
  geographical theory, 2–3, 171n5;
  moral, 163; Portuguese, 171, 207,
  218
Gerholm, Tomas, 46
Germanic peoples, 208, 211, 217
Gilroy, Paul, 171n7, 172n12
gitano (Gypsy), 12–13. See also Roma
Glazer, Nathan, 154
global, 2, 13, 20, 20n1, 225, 251,
  255, 264, 266, 274, 288n3, 288n6;
  citizenship, 251, 252, 266; flows,
  264; globalization and globalism,
  73n1, 154, 265, 266, 267n2;
  "globalization from below," 251,
  266; "glocality," 19; "local" versus,
  254, 265, 266, 267n2, 274–75,
  280; technologies, 266
Gmelch, George, 18
Goa, 72

Goffman, Erving, 262
Gonçalves, Nuno, 44, 50n9, 88
Gramsci, Antonio, 130
Graves, Lucia, 110–12, 116
Great Britain: colonial administration, 70; colonial rule of, 35, 67, 162; dominance of Portugal, 213; during World War II, 161; and ideology of superiority, 162–64. See also *Ultimatum*
Greeks, 7, 274, 280–81
Greenwood, Davydd J., 17, 18, 286
Gujaratis, 58
Gupta, Akhil, 2, 4–5

habitus, 33; ethnic habitus, 61
Halperin, Rhoda, 74n3
Handler, Richard, 83
Harris, Marvin, 212
Harvey, David, 3
hegemony, 2, 5, 20, 36, 210, 215, 228, 233, 244, 247n24, 257, 277, 278; bourgeois hegemony, 36; hegemonic, 6, 16, 130, 245, 260; "hegemonic masculinity," 17 (*see also* Almeida, Miguel Vale de)
Herri Batasuna, 268n9
Herzfeld, Michael, ix, 2, 64, 83, 89, 123–24, 129, 130, 134, 138, 146, 225, 227, 285
Hlabazahlangana Movement, the, 276
Hobsbawm, Eric, 64, 82, 92, 151–52, 155, 163
Holton, Kimberly DaCosta, 16, 19
hospitality, 49, 159, 165–66, 168
Huber, Mary Taylor, 2, 130
Hume, David, 217
humor, 202n11, 259; humor about Franco, 116, 121; jokes, 117–18, 121, 122, 123, 124, 125–26n6; political cartoons, 122, 169; and representations of a fascist

classroom, 101, 114, 116, 120, 122, 124
hyperamnesia, 49

Iberia, 2–21, 210, 226, 278, 281; Iberians, 7, 8, 9, 210–11; Iberian social landscape, 226; Iberian spaces, 8, 11–12, 20, 247n24, 272, 278; "*iberismo,*" 9; Iberos, 7, 9; and spatial vectors, 280–81, 283, 289n10
Iberian Peninsula, 2, 3, 7, 8, 33, 75n9, 108, 209–11, 218, 271–72
icon, 89, 190, 228, 247n24; Catholic, 179–204 (*see also* Catholicism; saints); iconic knowledge, 83; iconic representation, 89, 94; "iconicity," 64, 86, 89, 94 (*see also* Herzfeld, Michael); iconification, 89; iconoclasticism, 14; iconophilism, 14. *See also* Delgado Ruiz, Manuel
identity, 57, 62, 102, 153, 169, 171, 196, 218–19, 251, 286; "diffused identities," 12; disidentification, 75n10; displaced, 69; double identity, 64; hybrid identity, 59; hyper-identity, 33, 61; national identity, 36–37, 39–49, 62, 94, 95n6, 159, 205–20, 233, 281–82, 286; regional identity, 233; social identity, 10; state identity, 113; symbol of identity, 196; village identity, 199, 242. *See also* Basque; Kristang; Portuguese identity
ideology, 75n8, 89, 124, 200; authoritarian, 86, 110; ideological pluralism, 262; "ideology of return," 18; imperialist, 81–99, 283; language, 110, 261; of *Lusofonia*, 48; political ideology, 131, 133; of Portuguese national

ideology *(continued)*
decline, 39; racial, 205, 212, 280–81; transmission of, 81, 89, 91, 131, 133; and unspoken knowledge, 164
idioms: cultural, 1, 13, 102, 123, 129, 132, 136, 137, 138, 143, 144, 146n11
"imagined communities," 84, 95n5, 156. *See also* Anderson, Benedict
India, 41, 49n5, 76n13, 162, 170; Portuguese in 66, 72
indigenous peoples, 72, 265; colonized, 68; as exoticized others, 82, 85; "indigenous" as an ambiguous status, 64; "indigenous labor," 36
Indonesia, 6, 48; Larantuka and Tugu, 72; Portuguese presence in, 72
industrialism and industrialization, 207, 212, 213, 217, 281; Basque industrial center, 266; captains of industry, 92; industrial colonies, 18; industrial periphery, 206; Industrial Revolution,168, 282; industrialists and the promotion of exhibitions, 91, 96n13; and the working class, 206–7
Instituto do Vinho do Porto (Port Wine Institute), 245n3
intellectuals: Basque, 269n10; Portuguese, 47, 92, 94, 95n7, 178, 241; and racialist ideologies, 178, 205, 210, 218; Spanish, 125n3
"invention of tradition," 64, 82, 155. *See also* Hobsbawm, Eric and Ranger, Terence
Irigaray, Jose Angel, 253–54, 256–59, 261, 262, 268n3
irony, 1, 44, 83, 123–24, 284; ironic, 76n13, 124, 130, 137, 142, 186, 189, 196, 199, 202n8; non-ironic, 132

Isabella I of Castile, Queen, 109, 122
Islam, 209, 211; Islam in Iberia, 272; in Spain, 8, 117

Jerónimos Monastery, 44, 50n9
Jews, 108–9, 170, 202, 216, 217. *See also* anti-Semitism
John I of Portugal, King, 49n5
Jones, William, 212
journalism, 55, 86, 88, 225–49, 258

Kafe Antzokia, 251, 253–70, 274–75; Zenbat Gara, 254–55, 258, 263, 264, 268n6
Kaufman, Eric, 156
Keil, Alfred, 90
Kenny, Michael, 18–19
kinship relations, 15, 166, 237–39
Kristang, 33, 55–76; identity, 57–59, 60, 61, 62, 64, 67–68, 70, 72, 73, 74n4, 74n5, 75n9; language, 56. *See also* Malacca
korrika, 13. *See also* Basque

La Jonquera, 159
Laboa, Mikel, 268n4
Lamego, 228
L'Ametlla de Merola, 18–19
landscape, 14, 73, 155–56, 158, 177, 208, 216, 220n2, 221n17, 226, 228–29, 251, 276; "landscapes of inequality," 13; natural, 14; social, 226; symbolic, 163; urban, 69
Lavie, Smadar, 73
Lawrence-Zúñiga, Denise, 15
Leal, João, 11, 20n4, 21n5, 33, 35, 36, 42, 47, 49n1–4, 50n6–11, 85, 95n5, 208, 216, 218, 246n6, 282–83
Leão, Cunha, 47
Lefebvre, Henri, 3, 4, 164

left-wing, 9, 121, 139, 206, 262,
    268n9–10, 279
León, 11, 15, 278
Levine, Robert, 273
liminality, 13
Lisbon, 16, 17, 38, 56, 72, 84, 91,
    94n1, 178, 207, 209, 214–15, 217,
    219–20, 221–22n21, 246n6, 282;
    industrial periphery of, 206
Lisón Tolosana, Carmelo, 11, 12, 15
literacy, 277; cultural, 49; gender
    and, 246n15; social power and,
    236, 238, 242, 246n15, 247n19,
    277–78
local: as a spatial category, 12, 34,
    35, 69, 225, 227, 232, 254, 265,
    274–75, 285; delocalization, 58;
    extra-local reference, 231;
    "glocality," 19; identity, 159;
    interlocal difference, 285; "local
    ethnology," 46; locales, 1, 14, 17,
    141; localism, 244; locality, 1, 5,
    91, 95n10, 140, 142, 146n9, 178,
    203n12, 227–44, 247n22, 266,
    279, 285; locality and post-marital
    residence patterns, 15; local-
    regional slippage, 233; peripheral-
    ized locality, 230, 233;
    representation, 230; sacred
    locations, 14; social imaginary,
    160; supralocal, 177. See also space
Löfgren, Orvar, 49, 137, 144
Lomnitz-Adler, Claudio, 5
London, 3, 102, 151–70, 274, 286;
    "sacred centers" in, 163; suburb
    of Clapham, 161
ludic, 96n14, 251, 259, 263–64. See
    also space
Lugo, x, 130, 133, 137, 139, 146
Lusitanian, 209, 216; Lusitanian
    community, 66–67; Lusitanians, 7
Lusofonia, 48; Lusophone, 58

Maastricht Treaty, 231
Macau, 61, 63, 72
Maddox, Richard, 16, 21n7,
    247n24
Madrid, 18, 104, 136, 140–41, 286
magazines, 116, 165. See also media;
    newspapers; radio; television
Malacca, 55–80; Jalan Portugis, 69;
    kasta altu and kasta bassu, 33, 56–
    76; "Malacca Portuguese," 33, 55–
    76; Muzium Samudera; "Portuguese
    Settlement," 33, 55; rejidó (regedor),
    56; Porta de Santiago, 69; St. Paul's
    Church, 69; St. Peter's Church,
    69. See also Kristang
Malawi, 40
Malay identity, 62, 70
Malaysia, 55, 62–73, 74–75n7, 283–84
Malkki, Liisa H., 116, 157
Mallorca, 8, 110
Manuelino style, 45, 50n9
maps, 108, 162; mappings, 2, 3, 9.
    See also cartography
Maragall, Joan, 107
Marbeck, Celine, 72, 75n9
Marbeck, Joan, 72
Marco de Canaveses, 89, 96
Marcus, George E., 4, 155, 227
Marias of Portugal, 87
Martín, Annabel, 267n2
Marx, Karl, 3, 288n4; Marxism, 116;
    "Marxist hordes," 186, 200
McDonogh, Gary Wray, 16–17
Mead, Margaret, 42
Medeiros, António, x, 11, 34, 64, 81,
    87, 101, 246n6, 247n11, 283
media: mass media as public space,
    129, 234. See also magazines;
    newspapers; radio; television
Mediterranean, 6, 13, 42, 159, 209,
    277, 286; Portugal, 207–8. See also
    Atlantic

Melo, Daniel, 65–66
"melting pot," 154; *The melting pot,*
    171n4
memory, 82–84, 115, 116, 151–69,
    171n7, 181, 240–41, 275; "com-
    munity of memory," 116; memoir,
    101–2, 103, 112, 114–15, 125n4,
    153; memory politics, 1, 6, 20,
    101–2, 283; "poetics of remem-
    brance," 152; rote memorization,
    106. *See also* space
Menéndez-Reigada, Fray Albino
    González, 125n5
metaphor, 41, 84, 123, 124, 164,
    171n4, 190, 263–64; "metaphors
    of masculinity," 16 (*see also*
    Brandes, Stanley); spatial meta-
    phor, 19. *See also* trope
metonym, 101; metonymic misrep-
    resentation, 6; metonymy, 103,
    124, 131
"microcosmogony," 276
migration, 15, 18, 69, 213; emigra-
    tion, 18, 213–14, 272; immigrants,
    12–13, 16, 50n12, 102, 154, 157,
    166, 171n4, 266–67; migrants, 33;
    return migration, 18; temporary
    migration, 17
"militant middle ground," 225. *See
    also* Herzfeld, Michael
military, 9, 41, 49n5, 105, 121–22,
    129, 144, 162, 209, 213–14;
    academy, 105; army 116, 125n5,
    183; militaristic images, 108, 139;
    militarization, 108, 141; service,
    131
mimesis, 86–89, 96n15; burlesque
    mimesis, 87
Minho (region), 10, 34, 82, 86, 87–
    88, 90, 93, 210, 216; costume, 90,
    95n9; *minhotos,* 6. *See also* Entre-
    Douro-e-Minho

minoritized: groups, 255; language
    257, 267n3; spaces, 6
modern, 2, 3, 45, 61, 74n6, 81, 86,
    95n8, 96n15, 102, 105, 154,
    170n1, 197, 209, 256, 281; anti-
    modernist, 85; hyper-modernist,
    58; modernity, 16, 48, 85, 155,
    171n7; modernization, 55, 84,
    144; notions of the "modern,"
    92–93, 130–39, 143–45; states,
    129–30, 145, 156, 255
Mondego River, 221n13
Moors, 217, 221–22n21; *Mourolândia*
    ("Land of the Moors"), 207
Movimiento Nacional, 110. *Also see*
    Falange; Franco
Moynihan, Daniel, 154
Mozambique, 36, 213
municipality, 210, 231; municipal
    festivals, 65; municipal govern-
    ment, 115, 184, 187, 247n18
Murguía, Manuel, 217
music, 56, 58, 61, 63–64, 72, 75n11,
    90, 105, 139, 140, 253, 257, 265,
    269n11, 284; and class differentia-
    tion, 16, 38–39; creole music, 66,
    72; cultural crossings in music,
    265, 268n4, 268n14; *fado,* 38–39,
    41, 43, 56; folk, 41, 65, 135;
    hymns, 108, 113, 114; musical
    propaganda, 65, 67, 75n8; musical
    theater, 188, 256; patriotic, 107–
    08, 115, 117; songs, 66, 72, 74,
    89, 135, 172n12
Muslims, settlement in the Iberian
    Peninsula, 217

Narotzky, Susana, 7–8
Nash, Mary, 131, 144
nation, 1, 5, 39, 42, 48, 49, 75n10,
    84, 133, 155–56, 212, 260; as a
    category of spatial analysis, 225,

227, 232–33, 235, 246n6, 265,
282; class and ethnic diversity in,
212, 282; historic nations, 10;
nation building/nation questioning anthropology, 35–40, 46;
national autonomy, 35; national
identities, 8–9, 19, 33, 159,
221n11, 233, 286; national
imaginary, 261; nationality, 9, 34,
36, 153, 283; "non-state nation,"
227; stateless nations, 9
National Museum of Catalan
History, 103, 107
nationalism, 42, 60, 65, 67, 92, 104,
106–7, 114, 179, 209, 212–13;
Basque, 261–66, 268–69n10;
dissenting nationalists, 268n9; in
Malacca, 55–76, 94, 95n6–9, 102;
nationalist agendas in rural
training, 139–43; nationalist
discourse, 89; nationalist Left, 262,
268n9–10; "nationalization of
Portuguese art," 45; Portuguese
national redemption, 85; "race" as
the equivalent of nation, 216, 219,
221n10; reinscription of national
culture, 34; "training of the
national spirit" under Francoism,
107, 109–10, 113, 135;
transnational, 254, 258, 266. See
also Portuguese identity
Nazis, 219
newspapers: regional, 178, 225–50;
as sources, 87–96, 227–28, 258,
262, 285. See also magazines;
radio; television
Nora, Pierre, 151
North/South, 1, 281, 286; agriculture, 213–15, 217, 221n14;
differentiation in Portugal, 10–11,
15, 178; Europe, 212, 280; industrialization, 206, 217; Italy, 217;

and national identity in Portugal,
205–24, 281; northern Portugal
and regionality, 225–49; in
Portugal, 20–21n5, 34, 38, 42, 81–
83, 91, 94, 95n10, 178; in Spain,
182, 217; as vectored spaces, 273–
74, 280–82, 285, 287, 289n10
nostalgia, 1, 33, 42, 48–49, 56, 125–
26n6, 152, 156, 216, 279, 283,
286. See also saudade
nuns, 109–11, 202n8. See also
Catholicism; education

objectification, 83, 88
Old Man's Church, 276
Oliveira Martins, Joaquim Pedro, 11,
209–19
O'Neill, Brian Juan, x, 10, 11, 15, 18,
21n5, 33, 55, 75n10, 102, 283, 289n10
orientalism, 70, 76n13; indirect
orientalism, 70, 73; inverse
orientalism, 71, 73n1
Ortega y Gasset, José, 11, 272
Orwell, George, 125n4, 167
Ovar, 88

Paasi, Anssi, 227
parades, 86, 90, 95n8, 142; colonial
processions, 93–94; Entre-Douro-e-
Minho Regional Parade, 82, 90–
92; "ethnographic" processions, 81,
93–94, 94n3. See also exhibitions
Pardais, 17
parish, 11, 18, 20–21n5, 47, 243;
Administrative Commissions, 238;
council, 231, 239–40, 247n18,
247n21; government, 230, 238;
organization, 94, 243; political
crisis, 243
Parkhurst, Shawn S., x, 1, 15, 95n5,
146, 178, 201n2, 225, 226, 240,
247n20, 285

parody, 34, 93, 123. *See also* humor; irony; satire
Partido Nacionalista Vasco, 268n9
Partido Popular, 9, 103, 121–22
Pascoaes, Teixeira de, 46–48, 216–17, 219
patriotism, 105, 107, 243, 255, *patria*/fatherland, concept of, 43, 63, 114, 117, 119; patriotic call and response exercises, 117; songs promoting, 108, 115
Paulo, Heloísa, 75n8
Payne, Stanley G., 125n4
peasants, 19, 35, 93, 132, 134, 136, 138, 145, 166, 182, 186, 198–99, 283; households, 15; life, 130; peasant customs, 37–38, 40, 42–43, 46; Portuguese, 41, 46; women, 93, 137; worker-peasants, 133, 136–37, 144, 145
Peixoto, Rocha, 37–43, 87
Pereira, Duarte Pacheco, 40
Pereira, Nuno Álvares, 40, 49n5
Pereira, Rui, 36
Peso da Régua, 178, 225–29, 233, 235, 237, 244
Pessoa, Fernando, 50n15
Phoenicians, 212, 216
pilgrimage, 17, 181, 188, 191, 194, 200
Pi i Sunyer, Carles, 125n4, 156, 160, 171n9
Pina-Cabral, João de, 6, 10, 11, 12, 15, 36, 138, 227
Pinhão, 230
Pintado, Father Manuel Joaquim, 55–56, 63, 69, 75n9
Pi-Sunyer, Carolina, 166
Pi-Sunyer, Núria, 166
Pi-Sunyer, Oriol, ix, 10, 17, 68, 102, 121, 124, 151, 171n6, 274–76, 285–86

Pitt-Rivers, Julian, 12
popular culture, 65, 86, 92, 95n8, 154. *See also* folk culture
port wine, 178, 225–26, 230–31, 232, 245n3
Porto, 81–96, 178, 206–9, 213, 217, 219–20, 221–22n21, 226, 228, 232, 237, 242, 246n6; Bishop of Porto, 96n13; Palácio de Cristal (Porto), 81, 84; uprising of 1891, 213. *See also* exhibitions
Portucale, 209, 232, 246n11
Portuguese identity, 33, 36–37, 39–42, 46–49, 57, 63–64, 69–70, 94, 205, 207, 211, 218–19, 281–82, 289n10; and North/South distinctions, 205–24
Portuguese national character, discourses on, 37–47, 209
Portuguese Revolution of 1974, 48, 83
postmodern, 154, 265; capitalism, 4; postmodernism, 5; postmodernist theory, 4
power, 1–5, 60, 70, 89, 91, 94, 102, 129–31, 170n3, 190, 264, 287, 289n11; "aesthetics of," 102, 143; colonial, 71; domains of, 70; gender and, 17, 226; mechanisms of, 70, 89, 123–24; military, 39, 49n5, 214; political, 34, 84, 94, 122, 125n1, 129, 130–31, 178, 201n2, 219; "power region," 5; powerlessness, 170n2; relationships to space and culture, 6, 13, 33, 94, 177, 281; representations of, 162, 199; social power, 130–31, 212; spiritual power, 275, 284; state power, 130–31
praxis, 73
Pred, Allan, 4
Primo de Rivera, José Antonio, 108, 111, 131

Primo de Rivera, Miguel, dictatorship of, 2, 106
Primo de Rivera, Pilar, 131. *See also* Sección Femenina
Protestantism, 111, 117, 281
Pujadas, Joan Josep, 13
Pyrenees, 11, 13, 21n6, 153, 160, 171n8

race, discourses on, 46, 75n9, 107, 114, 154, 209–12, 215–19, 220n3–6, 221n10–11; racialization, 13
racism, 12, 116, 170, 212, 221n8, 281–82; *See also* antiracism
radio, 129, 256, 269n14; *Emissora Nacional*, 94n2. *See also* magazines; media; newspapers; television
railroad: Portuguese railroad, 231, 241
Ramos, Rui, 246n15
Ramosierra, 18
Ranger, Terence, 64, 82, 92, 155, 163
refugees, 102, 152, 153–54, 157, 160–61, 165, 167, 169, 170n2, 171n8, 172n11
regionality, 1, 5–6, 20, 178, 199; cultural production of, 225–49; North-South divisions of, 205–24; urban and rural, 181–204. *See also* North/South
reinscription, processes of, 251, 264; rescripting, 73; scripting, 264
Renan, Ernest, 49
republicanism, 2, 9, 101, 102, 106, 107, 111, 116, 124n1, 157, 160–61, 165, 169, 186, 200, 205–6, 213–14, 236
resistance, 1, 13, 20, 72, 73, 114, 120, 123–24, 130, 161, 269n12; cultural, 113, 257, 282

Ribatejo, 86
Ribeiro, Luís, 45–46, 50n11
Ribeiro, Orlando, 207–8
Riegelhaupt, Joyce, 17
right-wing, 85, 95n7, 103, 111, 121–22, 171n9, 206, 261
Risco, Vicente, 11
rituals, 13–14, 47–48, 50n13, 112, 187, 189, 200, 276; family rituals, 102. See also *Encomendação das almas*; *korrika*
Rodrigues, Sarmento, 64, 66
Roma, 12
Romans, 208, 216, 218, 230; Romanization, 8, 211
Roseman, Sharon R., ix, 1, 10, 14, 101–2, 129, 133, 134, 138, 145, 177, 226, 227, 284–85
rural, 12, 13, 14, 18, 19, 37, 38, 47, 71, 89, 90, 91, 93, 96n13, 101–2, 129–49, 182, 183, 190, 198, 226, 276, 277, 280, 284; brotherhoods, 183, 190, 195, 198, 199; conceptions of rurality, 84, 85, 87, 108, 132, 199, 266, 268; customs, 48, 87, 96n15; instructors, 134, 137; shrines, 14; social and economic organization of rural communities, 37; "the rural house," 137; zones, 85–86. *See also* space; spatiality

Sahlins, Marshall, 5
Sahlins, Peter, 21n6, 170n3
Said, Edward, 71, 73, 156, 164
saints, 12, 14, 17, 201n2; Ávila "City of Saints," 3, 201; patron saint festivals, 12, 138–39, 143, 177, 263; popular saints, 231; Saint Zoilo of Córdoba, 182; Virgin of Czestochowa, 171n9; Virgin of Montserrat, 171n9. *See also* Teresa of Ávila; Virgin of Sonsoles

Salazar, António de Oliveira, 34, 64,
    66, 87, 94, 230; Salazar-Caetano
    regime, 238, 240; Salazar dictator-
    ship, 2, 88, 219, 283; Salazarism,
    65; Salazar regime, 19, 34–36, 93,
    230, 240. *See also* Estado Novo
Sampaio, Alberto, 215, 217, 219
Sampson, Anthony, 163
San Martín, 18
San Román, Teresa, 12
San Sebastián. *See* Donostia
Sánchez Carrión, José María
    (Txepetx), 251, 259–60, 268n6
Sanskrit, 12
Santa Maria, Bernard, 72
Santa Maria, Joseph, 72
Santos, Boaventura de Sousa, 48,
    50n15
São João das Lampas, 17
Sarasua, Jon, 268n6
Sardinha, António, 218
Sarkissian, Margaret, 57, 64, 75n11
Sarmento, Francisco Martins, 218
satire, 101, 118, 120, 257; commen-
    tary, 124; as resistance, 123, 257;
    satirical performance, 101
saudade, 33, 42, 46–47, 49, 50n8,
    50n12, 216, 283; *saudosismo*, 47
Schama, Simon, 170
Schlegel, Friedrich, 212
Scott, James C., 72
Sección Femenina, 101, 111, 129–
    47, 284–85
Senegalese, 13
Sérgio, António, 218–19
Serra da Estrela, 90
Shaw, George Bernard, 167
shrines, 12, 14; and the Virgin of
    Sonsoles, 182, 184–86, 193–94,
    196, 284
Sieber, Timothy R., 16
Silva, Agostinho da, 47

Silva, Baldaque da, 45
Singapore, 61
Smith, Anthony, 163
Soares, Mário, 232
Sobral, José Manuel, x, 11, 21n5,
    177–78, 205, 246n6, 281–82,
    289n10
Social Democrats, 238
socialism, 2, 106, 206, 238, 288;
    postsocialist societies, 2
Soja, Edward W., 3–4, 225
Sollors, Werner, 171
Soria, 18
space: aesthetic space, 61, 160;
    archetypical space, 264; "Basque-
    only" spaces, 251; colonial space,
    1, 3, 5, 8, 35, 37, 57, 66, 72, 81,
    84, 213, 275–76; "counterspace,"
    1, 102, 164, 167 (*see also* Lefebvre,
    Henri); "cultural space," 5, 16, 89,
    251, 272, 286, 287 (*see also*
    Maddox, Richard); culture and,
    5–6, 9, 14, 19, 20, 33, 102, 271–
    72, 279, 280, 285; ecological, 278;
    of encounter, 265; "epoch of
    space," 4 (*see also* Foucault,
    Michel); ethnic, 61; "frontier
    spaces," 13; and gender, 16–17;
    geographic, 3, 61, 69, 220, 282;
    geopolitical, 278; and historical
    process, 6; hybrid space, 168;
    Iberian, 2, 6, 8, 11, 247n24, 272,
    278; ideological space, 160;
    imperial space, 283, 286; informal,
    16; interactive spaces (town and
    country), 273, 284, (*see also* Caro
    Baroja, Julio; Williams, Raymond);
    kinesthetics of space, 287; local,
    13, 275; ludic, 103, 251, 259, 264;
    mental, 69, 155, 227; noninstitu-
    tional, 257; physical, 1, 3, 13, 17,
    19, 20n1, 69, 102, 196, 251, 256;

and place distinctions, 20n1, 271–72, 286, 288n3; political, 103; Portuguese, 178, 207, 212, 246n11; postcolonial space, 5; power in space, 1, 3, 5, 13, 94, 177; private, 4, 108, 165; public, 17, 129, 165, 264, 269n11; "quality space," 285–87, 289n11; regional, 11, 94, 177; rural, 12, 18, 101, 130–31, 140, 288n4; semantic, 19; and sociality, 12, 139; space of memory 101, 103, 123, 156–57, 160, 284; space of pluralist coexistence, 262; "space on the side of the road," 6, 160 (see also Stewart, Kathleen); synesthesia of space, 287; theories of, 2–5, 19; transcultural space, 254; urban, 12, 17, 18, 19, 102, 129–49, 177, 242, 267, 269n11, 273, 284–85 (see also Caro Baroja, Julio; Williams, Raymond); urban/rural distinctions of, 12, 14, 18, 101, 267, 277, 284, 285, 286, 287; woman-only space, 257

spaces: of alterity, 267; of everyday life, 1, 16, 132, 164, 259; of linguistic diversity, 251; symbolic, 61, 163; of usage, 260, 262; vectored spaces, 271–90

Spanish Civil War (1936–39), 14, 102, 124n1, 152–53, 185, 200, 202n9, 274, 286

spatiality, 12, 15, 287; rural, 18, 101, 130–31, 140, 143; spatial: concretization, 16; dialectic, 19; displacement, 278; dynamics, 273–74; metaphor, 19; opposition, 289n10; politics, 177; practices, 4; preoccupation, 19; register, 19; relations, 3; "sociospatial segmentation," 13; spatialized accounts,

219–20; specificity, 3, 7, 92; symbols, 69; trope, 271; urban spatiality, 12, 18, 19, 102, 269

sports, 129, 139–40, 163, 230; gymnastics, 111–12; 142–43; Lisbon soccer teams, 207; Porto soccer club, 207; Sección Femenina training in, 111–12, 142, 143. See also competitions; Sección Femenina

Sri Lanka, 72

stages, 16, 74n2, 75n11, 93, 256–57

state, 6, 8, 18, 21n6, 71, 81, 83, 84, 102, 129–31, 135, 143–45, 154, 170n3, 202n9, 267–68n3; identity, 113; nation-state, 10, 255; nation-state institutions, 2; Portuguese state, 9, 36, 48, 216, 225; Portuguese state-formation, 48, 209, 214, 218; Spanish state, 9–10, 12, 103, 105, 122, 124–25n1, 257, 258

Stendhal, Henri Mari Beyle, 73, 76n14

stereotypes, 4, 6, 47, 49, 82, 130, 246n6, 285; ethnic, 207; regional, 75n8, 178, 227

Stewart, Kathleen, 6, 160. See also space

Stocking, George W., 35

Stoller, Paul, 123

"structure of feeling," 116, 125–6n6. See also Williams, Raymond

Suárez-Navaz, Liliana, 13

Sutton, David E., 152, 159

symbols, 6, 14, 69, 75n8, 155, 163; fascist, 116, 121; public, 229

synecdoche, 19

Swedenburg, Ted, 73

Tamils, 58

Taussig, Michael, 96n15, 164

Teles, Basílio, 178, 213–19, 221n13–16

television, 129, 254. *See also* magazines; media; newspapers; radio

Teresa of Ávila, Saint, 181–202

Terradas Saborit, Ignasi, 18–19, 110

territory, 13, 36, 39, 69, 86, 154–55, 162, 182, 198, 200, 209, 213, 215, 220n1, 251, 255, 261; deterritorialization, 58; divine territory, 185; "territoriality of words," 19, (*see also* Fernandez, James W.); territorialization, 14; "transterritorial community," 12 (*see also* San Román, Teresa)

Teruel, 116

texts, 3, 8, 9, 45, 50n7, 64, 72, 74n5, 162, 193, 246n6, 265; textbooks, 104, 107–9, 116–20, 131; "textual hailing," 229. *See also* education

theatre, 12, 85, 103, 139, 143, 231, 241–42, 253, 256; *El florido pensil*, 115, 120; plays, 1, 101, 103, 115, 120, 171n4, 264, 269n12

"thick description," 123. *See also* Geertz, Clifford

Thierry, Augustin, 211, 220n5–6

topography: topographic differences, 10, 208; (*see also* North/South); "topographic logic," 14. *See also* Delgado Ruiz, Manuel

toponymy, 14, 17

tourism, 17, 57, 60, 64, 65, 72, 75n8, 279, 280

tradition, 8, 14, 16, 38, 40, 63, 73–74n2–4, 95n6, 163, 171n7, 200, 210, 231, 242, 247n24, 263, 265, 277; anthropological, 35, 37, 46, 50n11; contested tradition, 14; "folk traditions," 35–37, 65, 92, 211, 256; intellectual traditions, 3, 155, 217, 271; literary tradition,

107; and material culture, 37, 38, 163; as an object of study, 35–45; 'officialized' popular traditions, 64–65, 75n8; politics of, 16; traditional poetry, 41, 43. *See also* Hobsbawm, Eric; "invention of tradition"; Ranger, Terence

Trás-os-Montes, 10, 86, 88, 235

trope, 48, 123, 154, 272, 284. *See also* irony; metaphor

Tsing, Anna Lowenhaupt, 4, 6, 265

Tugu, 72

Turner, Terence, 233, 246n13

Ugresic, Dubravka, 153

Ultimatum, 39–40

urban, 12, 15, 18, 55, 61, 69, 101, 102, 125n4, 145, 177, 242, 254, 266–67, 279, 284, 285; "deurbanization of industry," 18; elites, 178; ghettos, 55; individuals, 47, 101, 132–33, 137, 138, 145, 177, 178, 185, 187, 284; interests, 177; periurban, 276; suburban, 161; urban/rural fiestas associated with the Virgin of Sonsoles, 189, 198–99, 284; urbanites, 187; urbanity/rusticity, 277, 286, 287; urbanization in the countryside, 199; urbanization of the countryside, 288n5; values, 137. *See also* space

Urla, Jacqueline, ix, xi, 10, 146n11, 251, 253, 269n12–14, 274

Van der Veer, Peter, 76

Varenne, Hervé, 154

Vasconcelos, Leite de, 87

Vatuas, 93

Vercingectórix, 221n19

Viana, Abel, 92

Viana do Castelo, 15, 90

Vicens Vives, Jaume, 104
Vila Branca, 15
Vila Nova de Gaia, 226, 232
Vila Real, 228, 233
Vilhena, Júlio de, 210–12, 215
villages, 3, 6, 12, 18, 19, 21n5, 178–
  179, 226, 233, 236, 241–42, 266,
  272, 277–80, 288n3; celebration
  and identity, 199; as exhibits, 82,
  88–89; factionalism within, 240;
  inter-village conflict, 226, 231,
  243; modernizing educational
  programs in, 1, 132–45, 146n11;
  offerings and the brotherhoods in,
  189–91, 202n12; and regional
  representations, 242, 244–45
Villas Boas, Count of, 90–91
Virgin of Sonsoles, 177, 179–204,
  284
Viriato, 218, 221n19
Völkerkunde, 35. *See also* "anthropologies of empire building."

Volkskunde, 35. *See also* "anthropologies of nation building."

Williams, Raymond, 116, 244,
  247n24, 273, 284, 288n4–5. *See
  also* "structure of feeling."
Wolf, Eric R., 2, 3, 5
World War I, 85, 163, 170

Yaeger, Patricia, 20n1, 288n3
youth, 18, 107, 119, 231; activities,
  140, 256; and educational strategies, 135; and military sacrifice,
  108, 114

Zangwill, Israel, 171n4
Zimbabwe, 39
Zimmer, Oliver, 156
Zulaika, Joseba, ix, 253, 269n12,
  274–75, 288n6
Zulu, 277, 288n7; Zionists among
  the, 276